A+ CoursePrep
StudyGuide/ExamGuide
2003 Core Exam and OS Exam
Second Edition

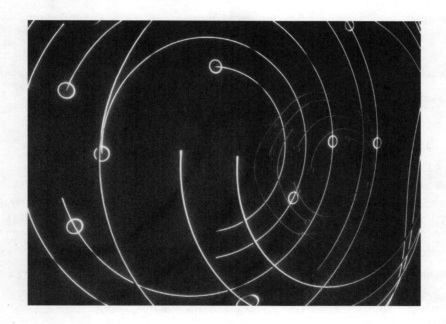

THOMSON
COURSE TECHNOLOGY

CompTIA Certified

Australia • Canada • Mexico • Singapore • Spain • United Kingdom • United States

THOMSON
COURSE TECHNOLOGY ™

A+ CoursePrep StudyGuide and CoursePrep ExamGuide, 2003 Core Exam and OS Exam, Second Edition

by Jean Andrews, Wally Beck, Greg Tomsho is published by Course Technology

Senior Product Manager:
Laura Hildebrand

Product Manager:
Tim Gleeson

Senior Editor:
William Pitkin III

Product Marketing Manager:
Jason Sakos

Associate Product Manager:
Nick Lombardi

Development Editor:
Jill Batistick

Manufacturing Coordinator:
Trevor Kallop

Production Editor:
Summer Hughes

Cover Design:
Steve Deschene

Compositor:
GEX Publishing Services

Disclaimer
Course Technology reserves the right to revise this publication and make changes from time to time in its content without notice.

ISBN 0-619-18622-4
ISBN 0-619-18623-2

TABLE OF CONTENTS

The A+ CoursePrep ExamGuide and StudyGuide are the very best tools to use to prepare for exam day. Both products provide thorough preparation for the newly revised 2003 A+ certification exams created by CompTIA. These products may be used on their own or with any of Jean Andrews' core PC Repair texts, including the core "Guide to" textbook, *A+ Guide to Managing and Maintaining Your PC, Fourth Edition* (ISBN 0-619-18617-8). CoursePrep ExamGuide and CoursePrep StudyGuide provide you ample opportunity to practice, drill, and rehearse for the exam!

COURSEPREP EXAMGUIDE

The *A+ CoursePrep ExamGuide, Second Edition* (ISBN 0-619-18623-2) provides the essential information you need to master each exam objective. The ExamGuide devotes an entire two-page spread to each certification objective for the newly revised 2003 A+ exams, helping you to understand the objective and giving you the bottom line information—what you *really* need to know. Learn these facts and bulleted points before heading into the exam. In addition, there are seven practice test questions for each objective on the right page: more than 850 questions total! The CoursePrep ExamGuide provides the exam fundamentals to get you up to speed quickly. If you are seeking even more opportunity to practice and prepare, we recommend that you consider our most complete solution—the CoursePrep StudyGuide, which is described next.

COURSEPREP STUDYGUIDE

The *A+ CoursePrep StudyGuide, Second Edition* (ISBN 0-619-18622-4) offers an even more robust solution. This offering includes all of the same great features you get with the CoursePrep ExamGuide, including the unique two-page spread, bulleted memorization points, and practice questions. In addition, you will be provided with a password valid for six months of practice on CoursePrep, a dynamic test preparation tool. The password is provided in an envelope in the back cover of the CoursePrep StudyGuide. CoursePrep is a Web-based pool of hundreds of sample test questions. CoursePrep exam simulation software mimics the exact exam environment. The CoursePrep software is flexible and allows you to practice in several ways as you master the material. Choose from Certification Mode to experience actual exam-day conditions or Study Mode to request answers and explanations to the practice questions. Custom Mode lets you set the options for the practice test, including number of questions, content coverage, and ability to request answers and explanation. Follow the instructions on the inside back cover to access the exam simulation software. To see a demo of this dynamic test preparation tool, visit *www.courseprep.com*.

FEATURES

The *A+ CoursePrep ExamGuide* and *A+ CoursePrep StudyGuide* books include the following features:

List of domains and objectives taken directly from the CompTIA web site. The content is divided into two sections: one section is devoted to the Core Hardware exam, and one section is devoted to the OS Technologies exam. Each section begins with a description of the domains covered on the exam. The objectives under each domain are found within the sections. For more information about the A+ Exams, visit CompTIA's web site at *www.comptia.org*.

Detailed coverage of the certification objectives in a unique two-page spread. The CoursePrep ExamGuide and StudyGuide allow you to study strategically by really focusing on the A+ certification objectives. To enable you to do this, a two-page spread is devoted to each certification objective. The left page provides the critical facts you need, while the right page features practice questions relating to that objective. You'll find that the certification objective(s) and sub-objectives(s) are clearly listed in the upper left-hand corner of each spread.

 Hardware Icon: This icon appears to the left of the certification objectives that are hardware related.

 Software Icon: This icon appears to the left of certification objectives that are software related.

An overview of the objective is provided in the ***Understanding the Objective*** section. Next, ***What you Really Need to Know*** lists bulleted, succinct facts, skills, and concepts about the objective. Learning these facts will be important for your success when taking the exam. ***Objectives on the Job*** places the objective in an industry perspective and tells you how you can expect to use the objective on the job. This section also provides troubleshooting information.

Practice Test Questions. Each right page contains seven practice test questions designed to help you prepare for the exam by testing your skills, identifying your strengths and weaknesses, and demonstrating the subject matter you will face on the exams and how it will be tested. These questions are written in a similar fashion to real A+ Exam questions. The questions test your knowledge of the objectives described on the left page and also the information in the *A+ Guide to Managing and Maintaining Your PC, Comprehensive, Fourth Edition* (ISBN 0-619-18617-8). You can find answers to the practice test questions at the end of the ExamGuide/StudyGuide.

Glossary: Boldfaced terms used in the book and other terms that you need to know for the exams are listed and defined in the glossary.

For more information: This book evolved from *A+ Guide to Managing and Maintaining Your PC, Fourth Edition* (ISBN 0-619-18617-8). Please refer to that book for more in-depth explanation of concepts or procedures presented here. Course Technology publishes a full series of PC Repair and A+ products that provide thorough preparation for the newly-revised A+ Exams. For more information, visit *www.course.com/pcrepair* or contact your sales representative.

HOW TO USE THIS BOOK

The *A+ CoursePrep ExamGuide* and *A+ CoursePrep StudyGuide* are all you need to successfully prepare for the A+ Certification exams if you have some experience and working knowledge of supporting and maintaining personal computers. These products may be used on their own or with any of Jean Andrews' core PC Repair texts, including the core "Guide to" textbook, *A+ Guide to Managing and Maintaining Your PC, Fourth Edition* (ISBN 0-619-18617-8). If you are new to this field, use this book as a roadmap for where you need to go to prepare for certification—use the *A+ Guide to Managing and Maintaining Your PC* to give you the knowledge and understanding that you need to reach your goal.

ACKNOWLEDGMENTS

Jean Andrews

Studying for exam day can be stressful, but the rewards are well worth the efforts. This book is dedicated to the people who are using it to get certified. Best to you!

Wally Beck

I'd like to thank Jill Batistick, Tim Gleeson, and Laura Hildebrand from Course Technology whose encouragement, support, and experience made this edition possible. And thank you to Jean Andrews for originally inviting me to take part in a truly exciting and rewarding venture. Many thanks to Rick Coker and Brandon Haag from Gainesville College for providing me with an opportunity to learn and grow. Most importantly, I'd like to dedicate this book to my wonderful wife, Renee. Her love and support has helped me through many demanding times. She's the best! And to my extraordinary mother, who is also the best!

Greg Tomsho

I would like to thank Product managers Tim Gleeson and Laura Hildebrand for giving me the opportunity to work on this project. Thanks to Jill Batistick, Development Editor, for doing such a fine job organizing the material, which made my job so much easier. As always, I want to thank my lovely wife, Julie, for being so supportive in all I do.

CORE HARDWARE

A+ Core Hardware Exam Objectives

Descriptions of the A+ Core Hardware exam objective can be found on the CompTIA Web site at *www.comptia.org/certification/A/objectives.asp*.

	% OF EXAM
DOMAIN 1.0 INSTALLATION, CONFIGURATION, AND UPGRADING	35%
DOMAIN 2.0 DIAGNOSING AND TROUBLESHOOTING	21%
DOMAIN 3.0 PREVENTIVE MAINTENANCE	5%
DOMAIN 4.0 MOTHERBOARD/PROCESSORS/MEMORY	11%
DOMAIN 5.0 PRINTERS	9%
DOMAIN 6.0 BASIC NETWORKING	19%

1.1 Identify the names, purpose, and characteristics, of system modules. Recognize these modules by sight or definition.

MOTHERBOARD • PORTS

UNDERSTANDING THE OBJECTIVE

The motherboard is the most important and largest circuit board inside the computer case. All hardware components must connect to the motherboard because on it is the central processing unit (CPU), the most important integrated circuit (IC) of the computer, through which all data and instructions must pass for processing.

WHAT YOU **REALLY** NEED TO KNOW

◆ There are two kinds of ICs on a motherboard and other circuit boards: complementary metal-oxide semiconductor (CMOS) chips and transistor-transistor logic (TTL) chips.

◆ CMOS chips require less electricity, hold data longer after the electricity is turned off, are slower, and produce less heat than TTL chips do.

◆ Names for the motherboard include main board, main logic board, motherboard, and planar board.

◆ Motherboard components can include a slot or socket for the CPU, a chip set, RAM, ISA, PCI, accelerated graphics port (AGP), and Video Electronics Standards Association (VESA) expansion slots, a ROM BIOS chip, power connections, a keyboard port, and so forth. You should be able to recognize these on a diagram.

◆ The CPU is installed on the motherboard in a socket or slot and sometimes requires a voltage regulator to step down the voltage from the motherboard before it is used by the CPU.

◆ Some CPUs have a fan or temperature sensor connected to the CPU housing that requires a voltage connection to the motherboard.

◆ The boot process and many basic I/O operations are controlled by the system BIOS stored on the ROM BIOS on the motherboard.

◆ Communication of control information, timing of activities, data, address information, and electrical power for components on the motherboard take place over a **bus**.

◆ Configuration information about hardware and user preferences is stored on a motherboard in the CMOS RAM chip, **DIP switches**, and **jumpers**. Many motherboards today use JumperFree mode whereby configuration is done primarily in CMOS setup.

◆ The **system clock** is responsible for timing activities on the motherboard.

◆ A motherboard normally has several built-in, on-board ports including one or more serial, parallel, keyboard, mouse, and USB ports.

◆ On-board ports can be enabled, disabled, and configured in CMOS setup. Sometimes an unused, on-board port must be disabled if it is using an IRQ needed by another device. When troubleshooting a problem with an on-board port, verify the port is enabled in CMOS setup.

OBJECTIVES ON THE JOB

When replacing a motherboard, use the same size board that was removed and one that accommodates the CPU, memory, and circuit boards. Jumpers and DIP switches are set when the motherboard is first installed and should not need to be changed after that.

PRACTICE TEST QUESTIONS

1. **Which statement about the motherboard is false?**
   a. The motherboard is sometimes called the motherboard, planar board, or main logic board.
   b. The motherboard is a field-replaceable unit.
   c. The motherboard contains the CPU.
   d. The motherboard requires 115 volts of power.

2. **In the drawing at the right, item 1 is a(n):**
   a. floppy drive connector
   b. PCI bus slot
   c. CPU socket
   d. cache memory chip

3. **In the drawing at the right, item 2 is a(n):**
   a. IDE connection
   b. keyboard connection
   c. bank of jumpers
   d. sound card connection

4. **In the drawing at the right, item 3 is a(n):**
   a. IDE connection
   b. ISA expansion slot
   c. PCI expansion slot
   d. CPU socket

5. **In the drawing at the right, item 4 is a(n):**
   a. ROM BIOS chip
   b. keyboard port
   c. jumper bank
   d. DIMM slot

6. **A FRU that is installed on the motherboard is:**
   a. the CPU
   b. a PCI expansion slot
   c. the CPU Socket 7
   d. the motherboard chipset

7. **Timing on the motherboard is controlled by the:**
   a. CPU
   b. system BIOS
   c. real-time clock
   d. system clock

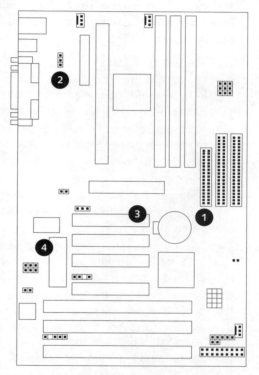

1.1 Identify the names, purpose, and characteristics, of system modules. Recognize these modules by sight or definition.

FIRMWARE

UNDERSTANDING THE OBJECTIVE

Firmware is software stored on microchips on the motherboard and other circuit boards and devices. It contains instructions used to control basic input and output operations of the PC and includes the system BIOS (basic input output system). One CMOS chip on the motherboard holds configuration information about the PC even when power is off, and is commonly known as CMOS setup or simply CMOS.

WHAT YOU **REALLY** NEED TO KNOW

- The BIOS is the set of programs called firmware that performs many fundamental input and output operations; BIOS on the motherboard can be permanently etched onto a ROM microchip or can be changed electronically.
- ROM chips that can be changed electronically are called **Flash ROM** or **electrically erasable programmable read-only memory (EEPROM)**.
- Flash ROM allows you to upgrade the programs in ROM without replacing the chip.
- The CMOS chip is a type of RAM storage for configuration information about the computer system; BIOS contains the CMOS setup programs to alter CMOS.
- Startup BIOS performs **power on self test (POST)** and includes programs to access CMOS setup.
- The motherboard contains the system BIOS, but expansion boards can also contain BIOS, which provides software to perform the most basic instructions to hardware and sometimes serves as the interface between higher-level software and hardware.
- When upgrading BIOS, be certain to use the BIOS upgrade compatible with your computer. You can download the upgrade from the Web site of the BIOS or computer manufacturer. You often copy these files to a floppy disk, which makes the disk bootable. Next, boot from the floppy disk to display a menu allowing you to select the option to complete the upgrade.
- The BIOS is responsible for the boot process until it loads the operating system. During startup, the BIOS performs POST, a check of essential hardware devices, and communicates problems encountered by error messages displayed on the screen. If errors occur early in the boot process before video is available, errors are communicated as a series of beeps. These beep codes are different for each BIOS manufacturer; some computer manufacturers alter these beep codes as well.

OBJECTIVES ON THE JOB

Verifying, changing, and optimizing settings in CMOS setup is an essential skill of a PC technician. Upgrading BIOS is sometimes necessary, especially on older systems. Interpreting the BIOS beep codes is an essential skill in troubleshooting problems with a PC during the boot process. The best source of information about beep codes and BIOS error messages and their meaning is the Web site of the BIOS or computer manufacturer.

PRACTICE TEST QUESTIONS

1. **When the PC loses setup information each time it is booted, a possible cause of this problem is:**
   a. the BIOS is Plug and Play
   b. the CMOS battery is weak and needs replacing
   c. the CPU is loose in its slot or socket
   d. BIOS is corrupted and needs to be refreshed or upgraded

2. **The system date and time can be set using:**
   a. DOS commands
   b. jumpers on the motherboard
   c. CMOS setup
   d. either a or c

3. **One reason you might flash ROM is to:**
   a. install a larger hard drive
   b. change the system clock frequency
   c. install a second floppy drive
   d. install Windows XP

4. **Plug and Play is a feature of:**
   a. ROM BIOS
   b. Windows XP
   c. some hardware devices
   d. all of the above

5. **How do you access CMOS to view settings and make changes?**
   a. Press a certain key combination during booting.
   b. Press a certain key combination after the OS loads.
   c. Press the Esc key as you turn off the power to the system.
   d. Use a setup CD that comes with the operating system.

6. **The program to change CMOS can be stored:**
   a. on the hard drive in a special partition
   b. on the ROM BIOS
   c. on a floppy disk
   d. all of the above

7. **The type of ROM BIOS that can be changed without exchanging the chip is called:**
   a. Change BIOS
   b. ROM BIOS
   c. Flash ROM
   d. EEPROM

1.1 Identify the names, purpose, and characteristics, of system modules. Recognize these modules by sight or definition.

POWER SUPPLY

UNDERSTANDING THE OBJECTIVE

The power supply provides power to all components inside the computer case (for example, the motherboard, circuit boards, hard drive, and so forth) and some outside the case (for example, the keyboard).

WHAT YOU **REALLY** NEED TO KNOW

◆ Power to the motherboard comes from the power supply by way of power cords connected to a P1 connection for **ATX motherboards** and P8 and P9 connections for **AT motherboards**.

◆ A power supply converts 115-volt **alternating current (AC)** to distinct **direct current (DC)** outputs.

◆ The AT power supply provides the system with +12 v, –12 v, +5 v, and –5 v.

◆ The ATX power supply provides the above four voltages and also +3.3 volts.

◆ Most ATX power supplies have a wire that runs from the front of the computer case to the ATX motherboard lead. This wire must be connected before powering the system.

◆ A **resistor, capacitor, diode, transistor,** and **ground** are all electrical components. You should be able to define and recognize their symbols.

◆ Hot, neutral, and **ground** have to do with house circuit, and you should understand these terms and recognize the symbol for ground.

◆ **Amperes (A), ohms, farads, volts,** and **watts** are electrical measurements that you should be able to define and identify the relationships between them.

◆ A power supply contains a fan that helps cool the inside of the computer case. Never allow a PC to run without a working fan because it can overheat; instead, replace the power supply. If the fan on the new power supply quickly fails, the problem might not be caused by a faulty fan, but by a short somewhere else in the system that draws too much power. Try disconnecting other components inside the computer case and connected to the motherboard. If disconnecting one of these components causes the fan to start working, then the disconnected component most likely has a short and should be replaced.

◆ When a motherboard fails, always consider that a faulty power supply might have damaged the motherboard. Check for correct voltage output of the power supply before installing a new motherboard.

◆ When replacing a power supply, use the same type of power supply—either an AT or ATX. Also consider the total wattage requirement of the system and use a new power supply that is rated at a wattage to run at about 60 percent capacity.

OBJECTIVES ON THE JOB

The power supply is an essential PC component. Understanding how it works and knowing about the different types of power supplies are essential pieces of knowledge for a PC technician.

PRACTICE TEST QUESTIONS

1. **Which power supply provides 3 volts of DC current to a motherboard?**
   a. the AT power supply
   b. the CPU power supply
   c. the ATX power supply
   d. Only AC current is supplied to a motherboard.

2. **What is the relationship between power, current, and voltage?**
   a. Power is directly proportional to current and inversely proportional to voltage.
   b. Power is directly proportional to current and directly proportional to voltage.
   c. Power is inversely proportional to current and directly proportional to voltage.
   d. Power is inversely proportional to current and inversely proportional to voltage.

3. **What is the unit of measure for the capacitance of a capacitor?**
   a. volts
   b. ohms
   c. coulombs
   d. microfarads

4. **Which statement is true about the power from an ATX power supply to a motherboard?**
   a. There are two power connections named P8 and P9.
   b. There is a single power connection named P1.
   c. The power goes to the motherboard by way of the CPU voltage regulator.
   d. The motherboard does not get its power from an ATX power supply.

5. **Which statement is true about a power supply?**
   a. A power supply converts AC to DC.
   b. A power supply converts DC to AC.
   c. A power supply is a large transistor.
   d. A power supply can supply power to the system for 30 seconds after a power outage.

6. **The voltage used by a floppy disk drive is:**
   a. +3 volts
   b. −12 volts
   c. +5 volts
   d. 0 volts

7. **An AT motherboard uses which voltages?**
   a. +12, −12, +5, and −5 volts
   b. +12 and −12 volts
   c. +3.3 volts
   d. +12, −12, +5, −5, and +3.3 volts

1.1 Identify the names, purpose, and characteristics, of system modules. Recognize these modules by sight or definition.

PROCESSOR/CPU

UNDERSTANDING THE OBJECTIVE

The CPU—also known by its shorthand name of "processor"—is the most important part of a computer system. All data and instructions pass through the CPU for processing.

WHAT YOU **REALLY** NEED TO KNOW

◆ Names for the CPU include central processing unit, microprocessor, and processor.

◆ CPUs are rated by internal and external speeds in MHz, special functionality such as MMX technology, size of data paths, the amount of memory cache included inside the CPU housing or on the CPU chip itself, and the voltage requirements.

◆ A CPU can run in either **real mode** or **protected mode**.

◆ When a CPU runs in protected mode, two programs can run without interfering with each other's memory space.

◆ Hyper-Threading Technology is used in several Intel CPUs to improve multitasking performance by allowing the chip to run two software threads simultaneously.

◆ Intel Centrino Mobile Technology (Pentium III M, Pentium M, Pentium 4 M) improves mobile computing by adding support for wireless LAN access and uses Intel SpeedStep technology to perform real-time adjustment of CPU speed to meet application demands and conserve power.

◆ Memory cache included on the CPU microchip is called internal cache, primary cache, Level 1 or L1 cache. Cache outside the CPU microchip is called external cache. This is called Level 2 (L2 cache), depending on the CPU.

◆ Intel's first 64-bit CPU is the Itanium. Its external L3 cache starts at 1.5 MB.

Table of Intel Pentium CPUs

CPU	Speed (MHz)	Primary L1 Cache	Secondary L2 Cache	System Bus Speeds (MHz)
Celeron	266 and up	32K	128K, 256K	66, 100, 133, 400
Pentium Xeon	400 and up	32K	512K, 1 MB, or 2 MB	400, 533
Pentium III	400 and up	32K	256K, 512K	100, 133
Pentium III Xeon	500 and up	32K	256K to 2 MB	100, 133
Pentium 4	1.3 GHz and up	12K	256K to 512K	400, 533
Pentium III M	1.0 GHz and up	32K	512K	133
Pentium M, 4 M	1.3 GHz and up	12K	512K, 1 MB	133, 400
Itanium	733 and up	32K	96K	266
Itanium 2	900 and up	32K	256K	400

OBJECTIVES ON THE JOB

A PC technician must understand what a CPU does, know how to select the best CPU for a system, and be able to troubleshoot problems with the CPU.

PRACTICE TEST QUESTIONS

1. Running a motherboard at a higher speed than that suggested by the manufacturer is called:
   a. turbo mode
   b. over-clocking
   c. MMX technology
   d. cache mode

2. What does the CPU do?
   a. controls the power to the other components on the motherboard
   b. executes program instructions
   c. controls which keys can be pressed on the keyboard
   d. all of the above

3. Which CPU technology is used to improve software multitasking performance?
   a. MMX
   b. SSE
   c. 3DNow!
   d. Hyper-Threading

4. If the CPU is running at 300 MHz and the system bus is running at 100 MHz, then the multiplier is:
   a. 1/3
   b. 100
   c. 3
   d. 300

5. Typical speeds for today's system bus are:
   a. 60, 66, and 100 MHz
   b. 133, 400, and 533 MHz
   c. 400, 500, and 1,000,000 MHz
   d. 20, 40, and 80 MHz

6. RISC stands for:
   a. reduced instruction set computer
   b. random instruction set computing
   c. RAM increasing storage container
   d. random instruction system computer

7. A memory cache stored on the CPU microchip is called:
   a. L1 cache
   b. L3 cache
   c. CPU cache
   d. Discrete cache

1.1 Identify the names, purpose, and characteristics, of system modules. Recognize these modules by sight or definition.

MEMORY • DISPLAY DEVICES

UNDERSTANDING THE OBJECTIVE

Data and instructions (programs) are permanently stored in secondary storage devices (hard drive, floppy disk, CD–ROM, and so forth) even when the PC is turned off, but must be moved to memory on the motherboard before the CPU processes them (this memory is called primary storage). A monitor is the primary output, or display, device of a PC.

WHAT YOU **REALLY** NEED TO KNOW

On memory:

◆ Memory or RAM is stored on the motherboard in a memory module called a SIMM, DIMM, or RIMM. In addition to RAM, a memory cache to speed up memory access is contained on older motherboards in microchips or memory modules, or inside the CPU housing as L1 or L2 cache.

◆ Know the definitions of these terms that apply to DOS and Windows 9x memory management (not Windows 2000 memory management): **high memory area (HMA), conventional** or **base memory, upper memory, extended memory (EMS),** and **expanded memory**.

◆ HMA is between 1024K and 1088K and is used to load part of DOS away from conventional memory, thus allowing for more program/data space in conventional memory.

◆ Conventional or base memory is between 0K and 640K and is used to load legacy device drivers, part of the operating system kernel, user-configurable parameters, and program/data files.

◆ Upper memory (also called reserved memory) is between 640K and 1 MB, and is used to load real mode device drivers and system BIOS.

◆ Extended memory is all memory above 1024K.

◆ In Windows 9x, Windows 2000, and Windows XP, **virtual memory** is space on the hard drive that is used as if it were RAM.

◆ Windows 2000 and Windows XP manage memory and virtual memory as one continuous memory space that is made available to applications.

◆ Himem.sys is a DOS memory manager that acts like a **device driver** (managing the "device" memory) making memory above 1024K available to programs.

On display devices:

◆ **Dot pitch** is the distance between dots of color on a display screen and is measured in millimeters.

◆ A **pixel** is a group of dots and the smallest addressable spot on the display device.

◆ Common display **resolutions** are 800 × 600 pixels and 1024 × 768 pixels.

◆ **Interlaced** display devices compensate for a slow **refresh** rate.

OBJECTIVES ON THE JOB

Monitors are considered "black boxes" by a PC technician who is not trained to service one. Don't open them in the field as they can contain high electrical charges even after the power is off. Upgrading memory is a common task for PC technicians. Generally, adding memory to a sluggish system can improve performance.

PRACTICE TEST QUESTIONS

1. **Another name for reserved memory is:**
   - a. base memory
   - b. extended memory
   - c. expanded memory
   - d. upper memory

2. **Which type of monitor provides the highest quality performance?**
   - a. VGA
   - b. CGA
   - c. SVGA
   - d. HGA

3. **A parity error is most likely caused by what device?**
   - a. a hard drive
   - b. RAM
   - c. ROM
   - d. a CPU

4. **Which device is not considered a field-replaceable unit?**
   - a. RAM
   - b. a CPU
   - c. a motherboard
   - d. a soldered cache IC

5. **Which DOS device driver is used to gain access to extended memory?**
   - a. Emm386.exe
   - b. Himem.sys
   - c. Command.com
   - d. Ramdrive.sys

6. **Space on the hard drive that is used as though it were RAM is called:**
   - a. RAM space
   - b. drive memory
   - c. RAM Drive
   - d. virtual memory

7. **Which memory module is used to hold memory cache on the motherboard?**
   - a. SIMM
   - b. DIMM
   - c. COAST
   - d. RIMM

1.1 Identify the names, purpose, and characteristics, of system modules. Recognize these modules by sight or definition.

STORAGE DEVICES

UNDERSTANDING THE OBJECTIVE

Data and instructions (programs) are stored in secondary storage devices (hard drive, floppy disk, CD–ROM, and so forth) even when the PC is turned off. Before this data (or programs) can be used or executed, they must be copied from secondary storage into memory.

WHAT YOU **REALLY** NEED TO KNOW

◆ Most hard drives use **IDE** technology in which the hard drive controller is permanently attached to the hard drive and controls where data is physically stored on the drive without interference from system BIOS or the OS.

◆ **SCSI** is another type of hard drive technology that uses a SCSI bus that can be connected to other SCSI devices.

◆ A PC must boot from an operating system stored on a secondary storage device, called the bootable device. Examples of bootable devices are floppy disks, hard drives, CD-ROM drives, and removable drives.

◆ Boot priority or boot sequence is determined in CMOS setup and is the order that the system BIOS uses to attempt to boot from a bootable secondary storage device.

◆ A SCSI hard drive cannot be the bootable device unless this feature is supported by the system BIOS.

◆ Some examples of external removable drives are Iomega Zip drives, Iomega Jaz drives, Imation SuperDisk, USB memory keys, tape backup drives, writeable CD-ROM drives (CD-R), and rewriteable CD-ROM drives (CDRW).

◆ An Imation SuperDisk can use a floppy disk or a 120 MB disk. Iomega Zip disks range from 100 MB to 750 MB. USB memory keys plug into USB ports and currently hold 64 MB or more.

◆ Initially, only hard drives used IDE technology. New standards mean that other secondary storage devices such as Zip and CD-ROM drives can use an IDE connection to the motherboard. These **ATAPI** standards have to do with the interface protocol between the device and the CPU, which must be supported by the OS.

OBJECTIVES ON THE JOB

PC technicians are expected to install, support, and troubleshoot secondary storage devices on a regular basis on the job. They need to know that the operating system is loaded from a secondary storage device. For DOS or Windows 9x, a FAT file system is installed on the storage device that includes track and sector markings on the storage media, a master boot program, a FAT, a root directory, and system files. When the PC boots, BIOS checks a specified device to see if it contains the operating system. If the device does not contain the file system and the system files, BIOS displays an error. When you get this error, replace the floppy disk with a good system disk or boot from the hard drive.

PRACTICE TEST QUESTIONS

1. **What is the purpose of ATAPI standards?**
   a. They determine how data is stored on a hard drive.
   b. They provide protocol standards that are used when a device using an IDE interface communicates with the CPU.
   c. They determine how data is stored on a CD.
   d. They control how the CPU communicates with a hard drive.

2. **What is a Jaz drive?**
   a. a removable secondary storage device
   b. a very fast hard drive
   c. a drive used to store music files
   d. a floppy disk drive designed for extra high density disks

3. **Which statement is true about an IDE hard drive and a SCSI hard drive?**
   a. A SCSI drive is generally faster than an IDE drive because of the way data is stored on the drive.
   b. A SCSI drive is generally faster than an IDE drive because of the bus used by the drive.
   c. An IDE drive is always faster than a SCSI drive.
   d. An IDE drive is generally faster than a SCSI drive because of the way data is stored on the drive.

4. **How can you change the boot priority of a system?**
   a. change a parameter in the Windows XP registry
   b. make the change using a jumper on the hard drive
   c. make the change in CMOS setup
   d. change the way the data cable is connected to the hard drive

5. **What is boot priority?**
   a. the most important task for the user to do after the PC boots up
   b. the order that system BIOS uses to find a boot device
   c. the first task BIOS performs when the PC is turned on
   d. the order of operating systems stored on the hard drive

6. **Which statement is true about Zip drives and Jaz drives?**
   a. Zip drives hold more data than Jaz drives.
   b. A Zip drive is an internal drive and a Jaz drive is an external drive.
   c. A Jaz drive holds more data than a Zip drive.
   d. Zip drives and Jaz drives always use a parallel cable connection.

7. **Which statement is true about secondary storage?**
   a. Secondary storage always uses magnetic media.
   b. Secondary storage can use magnetic media or optical media.
   c. Secondary storage is not permanent storage.
   d. There is always more primary storage in a system than there is secondary storage.

1.1 Identify the names, purpose, and characteristics, of system modules. Recognize these modules by sight or definition.

ADAPTER CARDS • CASES • RISER CARDS

UNDERSTANDING THE OBJECTIVE

In some computers, adapter cards plug into a riser card that in turn plugs into a connector on the motherboard. Riser cards are often used in computers with smaller, more compact cases. Adapter cards and riser cards are field–replaceable units.

WHAT YOU **REALLY** NEED TO KNOW

- There are three major categories of computer cases: desktop cases, tower cases, and notebook cases.
- Many cost-efficient desktop computers have compact cases sometimes referred to as **low-profile** or **slimline cases**. These cases have fewer drive bays and adapter card slots, but are more space-efficient. Low-profile cases require the use of low-profile adapter cards. Normal adapter cards cannot fit into a low-profile case.
- Some low-profile desktops and tower cases use a **riser card** which plugs into a connector on the motherboard. In this situation, all expansion slots are placed on the riser card, not the motherboard. As a result, full-size adapter cards run parallel to the motherboard, as viewed from the rear of the computer case.
- Low-profile cases use the NLX, LPX, or Mini-LPX motherboard form factor.
- There are three main categories of adapter card connectors: ISA, PCI, and AGP. ISA connections are being phased out and are no longer available on most new computers. The majority of adapter cards on the market fit PCI connectors.
- Video adapters on most new computers have a dedicated connector called the **accelerated graphics port (AGP)** slot.
- Some adapter cards cannot be replaced because they have been integrated into the motherboard. Examples of integrated cards include sound adapters, network adapters, modems, and video adapters. If the adapter card is integrated into the motherboard, then it is not a field-replaceable unit.
- In the event of a failed integrated device, the entire motherboard must be replaced.
- Riser cards that are mounted onto the computer case often use spaces or **standoffs** to prevent the riser from coming in contact with the computer case.

OBJECTIVES ON THE JOB

Adapter cards and riser cards are considered to be field-replaceable units, so a PC technician should know how to recognize a failed system component and replace it. Riser cards can be replaced when the motherboard, power supply, memory, CPU, ROM BIOS chip, hard drive, and floppy drive have all been eliminated as the source of a hardware failure that prevents the system from booting. Faulty adapter cards can be checked by testing the system with a known–good adapter card of the same make and model.

PRACTICE TEST QUESTIONS

1. **Low-profile cases use which motherboard form factors?**
   a. NLX
   b. LPX
   c. Mini-LPX
   d. All of the above

2. **In which direction do adapter cards run when used in conjunction with a riser card?**
   a. parallel to the motherboard
   b. perpendicular to the motherboard
   c. parallel to the riser card
   d. all of the above

3. **Which types of adapter cards may have BIOS that run before POST?**
   a. sound card
   b. video card
   c. network interface card
   d. all of the above

4. **The modem command to hang up the phone is:**
   a. ATD
   b. ATH
   c. ATM
   d. ATZ

5. **An external modem connects to:**
   a. the parallel port
   b. a game port
   c. a serial port
   d. a special adapter card made for modem interfaces

6. **Which of the following is NOT an adapter card?**
   a. IEEE 1394/FireWire
   b. the CPU
   c. NIC
   d. Sound

7. **Which adapter card uses a 15-pin 3 row port?**
   a. SCSI card
   b. PCI card
   c. video card
   d. serial port

1.2   Identify basic procedures for adding and removing field-replaceable modules for desktop systems. Given a replacement scenario, choose the appropriate sequences.

MOTHERBOARD

UNDERSTANDING THE OBJECTIVE

When installing a new motherboard in a PC, memory and the CPU are installed on the board, jumpers are set to communicate how the motherboard is configured, the motherboard is installed inside the case, and power, circuit boards, and LED wires are connected to it.

WHAT YOU **REALLY** NEED TO KNOW

◆ The **field-replaceable units (FRUs)** on the motherboard are the CPU, cache memory modules (on older boards only), RAM modules, CMOS battery, and ROM BIOS chip.

◆ When selecting the motherboard, use an AT board with an AT power supply and an ATX board with an ATX power supply.

◆ Connect Pin 1 on the system board IDE or floppy drive connection with the colored edge of the ribbon cable.

◆ An IDE connection has 40 pins and a floppy drive connection has 34 pins.

◆ When replacing a damaged motherboard, verify the power supply is good because it might be the problem and thus damage the new board.

◆ Steps to install a motherboard:

1. Carefully read the documentation that comes with the motherboard. If you have questions, get answers before you begin the installation.
2. Prepare a work place and take precautions to protect against electrostatic discharge (ESD).
3. Set the jumpers on the motherboard. Jumpers may be used for the type of CPU, the speed of the CPU or its multiplier, how much memory cache is installed, what voltage the CPU will use, and other power features.
4. Install the CPU and fan or heat sink. Then, install DIMMs, SIMMs or RIMMs.
5. An optional memory test can be performed at this point to verify that the motherboard is good.
6. Install the motherboard in the computer case.
7. Use spacers or standoffs to insulate the motherboard from the computer case, but make sure that the motherboard is properly grounded to the case by a metallic connection and firmly connected to the case.
8. Attach the power cords and front panel connectors to the motherboard.

OBJECTIVES ON THE JOB

The motherboard is considered a field-replaceable unit, so a PC technician should know how to recognize a failed motherboard and replace it. A motherboard needs replacing when the power supply, memory, CPU, ROM BIOS chip, hard drive, and floppy drive have all been eliminated as the source of a hardware failure that prevents the system from booting. Replace a motherboard with one that can use the same CPU and memory modules as the old board and has the same form factor as the old board.

PRACTICE TEST QUESTIONS

1. **The purpose of a standoff is to:**
   a. prevent components on the motherboard from contacting the computer case
   b. ground the motherboard to the computer case
   c. hold the power supply connections to the motherboard
   d. provide a ground for the CPU

2. **Which of the following devices are considered FRUs?**
   a. a motherboard
   b. a video card
   c. a power supply
   d. all of the above

3. **Before replacing a dead motherboard, one thing you should do is:**
   a. back up all the data on the hard drive
   b. boot the system and verify all is working
   c. verify that the printer is working
   d. measure the voltage output of the power supply

4. **What is one thing that might cause damage to a motherboard as you service a PC?**
   a. not using an ESD bracelet
   b. not backing up critical data on the hard drive
   c. not backing up CMOS
   d. not verifying that the hard drive power cord is connected properly

5. **When installing AT power supply connections to a motherboard, what should you remember?**
   a. The power connections will only connect in one direction, so you can't go wrong.
   b. the black-to-black rule
   c. the red-to-red rule
   d. the P1 connection aligns with Pin 1 on the system board

6. **When installing a motherboard, which is installed first?**
   a. the power lead from the front panel
   b. the CPU
   c. the hard drive
   d. the case cover

7. **When exchanging a motherboard, why is it important to remove other components?**
   a. It's dangerous to leave other components inside the case while the motherboard is not present.
   b. The speaker might be damaged when the motherboard is removed.
   c. Removing them protects the power supply from damage.
   d. It is not important; remove other components only as necessary to expose the system board.

1.2 Identify basic procedures for adding and removing field-replaceable modules for desktop systems. Given a replacement scenario, choose the appropriate sequences.

STORAGE DEVICE: FDD, HDD, CD/CDRW, DVD/DVDRW, TAPE DRIVE, AND REMOVABLE STORAGE

UNDERSTANDING THE OBJECTIVE

When storage devices are installed inside a PC, the resources needed by the device and available system resources (IRQ, DMA channels, and I/O addresses) must be determined. The device must be physically installed and logically configured. External storage devices can connect by way of a serial, parallel, USB, IEEE 1394 or infrared port. A hard drive, CD/CDRW, DVD/DVDRW, tape drive, and removable storage drives can be either an IDE or SCSI device.

WHAT YOU **REALLY** NEED TO KNOW

- ◆ Hard disk drives (HDD), CD-ROM drives, CD-R/CDRW drives, DVD/DVDRW drives, tape drives, floppy disk drives (FDD), removable storage drives, controller cards, and data cables are all considered field-replaceable.
- ◆ When using an IDE connector with a storage device, the device jumpers can be set to Master, Slave, or Cable Select, depending on the location on the IDE ribbon.
- ◆ The BIOS on older systems may not support large hard drives and might need upgrading.
- ◆ To install an IDE hard drive:
  1. Step through the entire installation before you begin working to make sure you have everything you need and know the answers to any questions that might arise as you work.
  2. If you are removing an existing hard drive, back up the data.
  3. Turn off the power and remove the computer case cover.
  4. Set the IDE master/slave/CSEL jumpers on the drive.
  5. Fit the drive into the bay and install screws to secure the drive.
  6. Connect the data cable to the IDE connection on the back of the hard drive and to the IDE adapter card or connection on the system board, connecting Pin 1 on the connections to the edge color on the data cable.
  7. Connect the power cord from the power supply to the power connection on the drive.
  8. Replace the computer case cover and turn on the power. If CMOS supports auto detection, then verify that CMOS detected the drive correctly.
  9. If CMOS does not support auto detection, then record the drive parameters in CMOS setup.
  10. After the drive is physically installed, use FDISK to create partitions on the drive, format each partition, and install the OS.
  11. Verify that the drive is working.

OBJECTIVES ON THE JOB

Installing storage devices is a common task for a computer repair technician. Most storage devices use an IDE interface with the system board, a USB port, or SCSI connection for hard drives in high-end systems to improve speed and performance.

PRACTICE TEST QUESTIONS

1. If a system has two IDE hard drives that each have primary and extended partitions with one logical drive in each partition, what is the drive letter assigned to the primary partition of the second hard drive?
   a. C
   b. D
   c. E
   d. F

2. After performing a low-level format of a hard drive, what is the next step in the installation process?
   a. format the drive
   b. partition the drive using FDISK
   c. install the operating system
   d. enter the drive parameters in CMOS

3. What kind of cable is a 34-pin data cable?
   a. IDE hard drive cable
   b. SCSI hard drive cable
   c. IDE CD-ROM cable
   d. floppy drive cable

4. How many pins does an IDE data cable have?
   a. 25
   b. 34
   c. 40
   d. 50

5. When a CD-ROM drive and an IDE hard drive are sharing the same data cable:
   a. set the hard drive to master and the CD-ROM drive to slave
   b. set the CD-ROM drive to master and the hard drive to slave
   c. set both drives to master
   d. set both drives to slave

6. A port on the back of a PC has 50 pins. What type port is it?
   a. IDE port for an external hard drive
   b. SCSI port
   c. Parallel port
   d. IEEE 1394

7. Which IRQ does the primary IDE channel use?
   a. IRQ 5
   b. IRQ 7
   c. IRQ 14
   d. IRQ 15

1.2 Identify basic procedures for adding and removing field-replaceable modules for desktop systems. Given a replacement scenario, choose the appropriate sequences.

POWER SUPPLY: AC ADAPTER AND AT/ATX • DISPLAY DEVICE • INPUT DEVICES: KEYBOARD, MOUSE/POINTER DEVICES, AND TOUCH SCREEN

UNDERSTANDING THE OBJECTIVE

When installing a power supply, match the power supply type to the system board and its case. Input devices are connected to the system board by way of ports (serial, parallel, IEEE 1394, USB, DIN, mini–DIN, and so forth) connected directly to the system board or to ports on the circuit boards. Display devices (monitors and LCD screens) are attached to the rear of the computer by way of the video port on the video adapter card.

WHAT YOU **REALLY** NEED TO KNOW

◆ The power supply is a field-replaceable unit. If there is a problem with the fan or other component inside it, replace the entire power supply.

◆ When removing a power supply from a computer case, look on the bottom of the case for slots that are holding the power supply in position. Often the power supply must be shifted in one direction to free it from the slots.

◆ AT power supplies have several connectors. Be sure to note which connector is P8 and which is P9 when installing a power supply.

◆ ATX power supplies are powered on by the motherboard and have a single power line (called P1) connecting to the motherboard.

◆ An AC adapter is used to power a notebook computer.

◆ Touch screens have a touch screen sensor, an adapter card, and software drivers.

◆ If you install a new input device and it does not work, check the following:
  - Verify that the port it is using is enabled in CMOS setup.
  - Verify that there are no conflicts with the port's system resources.

◆ A mouse is powered by current received from the power supply by way of the system board, mouse port, and mouse cable.

◆ DOS requires loading a device driver for a mouse, but Windows 9x, Windows 2000, and Windows XP have internal support for a mouse.

◆ When a key is first pressed on a keyboard, a **make code** is produced. When the key is released, a **break code** is generated. The chip in the keyboard processes these actions to produce a scan code that is sent to the CPU.

◆ One pin in a keyboard cable carries +5 volts of current that comes from the power supply by way of the system board and is used to power the keyboard. Other pins in the keyboard cable are used for grounding, the keyboard clock, and keyboard data.

OBJECTIVES ON THE JOB

Installing a power supply is complex because often the entire computer must be disassembled to access the power supply. If a key on a keyboard does not work, after making a reasonable effort to clean the key, replace the keyboard. A mouse often gets dirt inside the ball mechanism and needs cleaning.

PRACTICE TEST QUESTIONS

1. **The ESD bracelet is designed to protect:**
   - a. the hardware from damage
   - b. the PC technician from harm
   - c. both the hardware and the technician
   - d. neither the hardware nor the technician

2. **If a monitor does not power on, what should you check?**
   - a. make sure the monitor is turned on
   - b. make sure the monitor is connected to a video card
   - c. make sure the monitor is plugged into a working power outlet
   - d. all of the above

3. **Before exchanging a power supply, you should:**
   - a. measure the voltage output of the old power supply
   - b. measure the capacitance of the old power supply
   - c. back up critical data on the hard drive
   - d. both a and c

4. **If the cable connector on a keyboard does not fit the keyboard port on the system board, then:**
   - a. the keyboard cannot be used on this system
   - b. use a DIN/mini-DIN adapter to make the connection
   - c. connect the keyboard using a serial port
   - d. change the keyboard port in CMOS

5. **If the mouse port on a system board does not work, then:**
   - a. check CMOS to see that the port is enabled
   - b. try using a serial port mouse
   - c. reboot the computer and try again
   - d. all of the above

6. **What ports can a mouse use?**
   - a. DIN
   - b. mini-DIN
   - c. serial port
   - d. all of the above

7. **How does a keyboard get its power?**
   - a. from the system board by way of the keyboard port
   - b. from an AC adapter connected to the keyboard
   - c. the keyboard does not need power
   - d. from a battery inside the keyboard

1.2 Identify basic procedures for adding and removing field-replaceable modules for desktop systems. Given a replacement scenario, choose the appropriate sequences.

COOLING SYSTEMS: FANS, HEAT SINKS, AND LIQUID COOLING • PROCESSOR/CPU • MEMORY

UNDERSTANDING THE OBJECTIVE

Both the processor/CPU and memory are installed on the system board. Both must match the type and size that the system board supports, and both are very susceptible to ESD, so caution must be taken as you work.

WHAT YOU **REALLY** NEED TO KNOW

◆ Protect memory modules and the CPU against ESD as you perform the installation; always use an anti-static **ground bracelet** as you work.

◆ **Liquid cooling** can be used to draw heat from a heat sink that cools a CPU.

◆ When installing a CPU:
- Install the **heat sink** or CPU fan on the CPU housing, following the directions accompanying the heat sink or fan.
- For a socket, before inserting the CPU, open the socket by lifting the **ZIF handle**, and for Slot 1, open the side braces on both ends of the slot.
- For a fan, attach the power lead from the fan to the pins on the system board.
- After installing the CPU, if the system appears dead or sounds beep codes, suspect that the CPU is not securely seated. Turn off the PC and reseat the CPU.

◆ When installing memory:
- For RIMM memory, all memory sockets must be filled. If the socket does not hold a RIMM, install a C-RIMM (continuity RIMM). The C-RIMM serves as a placeholder to achieve continuity throughout all sockets.
- Memory modules have spring catches on both ends of the memory slot.
- Look for notches on the memory module to exactly fit notches on the memory slot. This will indicate the correct orientation as well as the type of memory the slot can accomodate.
- Don't force modules into a memory slot; they are probably the wrong type of module if they don't fit easily into the slot.
- After installation, if the count is not correct for the new memory, turn off the PC, reseat the memory (for a DIMM, move the module to a new slot).
- To remove a module, release the latches on each side and for a SIMM, gently rotate the module out of the socket at an angle. For a DIMM, lift the module straight up and out of the slot.
- For some systems, you must tell CMOS setup how much memory is installed.

OBJECTIVES ON THE JOB

A CPU might be replaced if the old CPU is bad or you are attempting to improve performance with an upgraded CPU. Before upgrading either a CPU or memory, verify that the new component is compatible with the system board and the other components already installed.

PRACTICE TEST QUESTIONS

1. **A system has two SIMMs installed and two SIMM slots are still open. Which is correct?**
   a. You can install a third SIMM in one of the available slots.
   b. You must remove the two SIMMs and replace them with two larger SIMMs.
   c. You can install two more SIMMs in the empty slots, but they must match the already installed SIMMs.
   d. You can install two more SIMMs without matching the other SIMMs in any way.

2. **A system has four DIMM slots and one DIMM installed. Which statement is correct?**
   a. You can install one, two, or three more DIMMs of any memory size supported by the system board.
   b. You can install only one or three more DIMMs, but not two more.
   c. The additional DIMMs you install must match in memory size to the one DIMM already installed.
   d. The total amount of memory installed cannot exceed 64 MB.

3. **Which statement is true about RAM on a system board?**
   a. EDO and BEDO memory modules can exist together on a system board.
   b. SIMMs and DIMMs are protected against ESD by a coating on the tiny circuit boards.
   c. Most BIOS detect new RAM installed without manually changing CMOS settings.
   d. A single SIMM can be installed on a Pentium system board.

4. **After installing memory and booting the system, the memory does not count up correctly. The most likely problem is:**
   a. a memory module is bad
   b. the modules are not seated properly
   c. the CPU was damaged during the memory installation
   d. a circuit board became loose during the installation and needs reseating

5. **How many pins are there on a DIMM?**
   a. 30
   b. 64
   c. 72
   d. 168

6. **Without the system board documentation, how can you tell if a DIMM is the correct type of memory for a system board?**
   a. There is no way to tell; the documentation is the only source of that information.
   b. Match the notches on the DIMM to the notches in the memory slot.
   c. Look at the documentation that comes with the DIMM; it lists the system boards that the DIMM will work in.
   d. If the length of the DIMM and the DIMM slot are the same, it will work.

7. **Why does a Pentium system require that SIMMs be installed in pairs?**
   a. It takes two 32-bit SIMMs to accommodate a 64-bit data path.
   b. It takes two SIMMs to yield 8 MB of memory, which is required for a Pentium to work.
   c. Pentium system boards are designed to require at least two SIMMs so that the system will have enough memory for normal operation.
   d. None of the above; a SIMM can work on a Pentium system board as an individual module.

OBJECTIVES

1.2 Identify basic procedures for adding and removing field-replaceable modules for desktop systems. Given a replacement scenario, choose the appropriate sequences.

ADAPTERS: SOUND CARD, VIDEO CARD, SCSI, IEEE 1394/FIREWIRE, AND USB

UNDERSTANDING THE OBJECTIVE

Video cards are the interface between the CPU and the monitor and contain some memory to hold display data before it is sent to the monitor. Video cards today are installed in AGP slots, although older systems used PCI, VESA, or ISA slots. Sound cards, SCSI cards, USB cards, and IEEE 1394/FireWire cards are typically designed to fit PCI slots.

WHAT YOU **REALLY** NEED TO KNOW

- ◆ Many computers sold today have integrated sound, USB, and video support. In other words, PCI cards are no longer used. Therefore, replacing a component means replacing the motherboard in some situations. Many file servers have built-in support for a high-speed SCSI controller.
- ◆ The VESA bus slot was replaced with the PCI slot which has now been replaced with the AGP slot for video boards.
- ◆ The AGP bus connects directly to the CPU, running at the same speed as the system bus with a 32-bit data path.
- ◆ An AGP slot is a 132-pin slot, and the AGP Pro standard uses a wider 188-pin slot. The extra pins provide additional voltage to high-end graphics accelerators.
- ◆ Windows 98, Windows 2000, and Windows XP support AGP.
- ◆ When installing a video card on an older system, once the card is physically installed in the video slot, install the video card drivers. Use the drivers recommended by the manufacturer.
- ◆ SCSI and IEEE 1394/FireWire cards are used for high-speed data transfer (i.e. video capture) and plug into a PCI slot. They often require the installation of specific software drivers.
- ◆ USB ports are integrated into motherboards on newer computers and cannot be replaced. Support for USB 2.0 is provided in Windows XP Service Pack 1.
- ◆ Windows XP offers a unique feature called Device Driver Rollback. This feature offers administrators an opportunity to undo a device driver installation that may have caused a problem. The Device Driver Rollback option can be accessed under each individual component in Device Manager.
- ◆ To install a USB device, first plug in the USB device. You will then be prompted for device drivers.
- ◆ Hardware device drivers always contain at least one .inf file. The .inf contains a **device ID** string that is used to identify a specific hardware device and install supporting files.

OBJECTIVES ON THE JOB

If the video system fails, before exchanging the video card, check the simple things first including the on/off monitor switch, power to the monitor, monitor adjustments, video drivers, and video cable. Only then exchange the video card for a known–good card.

PRACTICE TEST QUESTIONS

1. **The fastest port used for video boards today is:**
    a. VESA
    b. PCI
    c. AGP
    d. IEEE 1394

2. **What is the difference in an AGP slot and an AGP Pro slot on a system board?**
    a. An AGP slot is wider than an AGP Pro slot.
    b. An AGP Pro slot is wider than an AGP slot.
    c. There is no difference; both slots are the same size and shape.
    d. The AGP slot has 188 pins and the AGP Pro slot has 132 pins.

3. **What is one thing you can do to speed up a sluggish system that is graphic intensive?**
    a. Add memory to the video board.
    b. Move the video board to a different slot on the system board.
    c. Buy a larger monitor.
    d. Upgrade the power supply.

4. **AGP 4X is defined by the AGP 2.0 specification. The 4X refers to:**
    a. data throughput that can be achieved by the video card
    b. the number of memory chips on an AGP video card
    c. the number of pins on the AGP slot
    d. the size of the video card

5. **What bus is no longer found on system boards today?**
    a. ISA
    b. PCI
    c. VESA
    d. Both a and c

6. **The video system does not work. What is the first thing you check?**
    a. Is the monitor turned on?
    b. Is the video cable good?
    c. Is the monitor adjusted correctly?
    d. Is the video card good?

7. **What is the name of the string identifier that is used to match a specific hardware device with its installation software?**
    a. Device ID
    b. .inf file
    c. Setup.exe
    d. none of the above

OBJECTIVES

1.2 Identify basic procedures for adding and removing field-replaceable modules for desktop systems. Given a replacement scenario, choose the appropriate sequences.

ADAPTERS: NETWORK INTERFACE CARD (NIC), MODEM, AND WIRELESS

UNDERSTANDING THE OBJECTIVE

Network interface cards (NICs), modems, and wireless cards all serve as the interface between your computer and the outside world. Network interface cards and modems can be installed in PCI slots, although newer systems integrate these devices into the motherboard. Wireless cards are used frequently in notebook computers to increase mobility.

WHAT YOU **REALLY** NEED TO KNOW

- Failed devices that are integrated into the motherboard cannot be replaced. Instead, the entire motherboard must be replaced.
- For network cards, use the network card that matches the network protocol and cabling type of the network.
- Install the network card in a PCI slot (ISA slots have been eliminated on newer computers) and then install the network card drivers. After the drivers are installed, turn off the PC, connect the network cable, and reboot the PC to connect to the network.
- Verify the network card is working by checking the lights on the card. One light stays lit when the PC is connected to the network, and another light flashes when data is being transmitted over the network.
- If a network card fails to work, try uninstalling and reinstalling the network card drivers. Verify with the network administrator that you are using the correct drivers.
- Wireless cards plug into PCI slots on desktop computers.
- It is important to configure a wireless NIC using the supplied software and documentation to set specific wireless network parameters.
- Using a wireless network connection requires that you remain within a certain distance of the wireless access point.
- Each network interface card and wireless card has its own unique identifier called a MAC adapter address.
- Modems are one of the most often replaced components on a computer. Users sometimes leave a phone line plugged into a modem. The phone line can carry an electrical surge that can damage a modem. Electrical surges can be the result of a direct or indirect lightning strike. The best method for testing a suspected faulty modem is to replace it with a known-good modem.
- It is recommended that you use a surge suppressor that includes a RJ-11 jack for protecting against phone line surges.

OBJECTIVES ON THE JOB

A network card sometimes fails and needs replacing, but first verify that the network cable is good and the network is working properly. If possible, replace the network cable with a known-good cable. Lightning frequently causes damage to modems. Wireless network cards vary in configuration. Always read documentation when configuring wireless network cards.

PRACTICE TEST QUESTIONS

1. **Which of the following techniques are useful for troubleshooting modem problems?**
   a. Ask the phone company to test the phone line.
   b. Replace the modem with a known-good modem.
   c. Reinstall the modem software.
   d. All of the above.

2. **What is the most common cause of modem failure?**
   a. upgrading Web browser
   b. lightning
   c. bad memory
   d. viruses

3. **What is one thing you can do to speed up sluggish bandwidth on a wireless network?**
   a. Add memory to the video board.
   b. Move closer to the network access point.
   c. Add more RAM.
   d. None of the above.

4. **What is the most common type of network cable used today?**
   a. RJ-45
   b. CAT 5
   c. RJ-11
   d. CAT 3

5. **Which bus can be used to install a modem?**
   a. ISA
   b. PCI
   c. VESA
   d. Both a and b

6. **How can users be authenticated on a wireless network?**
   a. They cannot be authenticated.
   b. by registering the MAC address of their wireless card
   c. by operating system
   d. by IRQ

7. **How can you tell that the network card is connected to and communicating with other network equipment on the network?**
   a. View resources in Network Neighborhood.
   b. View a shared printer in the Printer window.
   c. Check for a solid light on the network card.
   d. Check for a blinking light on the network card.

1.3 Identify basic procedures for adding and removing field-replaceable modules for portable systems. Given a replacement scenario, choose the appropriate sequences.

STORAGE DEVICES: FDD, HDD, CD/CDRW, DVD/DVDRW, AND REMOVABLE STORAGE • MEMORY

UNDERSTANDING THE OBJECTIVE

Notebook computers are generally purchased as a whole unit, including hardware and software. You are less likely to upgrade a notebook's hardware or OS, than you would a PC's. A notebook likely has the standard drives that a PC has including a floppy disk drive (FDD), hard disk drive (HDD), a CD-ROM drive, or a CDRW. More expensive notebook computers include DVD drives or DVD-Rewrite drives.

WHAT YOU **REALLY** NEED TO KNOW

◆ Floppy disk drives (FDD), hard disk drives (HDD), CD-ROM drives, CDRW drives, DVD drives, DVDRW drives, removable storage devices, and memory are all considered field-replaceable units.

◆ Some notebook computers come equipped with a modular drive bay which can support a variety of drives. Some examples of modular drives include a CD-ROM drive, a floppy disk drive, a Zip drive, a DVD drive, or DVDRW drive. Some notebook models include support for adding a second modular hard drive or second modular battery.

◆ Modular drives can be replaced by contacting the system manufacturer. If the problem is with the modular drive bay, then the notebook is usually serviced by the manufacturer.

◆ Modular drives are sometimes **hot-swappable** which means they can be switched without having to power down the notebook computer. A hot-swap utility is sometimes installed and running (check the system tray) on notebook computers to aid in swapping modular drives.

◆ Some notebook computers come equipped with an integrated drive bay. Integrated bays do not offer the flexibility of changing from one drive to another. If service is needed on a faulty integrated drive, contact the manufacturer to determine if the notebook must be serviced by the manufacturer. Failing to do so may void the warranty.

◆ Notebook computers use SO-DIMM (small outline DIMMs) memory which is much smaller than PC memory. There are four types of SO-DIMM memory: 72-pin, 144-pin, 160-pin, and credit card memory. It is important to check the documentation before attempting a replacement or upgrade of memory because the procedure varies from one make/model to another.

◆ Memory keys, a form of removable storage, have become a popular choice for moving files from one computer to another. Memory keys connect via the USB port. Higher capacity memory keys sometimes require USB 2.0.

OBJECTIVES ON THE JOB

Notebooks are very proprietary in design, which means the skills to support them are brand specific. A notebook's warranty can be voided if you open the notebook case or install hardware that was not made by, or at least authorized by, the notebook manufacturer.

PRACTICE TEST QUESTIONS

1. Which of the following devices is considered a field replaceable unit on a notebook computer?
   a. floppy disk drive
   b. memory
   c. CD-ROM drive
   d. all of the above

2. Which types of technology are often bundled together into a single drive?
   a. CD-ROM/Zip
   b. DVD/CDRW
   c. DVDRW/CDRW
   d. none of the above

3. To hot-swap an external storage device, which statement must be true?
   a. The notebook must be rebooted in order for it to sense the newly installed device.
   b. The OS must support hot-swapping or a hot-swap utility must be installed.
   c. The external device must be an IDE device.
   d. All the above.

4. What kind of memory do notebook computers use?
   a. SO-DIMM
   b. DSIMM
   c. SIMM
   d. RIMM

5. Which operating system provides the most comprehensive support for hot-swapping devices?
   a. Windows 98
   b. Windows ME
   c. Windows 2000
   d. Windows XP

6. Which of the following steps should be followed, given the following scenario? Upgrade notebook memory.
   a. Contact manufacturer to ensure upgrading memory is within the terms of the warranty.
   b. Order replacement memory from manufacturer.
   c. Read and follow all documentation before beginning upgrade.
   d. All of the above.

7. Which hardware or software listed below is typically proprietary to the make and model of the notebook computer?
   a. CD-ROM
   b. SO-DIMM
   c. restoration utilities provided by the manufacturer
   d. all of the above

1.3 Identify basic procedures for adding and removing field-replaceable modules for portable systems. Given a replacement scenario, choose the appropriate sequences.

PCMCIA/MINI PCI ADAPTERS: NETWORK INTERFACE CARD (NIC), MODEM, SCSI, IEEE 1394/FIREWIRE, USB, AND STORAGE (MEMORY AND HARD DRIVE)

UNDERSTANDING THE OBJECTIVE

Notebooks and their accessories cost more than desktop PCs with similar features because components are designed to be more compact and use less power. Many components such as NICs, modems, and USB ports are integrated into the motherboard on notebook computers. Other components such as SCSI and IEEE 1394/FireWire ports can be found on more expensive notebook computers. Additional memory and hard drive capacity can be added via a PC Card or USB memory key.

WHAT YOU **REALLY** NEED TO KNOW

- ◆ Additional devices, including a DVD/DVDRW drive, can be added to a notebook computer by way of way of a PC Card or USB port. This feature can greatly enhance the usability of a notebook that is equipped with integrated drives. External devices such as a DVD drive are connected to the notebook by way of a PC Card.

- ◆ Devices connected via the USB port can operate at fast speeds, comparable to internal devices, if USB 2.0 is available. USB 1.0 can be upgraded to USB 2.0 by installing Service Pack 1 on Windows XP.

- ◆ PCMCIA (Personal Computer Memory Card International Association) cards can be used to add peripherals such as a network interface card, modem, SCSI controller, IEEE 1394/FireWire controller, USB controller, extra memory (RAM), and hard drive capacity.

- ◆ PCMCIA (also called PC Cards) can be hot-swapped. It is important to first turn off a PC Card before swapping it with another PC Card. This can be accomplished in Windows XP by using the Safely Remove Hardware icon located in the system tray. In Windows 2000, use the Add/Remove Hardware icon in the Control Panel to disable PC Cards. In Windows 9x, use the PC Card icon in the Control Panel.

- ◆ PCMCIA cards are considered to be field-replaceable units. Troubleshooting can be easily performed by replacing the PC Card with a known-good PC Card.

- ◆ The latest PCMCIA specification is called CardBus. It improves performance while remaining backward compatible with older specifications.

- ◆ Mini-PCI is a standard that provides integrated support for devices such as network interface cards and modems in notebook computers. If a software or device driver modification fails to solve issues with an integrated device, return the notebook computer to the manufacturer for repair.

OBJECTIVES ON THE JOB

It is likely that you will be asked to upgrade components that are by way of the USB port or a PC Card. This may require device driver installation and good software troubleshooting skills. Windows XP provides excellent device driver support. The manufacturer provides restoration utilities on a CD–ROM or floppy disk that are customized to a specific notebook computer model and operating system.

PRACTICE TEST QUESTIONS

1. **Which of the following operating systems support USB 2.0 via a Microsoft patch or service pack?**
   a. Windows XP
   b. Windows 2000
   c. Windows 98
   d. Both a and b

2. **Which of the following techniques is useful in troubleshooting issues with a PCMCIA card?**
   a. Replace the PCMCIA with a known-good card.
   b. Visit the PCMCIA manufacturer's Web site and review support information.
   c. Reboot the notebook computer.
   d. All of the above.

3. **To hot-swap an external storage device, which statement must be true?**
   a. The notebook must be rebooted in order for it to sense the newly installed device.
   b. The OS must support hot-swapping.
   c. The external device must be an IDE device.
   d. All the above.

4. **If a notebook does not have an internal modem included in the hardware, how is a modem typically added to the system?**
   a. as an external IDE device
   b. connected to the notebook using the serial port
   c. as a PC Card
   d. connected to the notebook using the USB port

5. **What is the Windows XP feature that allows you to share an Internet connection between two computers?**
   a. Multilink Channel Aggregation
   b. Microsoft Exchange
   c. Internet Connection Sharing
   d. Virtual Phone Lines Aggregation

6. **Which of the following operating systems support USB 1.0?**
   a. Windows 98
   b. Window ME
   c. Windows 2000
   d. All of the above

7. **What is important to first determine before servicing or upgrading a notebook computer?**
   a. What is the warranty agreement?
   b. What are the latest updates to the OS installed on the notebook and is the OS the most current version?
   c. How long has it been since the battery was replaced or recharged?
   d. Is all software installed on the notebook properly registered with the software manufacturer?

1.3 Identify basic procedures for adding and removing field-replaceable modules for portable systems. Given a replacement scenario, choose the appropriate sequences.

POWER SOURCES: AC ADAPTER, DC ADAPTER, AND BATTERY • LCD PANEL

UNDERSTANDING THE OBJECTIVE

Notebook computers use thin LCD panels instead of CRTs for displaying information. LCD panels vary in quality depending upon the technology used and can be easily damaged. They are expensive to repair. Notebook computers can use a variety of power sources which include an AC adapter, DC adapter, and a battery.

WHAT YOU **REALLY** NEED TO KNOW

◆ A battery is the standard choice for powering a notebook computer. Battery life varies typically from one hour to three hours, depending upon several factors. These include the size and type of the LCD panel, the processor speed, and the operating system—among other factors.

◆ Windows XP is the ideal choice for preserving battery life on notebook computers. It does a better job of monitoring remaining battery life than previous operating systems. Standby mode also helps by powering down the monitor and hard drive when not in use.

◆ Hibernation mode is a greater attempt at saving power and can save all open files before powering down the notebook computer. If needed, hibernation mode can be disabled under Windows XP by entering the Control Panel and choosing Power Options. Then, uncheck the "enable hibernation" option.

◆ Notebook batteries include the now obsolete Ni-Cad (Nickel Cadmium) that had memory problems, NiMH (Nickel-Metal-Hydride), and Lithium Ion. Lithium Ion batteries provide two to three hours of power on most notebook computers. Multiple batteries can be added to some notebooks to extend uptime. Current research may yield Lithium Metal batteries that offer a long shelf life with greater efficiency.

◆ Some notebook computers come equipped with a modular drive bay that is capable of supporting a second battery. The battery is considered to be a field-replaceable unit and should only be replaced after contacting the manufacturer and reading accompanying documentation.

◆ Instead of a battery, you can use an AC adapter to power a notebook. The AC adapter recharges the battery. A DC adapter can be used to power a notebook computer via an automobile's cigarette outlet.

◆ LCD panels vary in size, but are typically from 12.1" to 15.4" while display types vary from dual-scan passive matrix to active matrix (called thin film transistor or TFT). Active matrix provides a higher quality image.

OBJECTIVES ON THE JOB

An LCD panel should only be replaced after contacting the manufacturer. If the notebook is still under warranty, the manufacturer may perform the necessary repairs at no charge. Some warranties also cover replacement costs associated with dead pixels.

PRACTICE TEST QUESTIONS

1. **Which type of battery is most often shipped with state-of-the-art notebook computers?**
   a. NiMH
   b. Lithium Ion
   c. Ni-Cad
   d. None of the above

2. **Which types of notebook batteries typically experienced memory problems?**
   a. NiMH
   b. Lithium Ion
   c. Ni-Cad
   d. All of the above

3. **Which of the following is true concerning LCD panels?**
   a. The larger the LCD panel, the greater the cost of replacement.
   b. LCD panels can be easily damaged.
   c. It is not uncommon for an LCD panel to have one or two dead pixels.
   d. All the above.

4. **Which of the following technologies produce a sharper image?**
   a. Active matrix
   b. Dual-scan passive matrix
   c. Positron balanced
   d. None of the above

5. **Which of the following can be used to power a notebook computer?**
   a. DC adapter
   b. battery
   c. AC adapter
   d. all the above

6. **What is the danger in using the AC adapter too much to power a notebook?**
   a. The AC adapter will burn out prematurely.
   b. The notebook will waste too much electricity.
   c. The change of damage from ESD is increased.
   d. The battery will not last as long between charges.

7. **Which of the following steps should you take if an LCD panel is cracked?**
   a. Contact the manufacturer to see if this is covered under the warranty.
   b. Contact the manufacturer to order a replacement LCD panel—if out of warranty.
   c. Consider purchasing the LCD panel from a third party—if out of warranty.
   d. All the above.

1.3 Identify basic procedures for adding and removing field-replaceable modules for portable systems. Given a replacement scenario, choose the appropriate sequences.

DOCKING STATION/PORT REPLICATORS • INPUT DEVICES: KEYBOARD, MOUSE/POINTER DEVICES, AND TOUCH SCREEN • WIRELESS: ADAPTER/CONTROLLER AND ANTENNAE

UNDERSTANDING THE OBJECTIVE

Wireless adapter cards add greater mobility to notebook computers by allowing users to transfer files and access the Internet from almost any location. Docking stations and port replicators can turn a notebook computer into a desktop computer where additional devices are easily supported. Input devices such as a keyboard, mouse, and touch screen can be added.

WHAT YOU **REALLY** NEED TO KNOW

◆ A docking station can be used to essentially turn a notebook computer into a desktop computer by providing additional PCI slots and expansion bays. A full-size keyboard can also be utilized. Docking stations are manufactured to fit specific notebook models. Windows XP has been optimized for use with docking stations by allowing users to connect or disconnect without having to modify hardware configurations or reboot.

◆ A notebook can have a video-out port so that you can use a monitor as an alternative display device.

◆ Notebook computers can be equipped with a wireless adapter card that connects to an access point. An access point (AP) is a hardware device that provides users with a mobile network connection to the local area network. APs provide users with a limited range to access network bandwidth. The greater the distance from an AP, the lower the network bandwidth. Access points also provide administrators with a means of applying security protocols to authenticate users.

◆ Wireless controllers are hardware devices that are used to configure and manage multiple access points across a local area network.

◆ Access points use antennae to transmit RF (radio frequency) signals to wireless cards in notebook computers. Antennae typically transmit RF signals in an omni-directional or directional pattern. Omni-directional signals provide the widest coverage by transmitting signal in a 360-degree horizontal direction (signals are not transmitted vertically). Therefore, for omni-direction transmission, the antennae should be perpendicular to the ground to maximum range. Directional transmission is often used for point-to-point links between buildings.

◆ Notebooks have a pointing device such as a touchpad or trackball embedded near the keyboard, but a user can install a mouse using a mouse or serial port as an alternate pointing device. Many notebooks offer touch screen capability that lets users interact with software by applying pressure to the LCD panel.

OBJECTIVES ON THE JOB

You should be able to troubleshoot software and hardware issues that may occur between a notebook computer and a docking station. Setup and configuration of wireless adapters vary by manufacturer. Always refer to included documentation which may reference using an included software utility to configure the wireless adapter.

PRACTICE TEST QUESTIONS

1. **Which Intel processor is integrating support for wireless LANs?**
   a. Intel Pentium III
   b. Intel Pentium 4
   c. Intel Pentium 4 M
   d. None—the technology does not exist.

2. **How should an antenna that transmits an omni-directional be physically positioned?**
   a. parallel to the floor
   b. perpendicular to the wall it's mounted on
   c. perpendicular to the floor
   d. none of the above

3. **How can a PCI card be added to a notebook computer?**
   a. via a PCMCIA card
   b. docking port
   c. via the USB port
   d. none of the above

4. **What do access points use to transmit RF signals to wireless cards in notebook computers?**
   a. antennae
   b. transfer files
   c. docking station cards
   d. wireless stations

5. **Which operating system provides the most comprehensive support for wireless network cards?**
   a. Windows 98
   b. Windows ME
   c. Windows 2000
   d. Windows XP

6. **Which notebook hardware listed below is considered a field-replaceable unit?**
   a. mouse
   b. keyboard
   c. wireless adapter
   d. all of the above

7. **Which hardware or software listed below is typically proprietary to the make and model of the notebook computer?**
   a. docking station
   b. port replicator
   c. restoration utilities provided by the manufacturer
   d. all of the above

1.4 Identify typical IRQs, DMAs, and I/O addresses, and procedures for altering these settings when installing and configuring devices. Choose the appropriate installation or configuration steps in a given scenario.

LEGACY DEVICES (E.G., ISA SOUND CARD) • SPECIALIZED DEVICES (E.G., CAD/CAM) • MULTIMEDIA DEVICES

UNDERSTANDING THE OBJECTIVE

Before installing a new device, determine what system resources (IRQ, DMA channel, or I/O address) are in use. For DOS, use MSD, and for Windows, use Device Manager. Legacy devices are configured to use these resources by DIP switches or jumpers on the devices themselves. Newer Plug and Play devices are automatically configured and sometimes prompt the user for device drivers.

WHAT YOU **REALLY** NEED TO KNOW

- ◆ **IRQs** 8 through 15 cascade to IRQ 2, which is not available for I/O devices. IRQ 9 is wired to the pin on the ISA bus previously assigned to IRQ 2.
- ◆ The 8-bit ISA bus only has wires for the first 8 IRQs. The 16-bit ISA bus has wires for all 16 IRQs.
- ◆ Legacy devices such as ISA sound cards, ISA modems, and ISA SCSI cards typically use factory default settings in terms of IRQ addresses, DMA channels, and I/O addresses. The factory default resource settings can be altered by re-adjusting DIP switches or jumpers.
- ◆ ISA devices cannot share system resources. For this reason, you may be forced to disable devices in system CMOS or remove other legacy devices in order for an ISA device to work correctly.
- ◆ Multimedia devices that utilize PCI technology can often share resources with other PCI devices and are usually automatically configured by the operating system via Plug and Play. For example, a sound card sometimes reserves IRQ 9 and can share this resource with a NIC.
- ◆ It is strongly recommended to upgrade legacy devices since 16-bit ISA slots do not exist on newer computers.
- ◆ A SCSI bus system uses a single set of resources (an IRQ, I/O addresses and possibly a DMA channel). All SCSI devices on the bus share these resources. A USB bus system works the same way.
- ◆ Specialized devices such as CAD/CAM devices, video capture cards, security card readers, and temperature sensors can be installed in much the same manner as common devices. Always refer to their documentation.
- ◆ Here are some common IRQ and I/O addresses:

IRQ	I/O Address	Device
5	278-27F	Sound card or other multimedia device, legacy or specialized device
9-10	varies	Sound card or other multimedia device, legacy or specialized device
11	varies	Sound card or other multimedia device, legacy or specialized device

OBJECTIVES ON THE JOB

Resolving resource conflicts on legacy devices is a challenge for a PC technician. Determine which current resources are being used. You must then force conflicting devices to use a different resource. If this is not possible, then set the device back to its original factory settings and start moving or eliminating other devices to open resources.

PRACTICE TEST QUESTIONS

1. **Which of the following statements is true?**
   a. PCI devices cannot share resources.
   b. ISA devices cannot share resources.
   c. ISA devices can share resources.
   d. Both a and c.

2. **Which of the following IRQs is typically available:**
   a. IRQ 9
   b. IRQ 10
   c. IRQ 11
   d. All of the above

3. **In this scenario, choose a common technique to modify resource settings (either on the computer or device itself) for a common device such as a sound card.**
   a. modify resources using device manager
   b. modify resources using CMOS
   c. modify resources by moving the PCI card to another PCI slot
   d. all of the above

4. **The purpose of an IRQ is to:**
   a. give the CPU a way to communicate with a device
   b. give the device a way of interrupting the CPU for service
   c. pass data from the device to the CPU
   d. give a device a way to pass data to memory

5. **The purpose of an I/O address is to:**
   a. give the CPU a way of communicating with a device
   b. give a device a way of requesting service from the CPU
   c. give a device a way of sending data to the CPU
   d. allow a device to pass data to the CPU

6. **Which IRQ can a device using an 8-bit ISA bus NOT use?**
   a. 5
   b. 4
   c. 7
   d. 10

7. **On the 16-bit ISA bus, IRQ 2 is used to cascade to the higher IRQs, so its position on the ISA bus is taken by which IRQ?**
   a. IRQ 0
   b. IRQ 7
   c. IRQ 9
   d. IRQ 15

1.4 Identify typical IRQs, DMAs, and I/O addresses, and procedures for altering these settings when installing and configuring devices. Choose the appropriate installation or configuration steps in a given scenario.

INTERNAL MODEMS • FLOPPY DRIVE CONTROLLERS • HARD DRIVE CONTROLLERS • NICS

UNDERSTANDING THE OBJECTIVE

Internal modems and NICs require proper resource configuration in order to work properly. Their resource settings can be configured in Windows from Device Manager. Floppy drive controllers are located on the system board, and hard drive controllers are usually located on the device itself. Use CMOS setup to modify resources or enable/disable a controller on the motherboard as needed.

WHAT YOU **REALLY** NEED TO KNOW

- ◆ Internal modems can sometimes conflict with a COM port on the system board. If this occurs, use CMOS setup to disable the conflicting COM port on the system board. Then, restart the computer and verify that the modem is working properly.
- ◆ Older internal modems can sometimes be configured to use U.S. Robotics drivers. If using these drivers fails to solve the problem, contact the computer manufacturer for a correct set of device drivers.
- ◆ To modify resource settings for PCI devices such as internal modems or NIC, move the device card to another PCI slot. Then, reboot the computer and verify that the device is no longer conflicting.
- ◆ Floppy drive controllers and hard drive controllers do not typically conflict with many devices. If a conflict occurs, remove all ISA and PCI cards from your computer and reboot. If this fails to solve the conflict, then delete the conflicting controller and reboot. If this still fails to solve the conflict, then you may have a faulty controller on the system board. Contact the computer manufacturer.
- ◆ If an ISA NIC is conflicting, consider upgrading to a PCI NIC.
- ◆ Here are some common IRQ and I/O addresses for devices listed in this section:

IRQ	I/O Address	Device
3	2F8-2FF	COM2, Internal Modem
4	3F8-3FF	COM1, Internal Modem
6	3F0-3F7	Floppy drive controller
9-10		NICs
11		NICs
14	1F0-1F7	Primary IDE hard drive
15	170-170	Secondary IDE hard drive

OBJECTIVES ON THE JOB

Troubleshooting controller issues can be difficult, especially if the floppy disk controller or hard drive controller is faulty. The best approach to troubleshooting any conflicting device is to remove all devices. Then, reboot the computer and slowly add one card at a time while rebooting after each addition. Once the conflicting card is pin-pointed, either move it to another PCI slot or its adjust jumper settings (for ISA cards).

PRACTICE TEST QUESTIONS

1. A disk drive can access primary memory without involving the CPU by using a(n):
   a. IRQ
   b. port address
   c. DMA channel
   d. I/O address

2. IRQ 14 is reserved for:
   a. the coprocessor
   b. a mouse
   c. the secondary IDE controller
   d. the primary IDE controller

3. IRQ 15 is reserved for:
   a. the coprocessor
   b. a mouse
   c. the secondary IDE controller
   d. the primary IDE controller

4. IRQ 4 is reserved for:
   a. the coprocessor
   b. a COM port
   c. an internal modem
   d. b and c

5. Given the following scenario, which of the following steps should you take to solve the problem? An ISA modem is conflicting.
   a. Upgrade to a PCI modem.
   b. Remove all devices and slowly add a device—rebooting the computer after each addition.
   c. Disable the COM port using CMOS setup.
   d. All of the above.

6. IRQ 9 is reserved for:
   a. It is not reserved for any particular device and is available.
   b. internal modem
   c. mouse
   d. hard drive controller

7. Which of the following statements are true?
   a. A PCI NIC can share its resources with another PCI device.
   b. A PCI NIC can share its resources with another ISA device.
   c. A PCI NIC can share its resource with any other device.
   d. All of the above.

OBJECTIVES

1.4 Identify typical IRQs, DMAs, and I/O addresses, and procedures for altering these settings when installing and configuring devices. Choose the appropriate installation or configuration steps in a given scenario.

I/O PORTS: SERIAL, PARALLEL, USB PORTS, IEEE 1394/FIREWIRE, AND INFRARED

UNDERSTANDING THE OBJECTIVE

Serial ports, parallel ports, USB ports, IEEE 1394/FireWire ports, and infrared ports are often integrated into the system board and share resources with other devices including PCI devices. USB ports, IEEE 1394/FireWire ports, and other ports can be added to a computer with the addition of a special PCI card. Configuration of port resources is performed from CMOS setup and can also be performed from Windows Device Manager. Ports can be enabled or disabled as needed.

WHAT YOU **REALLY** NEED TO KNOW

- ◆ An I/O controller card can be used to add serial or parallel ports.
- ◆ Newer computers are usually equipped with two or more USB ports and a single COM port.
- ◆ A **parallel port** can be found on nearly every computer—regardless of age. They can be configured as LPT1, LPT2, or LPT3.
- ◆ Serial ports can be configured as COM1, COM2, COM3, or COM4.
- ◆ IRQ settings and I/O address assignments can sometimes be modified in CMOS setup.
- ◆ An infrared transceiver can use the resources of a serial port and provide virtual ports for infrared devices. These virtual ports are assigned their own individual resources.
- ◆ The USB bus is controlled by a USB host controller that is integrated into the chipset. A single IRQ, I/O address, and DMA channel are used by the USB host controller which in turn can support up to 127 USB devices.
- ◆ IEEE 1394/FireWire has greater data transfer speeds than USB and uses a single set of resources (similar to USB) to manage all FireWire devices.
- ◆ Here are some common IRQ and I/O addresses for devices listed in this section:

IRQ	I/O Address	Device
3	2F8-2FF	COM2
3	2E8-2EF	COM4
4	3F8-3FF	COM1
4	3E8-3EF	COM3
5	278-27F	Parallel port LPT2
7	378-37F	Printer parallel port LPT1
9-10		USB Ports, available
11		available
12	238-23F	System-board PS/2 mouse
13	0F8-0FF	Math coprocessor

OBJECTIVES ON THE JOB

I/O ports are undergoing rapid change with the introduction of USB and FireWire ports. Serial and parallel ports are destined to be legacy ports. Port resource settings can sometimes be modified in CMOS setup.

PRACTICE TEST QUESTIONS

1. **IRQ 5 is reserved for:**
   a. a COM port
   b. a parallel port
   c. the secondary IDE controller
   d. the primary IDE controller

2. **IRQ 3 is reserved for:**
   a. a COM port
   b. a parallel port
   c. a USB port
   d. the primary IDE controller

3. **In this scenario, choose a common technique to modify resource settings (either on the computer or device itself) for a common device such as an IEEE 1394/FireWire card.**
   a. modify resources using device manager
   b. modify resources using CMOS
   c. modify resources by moving the PCI card to another PCI slot
   d. all of the above

4. **IRQ 9 is reserved for:**
   a. a COM port
   b. a parallel port
   c. a USB port
   d. the primary IDE controller

5. **Given the following scenario, which of the following steps should you take to solve the problem? Under Windows 2000/XP, a USB device is not being detected after being plugged into a USB port.**
   a. Log on with local administrator permissions and plug the device in again.
   b. Check Device Manager to ensure the USB Host controller is not conflicting with another device.
   c. Plug the device into a different USB port.
   d. All of the above.

6. **Which of the following operating systems have offered native support for USB ports?**
   a. Windows XP
   b. Windows 2000
   c. Windows NT
   d. Both a and b

7. **Which of the following operating systems have offered native support for FireWire ports?**
   a. Windows XP
   b. Windows 98
   c. Windows NT
   d. All of the above

OBJECTIVES

1.5 Identify the names, purposes, and performance characteristics, of standardized/common peripheral ports, associated cabling, and their connectors. Recognize ports, cabling, and connectors, by sight.

PORT TYPES: SERIAL, PARALLEL, USB PORTS, IEEE 1394/FIREWIRE, AND INFRARED

UNDERSTANDING THE OBJECTIVE

Older ports such as serial and parallel ports are being phased out in favor of newer, faster ports such as USB ports and IEEE 1394/FireWire ports. An infrared transceiver usually connects to the serial port or COM port and supports wireless input devices.

WHAT YOU REALLY NEED TO KNOW

◆ Serial ports are sometimes used to support devices such as an external modem, Palm Pilot, or game controller and are usually connected directly to the system board. A game port has a 15-pin female connector.

◆ There are three types of printer ports: A normal printer port (also called a Centronics port), an Enhanced Parallel Port (EPP), and an Extended Capabilities Port (ECP). A standard parallel port allows data to be transmitted in a single direction. EPP and ECP ports can transmit data in both directions (called bi-directional).

◆ IEEE 1284 compliant printer cables must be used with EPP and ECP printers.

◆ The A-Male connector is flat/wide and attaches to the USB port on the computer. The B-Male connector is square and attaches to the USB device.

◆ FireWire ports use two types of connectors. The 6-pin connector provides voltage to the device and is larger than the 4-pin connector which does not provide voltage to the device. The cable consists of two pairs of shielded twisted pair cable that is similar to Ethernet.

Port Type	Performance	Connector	Max Cable Length
Serial	115.2 Kbps	9-pin male, 25-pin male, 15-pin female (game port)	Varies—up to 150 ft
Parallel	1.5 Mbps	25-pin female	4.5 meters (15 feet)
USB 1.0	12 Mbps	A-Male, B-Male	3 meters
USB 2.0	480 Mbps	A-Male, B-Male	5 meters
IEEE 1394	1.2 Gbps	4-pin, 6-pin (provides voltage)	4.5 meters (15 feet)
Infrared		5-pin (integrated into system board)	See USB or Serial

OBJECTIVES ON THE JOB

Recognizing port types is critical to matching device needs and restrictions. USB ports are destined to replace serial and parallel ports. IEEE 1394/FireWire may eventually replace SCSI connectors.

PRACTICE TEST QUESTIONS

1. Serial ports can support:
   a. large hard drives
   b. a second floppy drive
   c. a Palm Pilot
   d. a ROM upgrade

2. A normal printer port is also known as a(n) ____ port.
   a. Centronics
   b. 9-pin male
   c. BIOS
   d. routine

3. EPP and ____ ports can transmit data in both directions.
   a. A-Male
   b. EDO
   c. DRAM
   d. ECP

4. A USB cable has only ____ wires.
   a. two
   b. three
   c. four
   d. five

5. The maximum usable length of a parallel cable is ____ meters.
   a. 4.5
   b. 5.5
   c. 6.5
   d. 7.5

6. The maximum usable length of a USB 1.0 cable is ____ meters.
   a. 10
   b. 7
   c. 3
   d. 2.5

7. The maximum usable length of an IEEE cable is ____ meters.
   a. 2.5
   b. 3.5
   c. 4.5
   d. 5.5

Identify the names, purposes, and performance characteristics, of standardized/common peripheral ports, associated cabling, and their connectors. Recognize ports, cabling, and connectors, by sight.

CABLE TYPES: SERIAL (STRAIGHT THROUGH VS. NULL MODEM), PARALLEL, AND USB • CONNECTOR TYPES: SERIAL (DB-9, DB-25, RJ-11, AND RJ-45), PARALLEL (DB-25 AND CENTRONICS (MINI, 36)), PS2/MINI-DIN, USB, AND IEEE 1394

UNDERSTANDING THE OBJECTIVE

Common peripheral ports include parallel, 9–pin and 25–pin serial (DB–9 and DB–25), USB, game port, DIN, mini–DIN (PS/2), video port, wide and narrow SCSI, phone line (RJ–11 or RJ–12) connectors, network connections (RJ–45), and IEEE–1394.

WHAT YOU **REALLY** NEED TO KNOW

◆ Parallel cables can be mono- and bi-directional and have a 25-pin female connection (DB-25) at the computer end and a 36-pin Centronics connection at the printer end.

◆ A parallel port can be configured as bi-directional, **extended capabilities port (ECP)**, or **enhanced parallel port (EPP)**.

◆ An ECP parallel port uses a DMA channel to speed up data transmission.

◆ **Null modem cables** use serial ports and connect two DTE devices (i.e. PCs). The cable has several wires that are cross-connected to simulate a modem connection. Standard serial cable wires run straight and do not cross.

◆ The 5-pin DIN connection and the 6-pin mini-DIN or PS/2 connection are both used for a mouse or a keyboard.

◆ A phone line connection looks like a phone jack. It is type **RJ-11** or **RJ-12**.

◆ A RJ-45 connection is used with twisted-pair cable by Ethernet 10BaseT (Twisted pair) and Ethernet 100BaseT (Fast Ethernet) networks and looks like a large phone jack.

Port Type	Performance	Connector	Max Cable Length
Serial	115.2 Kbps	9-pin male, 25-pin male, 15-pin female (game port)	50 ft
Parallel	1.5 Mbps	25-pin female	4.5 meters (15 feet)
USB 1.0	12 Mbps	A-Male (flat/wide to PC), B-Male (square)	3 meters
USB 2.0	480 Mbps	A-Male (flat/wide to PC), B-Male (square)	5 meters
IEEE 1394	1.2 Gbps	4-pin, 6-pin (provides voltage)	4.5 meters (15 feet)
Infrared		5-pin (integrated into system board)	See USB or Serial

OBJECTIVES ON THE JOB

A PC technician should be able to identify different cables and ports and know how to use them. Ports require system resources and can be enabled and disabled in CMOS setup. To know what resources a port is using, for DOS use MSD; for Windows 2000/XP use Device Manager.

PRACTICE TEST QUESTIONS

1. A 25-pin female port on the back of your computer is most likely to be a:
   a. parallel port
   b. serial port
   c. video port
   d. game port

2. What component controls serial port communication?
   a. the ISA bus
   b. the PCI bus
   c. UART
   d. BIOS

3. Which port provides the faster data transmission speeds?
   a. serial
   b. parallel
   c. USB
   d. IEEE 1394/FireWire

4. Which port cannot support a printer?
   a. COM1
   b. COM2
   c. LPT2
   d. the game port

5. Which port provides the fastest data transmission rate for a printer?
   a. RS-232
   b. parallel
   c. serial
   d. DIN

6. Which device can use a DMA channel?
   a. the serial port
   b. the parallel port
   c. the keyboard
   d. the mouse

7. Which device uses a 9-pin data cable?
   a. the parallel port
   b. the serial port
   c. the keyboard
   d. the SCSI port

OBJECTIVES

1.6 Identify proper procedures for installing and configuring common IDE devices. Choose the appropriate installation or configuration sequences in given scenarios. Recognize the associated cables.

IDE INTERFACE TYPES: EIDE, ATA/ATAPI, SERIAL ATA, AND PIO • RAID (0, 1, 5) • MASTER/SLAVE /CABLE SELECT • DEVICES PER CHANNEL • PRIMARY/SECONDARY • CABLE ORIENTATION/REQUIREMENTS

UNDERSTANDING THE OBJECTIVE

An Enhanced IDE (EIDE) system can support up to four devices. When installing IDE devices, it's important to set the device jumper correctly and understand cable orientation requirements. IDE interface types have evolved over the years from PIO (Programmed I/O) modes implemented under the ATA and ATA-2 standards to the latest Serial ATA standard which uses a smaller cable and fewer pins. The most common types are EIDE and ATA/ATAPI. RAID technology is used on high-end server and workstations to provide fault tolerance for data.

WHAT YOU **REALLY** NEED TO KNOW

◆ Up to four IDE devices can be installed on an **EIDE system** using the two IDE channels (primary and secondary).

◆ Each IDE channel has a master and a slave device. Typically, the jumper on one device is set to master and the other device is set to slave. A 40-pin cable is used to connect the devices to the system board.

◆ On newer computers that use the ATA/ATAPI-4 standard, the hard drive is connected via a 40-pin Ultra DMA IDE/ATA interface cable that contains 80-conductor wires. The extra wires help reduce cross-talk between wires which greatly increases data transfer speeds.

◆ Devices that use the Ultra DMA interface cable (typically hard drives) can have their jumpers set to cable select. Then, the hard drive would be connected to the master connector (black) and the other device would be connected to the slave connector (grey). Finally, the blue connector would plug into the system board.

◆ Earlier IDE/ATA standards only apply to hard drives, but newer standards apply to many devices including ATAPI CD-ROM drives.

◆ Variations of the IDE/ATA standards developed by ANSI include ATA, ATA-2, Fast ATA, Ultra ATA, and Ultra DMA.

◆ RAID 0 (disk striping without parity) writes data to two or more hard drives and treats them as a single drive. RAID 1 (disk mirroring or duplexing) writes data twice to two drives. RAID 5 provides the highest level of fault tolerance.

OBJECTIVES ON THE JOB

IDE is currently the most popular interface for storage devices in computer systems. A PC technician must be comfortable with installing and configuring IDE devices.

When installing an IDE drive, remember that the red stripe down the data cable aligns with Pin 1 on the drive and on the IDE connection. Pin 1 on the hard drive is usually next to the power connector.

PRACTICE TEST QUESTIONS

1. **When installing a second IDE device on an IDE channel, you must:**
   a. use CMOS setup to set the second device as the slave
   b. use CMOS setup to set the second device as drive D:
   c. use jumpers on the device to set it to slave
   d. use software that comes with the device to set it to slave

2. **How many EIDE devices can be installed in a system?**
   a. 1
   b. 2
   c. 4
   d. 8

3. **A system has a single IDE device installed on the primary IDE channel, and a new IDE device is installed on the secondary IDE channel. The new device does not work. What might be a cause of the problem?**
   a. The secondary IDE channel cannot be used until at least two devices are installed on the primary IDE channel.
   b. The second device should be set to slave.
   c. The secondary IDE channel might be disabled in CMOS setup.
   d. Both IDE devices are using the same IRQ.

4. **Which RAID level is used to write the same data to two hard drives?**
   a. RAID 0
   b. RAID 1
   c. RAID 5
   d. RAID 10

5. **Two IDE devices share a data cable. Which statement is true?**
   a. One device is using the primary IDE channel and the other device is using the secondary IDE channel.
   b. The data cable has 34 pins.
   c. The devices are sharing an IRQ.
   d. Both devices are set to slave.

6. **When connecting a floppy drive data cable to a system board connection, how do you know the correct orientation of the cable to the connection?**
   a. The red color on the cable goes next to the power supply.
   b. The edge color on the cable goes next to pin 1 on the connection.
   c. The orientation does not matter.
   d. Use the black-to-black rule.

7. **A CD-ROM drive that uses an IDE interface to the system board is following what specifications?**
   a. Ultra ATA
   b. ATAPI
   c. ANSI
   d. ATA-2

1.7 Identify proper procedures for installing and configuring common SCSI devices. Choose the appropriate installation or configuration sequences in given scenarios. Recognize the associated cables.

SCSI INTERFACE TYPES: NARROW, FAST, WIDE, ULTRA-WIDE, LVD, AND HVD • RAID (0, 1, 5)

UNDERSTANDING THE OBJECTIVE

Never attach an HVD device on a SCSI bus with SE or LVD devices. The higher voltage used by an HVD device can damage LVD devices. Ultra Wide SCSI can also be referred to as Wide Ultra SCSI or Fast–20 Wide SCSI.

WHAT YOU **REALLY** NEED TO KNOW

- ◆ Narrow SCSI uses an 8-bit data path and 50-pin cables. Wide SCSI uses a 16-bit data path and 68-pin cables. SCSI-1, SCSI-2, and SCSI-3 can have up to eight devices on a bus. Fast Wide SCSI and Ultra-Wide SCSI can support up to 16 devices.

- ◆ RAID 0,1, and 5 can be setup under Windows NT Server, Windows 2000, and Windows XP by way of the disk management GUI interface. Consult Windows Help for more information on configuring fault tolerance.

- ◆ SCSI-1 is commonly know as Regular SCSI. SCSI-2 is also known as Fast SCSI or Fast Narrow SCSI. SCSI-3 is also known as Ultra SCSI, Ultra Narrow SCSI, or Fast-20 SCSI.

- ◆ Twisted pair wires on differential cables carry voltages whose difference is the signal. HVD (High Voltage Differential) signaling has been replaced by LVD (Low Voltage Differential) based upon the newer SCSI-3 standards. In HVD signaling, a large voltage could possibly burn out hardware. LVD used a lower voltage signal and is required by Ultra SCSI standards.

- ◆ The following table summarizes SCSI standards:

Names for the SCSI Interface Standard	Bus width Narrow=8 bits Wide=16 bits	Maximum Length of Single-ended Cable (meters)	Maximum Length of Differential Cable (meters)	Maximum Number of Devices
SCSI-1 (Regular SCSI)	Narrow	6	25	8
SCSI-2 (Fast SCSI)	Narrow	3	25	8
Fast Wide SCSI	Wide	3	25	16
SCSI-3 (Ultra SCSI)	Narrow	1.5	25	8
Ultra-Wide SCSI	Wide	1.5	25	16
Ultra2 SCSI	Narrow		12 LVD*	8
Wide Ultra2 SCSI	Wide			16
Ultra3 SCSI	Narrow		12 LVD*	8
Wide Ultra3 SCSI	Wide		12 LVD*	16

* LVD: Low voltage differential cable allows for lengths of up to 12 meters.

OBJECTIVES ON THE JOB

When purchasing and installing SCSI devices, a technician must know which SCSI standards are compatible with other SCSI standards and not mix standards on the same SCSI bus that are incompatible. These standards apply to device drivers, the host adapter, cabling, termination devices, and SCSI devices.

PRACTICE TEST QUESTIONS

1. **SCSI-2 can support how many devices?**
   a. 1
   b. up to 6
   c. up to 8
   d. up to 16

2. **The data path of Wide Ultra SCSI is:**
   a. 4 bits
   b. 8 bits
   c. 16 bits
   d. 32 bits

3. **Which is the fastest SCSI standard?**
   a. Regular SCSI
   b. Fast SCSI
   c. Fast-20 SCSI
   d. Wide Ultra3 SCSI

4. **Which of the following is a difference between a single-ended SCSI cable and a differential SCSI cable?**
   a. The single-ended SCSI cable can be longer than the differential SCSI cable.
   b. The single-ended SCSI cable can be used with Regular SCSI, but the differential SCSI cable cannot.
   c. Differential SCSI cable is more popular than single-ended SCSI cable because it is less expensive.
   d. Data integrity is greater for a differential SCSI cable than for single-ended SCSI cable.

5. **What is true about SCSI termination?**
   a. Each end of the SCSI chain must be terminated.
   b. Each SCSI device must be terminated.
   c. The SCSI host adapter is always terminated.
   d. Terminators will always be installed inside the computer case.

6. **Which major SCSI standard does not include a standard for 16-bit data transmission?**
   a. SCSI-1
   b. SCSI-2
   c. SCSI-3
   d. All SCSI standards can use 16-bit data transmission.

7. **How many pins does a Narrow SCSI data cable have?**
   a. 50
   b. 9
   c. 68
   d. none of the above

1.7 Identify proper procedures for installing and configuring common SCSI devices. Choose the appropriate installation or configuration sequences in given scenarios. Recognize the associated cables.

INTERNAL VERSUS EXTERNAL • SCSI IDS: JUMPER BLOCK/DIP SWITCH SETTINGS (BINARY EQUIVALENTS) AND RESOLVING ID CONFLICTS • CABLING: LENGTH, TYPE, AND TERMINATION REQUIREMENTS (ACTIVE, PASSIVE, AUTO)

UNDERSTANDING THE OBJECTIVE

Small Computer Systems Interface (SCSI) is a type of closed bus. SCSI devices are connected to a host adapter. Within a physical device, each virtual device is assigned a logical unit number (LUN). Of the several SCSI standards, some are compatible with one another.

WHAT YOU **REALLY** NEED TO KNOW

♦ SCSI-1, SCSI-2, and Fast SCSI devices connect using a Centronics-50 or DB-25 male connector. All wide SCSI devices use a 68-pin connection.

♦ Both narrow and wide SCSI can use either single-ended or differential cables. A differential cable can be up to 25 meters long and a single-ended cable can be up to 6 meters long, depending on the SCSI standard.

♦ Eight or 16 devices (including the host adapter) can be chained on a SCSI bus, depending on the standard used (SCSI IDs are 0 through 15).

♦ The SCSI host adapter is assigned SCSI ID 7 or 15, and a bootable SCSI hard drive is assigned SCSI ID 0.

♦ A SCSI device is assigned a single SCSI ID, but one physical device can have multiple units or virtual devices in it, each assigned a LUN. For example, a 12-tray CD changer or juke box is assigned a single SCSI ID, but each tray in the changer is assigned a LUN.

♦ A SCSI ID is set by setting jumpers, device DIP switches, or software. Some devices include documentation that shows the relationship of dip switch settings to a binary equivalent (ON or OFF).

♦ The SCSI chip on a hard drive that controls the transfer of data over the SCSI bus is a **SCSI bus adapter chip (SBAC)**.

♦ A SCSI device can be an internal device or an external device, and the host adapter can be anywhere in the SCSI daisy chain.

♦ To resolve device ID conflicts, make sure that each device has its own SCSI ID. Slower devices, CD recording devices, and video capture devices should typically be assigned the highest SCSI ID. The device ID priority sequence (highest to lowest) for wide SCSI is 7, 6, 5, 4, 3, 2, 1, 0, 15, 14, 13, 12, 11, 10, 9, 8. Narrow SCSI is 7, 6, 5, 4, 3, 2, 1, 0.

♦ A SCSI bus requires **termination** at each end of the SCSI bus to eliminate electrical noise. There are three types of cable termination: passive (now obsolete), active (widely used with wide SCSI and required with fast SCSI), and forced perfect termination (most reliable). Some devices have automatic support for termination by use of an internal terminator.

OBJECTIVES ON THE JOB

SCSI devices are popular because they are generally faster than similar devices that don't use SCSI technology, but SCSI installations can be more complex than other installations.

PRACTICE TEST QUESTIONS

1. A SCSI ID is set on a SCSI device using three jumpers. If the ID is set to 6, what will be the jumper settings?

   a. On, On, and Off
   b. On, On, and On
   c. Off, On, and On
   d. Off, Off, and On

2. Which statement about a SCSI configuration is true?

   a. The host adapter must be at one end of the SCSI chain.
   b. The host adapter must *always* be terminated.
   c. A SCSI chain cannot have both internal and external devices on the same chain.
   d. A SCSI chain can have both internal and external devices and the host adapter can be anywhere in the chain.

3. Two SCSI hard drives are installed on the same SCSI bus. Which statement is true?

   a. The two SCSI drives must have the same SCSI ID.
   b. The two SCSI drives must have different SCSI IDs and one must have SCSI ID 7.
   c. The two SCSI drives must have different SCSI IDs.
   d. It does not matter which SCSI IDs the drives have.

4. How many devices can be used on a single SCSI bus, including the host adapter?

   a. 6
   b. 8
   c. 14
   d. 10

5. A SCSI CD-ROM drive is installed on an existing SCSI bus in a system. Which statement is true?

   a. The CD-ROM SCSI ID must be different than any other SCSI ID already assigned.
   b. The CD-ROM SCSI ID must be set to zero.
   c. A new host adapter must be installed that supports CD-ROM drives.
   d. It does not matter which SCSI ID is assigned to the CD-ROM drive.

6. How can a SCSI ID be set on a SCSI device?

   a. by software
   b. by jumpers on the device
   c. by DIP switches on the device
   d. all of the above

7. A SCSI bus has three SCSI devices and a host adapter. Which device(s) can communicate with the CPU?

   a. Only the host adapter communicates with the CPU: all communication goes through it.
   b. Each device on the SCSI bus can communicate directly with the CPU.
   c. Hard drives can communicate with the CPU, but all other SCSI devices must communicate through the host adapter.
   d. Only two devices on a SCSI bus can communicate with the CPU: the host adapter and one other device.

1.8 Identify proper procedures for installing and configuring common peripheral devices. Choose the appropriate installation or configuration sequences in given scenarios.

MODEMS AND TRANSCEIVERS (DIAL-UP, CABLE, DSL, ISDN) • MONITORS

UNDERSTANDING THE OBJECTIVE

A video subsystem includes the video card, monitor, and monitor cable. Video drivers must be compatible with the OS and the video card. They can be included by the OS or provided by the video card manufacturer. A modem can be installed as an external device or an internal circuit board. Installation includes assigning system resources, physically installing the hardware, and installing device drivers to interface with the device.

WHAT YOU **REALLY** NEED TO KNOW

- ◆ Cable, DSL, and ISDN modems offer greater bandwidth than dial-up modems. Cable and DSL modems are the most prevalent technologies for home users.
- ◆ To install a video card:
  1. After physically installing the video card in the slot, connect the monitor data cable to the port on the back of the card.
  2. Turn on the power to the computer and the monitor.
  3. Install the device drivers for the video card. For DOS, run the installation disk. For Windows 9x, Windows 2000, and Windows XP, the OS recognizes a new device and automatically performs the installation. You can use the setup disk from the video card manufacturer in the installation process.
  4. Set display properties for the monitor to user preferences.
- ◆ In Windows, know the menu path to the Display Properties dialog box.
- ◆ A modem can be an external device, which most commonly uses a serial port. An external modem using a serial port uses the IRQ and I/O addresses assigned to the serial port. An internal modem must be assigned an IRQ and I/O addresses by the system. Most modem cards are Plug and Play, so the system automatically assigns the resources.
- ◆ After physically installing the modem, install device drivers using the setup disk that comes with the modem.
- ◆ To test a newly installed modem in Windows, use HyperTerminal to make a phone call. Know the menu path to HyperTerminal.
- ◆ When adding an infrared transceiver to a system, connect the transceiver to a port and reboot. Windows automatically detects and installs drivers.
- ◆ To activate an infrared transceiver, double-click the Infrared icon in Control Panel.

OBJECTIVES ON THE JOB

Installing a video card, monitor, and modem are common tasks expected of PC technicians. Both a video card and a modem require device drivers to operate. Windows 9x has drivers for many video cards and modems, but, when given the option, you should use those provided by the device manufacturer. Windows XP offers the widest support of drivers for new devices.

PRACTICE TEST QUESTIONS

1. **An external modem will most likely use which port on a PC?**
   - a. serial
   - b. parallel
   - c. SCSI
   - d. DIN

2. **Video cards are normally installed in which bus expansion slot?**
   - a. ISA
   - b. PCI
   - c. AGP
   - d. Either b or c

3. **A VESA bus expansion slot:**
   - a. is never used for a video card
   - b. is found on older systems but not used on newer systems
   - c. is slower than an ISA expansion slot
   - d. has a 16-bit data path

4. **The AGP expansion slot:**
   - a. is used only for video cards
   - b. has a data path of 64 bits
   - c. is slower than a PCI expansion slot
   - d. runs asynchronously with the system clock

5. **What IRQ does an external modem use?**
   - a. the IRQ assigned to its serial port
   - b. IRQ 10
   - c. An external modem does not need an IRQ because it is an external device.
   - d. IRQ 7

6. **Which device does not require an IRQ?**
   - a. a modem
   - b. a sound card
   - c. a monitor
   - d. a keyboard

7. **Describe the port typically used by a monitor on today's systems.**
   - a. 9-pin female with two rows of pins
   - b. 15-pin female with three rows of pins
   - c. 15-pin male with three rows of pins
   - d. 25-pin female with two rows of pins

OBJECTIVES

1.8 Identify proper procedures for installing and configuring common peripheral devices. Choose the appropriate installation or configuration sequences in given scenarios.

EXTERNAL STORAGE • DIGITAL CAMERAS • PDAS • WIRELESS ACCESS POINTS

UNDERSTANDING THE OBJECTIVE

Common storage devices are floppy disk drives, hard drives, DVD drives, and CD-ROM drives, which can be either internal or external devices. Installation includes assigning resources, configuring the drive and the system, and the physical installation. PDAs and digital cameras have become popular accessories on many computers.

WHAT YOU **REALLY** NEED TO KNOW

- ◆ Floppy drives and hard drives don't normally require the manual installation of device drivers because the OS and/or BIOS interfaces directly with the drive.
- ◆ CMOS setup is configured to detect a floppy drive or hard drive. CMOS may need to be changed or may automatically detect the new drive (as with hard drive auto detection, if available).
- ◆ When installing data cables for drives, connect pin 1 on the connection to the edge color on the data cable.
- ◆ For a CD-ROM installation, if the system has a sound card, connect the audio wire from the sound card to the CD-ROM drive.
- ◆ Software is usually bundled with a digital camera that will allow the user to transfer images to a computer.
- ◆ There is a wide variety of methods and technologies for storing and transferring digital images. Some digital cameras are bundled with a cable (serial, parallel, FireWire, or USB) that can be used to transfer images directly to a computer. Some digital cameras use a flash RAM card such as CompactFlash, SmartMedia, or Sony Memory Sticks. Older Sony Mavica digital cameras store images on floppy disks that can be inserted directly into the camera. SmartMedia cards can be inserted into a FlashPath device which can then be inserted into a floppy disk drive.
- ◆ If a new external storage device does not work after an installation, verify the port is enabled in CMOS, and test the port using diagnostic software and loop-back plugs.
- ◆ **Wireless access points** can be accessed from any computer with a wireless adapter. Installation of wireless adapters is similar to most adapter cards and usually requires an open PCI slot.
- ◆ PDAs (Personal Digital Assistants), such as a Palm Pilot or Pocket PC, can be connected to a computer by way of a serial or USB port. Then, you usually have to install manufacturer's software to support synchronization of files between the computer and PDA. The software is usually bundled with the PDA. Be sure that the included software is certified to be installed on your operating system. If it cannot be installed, visit the manufacturer's Web site to download a version that is compatible with your operating system.

OBJECTIVES ON THE JOB

Installing peripheral devices on a PC is a common task for a PC technician.

PRACTICE TEST QUESTIONS

1. **After physically installing a floppy drive, the next step is to:**
   a. install the floppy drive device drivers
   b. inform CMOS setup of the new drive
   c. upgrade BIOS to support the drive
   d. disconnect the power cord to the hard drive

2. **You attach a Palm Pilot to the serial port on your computer and would like to synchronize files between your computer and PDA. How can this be accomplished?**
   a. Copy files by way of Windows Explorer.
   b. Install Palm Pilot software that enables files synchronization.
   c. Synchronization can only be achieved by using a USB port.
   d. None of the above.

3. **An IDE Zip drive data cable has how many pins?**
   a. 9
   b. 25
   c. 34
   d. 40

4. **You install an internal CD-R drive on a computer that already has an internal CD-ROM drive. To which IDE ribbon should the CD-R drive be connected in order to optimize performance?**
   a. The CD-R drive and CD-ROM drive should be on the same IDE ribbon.
   b. The CD-R drive and CD-ROM drive should be on different IDE ribbons.
   c. The CD-R drive should be added to the floppy disk drive ribbon.
   d. None of the above.

5. **You install a floppy drive and reboot the PC. The drive light on the floppy drive stays lit and the system hangs. What is the most likely source of the problem?**
   a. The floppy drive data cable is not connected correctly.
   b. The power cord to the floppy drive is not connected.
   c. The hard drive was damaged during the installation.
   d. The floppy drive is installed upside down.

6. **You have installed an IDE CD-ROM drive as the only device using the secondary IDE channel, and the drive is not recognized by the system. What is likely to be wrong?**
   a. The jumper setting on the CD-ROM drive is set to master and should be set to slave.
   b. The secondary IDE channel is disabled in CMOS setup.
   c. There is an IRQ conflict with the keyboard.
   d. The drive was damaged by ESD during the installation.

7. **You have installed an external Zip drive using a second parallel port in a system, and you cannot get the system to recognize the drive. What is likely to be wrong?**
   a. A Zip drive cannot use a parallel port but must be installed as a SCSI device.
   b. The parallel port has a resource conflict; check Device Manager.
   c. The parallel port is disabled in CMOS setup or configured wrong; check setup.
   d. Either b or c.

1.8 Identify proper procedures for installing and configuring common peripheral devices. Choose the appropriate installation or configuration sequences in given scenarios.

INFRARED DEVICES • PRINTERS • UPS (UNINTERRUPTIBLE POWER SUPPLY) AND SUPPRESSORS

UNDERSTANDING THE OBJECTIVE

Printers are usually connected by way of a USB cable or parallel cable. Newer printers are not supported by most operating systems and require installation software that contains printer drivers. UPS and surge suppressors provide help to protect against data and equipment loss. Infrared devices can be added to support wireless devices such as a keyboard or mouse.

WHAT YOU **REALLY** NEED TO KNOW

- ◆ Windows XP has built-in support for more printers than any other Microsoft operating system.
- ◆ Up to 127 USB devices can be daisy-chained together off a single USB port. One USB device can provide a port for another device, or a device can serve as a hub, connecting several devices. The maximum length for a USB cable is five meters.
- ◆ Windows 95 with the USB update, Windows 98, Windows 2000, and Windows XP support USB, but Windows NT does not.
- ◆ A surge suppressor provides a row of power outlets that can be used to protect computers and accessories from being damaged from a voltage spike. You can expect to pay at least $50 for a high quality surge suppressor.
- ◆ A UPS (Uninterruptible Power Supply) can power a computer and other accessories and supply a limited amount of power in the event of a power failure. UPS devices contain heavy rechargeable batteries and have several power outlets for powering devices. On Windows 2000 and Windows XP, a UPS can be configured to automatically perform a proper power down of the computer in the event of a power failure.
- ◆ IEEE 1284 is a standard for parallel ports and cables, and includes specifications for EPP (enhanced parallel port) and ECP (extended capabilities port). EPP is a bi-directional parallel port standard.
- ◆ ECP increases performance by using a DMA channel. Control the DMA channel used and enable and disable ECP using CMOS setup.
- ◆ Infrared devices are assigned virtual ports such as COM4 or LPT3.

OBJECTIVES ON THE JOB

To install a new printer, first assembly the printer and printer cartridges. Then, plug the printer into a power outlet and attach the printer to the computer by way of a USB or parallel cable. Finally, install the appropriate printer software.

PRACTICE TEST QUESTIONS

1. Which of the following techniques can be used to troubleshoot printing problems on an ink-jet printer?
   a. Uninstall and reinstall the printer driver software.
   b. Use printer software to test communication between the printer and computer.
   c. Replace the printer cartridge.
   d. All of the above.

2. When does a parallel port require a DMA channel?
   a. when the parallel cable is bi-directional
   b. when ECP is enabled in CMOS setup
   c. when EPP is enabled in CMOS setup
   d. None of the above; a parallel port never uses a DMA channel.

3. You use an UPS to supply power to your Windows XP computer and would like to enable the UPS to automatically shutdown the computer in the event of a power failure. What should you do?
   a. Read all documentation provided with your UPS.
   b. Configure Windows XP UPS options to support your UPS model.
   c. Attach a serial cable to the COM port.
   d. All of the above.

4. You install a printer, but the PC cannot communicate with the printer. What is one thing to check?
   a. The parallel port does not have conflicting resources in Device Manager.
   b. The parallel port is enabled in CMOS setup.
   c. The printer is online.
   d. All of the above.

5. Surge suppressors can protect which of the following devices?
   a. computers
   b. modems
   c. printers
   d. all of the above

6. What port on the back of a computer allows you to use a keyboard or other input device without a connecting cord to the computer?
   a. the USB port
   b. the remote serial port
   c. the PC Card port
   d. the infrared port

7. Which of the following techniques can be used to troubleshoot problems with infrared devices?
   a. If the remote device uses a battery, replace it with a new one.
   b. Check CMOS and make sure the COM ports are enabled.
   c. Determine if another infrared device is interfering with the signal.
   d. All of the above.

1.9 Identify procedures to optimize PC operations in specific situations. Predict the effects of specific procedures under given scenarios.

COOLING SYSTEMS: LIQUID, AIR, HEAT SINK, AND THERMAL COMPOUND • MEMORY • ADDITIONAL PROCESSORS

UNDERSTANDING THE OBJECTIVE

Cooling systems keep CPUs and other chips below the maximum temperature of 185 degrees Fahrenheit, as recommend by Intel. If the temperature rises above this level, the CPU and other components could become damaged. Adding memory to your computer helps the operating system perform faster. Some motherboards can support more then one processor.

WHAT YOU **REALLY** NEED TO KNOW

- ◆ Motherboards that support multiple processors require a special chipset which coordinates the processing power of the entire system to maximize efficiency. They also have one or more extra slots to add multiple processors.

- ◆ Multiple processors are also managed by the operating system. Typically, multiple processor systems are configured to be file servers running Windows 2000 Server or Windows 2003 Server. However, operating systems such as Windows 2000 and Windows XP can support multiple processors.

- ◆ Multiple processor systems also share the same memory. File servers often use ECC (error checking and correction) memory that helps improve performance while reducing errors.

- ◆ Windows 2000 and Windows XP perform best when memory is upgraded to at least 256 MB.

- ◆ Windows 9x performs best when memory is upgraded to at least 128 MB.

- ◆ When upgrading memory, it is highly recommended that you select memory that is optimized for use on your motherboard. This can be accomplished by searching for memory that fits the make and model of your computer.

- ◆ Cooling systems such as fans, heat sinks, and thermal compounds are used on both desktop computers and file servers. Fans are often mounted to the processor and power supply to help maintain proper air flow. Heat sinks are attached to help dissipate heat quickly. Thermal compounds are often applied between a heat sink and processor to increase heat flow to the heat sink.

- ◆ Some computer hobbyists attempt to over-clock processors to increase performance. This results in a great increase in temperature and will damage a CPU. One solution that is often used to aggressively dissipate heat is a liquid cooling system. In this system, distilled water is pumped over the CPU to keep it cool.

OBJECTIVES ON THE JOB

Improper ventilation can cause a computer to overheat, damaging the processor and other components. This may cause the computer to repeatedly freeze when in use. Be sure that airflow is not obstructed and that dust is regularly removed from all vents on a computer.

PRACTICE TEST QUESTIONS

1. **Given the following scenario, predict the outcome. You upgrade the memory to 256 MB of PC100 RAM on a computer with a system bus of 133 MHz.**
   a. The computer will boot but memory is not optimized for the speed of the system bus.
   b. The computer will not boot and POST will sound errors.
   c. The computer will boot but will not recognize the PC100 memory.
   d. None of the above.

2. **Given the following scenario, predict the outcome. You over-clock your CPU by 25 percent.**
   a. Your computer will run faster and no damage will result.
   b. Your computer will run faster and your system may occasionally freeze.
   c. Your computer will run faster and your CPU will be damaged.
   d. Both b and c.

3. **Given the following scenario, predict the outcome. You add a second processor to a file server without adding a fan.**
   a. Both CPUs may become damaged.
   b. The server is already configured to support multiple processors and no damage will occur.
   c. You leave the case open and no damage will occur.
   d. None of the above.

4. **Given the following scenario, predict the outcome. After installing Windows XP, you add a second processor to your computer.**
   a. Windows XP will detect the new processor and install support for it.
   b. Windows XP will boot up to a STOP error (blue screen of death).
   c. Windows XP will detect the new processor and prompt for support files.
   d. None of the above.

5. **What is the minimum amount of memory for Windows XP, as recommended by Microsoft?**
   a. 64 MB
   b. 128 MB
   c. 256 MB
   d. 512 MB

6. **What is the best practice when choosing memory for an upgrade?**
   a. Purchase the cheapest memory available.
   b. Purchase the memory that is designed to work with your make and model of computer.
   c. Purchase generic memory.
   d. All of the above.

7. **Given the following scenario, predict the outcome. Your computer keeps freezing and you suspect that it may be caused by faulty memory. Which of the following techniques are useful in troubleshooting this problem?**
   a. Replace the memory with a known-good memory module.
   b. Test the memory using a DOS-based memory tester (such as MemTest) for a few hours.
   c. Contact your computer manufacturer and report the problem.
   d. All of the above.

1.9 Identify procedures to optimize PC operations in specific situations. Predict the effects of specific procedures under given scenarios.

DISK SUBSYSTEM ENHANCEMENTS: HARD DRIVES, CONTROLLER CARDS (E.G., RAID, ATA-100, ETC.), AND CABLES • NICS • SPECIALIZED VIDEO CARDS

UNDERSTANDING THE OBJECTIVE

There are many standards for IDE hard disks. Controller cards were used on older motherboards that did not have support for IDE devices. NICs are typically PCI cards but have become integrated on newer motherboards. Graphics accelerator cards have their own processor and are specially designed to handle graphic–intensive software.

WHAT YOU **REALLY** NEED TO KNOW

◆ IDE hard drives have a hard drive controller that is mounted directly on or inside the hard drive itself. The hard drive is then connected directly to the motherboard by way of an IDE cable. Hard drive IDE cables on older computers attached directly to an adapter card which plugged into an ISA slot on the motherboard. A PCI host adapter card can be added to today's computers if support is needed for more than four IDE devices.

◆ IDE hard drives on today's computers use a special 40-pin cable that actually contains 80 wires. This helps increase performance by reducing crosstalk.

◆ Common IDE standards for hard drives include Ultra ATA/66 (also called Ultra DMA/66) which runs at 66.6 Mbps. Ultra ATA/100 runs at 100 Mbps. Ultra ATA/133 runs at 133 Mbps. The system bus on the motherboard must support the data transfer speed of the hard drive.

◆ Implementing **RAID** is a good method for protecting against hardware loss and data corruption. There are three RAID levels (0, 1, 5) that are supported under Windows 2000 Server, Windows 2003 Server, Windows 2000, and Windows XP.

◆ Newer computers integrate the NIC into the motherboard. If an integrated NIC fails, it can usually be disabled in CMOS setup. Then, a NIC can be inserted into a PCI slot on the motherboard. You may then be prompted for device drivers so be prepared to provide the correct drivers for your operating system.

◆ Specialized video cards called graphics accelerators can be added to a computer to speed up video processing. A graphics accelerator card may be needed for 3-D gaming, AutoCAD, Adobe Photoshop, or other graphics intensive software.

OBJECTIVES ON THE JOB

It is usually not feasible to add a newer hard drive to an older computer because the motherboard bus speed and processor will still limit the data transfer rate. Also, sometimes older motherboard BIOS does not support larger hard drives. The BIOS can sometimes be upgraded to support larger hard drives if needed.

PRACTICE TEST QUESTIONS

1. Given the following scenario, predict the outcome. You add a graphics accelerator card to your computer.
   a. You will be prompted for a device driver after the computer loads the operating system.
   b. Video processing will greatly increase.
   c. The CPU performance will increase because it is not processing as much video information.
   d. All of the above.

2. Which of the following is false?
   a. Windows 98 supports various RAID levels.
   b. Windows 2000 Server supports various RAID levels.
   c. Windows 2000 supports various RAID levels.
   d. Windows XP supports various RAID levels.

3. Which of the following is not a standard for IDE drives?
   a. Ultra ATA/66
   b. Ultra ATA/100
   c. Ultra ATA/133
   d. None of the above.

4. How many pins are in an 80 wire IDE cable?
   a. 80
   b. 40
   c. 60
   d. 20

5. Given the following scenario, predict the outcome. The integrated NIC has failed. How can you replace the NIC?
   a. Use a Phillips head screwdriver.
   b. You cannot. You must instead disable the integrated NIC from CMOS setup.
   c. Replace the motherboard.
   d. Both b and c.

6. Where is the hard drive controller located on newer computers?
   a. the motherboard
   b. the fatherboard
   c. the hard drive
   d. none of the above

7. Given the following scenario, predict the outcome. Video processing is slow. What can be done to increase performance?
   a. Add memory.
   b. Add a video graphics card.
   c. Decrease the video resolution.
   d. All of the above.

OBJECTIVES

1.10 Determine the issues that must be considered when upgrading a PC. In a given scenario, determine when and how to upgrade system components.

CPU • PROCESSOR SPEED AND COMPATIBILITY• MEMORY • MEMORY CAPACITY AND CHARACTERISTICS • MOTHERBOARDS • CACHE IN RELATIONSHIP TO MOTHERBOARDS • BUS TYPES AND CHARACTERISTICS

UNDERSTANDING THE OBJECTIVE

Memory is optimized when the system has a large amount of dynamic RAM (DRAM) and some static RAM (SRAM). Older systems store SRAM on the motherboard, which can be upgraded. Newer systems contain SRAM inside the CPU housing and, therefore, cannot be changed. For older systems, install enough SRAM to speed up memory access. For all systems, install additional DRAM so that software and data have enough room in RAM without having to rely too heavily on virtual memory. The optimum CPU for a system is determined by the system board, what CPUs it supports, and the intended purpose of the system.

WHAT YOU **REALLY** NEED TO KNOW

◆ Local I/O buses support fast devices such as PCI video cards or hard drives and are synchronized with the system clock and CPU. Examples of local I/O buses include the system bus, memory bus, PCI bus, AGP bus, and FireWire bus.

◆ Expansion buses support devices such as ISA video cards or USB devices and work asynchronously with the CPU at a much slower speed. Examples of expansion buses include the EISA bus, 8-bit ISA bus, 16-bit ISA bus, and USB bus.

◆ Motherboard types include the AT (very old) which uses P8 and P9 power connectors, the Baby AT which is a small version of the AT and uses the P8 and P9 power connectors, the ATX (rotated 90 degrees from Baby AT style and designed for Pentium CPUs) which uses the P1 power connector, and the Mini ATX (very compact) which again uses P1.

◆ For Windows 9x, use at least 64 MB of RAM; 128 MB is optimal. For Windows 2000 and Windows XP, use at least 128 MB of RAM; 256 MB is optimal.

◆ Upgrading memory means to add more RAM to a computer system. You can install DIMMs, SIMMs, and RIMMs in empty memory slots or you can exchange existing modules that hold small amounts of memory with those that hold more.

◆ The two kinds of SRAM are **primary cache** (L1 cache, internal cache) located on the CPU microchip and **secondary cache** (L2 cache, external cache) located on the system board or, for newer Pentium systems, on a tiny circuit board contained within the CPU housing.

◆ SRAM is installed in multiples of 256K. Optimal SRAM depends on the system, but 512K is commonly recognized as adequate for most systems.

OBJECTIVES ON THE JOB

Upgrading memory is a simple and relatively inexpensive method of improving the overall performance of a computer system and an expected skill of PC technicians.

PRACTICE TEST QUESTIONS

1. Given the following scenario, determine how to upgrade system components. Which of the following steps is important in upgrading a motherboard?
   a. Determine the current type of motherboard and power supply.
   b. Purchase a motherboard that will fit correctly in the computer case.
   c. Purchase a motherboard that is supported by the power supply.
   d. All of the above.

2. Cache memory is usually installed on a system board in increments of:
   a. 1K
   b. 256K
   c. 1 MB
   d. 4 MB

3. What is a reasonable amount of cache memory on a system board?
   a. 1K
   b. 1 MB
   c. 512K
   d. 16 MB

4. L2 cache memory can exist in a system as:
   a. individual chips on the system board
   b. in a COAST module installed on the system board
   c. inside the housing of a Pentium II or higher CPU
   d. all of the above

5. What is the purpose of installing additional cache memory?
   a. to give applications more room for their data
   b. to speed up data access time
   c. to allow more applications to be open at the same time
   d. all of the above

6. Why do newer system boards not have cache memory installed?
   a. It is contained inside the CPU housing.
   b. DRAM no longer needs SRAM to operate at fast speeds.
   c. Cache memory is so expensive.
   d. Newer CPUs cannot use cache memory.

7. What can result if there is not enough RAM installed in a system?
   a. disk thrashing
   b. The system is slow.
   c. Some applications might not be able to load.
   d. all of the above

OBJECTIVES

1.10 Determine the issues that must be considered when upgrading a PC. In a given scenario, determine when and how to upgrade system components.

POWER SUPPLY OUTPUT CAPACITY • HARD DRIVES • HARD DRIVE CAPACITY AND CHARACTERISTICS • ADAPTER CARDS • DRIVERS FOR LEGACY DEVICES

UNDERSTANDING THE OBJECTIVE

Newer systems typically require that the IDE hard drive be connected by way of a 80-wire connector that supports fast data transfer speeds. For optimal use of hard drive space, the cluster size should be small. ISA slots are no longer available on newer computers so adapter cards should be upgraded accordingly. A power supply upgrade may be necessary if you are adding a large number of new devices.

WHAT YOU **REALLY** NEED TO KNOW

◆ After adding new devices, you can test your power supply by getting as many of the devices working at the same time. Try copying files from the hard drive to a floppy disk. If the devices do not work correctly, but work independently, you may need to replace the power supply.

◆ Power supplies range from 200 watts on a desktop computer to 600 watts for a file server.

◆ Defragment and back up data on a hard drive routinely.

◆ Protect hard drives from magnetic fields and extremely hot or cold temperatures.

◆ Windows 2000, Windows 98, and later versions of Windows 95 support FAT32, which can yield the optimal use of hard drive space because the cluster size is smaller than that of FAT16. Windows NT does not support FAT32.

◆ DOS and Windows 9x support FAT16 up to 2 GB hard drives. Windows NT, 2000, and XP support FAT16 up to 4 GB.

◆ Windows 2000 and Windows XP support FAT32 on hard drives up to 32 GB.

◆ When replacing or upgrading a hard drive on older computers, check to make sure the new hard drive is supported by the BIOS. If the hard drive is not supported by the BIOS, you may need to upgrade the BIOS to support the larger hard drive.

◆ When updating drivers for legacy devices, always contact the manufacturer or visit the manufacturer's Web site to determine if the device is supported under the new operating system or on the new computer.

◆ When replacing a hard drive, be sure to set the jumpers on the new hard drive so they match the setting on the old hard drive. Most hard drives on newer computers are set to CABLE SELECT and are plugged into the master IDE connector on the primary IDE channel.

OBJECTIVES ON THE JOB

Routinely defragment and scan a hard drive for errors, especially if the end-user typically works with a large number of files. Computer freezes are difficult to troubleshoot. It is best to use the process of elimination and replace a single component at a time.

PRACTICE TEST QUESTIONS

1. **Given the following scenario, determine when to upgrade system components. Which of the following problems may be related to a faulty power supply?**
   a. The computer freezes intermittently.
   b. The computer power is cut-off intermittently.
   c. The computer does not power on after depressing the power button.
   d. All of the above.

2. **Which storage device provides the fastest access time for large multimedia files?**
   a. the CD-ROM drive
   b. the IDE hard drive
   c. the SCSI hard drive
   d. the floppy drive

3. **Given the following scenario, determine when to upgrade system components. Which of the following problems may be related to a faulty hard drive?**
   a. The computer will not boot.
   b. The computer freezes intermittently.
   c. The computer reports errors when accessing data or is slow to respond.
   d. All of the above.

4. **Given the following scenario, determine how to upgrade system components. After upgrading to Windows XP an ISA device card no longer functions correctly.**
   a. Check the manufacturer's Web site for Windows XP compatible device drivers.
   b. Replace the ISA device card with a PCI device card.
   c. Contact the manufacturer to determine if the device is supported under Windows XP.
   d. All of the above.

5. **Given the following scenario, determine how to upgrade system components. You would like to replace a faulty hard drive. Which of the following steps are necessary to perform this task?**
   a. Unplug the computer.
   b. Set the jumper setting on the new hard drive so that it matches the jumper setting on the old hard drive.
   c. Read all documentation that is bundled with the new hard drive before starting the installation process.
   d. All of the above.

6. **What type of IDE cable is necessary to support hard drives on newer computers?**
   a. 40 pin, 40-wire IDE cable
   b. 40 pin, 80-wire IDE cable
   c. 40 pin, 120-wire IDE cable
   d. none of the above

7. **What size hard drive is supported under Windows XP if it is formatted FAT32?**
   a. 32 GB
   b. 20 GB
   c. 4 GB
   d. all of the above

1.10 Determine the issues that must be considered when upgrading a PC. In a given scenario, determine when and how to upgrade system components.

BIOS • SYSTEM/FIRMWARE LIMITATIONS

UNDERSTANDING THE OBJECTIVE

Older ROM BIOS microchips could only be upgraded by replacing the chip. Newer BIOS chips (EEPROM chips) can be electronically upgraded. This technology is called Flash ROM, and the process is sometimes called flashing ROM. Note that firmware is set in ROM.

WHAT YOU **REALLY** NEED TO KNOW

- ◆ Flash ROM allows you to upgrade BIOS without having to replace the chip.
- ◆ One reason to upgrade the BIOS is to install a hard drive with a capacity larger than the one supported by your current BIOS chip. Older BIOS only supported 504 MB or smaller drives.
- ◆ BIOS manufacturers often offer upgrades or fixes to their BIOS code. These upgrades can be downloaded from the manufacturer's Web site.
- ◆ The most popular manufacturers of BIOS software are Phoenix Software, Award Software, and American Megatrends (AMI).
- ◆ To identify the BIOS manufacturer of a BIOS chip, look for the manufacturer and model number written on top of the chip or look for the information written on the screen during booting.
- ◆ The ROM BIOS chip on the system board is larger than most chips and might have a shiny label on top.
- ◆ The BIOS on expansion cards written for 16-bit real mode DOS sometimes expects to use specific memory addresses in the upper memory address range from 640K to 1024K.
- ◆ Some real-mode device drivers will not work unless given specific memory addresses in upper memory.
- ◆ The BIOS for some devices only works when allowed to use specific IRQs, I/O addresses, DMA channels, or upper memory addresses.
- ◆ For standard devices, such as a floppy disk drive that uses IRQ 6, using specific resources is not a problem, but for other devices, a resource conflict can result when two legacy devices attempt to use the same system resource.

OBJECTIVES ON THE JOB

Upgrading BIOS is most often appropriate when attempting to install a large hard drive in an older system. Sometimes a BIOS manufacturer will offer an upgrade when there are known problems with a particular BIOS model or in order to support new hardware or software. In most environments, you will not often be called on to perform this task.

PRACTICE TEST QUESTIONS

1. **The major advantage of using Flash ROM is:**
   a. upgrading BIOS without replacing the chip
   b. not having to reload the operating system
   c. protected hard drives
   d. increased memory capacity

2. **One reason to upgrade a BIOS is to:**
   a. install a larger hard drive
   b. install a second floppy drive
   c. cause the system to use less power
   d. perform routine maintenance on a system

3. **You can find an upgrade for BIOS in:**
   a. the CD that came with the system board
   b. files in the \Windows\System folder that contain BIOS upgrades
   c. the Web site of the BIOS manufacturer
   d. the Microsoft Web site, because they keep all BIOS upgrades in stock

4. **How often does a PC technician perform a BIOS upgrade on a system?**
   a. very seldom, maybe never
   b. at least once a year
   c. whenever new hardware is installed
   d. whenever routine maintenance is scheduled

5. **To identify the BIOS manufacturer and model look:**
   a. on the top of the BIOS chip
   b. on the bottom of the system board
   c. on the power supply or the back of the computer case
   d. in the Word document stored in the root directory of the hard drive

6. **When upgrading the BIOS, the most likely way to get the BIOS upgrade is to:**
   a. read the upgrade file from the CD-ROM sent to you by the BIOS manufacturer
   b. download the upgrade from the Internet
   c. read the upgrade file from the system board setup CD-ROM
   d. type the code into a document on the screen

7. **When upgrading BIOS, what should you remember?**
   a. Be careful to not expose the ROM BIOS chip to light as you work; this can damage the chip.
   b. Be careful to not move the ROM BIOS chip in its socket, which can damage the chip.
   c. Be careful to upgrade using the correct upgrade from the manufacturer. Upgrading with the wrong file could make your system BIOS totally useless.
   d. Be careful to not type the wrong code into the BIOS program.

OBJECTIVES

1.10 Determine the issues that must be considered when upgrading a PC. In a given scenario, determine when and how to upgrade system components.

LAPTOP POWER SOURCES: LITHIUM ION, NIMH, AND FUEL CELL • PCMCIA TYPE I, II, III CARDS

UNDERSTANDING THE OBJECTIVE

Many add–on devices are installed in a notebook computer using PC Card slots (formally called PCMCIA slots). There are three sizes of PC Cards. Both NiMH (nickel–metal–hydride) and Lithium Ion notebook batteries can be replaced as they become worn out. Replaceable or refillable fuel cell batteries are currently under development and may be released by 2004.

WHAT YOU REALLY NEED TO KNOW

◆ A standard notebook battery usually lasts between two and four hours. Some notebook computers offer the ability to add a second battery.

◆ When replacing or adding a notebook battery, only use a battery that is recommended by the notebook manufacturer.

◆ Fuel cells called Direct Methanol Fuel Cells (DMFC) break down methanol molecules into protons, electrons, water, and carbon dioxide. Protons are passed through a specialized membrane and electrons are directed into a wire that powers the notebook computer. DMFCs will initially provide up to five hours of battery life. Future versions will provide up to 10 hours of battery life.

◆ DMFCs are electrically compatible with Lithium Ion batteries and therefore may be used on older laptops.

◆ PC Cards of Type I, II, and III have different thicknesses.

◆ A notebook's BIOS must provide **socket service** and **card service** to PC Cards.

◆ PC Cards require little power to operate and are **hot-swappable** (can be installed and removed without rebooting the computer).

◆ The first PC Cards used a 16-bit data path and followed the ISA bus standards. Newer PC Cards use CardBus technology, which offers a 32-bit data path and follows the PCI bus standards. Notebooks generally support both technologies.

◆ 16-bit and 32-bit PC Cards come in three sizes:

PC Card Type	Thickness	Devices That Use This Type
Type I	3.3 mm	Memory cards (oldest type)
Type II	5 mm	Network cards, modem cards
Type III	10.5 mm	Hard disk cards

OBJECTIVES ON THE JOB

Two common tasks for a PC technician supporting a notebook computer are replacing and adding notebook batteries and verifying that a PC Card device is configured and working correctly on the notebook.

PRACTICE TEST QUESTIONS

1. **Given the following scenario, determine how to upgrade system components. Which of the following steps is important in replacing a dead notebook battery?**
   a. Contact the manufacturer to determine what type of battery to purchase.
   b. Remove and recycle the dead notebook battery.
   c. Read all documentation bundled with the new battery and be sure to properly charge the battery before use.
   d. All of the above.

2. **Which PC Card is the thickest?**
   a. Type I
   b. Type 25
   c. Type II
   d. Type III

3. **Which type of PC Card is typically used for a modem?**
   a. Type I
   b. Type II
   c. Type III
   d. Type IV

4. **Hot-swapping refers to:**
   a. the ability to install a component without rebooting
   b. hard drives overheating and needing to be replaced
   c. a notebook computer providing support for a PC Card that serves as a hard drive
   d. quickly rebooting a computer when components are installed

5. **Given the following scenario, determine how to upgrade system components. Which of the following steps is important in upgrading a Lithium Ion battery with a fuel cell?**
   a. Contact the notebook manufacturer to determine which fuel cell is compatible.
   b. Properly dispose of or recycle the old Lithium Ion battery.
   c. Read all documentation that is bundled with the fuel cell before starting the installation process.
   d. All of the above.

6. **A power-saving feature of a notebook computer that turns the power off after a period of inactivity is:**
   a. sleep mode
   b. hibernation
   c. Screen Saver Plus
   d. PowerSave

7. **Which bus technology is CardBus based on?**
   a. ISA
   b. AGP
   c. PCI
   d. EISA

2.1 Recognize common problems associated with each module and their symptoms, and identify steps to isolate and troubleshoot the problems. Given a problem situation, interpret the symptoms and infer the most likely cause.

I/O PORTS AND CABLES: SERIAL, PARALLEL, USB PORTS, IEEE 1394/FIREWIRE, INFRARED, AND SCSI

UNDERSTANDING THE OBJECTIVE

Problems with a parallel port, serial port, USB port, FireWire (IEEE 1394) port, infrared port, or SCSI port can be physical or can be caused by errors in configuration or with how the port is used. Most ports can be configured by way of CMOS setup or Device Manager.

WHAT YOU **REALLY** NEED TO KNOW

◆ Always use a parallel printer cable that is rated IEEE 1284 compliant.

◆ A USB port must be enabled in CMOS, and there can be no conflicts with the resources used by the USB controller. The USB controller can be viewed using Device Manager.

◆ If a USB device fails to be detected when attached to a computer, plug the device into another USB port. If the device is still not detected, replace the USB cable with a known-good USB cable. Also, be sure the device is powered on. Under Windows 2000 and Windows XP, you must be logged in with local administrator permissions in order to install device drivers for a USB device.

◆ To check or modify the configuration of a port, check Device Manager from inside Windows. If the device is conflicting, then attempt the modify resource settings to eliminate the conflict. If this is not possible, then modify the resource settings of the conflicting device. PCI card resources can be modified by plugging the card into a different PCI slot. Other port resources can be modified from CMOS setup.

◆ Some ports such as USB, FireWire, infrared, or SCSI may require special drivers in order to be recognized and supported under an operating system. Visit the computer manufacturer's Web site to check for or download the needed drivers. For example, you may need to install the Intel Chipset drivers from Intel's Web site (*http://www.intel.com/design/software/drivers/platform/inf.htm*) in order to setup support for certain devices on the motherboard.

◆ A parallel port can be configured as bi-directional, extended capabilities port (ECP), or enhanced parallel port (EPP). If you are experiencing problems printing, access CMOS setup and change the printer port settings to use bi-directional mode.

◆ There is a known problem with supporting the SCSI port under Windows 2000. Your computer may hang due to a defect in the SCSI port driver file. To support SCSI, FireWire, USB, and Infrared ports, install the latest service pack.

◆ If you've installed the latest **service pack** for your operating system and are still experiencing communication problems with a device on a port, try using a new cable. If the problem still exists, then try replacing the device with a similar known-good device if possible.

OBJECTIVES ON THE JOB

Port configuration can usually be performed by accessing CMOS setup or by modifying the Device Manager setting from inside Windows 9x, Windows 2000, or Windows XP. If there are no port conflicts and you are still experiencing communication problems, try a new cable.

PRACTICE TEST QUESTIONS

1. How many bits of data are transmitted over a parallel port at one time?

    a. 1
    b. 8
    c. 16
    d. 32

2. Which IRQ does the parallel port LPT1 typically use?

    a. IRQ 0
    b. IRQ 7
    c. IRQ 10
    d. IRQ 14

3. What standard should a parallel printer cable meet?

    a. IEEE 1394
    b. IEEE 1284
    c. ECP
    d. Windows 98

4. Given the problem situation, interpret the symptoms and infer the most likely cause. A SCSI port resource is not listed under Device Manager.

    a. The SCSI port may not be natively supported by the operating system.
    b. The SCSI port is conflicting with another device.
    c. The SCSI port is damaged.
    d. None of the above.

5. Given the problem situation, interpret the symptoms and infer the most likely cause. A serial device has stopped communicating with the computer.

    a. The serial cable has gone bad. Replace it with a known-good cable.
    b. The serial port is disabled in CMOS setup.
    c. The serial cable has become detached from the computer or device.
    d. All of the above.

6. Given the problem situation, interpret the symptoms and infer the most likely cause. A USB device is not detected when it is attached to the computer.

    a. The USB port is disabled in CMOS setup.
    b. The USB port is conflicting with another device.
    c. The USB cable is defective.
    d. All of the above.

7. Given the problem situation, interpret the symptoms and infer the most likely cause. An infrared device has stopped communicating with the computer.

    a. The infrared port is conflicting with another device.
    b. The infrared port is disabled.
    c. Replace the batteries in the infrared device.
    d. All of the above.

2.1 Recognize common problems associated with each module and their symptoms, and identify steps to isolate and troubleshoot the problems. Given a problem situation, interpret the symptoms and infer the most likely cause.

MOTHERBOARDS: CMOS/BIOS SETTINGS AND POST AUDIBLE/VISUAL ERROR CODES

UNDERSTANDING THE OBJECTIVE

Problems with a system are divided into problems that occur during booting and problems that occur after booting completes. The BIOS performs a test of the CPU, CMOS, the system board, and other vital components during booting. Errors encountered before video is active are communicated by a series of beeps and, after video is active, by error codes and messages displayed on the screen.

WHAT YOU **REALLY** NEED TO KNOW

- ◆ Errors with a system board can be discovered by interpreting beep codes, POST error codes displayed on the screen, and BIOS error messages displayed on the screen.
- ◆ Sometimes a dead computer can be fixed by disassembling and reassembling parts, reseating expansion cards, reconnecting cables, and reseating DIMMs, SIMMs, RIMMs, and the CPU.
- ◆ Bad connections and corrosion are common problems. Dust buildup can cause a system to overheat and malfunction.
- ◆ Check jumpers, DIP switches, and CMOS settings. Look for physical damage on the system board.
- ◆ If the battery is dead or low, it may cause problems. The first indication of a failing battery is the system does not keep the correct time when the power is off.
- ◆ The following are error messages that might have to do with the CMOS and their meanings:

Error	Meaning of Error Message and What to Do
Configuration/CMOS error	Setup information does not agree with the actual hardware the computer found during boot
Fixed disk configuration error	The drive type set in CMOS setup is not supported by the BIOS, or the drive setup information does not match the hard drive type
Numeric POST code displays on the screen:	Troubleshoot the subsystem identified by the POST code
• Code in the 900 range	Parallel port errors
• Code in the 1100–1200 range	System board errors: Async communications adapter errors
• Code in the 1300 range	Game controller or joystick errors
• Code in the 1700 range	Hard drive errors
• Code in the 6000 range	SCSI device or network card errors
• Code in the 7300 range	Floppy drive errors

OBJECTIVES ON THE JOB

When attempting to solve problems during booting, use beep codes, POST error messages, and error codes to help in solving the problem. To interpret these beeps and codes, see the Web site of the system board manufacturer or the BIOS manufacturer.

PRACTICE TEST QUESTIONS

1. **A PC continuously reboots itself. What is the most likely cause of the problem?**
   a. corrupt operating system
   b. problems with the power source or power supply
   c. bad RAM
   d. corrupted hard drive

2. **POST error codes in the 1700 range indicate a problem with:**
   a. the hard drive
   b. a floppy drive
   c. a CD-ROM drive
   d. memory

3. **One long continuous beep or several steady long beeps most likely indicate a problem with:**
   a. the hard drive
   b. the CPU
   c. RAM
   d. the power supply

4. **You want to install a large hard drive on a system whose BIOS does not support large drives and you cannot upgrade the BIOS. What is the best solution?**
   a. Make the BIOS think the large drive is a SCSI drive.
   b. Use software that makes the BIOS think it is looking at a smaller drive.
   c. Replace the system board.
   d. Replace the entire PC.

5. **An error message, "Parity error," displays and the system hangs. The source of the problem is:**
   a. bad RAM
   b. bad CPU
   c. a corrupted hard drive
   d. a bad system board

6. **When a PC boots, the screen is blank and you hear a single beep. What is most likely to be the problem?**
   a. the system board or the CPU
   b. the video card
   c. the monitor
   d. ROM BIOS

7. **When a PC boots, the screen is blank and you hear several beeps. What is most likely to be the problem?**
   a. power to the PC
   b. a corrupted operating system
   c. the monitor
   d. RAM or the system board

2.1 Recognize common problems associated with each module and their symptoms, and identify steps to isolate and troubleshoot the problems. Given a problem situation, interpret the symptoms and infer the most likely cause.

PERIPHERALS • INPUT DEVICES: KEYBOARD, MOUSE/POINTER DEVICES, AND TOUCH SCREEN

UNDERSTANDING THE OBJECTIVE

A mouse, keyboard, and other peripherals and cables can sometimes fail. When isolating a problem, do the simple things first such as rebooting or exchanging a cable or external device before opening the case and exchanging parts inside the computer case. Work methodically when isolating a computer problem.

WHAT YOU **REALLY** NEED TO KNOW

◆ If a mouse does not work, try cleaning the ball cavity with a clean cloth and very small amount of mild soap.

◆ If Windows 2000 or Windows XP fails to load properly consider replacing the keyboard. If you're using a USB keyboard or USB mouse, consider replacing both with a standard keyboard and PS/2 mouse.

◆ Peripherals such as printers can sometimes stop working. If this occurs, try running diagnostic software to test the communication between the printer and computer. The diagnostic software can be run by accessing the printer's properties. Another option is to delete the printer icon from under Control Panel/Printers. Then, reboot and reinstall the printer drivers for your operating system.

◆ If you have just inserted a new ink-jet cartridge and the printer fails to print and blinks an error message, try replacing the cartridge. New ink-jet cartridges are sometimes defective.

◆ If a touch screen stops working, look under Device Manager for a resource conflict. If no conflicts exist, then reinstall device software for your operating system.

◆ When a keyboard is not working properly, after making a reasonable attempt to fix the problem, replace the keyboard.

◆ When keys do not work, try using compressed air or a vacuum to remove crumbs and other debris from underneath the keys.

◆ If a keyboard fails to work intermittently, consider a faulty power supply as the source of the problem because a keyboard receives its power from the power supply.

OBJECTIVES ON THE JOB

A good PC technician tries the simple things first. Always try replacing a cable or an external device such as a monitor before opening the computer case and replacing components.

PRACTICE TEST QUESTIONS

1. **If a peripheral stops working, what's one of the first things to check?**
   a. Device Manager, for a resource conflict.
   b. The NIC is communicating with other devices on the network.
   c. Network Neighborhood can access other hosts on the network.
   d. None of the above.

2. **What is one check you can make to be certain a printer is communicating properly with a computer?**
   a. Run diagnostic software to test printer communication.
   b. Power printer on.
   c. Make sure printer has paper.
   d. Device Manager reports the printer has no conflicts and is working properly.

3. **If a keyboard fails intermittently, what might be a source of the problem?**
   a. the mouse
   b. Windows 98 installation
   c. the power supply
   d. the NIC

4. **Video does not work. What are the things you should replace and the order you should replace them?**
   a. video cable, monitor, video card
   b. monitor, video cable, video card
   c. video card, monitor, system board
   d. video card, monitor, keyboard

5. **What standard should a parallel printer cable meet?**
   a. IEEE 1394
   b. IEEE 1284
   c. ECP
   d. Windows 98

6. **When a printer does not work, what are some things you can check?**
   a. Is the printer online?
   b. Is the printer cable connected securely at both ends?
   c. Is the printer installed correctly under Windows?
   d. All the above.

7. **You've just powered the computer on and receive a keyboard stuck error message. What is the first thing you should do?**
   a. Check the keyboard for a depressed or stuck key.
   b. Replace the mouse.
   c. Reboot the computer.
   d. All of the above.

2.1 Recognize common problems associated with each module and their symptoms, and identify steps to isolate and troubleshoot the problems. Given a problem situation, interpret the symptoms and infer the most likely cause.

COMPUTER CASE: POWER SUPPLY, SLOT COVERS, AND FRONT COVER ALIGNMENT

UNDERSTANDING THE OBJECTIVE

Problems with a power supply can cause the system to hang at unexpected times, the keyboard to not work, boot failures, or other intermittent errors.

WHAT YOU **REALLY** NEED TO KNOW

- ◆ **Line analyzers** can be used to eliminate suspected problems with power surges, spikes, and sags.
- ◆ After you have successfully tested a power supply using a multimeter, know that the power supply might still be the source of the problem because the problem might be intermittent.
- ◆ A power supply contains capacitors, which retain their charge even after the power is disconnected, so don't open the case of a power supply unless you are trained to service one.
- ◆ Before opening the case of a power supply, discharge the power supply by placing a high-voltage prong or insulated screwdriver across the hot and ground plugs.
- ◆ Don't wear an anti-static ground strap when servicing a power supply; you don't want to be ground for a discharge from the power supply.
- ◆ Problems with a power supply might look like:
  - The PC halts or hangs during booting, but after several tries, it boots successfully.
  - Error codes or beep codes occur during booting, but the errors come and go.
  - The computer stops or hangs for no reason. Sometimes it might even reboot itself.
  - Memory errors appear intermittently.
  - Data is written incorrectly to the hard drive.
  - The keyboard stops working at odd times.
  - The system board fails or is damaged.
  - The power supply overheats and becomes hot to the touch.
- ◆ Electrical problems can be caused by other devices (such as copy machines) on the same circuit as the computer and its equipment.
- ◆ After removing a PCI card, be sure to install a slot cover in the rear of the computer to cover the open slot.
- ◆ If the front cover is not seated properly, remove the front cover and re-align as necessary.

OBJECTIVES ON THE JOB

Problems with the power supply can sometimes appear as problems with peripheral devices or make the system unstable. Use a multimeter to test the power supply when a problem's source is not evident.

PRACTICE TEST QUESTIONS

1. **The device inside a power supply that retains a charge even after power is disconnected is a:**
   a. capacitor
   b. transistor
   c. rectifier
   d. transformer

2. **Covering empty slots on the back of a PC case with slot covers helps to:**
   a. prevent EMI from entering the case
   b. keep the heat inside the case so that components don't get too cold
   c. protect components from ESD
   d. prevent an electrical charge from leaving the case

3. **A power supply uses which IRQ?**
   a. 0
   b. 10
   c. 15
   d. A power supply does not use an IRQ.

4. **The IDE hard drive does not spin up when the PC is turned on. What is most likely to be the problem?**
   a. bad data cable
   b. a bad connection from the power supply
   c. a bad system board
   d. a virus

5. **A PC repeatedly reboots. You replace the power supply with one you know is good. What do you do next?**
   a. Use a line analyzer to eliminate the power line as the source of the problem.
   b. Replace the hard drive.
   c. Install a UPS.
   d. Install an operating system that can monitor the power input to the system.

6. **Which beep codes could indicate that there is a problem with the power supply?**
   a. one long beep, two short beeps
   b. three short beeps
   c. steady short beeps
   d. all of the above

7. **The computer system appears dead, with no lights on the front panel, nothing on the screen, and no beeps. What do you check first?**
   a. the system board
   b. the CPU
   c. the power supply
   d. the speaker

OBJECTIVES

2.1 Recognize common problems associated with each module and their symptoms, and identify steps to isolate and troubleshoot the problems. Given a problem situation, interpret the symptoms and infer the most likely cause.

STORAGE DEVICES AND CABLES: FDD, HDD, CD/CDRW, DVD/DVDRW, TAPE DRIVE, AND REMOVABLE STORAGE

UNDERSTANDING THE OBJECTIVE

Data and instructions (programs) are permanently stored in secondary (or removable) storage devices (hard drive, floppy disk, CD-ROM, DVD, and so forth) even when the PC is turned off. A DVD disc can hold up to 17 GB of data, enough for more than eight hours of video storage.

WHAT YOU **REALLY** NEED TO KNOW

◆ If the CD-ROM drive is sharing an IDE data cable with a hard drive, set the hard drive to master and the CD-ROM drive to slave. If the drives are connected by way of an 80-pin IDE cable, set both devices to cable select and make sure the hard drive is plugged into the primary IDE connector (black) and the CD-ROM drive is plugged into the slave IDE connector (gray).

◆ Mscdex.exe is a 16-bit real mode Microsoft CD-ROM extension to DOS and is loaded in Autoexec.bat and requires a real-mode CD-ROM device driver to be loaded from Config.sys.

◆ Windows XP, Windows 2000, and Windows 9x provide protected mode support for CD-ROM and DVD drives.

◆ A floppy drive is connected to a data cable, which can connect to a controller card (on very old systems) or directly to the system board using a 34-pin data cable.

◆ A floppy drive cable can support two floppy drives. The twist in the cable determines which drive is A: and which drive is B:.

◆ Floppy drive diagnostic software and floppy disks called digital diagnostic disks (data is written perfectly to these disks) can be used to check for problems with a floppy drive.

◆ A CD-ROM drive is read only. A CD-R drive can handle CD-Recordable (both read and write) discs. A CDRW drive manages rewriteable CDs, meaning that old data can be overwritten on the disc with new data.

◆ A DVD drive can require a decoder card to uncompress video and audio data stored on the DVD disc.

◆ You will not often encounter tape drives.

OBJECTIVES ON THE JOB

Installing and troubleshooting problems with CD-ROM drives is an essential skill of a PC technician. Know that Windows 95 does not automatically install the files necessary to access a CD-ROM drive on its Emergency Startup Disk (ESD). To access a CD-ROM drive in real mode from a command prompt, the ESD must include Mscdex.exe and the device driver file for the CD-ROM drive. Load Mscdex.exe from Autoexec.bat and the device driver from Config.sys. Windows 98 automatically includes these files on the ESD.

PRACTICE TEST QUESTIONS

1. **How is a real-mode device driver for a CD-ROM drive loaded?**
   a. from Config.sys
   b. from Autoexec.bat
   c. at the DOS prompt
   d. using the LOADHIGH command

2. **The DOS extension that manages a CD-ROM drive is:**
   a. Config.sys
   b. Mscdex.exe
   c. Cdrom.sys
   d. Io.sys

3. **What could cause the error message, "General failure reading drive A, Abort, Retry Fail?"**
   a. The file Command.com is missing from the disk.
   b. The floppy drive is faulty.
   c. The video system has a problem.
   d. There is a parity error in RAM.

4. **Possible sources of problems with reading a floppy disk include:**
   a. disk in drive is not formatted
   b. application currently running has an error
   c. power supply is bad
   d. all of the above

5. **The user reports that a floppy drive reads the first disk inserted into the drive after a reboot but does not read subsequent disks. What might be the problem?**
   a. The IRQ for the floppy drive is in conflict with another device.
   b. The floppy drive data cable is connected backwards.
   c. Device Manager does not recognize the drive.
   d. The power to the floppy drive is fluctuating.

6. **Which utility manages a CD-ROM drive for DOS?**
   a. Config.sys
   b. Command.com
   c. Mscdex.exe
   d. Io.sys

7. **Why is Mscdex.exe not used with Windows 9x?**
   a. It is replaced with Mscdex.sys.
   b. Windows 9x uses 32-bit protected mode support for CD-ROM drives.
   c. Mscdex.exe is required by Windows 9x.
   d. Windows 9x does not support CD-ROM drives.

2.1 Recognize common problems associated with each module and their symptoms, and identify steps to isolate and troubleshoot the problems. Given a problem situation, interpret the symptoms and infer the most likely cause.

COOLING SYSTEMS: FANS, HEAT SINKS, LIQUID COOLING, AND TEMPERATURE SENSORS • PROCESSOR/CPU • MEMORY

UNDERSTANDING THE OBJECTIVE

Problems with CPUs are rare but can occur if a computer is not properly ventilated or if the fans or heat sinks stop working. If you've installed a liquid cooling system or temperature sensors, be sure to properly maintain these systems, as suggested by the manufacturer. The BIOS performs a test of the CPU, CMOS, the system fans, and other vital components during booting. Errors encountered before video is active, such as a CPU that is not working, are communicated by a series of beeps.

WHAT YOU **REALLY** NEED TO KNOW

- ◆ Utilities can be downloaded that can test your CPU and memory. One popular memory testing software is called MemTest (*http://www.memtest.com*). In order to fully test memory, it should be allowed to run for several hours.

- ◆ Sometimes a POST beep error can be fixed by disassembling and reassembling parts, reseating expansion cards, reconnecting cables, and reseating DIMMs, SIMMs, RIMMs, and the CPU. Be sure to make sure that all fans are working properly.

- ◆ Bad connections and corrosion are common problems. Dust buildup can cause a system to overheat and malfunction.

- ◆ Another method for testing memory is to replace it with known-good memory. Then, perform tasks normally for several days to see if the problem occurs again.

- ◆ Fans tend to wear out after years of use. Be sure to replace any failed fan(s) immediately. Consult your computer manufacturer to obtain a proper replacement part.

- ◆ Heat sinks are typically attached to the CPU with thermal compound. This substance helps dissipate heat more quickly.

- ◆ Be sure to keep clean all computer ventilation holes on a regular basis. Never place a computer inside a closed cabinet without proper air circulation.

- ◆ If a computer running Windows 2000 or Windows XP continuously reboots itself, it has probably encountered an error from which it cannot recover. In order to view this error, you must uncheck "Automatically reboot" under the "Startup and Recovery" area of your system properties. After doing so, a blue or black screen containing specific information on the error will be displayed the next time a fatal error occurs. Use this information to search the Microsoft support Web site for more details on the error.

OBJECTIVES ON THE JOB

Troubleshooting CPU and memory problems is a very difficult and time-consuming task. Always replace one component or change one setting at a time and then test for several days. Through the process of elimination, you will be able to determine the root cause of the problem.

PRACTICE TEST QUESTIONS

1. **A Windows XP PC continuously reboots itself. What can you do to view a specific error message?**
   a. Reboot the computer.
   b. Uncheck "Automatically Reboot."
   c. Replace the RAM.
   d. None of the above.

2. **A computer keeps hanging or freezing for no apparent reason. Which of the following should you do to troubleshoot the problem?**
   a. Replace the RAM.
   b. Reboot the computer.
   c. Reinstall the operating system.
   d. None of the above.

3. **Which of the following utilities can be used to test RAM?**
   a. System Defragmenter
   b. MemTest
   c. ScanDisk
   d. None of the above

4. **Which of the following can be installed to monitor the inside temperature of your computer?**
   a. a temperature sensor
   b. a humidity sensor
   c. an EKG sensor
   d. all of the above

5. **An error message, "Parity error," displays and the system hangs. The source of the problem is:**
   a. bad RAM
   b. bad CPU
   c. a corrupted hard drive
   d. a bad system board

6. **Which of the following components is crucial to maintaining the proper temperature inside your computer?**
   a. the fan
   b. the CPU heat sink
   c. proper ventilation
   d. all of the above

7. **Which of the following tasks falls under the category of proper maintenance of your computer?**
   a. Clean dust for ventilation holes in computer case.
   b. Replace RAM.
   c. Replace CPU.
   d. All of the above.

2.1 Recognize common problems associated with each module and their symptoms, and identify steps to isolate and troubleshoot the problems. Given a problem situation, interpret the symptoms and infer the most likely cause.

DISPLAY DEVICE • ADAPTERS: NETWORK INTERFACE CARD (NIC), SOUND CARD, VIDEO CARD, MODEM, SCSI, IEEE 1394/FIREWIRE, AND USB

UNDERSTANDING THE OBJECTIVE

Problems with display devices (or ports, such as FireWire and USB) can be caused by either hardware or software failures and can occur during or after booting. To isolate the source of a problem, you can eliminate the unnecessary component, trade a suspected-bad component for a known-good component (a monitor, for example), or install a suspected-bad component into a known-good system.

WHAT YOU **REALLY** NEED TO KNOW

- Most problems with monitors and the video system are caused by simple things like loose cable connections and poorly adjusted brightness and contrast settings.
- If the LED light on the front of the monitor is lit, the monitor has power.
- Check that the fuse (if there is one) on the back of the monitor is not blown.
- Reseat an expansion card and try to boot again before exchanging the card.
- Check CMOS settings, reseat socketed chips, and replace suspected bad components. A USB port must be enabled in CMOS.
- Verify that Device Manager does not report any problems with the device or its port.
- To resolve resource conflicts, use MSD in DOS and Device Manager in Windows.
- If a musical CD does not play, check the audio wire between the CD-ROM drive and the sound card.
- If the sound does not work, try adjusting the volume in Windows and the amplifier or speakers.
- Before exchanging a NIC, first try exchanging the network cable.
- Before exchanging a NIC, first try uninstalling and reinstalling the network card drivers and the network protocol (for example, TCP/IP).
- You must often troubleshoot to solve problems when installing a modem. If the new modem does not work, check the following:
  - Is the PC short on hard drive space or RAM? Try closing all other applications currently running.
  - Is the modem set to the same COM port and IRQ as the software?
  - Is another device configured to the same COM port or IRQ as the modem?
  - Try moving an internal modem to a different expansion slot.
  - For an external modem, use a different serial cable.

OBJECTIVES ON THE JOB

Follow established troubleshooting procedures when attempting to isolate and solve problems with adapters.

PRACTICE TEST QUESTIONS

1. **If nothing is showing on the monitor screen, the first thing to do is:**
   a. check the monitor connections to the computer and the power
   b. reseat the video card in its expansion slot
   c. reinstall the video drivers
   d. reboot the PC

2. **If the LED light on the monitor is lit but the screen is blank, what is NOT a source of the problem?**
   a. the brightness or contrast settings
   b. video cable to the computer
   c. circuitry inside the monitor
   d. power to the monitor

3. **What IRQ does a sound card typically use?**
   a. 1
   b. 5
   c. 6
   d. 15

4. **Your modem was working fine until you installed a sound card; now neither the modem nor the sound card work. What is likely the problem?**
   a. The modem was accidentally disconnected while installing the sound card.
   b. There is a resource conflict between the two devices.
   c. The modem is the type that does not work if a sound card is installed in the system.
   d. The OS cannot support both devices at the same time.

5. **What IRQ does a monitor use?**
   a. 1
   b. 7
   c. 14
   d. A monitor does not use an IRQ.

6. **ESD is least likely to cause damage to what device?**
   a. an internal modem
   b. a keyboard
   c. a CPU
   d. RAM

7. **Which of the following is typically an input and output device?**
   a. a monitor
   b. a modem
   c. a mouse
   d. a keyboard

2.1 Recognize common problems associated with each module and their symptoms, and identify steps to isolate and troubleshoot the problems. Given a problem situation, interpret the symptoms and infer the most likely cause.

PORTABLE SYSTEMS: PCMCIA, BATTERIES, DOCKING STATIONS/PORT REPLICATORS, AND PORTABLE UNIQUE STORAGE

UNDERSTANDING THE OBJECTIVE

Troubleshooting a notebook computer is similar to troubleshooting a desktop computer. To isolate the source of a problem, you can eliminate the unnecessary component if possible, trade a suspected–bad component for a known–good component (a battery, for example), or install a suspected–bad component into a known–good system.

WHAT YOU **REALLY** NEED TO KNOW

◆ To troubleshoot PCMCIA cards, you must first identify if it is a software or hardware problem. This can be done by using a known-good PCMCIA card or by trying the suspected-bad card on another similar notebook computer.

◆ Windows XP has several problems dealing with devices, including PCMCIA cards, while in hibernation or sleep mode. To resolve these issues, download and install the latest service pack or visit Microsoft Window Update at *http://windowsupdate.microsoft.com*.

◆ If the notebook computer is running Windows 9x or Windows XP, load Msconfig.exe if you are troubleshooting a device that runs when the computer starts. Msconfig.exe can be helpful by allowing you to temporarily disable other devices that run at startup. By doing this, you may be able to identify which device is causing a conflict.

◆ If you are experiencing a problem with a battery, try reseating the battery into the notebook computer. If the battery still does not function and is relatively new, check with the manufacturer to determine if there was a recent battery recall alert issued. Older batteries tend to loose their ability to hold a charge and should be replaced with a new battery, as suggested by the notebook manufacturer.

◆ Troubleshooting docking stations can vary from notebook manufacturer. Always read the accompanying documentation. Contact the manufacturer or visit the support area of the manufacturer's Web site for additional details. There's a good chance that other individuals may have experienced the same configuration problem.

◆ Troubleshooting portable unique storage devices such as a Zip drive, CD-R drive, or memory key will vary depending upon the make and model of the device. 250 MB Zip drives can read/write to both 100 MB and 250 MB Zip disks. 750 MB Zip drives can read/write to 750 MB and 250 MB Zip disks and can only read from 100 MB Zip disks.

◆ CD-R discs can be read in almost any CD-ROM drive. Some older CD-ROM drives experience problems attempting to read CD-R discs. CDRW discs can only be read in CDRW drives.

OBJECTIVES ON THE JOB

Troubleshooting problems on notebook computers is sometimes brand specific. Be sure to read all documentation. Contact technical support if necessary to determine if a particular problem is a known issue or recall.

PRACTICE TEST QUESTIONS

1. Given the problem situation, interpret the symptoms and infer the most likely cause. You are unable to write to a 100 MB Zip disk using your 750 MB Zip drive.
   - a. The 100 MB Zip disk is defective.
   - b. The 750 MB Zip drive is defective.
   - c. This is a known limitation of the 750 MB drive.
   - d. None of the above.

2. Given the problem situation, interpret the symptoms and infer the most likely cause. A used notebook battery will not hold a charge.
   - a. The battery has lost its ability to hold a charge and should be replaced.
   - b. The battery charger unit is defective.
   - c. The battery charger is not plugged in.
   - d. None of the above.

3. Given the problem situation, interpret the symptoms and infer the most likely cause. A CD-R disc cannot be read in the notebook's CD-R drive.
   - a. The CD-R disc is scratched.
   - b. The CD-R disc is not formatted.
   - c. The CD-R drive is not capable of reading CD-R discs from other computers.
   - d. None of the above.

4. Given the problem situation, interpret the symptoms and infer the most likely cause. A CDRW disc cannot be read in the notebook's CD-R drive.
   - a. The CDRW disc is scratched.
   - b. The CDRW disc is not formatted.
   - c. The CD-R drive is not capable of reading CDRW discs.
   - d. None of the above.

5. A PCMCIA card is not detected after replacing another PCMCIA card on a running notebook computer. Given the situation, interpret the symptoms and infer the most likely cause.
   - a. You must stop one PCMCIA card before starting another.
   - b. The PCMCIA card is defective.
   - c. The PC Card slot is defective.
   - d. None of the above.

6. Given the problem situation, interpret the symptoms and infer the most likely cause. When you try to undock/eject your Windows XP computer by pressing the Undock/Eject button on your docking station, the computer does NOT undock. You receive a message similar to: "Problem Undocking from docking station. You cannot eject your computer because you do not have sufficient security privileges to do so."
   - a. You are using the Fast User Switching feature and are logged on as an additional user.
   - b. You are not logged on with local administrator permissions.
   - c. The docking station is defective.
   - d. All of the above.

7. Given the problem situation, interpret the symptoms and infer the most likely cause. The Windows 98 computer freezes when you attempt to write a large file to a 100 MB Zip disk using your 250 MB Zip drive.
   - a. The 100 MB Zip disk is defective.
   - b. The 250 MB Zip drive is defective.
   - c. This is a known limitation. Enable write-behind caching on the hard drive.
   - d. None of the above.

OBJECTIVES

2.2 Identify basic troubleshooting procedures and tools, and how to elicit problem symptoms from customers. Justify asking particular questions in a given scenario.

TROUBLESHOOTING/ISOLATION/PROBLEM DETERMINATION PROCEDURES • DETERMINING WHETHER A HARDWARE OR SOFTWARE PROBLEM

UNDERSTANDING THE OBJECTIVE

Approach each PC troubleshooting problem in a systematic way.

WHAT YOU **REALLY** NEED TO KNOW

- ◆ Determine if the problem occurs during or after the boot.
- ◆ When isolating a problem, eliminate the unnecessary and trade good for suspected bad or install a suspected-bad component into a known-good system.
- ◆ Here are some fundamental rules for PC troubleshooting:
  - **Approach the problem systematically.** Start at the beginning and walk through the situation in a thorough, careful way.
  - **Divide and conquer.** Isolate the problem by eliminating components until the problem disappears.
  - **Don't overlook the obvious.** Ask simple questions. Is the computer plugged in? Is it turned on? Is the monitor plugged in?
  - **Check the simple things first.** It is more effective to first check the components that are easiest to replace.
  - **Make no assumptions.** Check everything for yourself. Don't trust documentation or what the user tells you.
  - **Become a researcher.** Take advantage of every available resource, including online help, the Internet, documentation, technical support, and books such as this one.
  - **Write things down.** Keep good notes as you're working. Draw diagrams. Know that a problem can be hardware- and/or software-related.
  - **Establish your priorities.** Decide what your first priority is. Consult the user or customer for his or her advice when practical.
  - **Keep your cool.** In an emergency, protect the data and software by carefully considering your options before acting and by taking practical precautions to protect software and OS files.
  - **Know your starting point.** Before trying to solve a computer problem, know for certain that the problem is what the user says it is.

OBJECTIVES ON THE JOB

Good problem solving skills are the essence of a PC technician's skills.

PRACTICE TEST QUESTIONS

1. You install a second IDE hard drive in a system using the same IDE primary channel used by the first drive. When you boot up, the first drive works but the system fails to recognize the new drive. What is the most likely cause of the problem?
   a. The second drive is bad.
   b. The data cable is bad.
   c. You failed to change the IDE setting for the first drive from single to master.
   d. The second drive is not formatted, so the system doesn't recognize the drive.

2. A POST error code in the 6000 range indicates a problem with:
   a. the floppy drive
   b. the system board
   c. the IDE hard drive
   d. a SCSI device

3. POST is done when the computer is:
   a. shut down
   b. assembled
   c. turned on
   d. configured

4. POST is performed by:
   a. BIOS on the system board
   b. the operating system
   c. BIOS on the hard drive
   d. software on the hard drive

5. When you use a floppy drive cable with a twist, the order of connections on the data cable supporting two floppy drives is:
   a. system board, drive A:, drive B:
   b. system board, drive B:, drive A:
   c. drive A:, system board, drive B:
   d. The order depends on how CMOS sees the drive assignments.

6. A system appears dead but you notice that the small green light on the front of the monitor is on. What can you safely assume?
   a. The computer is receiving power.
   b. The monitor is receiving power.
   c. The system board is bad.
   d. The data cable from the computer to the monitor is loose.

7. You replace a system board because the old board is dead. You turn on the PC. It boots up correctly but hangs, dies, and refuses to reboot. What is most likely the source of the problem?
   a. The second system board was bad.
   b. There is a problem with the power. Check the power supply next.
   c. A failed hard drive caused the system to appear dead.
   d. The RAM you installed from the old board corrupted the new system board, destroying it.

2.2 Identify basic troubleshooting procedures and tools, and how to elicit problem symptoms from customers. Justify asking particular questions in a given scenario.

GATHERING INFORMATION FROM USER: CUSTOMER ENVIRONMENT, SYMPTOMS/ERROR CODES, AND SITUATION WHEN THE PROBLEM OCCURRED

UNDERSTANDING THE OBJECTIVE

When approaching a PC troubleshooting situation, first, interview the user and ask questions that will help you isolate the problem and know how to reproduce it. Get background information, such as when the problem first occurred and what has happened since the system last worked properly.

WHAT YOU **REALLY** NEED TO KNOW

- ◆ Follow these guidelines when working with the user:
  - Don't take drastic action like formatting the hard drive before you ask the user about important data on the hard drive that may not be backed up.
  - Provide the user with alternatives (where appropriate) before you make decisions affecting him or her.
  - Protect the confidentiality of data on the PC.
  - Don't disparage the user's choice of computer hardware or software.
  - If you have made a mistake or must pass the problem on to someone with more expertise, be honest.
  - Always ask the user for information about the problem and the situation when it first occurred. Don't assume you know what happened.
  - Never leave the customer's site unless you are certain you have left the PC in good working order; don't apply a fix and just assume it worked.
- ◆ Here are some helpful questions to ask the user when you are first trying to discover what the problem is:
  - When did the problem start?
  - Were there any error messages or unusual displays on the screen?
  - What programs or software were you using? Did you move your computer system recently?
  - Has there been a recent thunderstorm or electrical problem?
  - Have you made any hardware changes? Did you recently install any new software?
  - Did you recently change any software configuration setups?
  - Has someone else been using your computer recently?
  - Can you show me what you do when you see the error?
  - If you can't show me, can you describe what happened so I can reproduce the error?
- ◆ Make every attempt to reproduce the error in the presence of the customer so that you and the customer are in agreement as to the starting point of the problem.
- ◆ When interviewing the user, the goal is to gain as much information from the user as you can before you begin investigating the hardware and the software.

OBJECTIVES ON THE JOB

A satisfied customer is one who has been treated with respect and kindness. You can save a lot of time by carefully interviewing the customer before you begin troubleshooting. Discover all the information you can from the user about the problem and its source.

PRACTICE TEST QUESTIONS

1. **What question might you ask a user to help you locate a problem?**
   a. When was the PC purchased?
   b. Is the PC still under warranty?
   c. What software or hardware has recently been installed?
   d. Can you reproduce the problem so I can see it?

2. **How can the customer help you identify the source of an intermittent problem?**
   a. Call you the next time the problem occurs.
   b. Keep working until the problem recurs.
   c. Keep a log of when the problem occurs and what happened just before it occurred.
   d. Install diagnostic software to help you locate the problem.

3. **Which of the following questions is not appropriate to ask the user to help you locate the source of a problem?**
   a. When did the problem first begin?
   b. Has new hardware or software recently been installed?
   c. Why did you buy this brand of computer?
   d. What happened just before the problem began?

4. **You are late for an appointment with a customer. What should you do when you arrive?**
   a. Apologize for being late and immediately get to work.
   b. Immediately get to work without mentioning the fact you're late.
   c. Remind the customer that he or she is sometimes late, too.
   d. Spend the first 15 minutes at the customer site explaining why you're late.

5. **A hard drive has failed but you think you can fix it if you reformat the drive. What should you do first?**
   a. Check with the user to make sure that the data has been backed up.
   b. Immediately reformat the drive.
   c. Run diagnostic software in an attempt to save the data on the drive.
   d. Attempt to back up the data on the drive.

6. **What should you always do at a customer site?**
   a. Apply your fix and immediately leave the site.
   b. Apply your fix and test the system to make sure all is well.
   c. Apply your fix, reboot, and test the system to make sure all is well.
   d. Never admit to a customer that you made a mistake.

7. **When you first arrive at the customer's site, what is the first thing you should do?**
   a. Fill out all the paper work required by your boss.
   b. Listen carefully as the customer describes the problem.
   c. Disassemble the PC.
   d. Search the customer's desk for the PC documentation.

3.1 Identify the various types of preventive maintenance measures, products and procedures and when and how to use them.

LIQUID CLEANING COMPOUNDS • TYPES OF MATERIALS TO CLEAN CONTACTS AND CONNECTIONS • NON-STATIC VACUUMS (CHASIS, POWER SUPPLIES, FANS) • CLEANING MONITORS • CLEANING REMOVABLE MEDIA DEVICES • VENTILATION, DUST AND MOISTURE CONTROL ON THE PC HARDWARE INTERIOR

UNDERSTANDING THE OBJECTIVE

Performing routine preventive maintenance is a common task for most PC technicians. Know how and when to clean a system.

WHAT YOU **REALLY** NEED TO KNOW

◆ Dust inside a PC case can be dangerous because it acts like a blanket, insulating components and causing them to overheat. It's also important to make sure the PC is properly ventilated. Never place a PC inside a closed cabinet or in an area with high humidity. Excess moisture can conduct electricity and damage internal hardware components.

◆ There is disagreement in the industry about using a vacuum inside a computer case, and some believe a vacuum can cause ESD. When inside a PC case, always use a non-static vacuum to prevent ESD.

◆ Use compressed air to blow dust out of a system and vacuum the dust once it is outside the case. Be sure to clean dust from the chasis, power supply, and fans.

◆ Corrosion on the edge connectors of circuit boards can cause poor contact, which can cause the board to fail. Clean edge connectors with contact cleaner designed for that purpose.

◆ A monitor should be cleaned with a clean, dry, lint-free cloth. Never use an ammonia-based product with a cloth to clean a monitor.

◆ Almost all computer equipment can be cleaned with a soft, damp cloth using a small amount of mild detergent.

OBJECTIVES ON THE JOB

Routine maintenance on the computer system is a routine task expected of PC technicians. Below are a few general guidelines that a technician can follow as a regular preventive maintenance plan.

Component	Maintenance	How Often
Inside the case	Check air vents. Remove dust. Check that cards and chips are firmly seated.	Yearly
Removable devices, removable disks	Never place in direct sunlight. Do not jar or drop. Remove dust.	Monthly
CMOS setup	Back up to floppy disk.	Whenever changes are made
Keyboard, monitor	Clean with damp cloth.	Monthly
Mouse	Clean mouse rollers with damp cloth.	Monthly
Printers	Remove dust, bits of paper.	Monthly
Hard drive	Perform regular backups. Defragment and recover lost clusters. Place the PC where it will not be kicked, jarred, or bumped.	Weekly or daily Monthly

PRACTICE TEST QUESTIONS

1. **Which product should be used to clean fingerprints and dirt off a keyboard?**
   a. denatured alcohol
   b. all-purpose cleaner
   c. silicone spray
   d. contact cleaner

2. **Which product should be used to clean a notebook computer's LCD screen?**
   a. denatured alcohol
   b. ammonia window cleaner
   c. hair spray
   d. non-abrasive cleaner

3. **Which of the following is most likely to do damage to data stored on a removable disk such as a floppy disk or Zip disk?**
   a. a laser printer
   b. a CRT monitor
   c. a telephone
   d. an unshielded speaker

4. **Why is dust inside a computer case considered dangerous?**
   a. It can cause ESD.
   b. It can get inside the CPU and corrupt it.
   c. It can insulate components and cause them to overheat.
   d. It can get down inside expansion card slots and cause them to short out.

5. **The best way to remove dust from inside a computer case is to:**
   a. use a regular vacuum cleaner to remove the dust
   b. use compressed air to blow the dust out
   c. use a damp, soft cloth to clean up the dust
   d. use contact cleaner on a soft cloth to clean up the dust

6. **Preventive maintenance on a mouse includes:**
   a. exchanging the ball inside the mouse housing
   b. cleaning the rollers and ball inside the mouse
   c. reinstalling the mouse driver
   d. all of the above

7. **What should you use to clean a monitor screen?**
   a. ammonia window cleaner and a paper towel
   b. denatured alcohol
   c. mild soap and water on a clean cloth
   d. a clean, soft cloth

3.1 Identify the various types of preventive maintenance measures, products and procedures and when and how to use them.

HARD DISK MAINTENANCE (DEFRAGGING, SCAN DISK, CHKDSK) • VERIFYING UPS (UNINTERRUPTIBLE POWER SUPPLY) AND SUPPRESSORS

UNDERSTANDING THE OBJECTIVE

Use a UPS to provide uninterrupted power to the PC. Use a UPS, a line conditioner, or a surge suppressor to protect the system against power surges, lightning, and so forth. Hard disk maintenance includes defragging and running ScanDisk or CHKDSK to repair and recover data.

WHAT YOU **REALLY** NEED TO KNOW

◆ Some UPS models have the ability to perform a clean shutdown of your operating system in the event of a power failure. This feature is especially useful for file servers running Windows 2000 or Windows 2003 server.

◆ If the fan on the power supply stops working, suspect a device drawing too much power.

◆ Shorts in the circuit boards, devices, or the system board will cause an overloaded power system.

◆ All surge protection and battery backup devices should carry the UL (Underwriters Laboratory) logo, which ensures that the device has been tested for product safety.

◆ Devices that filter the AC input to computers are classified as surge suppressors, power conditioners, and uninterruptible power supplies (UPSs).

◆ Define these terms and know what distinguishes one device from another: **surge suppressor**, **UPS**, **standby UPS**, **inline UPS**, **line-interactive UPS**, the **buck-boost** UPS feature, **intelligent UPS**, **line conditioner**, spikes, brownouts, and sags in current.

◆ Data integrity errors such as bad sectors can be discovered and automatically repaired by running ScanDisk on Windows 9x computers and CHKDSK on Windows NT, Windows 2000, and Windows XP computers. To access ScanDisk or CHKDSK, right-click your system drive (usually C:), go to Properties, then Tools.

◆ Running disk defragmenter, also known as defragging a hard drive, reorganizes the way data is stored on your hard drive. This helps speed up the reading of files from your hard drive. You may need to disable anti-virus software in order to run disk defragmenter under Window 9x. To access disk defragmenter, right-click your system drive (usually C:), go to Properties, then Tools.

OBJECTIVES ON THE JOB

It may be necessary to defrag the data on your hard drive on a regular basis depending on the amount of file processing you perform. Running ScanDisk or CHKDSK is often helpful in solving or reducing computer problems related to accessing files or booting your computer. Managing environmental hazards caused by electricity, thunderstorms, and the like is an essential task of a PC technician.

PRACTICE TEST QUESTIONS

1. During a power outage, what should you do before the power is restored?
   - a. Unplug power cords to all equipment.
   - b. Turn off all equipment.
   - c. Close down all currently running software.
   - d. Unplug the monitor.

2. Which device helps prevent power surges to computer equipment?
   - a. a UPS
   - b. a line conditioner
   - c. a multimeter
   - d. a power strip

3. Which device prevents interruptions to power to computer equipment?
   - a. a UPS
   - b. a line conditioner
   - c. a multimeter
   - d. a power strip

4. How can computer equipment be completely protected from damage during an electrical storm?
   - a. with a surge protector
   - b. with an intelligent UPS system
   - c. by unplugging power cords
   - d. by turning off the AC power

5. What question do you ask to determine if power is getting to a computer?
   - a. Do you see lights on the front of the computer case?
   - b. Do you see anything displayed on the screen?
   - c. Do you hear beeps when the computer boots?
   - d. Do you see a light on the front of the CRT?

6. You're working at your computer and a thunderstorm begins. What do you do?
   - a. Keep on working because the power supply acts as a surge suppressor.
   - b. Keep on working because you have a surge suppressor installed.
   - c. Stop working and turn off the PC.
   - d. Stop working, unplug the PC, and unplug the phone line from the modem.

7. What utility is useful in reorganizing the way data is stored on your hard drive so it can be accessed more quickly?
   - a. disk defragmenter
   - b. ScanDisk
   - c. CHKDSK
   - d. all of the above

O B J E C T I V E S

3.2 Identify various safety measures and procedures, and when/how to use them.

ESD (ELECTROSTATIC DISCHARGE) PRECAUTIONS AND PROCEDURES: WHAT ESD CAN DO, HOW IT MAY BE APPARENT, OR HIDDEN, COMMON ESD PROTECTION DEVICES, AND SITUATIONS THAT COULD PRESENT A DANGER OR HAZARD

UNDERSTANDING THE OBJECTIVE

When working on a PC, you must protect the equipment from ESD, which can damage the hardware and data stored on storage devices. If all devices and you are properly grounded, then ESD is not a problem. Grounding devices include ESD bracelets and grounding mats.

WHAT YOU **REALLY** NEED TO KNOW

- ◆ The best protection against ESD is to use an ESD bracket (also known as a static bracelet, ground bracelet, ground strap, or ESD strap) that is grounded to the house ground line or to a bare metal part of the computer.
- ◆ Set the equipment on a grounding mat which is connected to the house ground. Sometimes an ESD bracelet can snap to a connection on the grounding mat.
- ◆ ESD can be high on carpets, when bringing equipment in from the cold, and around high-voltage equipment such as monitors or powerful, unshielded speakers. Wood, plastic, vinyl, and nylon can produce ESD.
- ◆ Always store or ship computer components in anti-static bags (ESD-safe bags). Do not remove a component from its anti-static bag until you are ready to use it.
- ◆ When you remove components from a computer system, set them on a ground mat or put them into an anti-static bag.
- ◆ Damage caused by ESD may not show up immediately and might cause intermittent problems that are hard to detect.
- ◆ **Electromagnetic interference (EMI)** is caused by the magnetic field that is produced as a side effect when electricity flows.
- ◆ EMI in the radio frequency range is called radio frequency interference (RFI) and can cause problems with radio and TV reception.
- ◆ Use a line conditioner to filter out the electrical noise that causes EMI. Note that ESD thrives in cold, dry air.
- ◆ ESD does permanent damage to equipment, but the damage caused by EMI is temporary.
- ◆ Know how to protect disks and other hardware against ESD as well as other hazards as you work.
- ◆ Always unplug the power cord, network cable, and modem cable from a computer before you open the case and begin working on its components.

OBJECTIVES ON THE JOB

It's extremely important to protect computer components against ESD as you work because damage created by ESD is permanent and not easily detected.

PRACTICE TEST QUESTIONS

1. **Damage from ESD can be caused by:**
   a. placing a CPU on a ground mat
   b. touching the computer case while the power is on
   c. placing a sound card in an anti-static bag
   d. placing an IC in a plastic bag

2. **To avoid damage from ESD as you work on a computer, you should:**
   a. keep anti-static bags close by
   b. wear an ESD bracelet
   c. touch the person next to you before picking up an IC
   d. leave the power to the PC on

3. **An ESD wrist strap contains a:**
   a. diode
   b. transistor
   c. resistor
   d. capacitor

4. **What is the best ground to use when working on a computer?**
   a. an AC outlet
   b. the computer case
   c. a ground mat
   d. an ESD wrist strap

5. **Which situation poses the worst possible potential danger from ESD?**
   a. hot, dry air
   b. cold, damp air
   c. cold, dry air
   d. air just after an electrical storm

6. **ESD is:**
   a. electrostatic discharge
   b. electrical storm damage
   c. electricity surge damage
   d. electrostatic device

7. **A human cannot feel ESD unless it reaches a charge of _____ volts.**
   a. 200
   b. 3000
   c. 20,000
   d. 50,000

O B J E C T I V E S

POTENTIAL HAZARDS AND PROPER SAFETY PROCEDURES RELATING TO: HIGH-VOLTAGE EQUIPMENT, POWER SUPPLY, AND CRTS

UNDERSTANDING THE OBJECTIVE

Power supplies, CRT monitors, and other high-voltage equipment contain capacitors that retain their charge even when power is disconnected. Unless you're trained to service these devices, don't open them.

WHAT YOU **REALLY** NEED TO KNOW

◆ A PC technician should not open a power supply or CRT unless trained to service one because of the danger of high charges inside these components.

◆ When working inside a CRT or power supply, don't wear an ESD bracelet because you don't want these strong electrical charges to flow through your body to the ground.

◆ Many devices including monitors, motherboards, and power supplies contain electrical components called capacitors. Capacitors are cylindrical-shaped components that have the ability to hold a charge long after the power has been turned off or disconnected. Some larger capacitors can be deadly and may hold a charge for up to 24 hours.

◆ Never try to insert any object into the vent holes of the power supply.

◆ Unplug a laser printer before opening the cover. Protect your eyes from a laser beam. If a printer uses an ozone filter, replace it as recommended by the manufacturer.

◆ Discharge a CRT monitor before disposing of it.

◆ When servicing printers, don't use an ESD bracelet, as you don't want to become the ground for the device.

OBJECTIVES ON THE JOB

Know the dangers of working on high-voltage equipment and don't attempt to work on them unless trained to do so. To protect against spikes, be sure to properly ground equipment. When grounded, high surges of electricity are diverted through the equipment to ground. To prevent these spikes from reaching the equipment, use a surge suppressor or line conditioner. Some types of uninterruptible power supply (UPS) equipment also provide surge protection, but not all UPS devices offer this protection. To protect modems against spikes in telephone lines, use a data line protector. Many surge protectors, line conditioners, and UPS devices include a connection for data line protection.

PRACTICE TEST QUESTIONS

1. **If the fan inside a power supply stops working, what should you do?**
   a. Replace the bad fan with a new one.
   b. Replace the power supply.
   c. Replace the computer case, which comes with a power supply already installed.
   d. Do nothing; the fan is not an essential device.

2. **When servicing a laser printer, why is it important to first unplug the printer?**
   a. because the current might damage the laser beam
   b. to reset the printer
   c. to prevent the printer from attempting to print while it is being serviced
   d. to prevent you from being shocked or your eyes damaged from the laser beam

3. **Why do you *not* wear an ESD bracelet while servicing a monitor?**
   a. The ESD bracelet might damage the components inside the monitor.
   b. The ESD bracelet might get tangled with the cords and wires inside the monitor.
   c. You don't want your body to be a ground for stray current.
   d. You want to create as clean a work environment as possible.

4. **A device that retains a high charge even after disconnected from power is:**
   a. a system board
   b. a CRT
   c. a power supply
   d. both b and c

5. **The electrical component that retains a charge after the power is turned off is:**
   a. a transistor
   b. a rheostat
   c. a capacitor
   d. an electrode

6. **When troubleshooting a monitor, one task a PC technician who is not trained to work inside the monitor can safely do is:**
   a. replace the cathode ray tube
   b. replace the fuse
   c. adjust the brightness and contrast settings
   d. both b and c

7. **The best way to ground an ESD bracelet when servicing a power supply is to:**
   a. connect the bracelet to the ground on an AC house outlet
   b. connect the bracelet to the side of the computer case
   c. connect the bracelet to a grounding mat
   d. None of the above; don't wear an ESD bracelet when servicing a power supply.

3.3 Identify environmental protection measures and procedures, and when/how to use them.

SPECIAL DISPOSAL PROCEDURES THAT COMPLY WITH ENVIRONMENTAL GUIDELINES: BATTERIES, CRTS, CHEMICAL SOLVENTS AND CANS, AND MSDS (MATERIAL SAFETY DATA SHEET)

UNDERSTANDING THE OBJECTIVE

There are legal guidelines designed to protect the environment that apply to the disposal of many computer components and chemicals. Know how to properly dispose of these things.

WHAT YOU **REALLY** NEED TO KNOW

◆ A **Material Safety Data Sheet (MSDS)** is written by the material manufacturer and contains information about how to safely use the material, what to do when accidents occur, and how to properly dispose of the material.

◆ A monitor retains a dangerous charge even after it has been unplugged.

◆ Before disposing of a monitor, disconnect it from the power supply and discharge capacitors in it by placing a screwdriver or high-voltage probe across the hot and ground prongs on the back of the monitor. Also have a technician qualified to open the monitor case discharge the CRT itself.

◆ Recycle batteries and CRTs according to local environmental guidelines.

◆ A Material Safety Data Sheet (MSDS) explains how to properly handle substances such as chemical solvents. It comes in packages with the chemical or you can order it from the manufacturer.

◆ A Material Safety Data Sheet (MSDS) can also be downloaded from the Internet. Two popular sites are MSDS-Search (*http://www.msdssearch.com/*) and Where to Find MSDS on the Internet (*http://www.ilpi.com/msds/*).

OBJECTIVES ON THE JOB

Disposing of used equipment is often expected of a PC technician. It's important to both your company and the environment that you follow regulated guidelines when doing so.

Use the following as general guidelines for disposing of computer parts.

Part	How to Dispose
Alkaline batteries including AAA, AA, A, C, D, and 9 volt	Normal trash
Button batteries used in digital cameras, Flash Path, and other small equipment Battery packs used in notebooks	These batteries can contain silver oxide, mercury, lithium, or cadmium and are considered hazardous waste. Dispose of these either by returning them to the original dealer or taking them to a recycling center. To recycle them, pack them separately from other items. If you don't have a recycling center nearby, contact your county for local regulations for disposal.
Computers Monitors Chemical solvents and cans	Check with local county or environmental officials for laws and regulations in your area for proper disposal of these items. The county might provide a recycling center that will receive them. Before disposing of a monitor, first discharge the monitor.

PRACTICE TEST QUESTIONS

1. **Which of the following statements are true?**
   a. A MSDS for a chemical solvent may be obtained at no charge from the distributor who sold you the chemical solvent.
   b. A MSDS for a chemical solvent may be obtained at no charge from the Internet.
   c. A MSDS for a chemical solvent may be shipped with the product.
   d. All of the above.

2. **Which component requires that you follow EPA environmental guidelines for disposal?**
   a. a sound card
   b. a CMOS battery
   c. a power supply
   d. a system board

3. **How do you recycle an alkaline battery?**
   a. Return it to the manufacturer.
   b. Take it to a county recycle center.
   c. Throw it in the trash.
   d. Mail it to the EPA.

4. **To know how to properly dispose of a can of contact cleaner, what do you do?**
   a. Research in the local library.
   b. Consult the product's MSDS.
   c. Ask the EPA.
   d. Call your county recycle center.

5. **How do you dispose of a CMOS battery?**
   a. Throw it in the trash.
   b. Return it to the manufacturer.
   c. Return it to the store where you purchased it.
   d. Take it to your local recycle center.

6. **Before disposing of a CRT, what must you do?**
   a. Remove the power cord from the CRT.
   b. Remove the CRT cover.
   c. Discharge the CRT.
   d. Let the CRT sit unplugged for one hour.

7. **When disposing of an entire computer system, which components need special attention?**
   a. the power supply, the CMOS battery, and the CRT
   b. the CPU, the system board, and the hard drive
   c. the floppy drive, the hard drive, and the CD-ROM drive
   d. the CRT, the CPU, and the CMOS battery

4.1 Distinguish between the popular CPU chips in terms of their basic characteristics.

POPULAR CPU CHIPS (PENTIUM CLASS COMPATIBLE) • SPEEDS (ACTUAL VS. ADVERTISED) • CACHE LEVEL I, II, III

UNDERSTANDING THE OBJECTIVE

The two main processor manufactures are Intel and AMD. The actual speed of each processor may vary from the advertised speed, sometimes as much as 5 MHz. It is critical to understand which processor can be installed in which system, the requirements of the CPU chips, and the performance to expect from it.

WHAT YOU **REALLY** NEED TO KNOW

◆ The following is a list of popular Intel and non-Intel processors and their characteristics (i.e. speeds, L1/L2/L3 cache, bus speeds in MHz, and which Intel processor it compares to, if applicable).

Processor	Latest Speeds	L1/L2/L3	Bus Speeds	Compares to
Classic Pentium	60 to 200MHz	16K/-/-	66	N/A
Pentium MMX	133 to 200MHz	32K/-/-	66	N/A
Pentium Pro	150 to 200MHz	16K/256K,512K,1MB/-	60,66	N/A
Pentium II	233 to 450MHz	32K/256K,512K/-	66,100	N/A
Celeron	850 to 1.8GHz	32K,ETC/128K,256KB/-	Up to 400	N/A
Pentium Xeon	400 to 3.0GHz	ETC/512K,1MB,2MB/-	Up to 533	N/A
Pentium III	450 to 1.33GHz	32K/256K,512K/-	100,133	N/A
Pentium III Xeon	600 to 1GHz	32K/256K,1MB,2MB/-	100,133	N/A
Xeon MP	1.4 to 1.6GHz	ETC/256K/512K,1MB,2MB	400	N/A
Xeon DP	1.8 to 2.4GHz	ETC/256K,512K/-	400	N/A
Pentium 4	1.4 to 3.0GHz	ETC/256K,512K/-	400,533,800	N/A
Itanium	733,800MHz	32K/96K/2MB,4MB	266	N/A
Itanium 2	900,1.0GHz	32K/256K/1.5MB,3MB	400	N/A
*Cyrix M II	300,333,350	64K/-/-	66 to 100	PII, Celeron
*Cyrix III	433 to 533	64K/-/-	66,100,133	PIII, Celeron
*VIA C3	Up to 1.0GHz	128K/64K/-	100,133	Celeron
*AMD-K6-III	350 to 450	64K/256K/-	100	Pentium II
*AMD Athlon	Up to 1.9GHz	128K/256K/-	200	Pentium III
*AMD Duron	1.0 to 1.3GHz	128K/64K/-	200	Celeron
*AMD Athlon MP	1.4 to 1.8GHZ	128K/512K/-	200 to 400+	Pentium III
*AMD Opteron		64K/1MB/-	1.4 to 1.8GHz	Itanium

* represents non-Intel processors, ETC represents Execution Trace Cache, PII represents Pentium II, and PIII represents Pentium III.

◆ To know what CPU is installed in a system on Windows, right-click My Computer icon and select Properties. Select the General tab.

OBJECTIVES ON THE JOB

Recognizing a CPU type and knowing what to expect of the CPU and what is needed to install and support the CPU is an important task of a PC technician.

PRACTICE TEST QUESTIONS

1. **Which processor is the most powerful?**
   a. AMD Athlon
   b. AMD-K6-2
   c. AMD-K6-III
   d. Cyrix M II

2. **Which processor is comparable to Intel's Itanium CPU?**
   a. VIA C3
   b. AMD Athlon MP
   c. AMD Opteron
   d. Intel Pentium 4

3. **How wide is the data path of the Pentium CPU?**
   a. 16 bits
   b. 32 bits
   c. 64 bits
   d. 128 bits

4. **How much L1 cache is there in a Pentium II CPU?**
   a. 16K
   b. 32K
   c. 128K
   d. 512K

5. **The Pentium II typically uses what clock bus speed?**
   a. 66 MHz
   b. 100 MHz
   c. 450 MHz
   d. 550 MHz

6. **Which processor has L3 cache?**
   a. Pentium III
   b. Pentium III Xeon
   c. Itanium
   d. Pentium Xeon

7. **Which processor does not have L2 cache included inside the processor housing?**
   a. Pentium III
   b. Pentium III Xeon
   c. Classic Pentium
   d. Pentium Xeon

4.1 Distinguish between the popular CPU chips in terms of their basic characteristics.

VOLTAGE • SOCKETS/SLOTS • VRM(S)

UNDERSTANDING THE OBJECTIVE

It is important to understand the relationship between CPUs, required sockets/slots, and voltage. A voltage regulator module (VRM) is a replaceable device that regulates the voltage supplied to the processor.

WHAT YOU **REALLY** NEED TO KNOW

◆ The following is a list of common sockets/slots and their required voltage.

Connector Name	Used by CPU	Voltage
Socket 4	Pentium 60/66	5V
Socket 5	Pentium 75/90/100/120/133	3.3V
Socket 7	Pentium MMX, Fast Classic Pentium, AMD KS	2.5V to 3.3V
Super Socket 7	AMD KS-2, AMD KS-III	2.5V to 3.3V
Socket 8	Pentium Pro	3.3V
Socket 370/PGA370	Pentium III FC-PGA, Celeron PPGA, Cyrix III	1.5V or 2V
Slot 1/SC242	Pentium II, Pentium III	2.8V, 3.3V
Slot A	AMD Athlon	1.3V to 2.05V
Socket A/462	AMD Athlon and Duron	1.1V to 1.85V
Slot 2/SC330	Pentium II Xeon, Pentium III Xeon	1.5V to 3.5V
Socket 423/478	Pentium 4	1.7V, 1.75V
Socket PAC418/PAC611	Intel Itanium, Intel Itanium 2	3.3V
Socket 603	Xeon DP and MP	1.5V, 1.7V

◆ SECC (Single Edge Contact Cartridge) is completely covered by a black housing that attaches to a heat sink and fan. It is used by Pentium II/III CPUs in slot 1 with 242 contacts. Also used by Pentium II/III Xeon CPUs with 330 contacts. SECC2 (Single Edge Contact Cartridge, version 2) does not have a heat sink plate. It's used on Pentium II/III with 242 contacts. SEP (Single Edge Processor) is similar to the SECC, but has an exposed circuit board at the housing bottom. It's used on Celeron in Slot 1 with 242 contacts.

◆ PPGA (Plastic Pin Grid Array) is a square box that fits into Socket 370. It's used by early Celeron CPUs with 370 pins. PGA (Pin Grid Array) has staggered pins that can only be inserted one way into the motherboard socket. It's used on Xeon CPUs with 423 pins. OOI/OLGA (Organic Land Grid Array) is similar to PGA, but dissipates heat more quickly. It's used on Pentium 4 CPUs with 423 pins.

◆ FC-PGA (Flip Chip Pin Grid Array) is a square box that fits into Socket 370. It's used by early Celeron CPUs with 370 pins. FC–PGA2 (Flip Chip Pin Grid Array 2) is similar to FC-PGA, but has a heat sink attached to the processor die. It's used by some Pentium III/4 and Celeron CPUs.

◆ PAC (Pin Array Cartridge) is a flat cartridge that uses a PAC418 socket with 418 pins or a PAC611 socket with 611 pins.

OBJECTIVES ON THE JOB

Recognizing a CPU slot or socket type and knowing the voltage requirements and what is needed to install and support the CPU is an important task of a PC technician.

PRACTICE TEST QUESTIONS

1. Which connector is used by Intel Xeon processors?
   a. PGA
   b. PPGA
   c. PAC
   d. SECC2

2. Which processor form factor fits into Socket 370?
   a. SECC2
   b. SECC
   c. PPGA
   d. SEP

3. Which processor uses 5 volts?
   a. Xeon
   b. Pentium 60/66
   c. Itanium
   d. Pentium 4

4. How much voltage does the Itanium processor require?
   a. 2.0V
   b. 3.3V
   c. 5V
   d. 1.5V

5. How many pins are used by the Intel Xeon processor?
   a. 423
   b. 611
   c. 370
   d. 242

6. Which slot or socket is *not* used by Intel processors?
   a. Socket 370
   b. Slot 1
   c. Slot 2
   d. Slot A

7. How many pins are used by the Intel Pentium 4 processor?
   a. 423
   b. 611
   c. 370
   d. 242

4.2 Identify the types of RAM (Random Access Memory), form factors, and operational characteristics. Determine banking and speed requirements under given scenarios.

TYPES: EDO RAM (EXTENDED DATA OUTPUT RAM), DRAM (DYNAMIC RANDOM ACCESS MEMORY), SRAM (STATIC RAM), VRAM (VIDEO RAM), SDRAM (SYNCHRONOUS DYNAMIC RAM), DDR (DOUBLE DATA RATE), AND RAMBUS

UNDERSTANDING THE OBJECTIVE

RAM memory modules are considered field-replaceable units. When replacing or upgrading these modules, it is important you understand what type of memory modules are available, how they are used, and when to use the different kinds of memory.

WHAT YOU **REALLY** NEED TO KNOW

- ◆ Extended data out (EDO) memory was used on early Intel Pentium computers. EDO RAM has to be added in pairs on Intel motherboards and is rated in terms of nanoseconds.
- ◆ Dynamic Random Access Memory (DRAM) is one of the most common types of RAM and requires refreshing. Refreshing RAM means that the CPU must rewrite data to the DRAM chip because it cannot hold its data very long.
- ◆ Synchronous DRAM (SDRAM) runs in sync with the system clock and is rated by clock speed. The SDRAM speed should match system bus speed.
- ◆ Variations of SDRAM include SDRAM II and SyncLink (SLDRAM). SDRAM II is also called Double-Data Rate (DDR SDRAM) memory and runs twice as fast as regular SDRAM.
- ◆ Direct Rambus DRAM (RDRAM or Direct RDRAM) uses a narrow 16-bit data path and transmits data in packets much like a network. RDRAM uses a proprietary memory module called a RIMM.
- ◆ The memory cache on the system board uses static RAM (SRAM). It has very low access times which helps speed up memory access. SRAM is very expensive and does not need to be refreshed by the CPU.
- ◆ Video RAM (VRAM) is a type of **dual-ported** memory used on video cards. Synchronous graphics RAM (SGRAM) is designed for graphics-intensive processing and can synchronize itself with the CPU bus clock.
- ◆ Windows RAM (WRAM) is a type of dual-ported RAM that is faster and less expensive than VRAM.

OBJECTIVES ON THE JOB

Upgrading memory is a typical job of a PC technician. With so many types of memory available, it's important that a technician be familiar with each type.

PRACTICE TEST QUESTIONS

1. **Which type of memory is fastest?**
   a. conventional memory
   b. BEDO
   c. FPM
   d. EDO

2. **Which type of memory runs in sync with the system clock?**
   a. FPM
   b. SDRAM
   c. EDO
   d. BEDO

3. **Which type of memory is especially designed to work on a video card?**
   a. EDO
   b. BEDO
   c. WRAM
   d. SDRAM

4. **Which type of memory uses a narrow 16-bit data path?**
   a. Rambus DRAM
   b. WRAM
   c. BEDO
   d. SDRAM

5. **The connection inside a SEC between the CPU and the L2 cache is called the:**
   a. memory bus
   b. frontside bus
   c. backside bus
   d. CPU bus

6. **Why must DRAM be refreshed?**
   a. because the power is turned off
   b. because the CPU overwrites memory with new data
   c. because DRAM cannot hold its data very long
   d. because SRAM erased the data in DRAM

7. **The Pentium II backside bus is:**
   a. visible on the system board
   b. completely inside the Pentium II housing
   c. completely contained on the CPU microchip
   d. completely contained on the Level 2 cache microchip

4.2 Identify the types of RAM (Random Access Memory), form factors, and operational characteristics. Determine banking and speed requirements under given scenarios.

FORM FACTORS (INCLUDING PIN COUNT): SIMM (SINGLE IN-LINE MEMORY MODULE), DIMM (DUAL IN-LINE MEMORY MODULE), SODIMM (SMALL OUTLINE DIMM), MICRODIMM, AND RIMM (RAMBUS INLINE MEMORY MODULE)

UNDERSTANDING THE OBJECTIVE

Newer computers use either DDR SDRAM or RDRAM and can often support either type of memory. When replacing or upgrading these modules, it is important you understand which types of memory modules should be used with a particular motherboard.

WHAT YOU **REALLY** NEED TO KNOW

- ◆ SIMM (Single In-Line Memory Module) is measured by the amount of time required for the CPU to receive a value in response to a request. The lower the access time, the faster the SIMM. Older SIMMs are conventional and use fast page memory which used 30 pins.

- ◆ DIMM (Dual In-Line Memory Module) such as SDRAM runs in sync with the system clock and is rated by clock speed. EDO DIMM is used by early Pentium systems running at 66, 100, 133, and 150 MHz. SDRAM is currently the most popular type of memory. It does not need to be added in pairs. DDR SDRAM is a type of SDRAM that runs at twice the clock (bus) speed. DDR SDRAM can be used on a motherboard with a system bus of up to 400 MHz.

- ◆ SODIMM (Small Outline DIMM) is used on notebook computers. Older notebook computers use 72-pin EDO SODIMMs. Newer notebook computers use 144-pin (up to 133 MHz bus) or 200-pin (up to 266 MHz bus) SODIMMs which support a 64-bit data path.

- ◆ MICRODIMM (Micro Dual-Inline Memory Module) is used on sub-compact notebook computers. It has a form factor over 50 percent smaller than SODIMMs running at up to 266 MHz.

- ◆ RIMM (Rambus Inline Memory Module) is sometimes called RDRAM or Direct RDRAM and offers a 16, 32, or 64-bit data path. RDRAM, often identified by its silver cover, can transfer data at speeds up to 1200 MHz.

Form Factor	Description	Pin Count
SIMM	Used mainly on EDO RAM with speeds of 30, 60, 70, or 80 nanoseconds.	72-pin
DIMM	Used on EDO RAM and SDRAM.	168 or 184-pin
SODIMM	Used in notebook computers.	72, 144, 200-pin
MICRODIMM	Used in sub-notebook computers.	144-pin
RIMM	Potential replacement for DDR SDRAM.	184, 232-pin

OBJECTIVES ON THE JOB

When upgrading memory or troubleshooting memory problems, it's important to know how to match the system board with the correct type of memory.

PRACTICE TEST QUESTIONS

1. Which type of memory is seen on newer computers?
   a. DDR SDRAM
   b. EDO
   c. FPM
   d. None of the above

2. Which type of memory is best suited for sub-notebook computers?
   a. SODIMM
   b. RDRAM
   c. EDO
   d. MICRODIMM

3. What is the current maximum bus speed that DDR SDRAM supports?
   a. 266 MHz
   b. 400 MHz
   c. 133 MHz
   d. 100 MHz

4. Which type of memory uses a 64-bit data path?
   a. SODIMM
   b. RIMM
   c. MICRODIMM
   d. All of the above

5. How many pins are found on RIMMs?
   a. 184
   b. 232
   c. 144
   d. a and b

6. How many pins are found on MICRODIMMs?
   a. 144
   b. 184
   c. 232
   d. 168

7. Which of the following is true about RIMM technology?
   a. Each memory socket must be filled.
   b. A C-RIMM (Continuity RIMM) can be used to fill unused memory sockets.
   c. A new version called nDRAM will support transfer speeds of up to 1.6 GHz.
   d. All of the above.

OBJECTIVES

4.2 Identify the types of RAM (Random Access Memory), form factors, and operational characteristics. Determine banking and speed requirements under given scenarios.

OPERATIONAL CHARACTERISTICS: MEMORY CHIPS (8-BIT, 16-BIT, AND 32-BIT), PARITY CHIPS VERSUS NON-PARITY CHIPS, ECC VS. NON-ECC, AND SINGLE-SIDED VS. DOUBLE-SIDED

UNDERSTANDING THE OBJECTIVE

A system board is designed to hold certain types of memory modules in banks that are limited to a certain quantity of memory. This information is important when replacing or upgrading memory chips.

WHAT YOU **REALLY** NEED TO KNOW

- ◆ DRAM comes in three types: parity, non-parity, or ECC (error checking and correction).
- ◆ Parity adds an extra single bit for every eight bits of data. This extra bit is used to check for errors. A BIOS setting is usually enabled to support parity. Parity can only detect single-bit errors and cannot detect multiple-bit errors.
- ◆ A parity error indicates a problem with a memory chip and brings the system to a halt. Never add parity and non-parity modules to the same computer.
- ◆ Parity memory will work on non-parity computers, but non-parity memory will not work on computers with parity enabled.
- ◆ Pentium and later model computers support both error detection and correction, called ECC. ECC is a method for detecting both single-bit and multiple-bit errors and will even correct single bit errors instantaneously. A BIOS setting is usually enabled to support ECC. Non-ECC memory cannot be used on a computer with ECC enabled.
- ◆ ECC memory usually requires a special chipset and can cause your computer to run a little slower when enabled. ECC is best suited for use with mission critical file servers or high-end workstations.
- ◆ The width of the data bus on a memory module is often listed as 8-bit, 16-bit, and 32-bit. This value can be used to determine the total amount of memory on a chip.
- ◆ Memory can be both single-sided and double-sided which means that memory chips can exist on one or both sides of the module.

OBJECTIVES ON THE JOB

Upgrading memory is a typical job of a PC technician. Being familiar with the types of memory, how they are physically contained, and their characteristics are important skills for a PC technician.

PRACTICE TEST QUESTIONS

1. Which of the following is a common width of a memory module data bus?
   - a. 8 bits
   - b. 16 bits
   - c. 32 bits
   - d. all of the above

2. Which type of memory has an error-checking technology that cannot repair the error when it is detected?
   - a. ECC memory
   - b. non-parity memory
   - c. parity memory
   - d. self-correcting memory

3. Which type of memory has an error-checking technology that can repair the error when it is detected?
   - a. ECC memory
   - b. non-parity memory
   - c. parity memory
   - d. self-correcting memory

4. Which type of memory has an error-checking technology that can detect multiple-bit errors?
   - a. ECC memory
   - b. non-parity memory
   - c. parity memory
   - d. self-correcting memory

5. If a system contains 64 MB of RAM in two banks of 2 SIMMs each, how much memory is on one SIMM?
   - a. 16 MB
   - b. 8 MB
   - c. 64 MB
   - d. 32 MB

6. Which of the following statements is true?
   - a. Double-sided memory is sometimes constructed as if two single-sided chips were wired back to back.
   - b. Single-sided memory has chips on both sides of the module.
   - c. Double-sided and single-sided memory cannot be used on the same computer.
   - d. None of the above.

7. Which of the following statements is true?
   - a. Parity memory and non-parity memory can be used on the same computer as long as parity is not enabled.
   - b. Parity memory and non-parity memory cannot be used on the same computer.
   - c. Parity memory and non-parity memory can be used on the same computer as long as parity is enabled.
   - d. None of the above.

4.3 Identify the most popular types of motherboards, their components, and their architecture (bus structures).

TYPES OF MOTHERBOARDS: AT AND ATX

UNDERSTANDING THE OBJECTIVE

There are two main types of system boards in use, AT and ATX. Each board has a smaller version, the Baby AT and Mini ATX. When installing or replacing a motherboard, it must match in size, options on the computer case, and power supply. The type of system board does not affect speed or performance.

WHAT YOU **REALLY** NEED TO KNOW

◆ AT system boards have two power connections, P8 and P9, but ATX system boards have only a single power connection, P1.

◆ Most ATX system boards have a remote switch connection which must be connected to the switch on the front of the computer case in order for power to work.

Type of System Board	Description
AT	Oldest type system board still commonly used Uses P8 and P9 power connections Measures 30.5 cm × 33 cm
Baby AT	Smaller version of AT; small size is possible because the system board logic is stored on a smaller chip set Measures 22 cm × 33 cm
ATX	Developed by Intel for Pentium systems Has a more conveniently accessible layout than AT boards Uses a single P1 power connection Measures 30.5 cm × 24.4 cm
Mini ATX	An ATX board with a more compact design Measures 28.4 cm × 20.8 cm

OBJECTIVES ON THE JOB

When building a system or replacing a system board, install the type of system board that is compatible with the computer case and power supply.

PRACTICE TEST QUESTIONS

1. **The AT power supply connects to the system board with:**
    a. two connections, P8 and P9
    b. one connection, P1
    c. 20 connections
    d. one connection, P8

2. **The ATX power supply connects to the system board with:**
    a. two connections, P8 and P9
    b. one connection, P1
    c. 20 connections
    d. one connection, P8

3. **Which type of motherboard is used in low-profile desktop computers?**
    a. AT
    b. Baby AT
    c. ATX
    d. Mini ATX

4. **What is one advantage that the ATX system board has over the AT system board?**
    a. Components are located on the ATX board in more convenient positions.
    b. The ATX board is much larger than the AT board.
    c. The ATX board requires less power than the AT board does.
    d. The ATX board uses more power connections than the AT board does.

5. **Which statement is true concerning the style of system board?**
    a. The Baby AT board can support more CPU types than the AT board.
    b. The ATX system board was developed by Intel for Pentium systems.
    c. The AT board measures 22 cm × 33 cm.
    d. The AT system board has a more convenient layout than the ATX system board.

6. **Which type of system board is required for a 500 MHz Pentium II that is using Slot 1?**
    a. the AT system board
    b. the Baby AT system board
    c. the ATX system board
    d. the Slot 1 system board

7. **Which type of system board measures 22 cm × 33 cm?**
    a. AT
    b. Baby AT
    c. ATX
    d. Mini ATX

OBJECTIVES

4.3 Identify the most popular types of motherboards, their components, and their architecture (bus structures).

MEMORY: SIMM, DIMM, RIMM, SODIMM, AND MICRODIMM • EXTERNAL CACHE MEMORY (LEVEL 2)

UNDERSTANDING THE OBJECTIVE

Every system board has slots for SIMMs, DIMMs, or RIMMs, and perhaps some external cache memory (Level 2).

WHAT YOU **REALLY** NEED TO KNOW

- ◆ SIMMs must be inserted in pairs in memory banks. SIMMs are usually inserted into the slot at a 45-degree angle and are held in place by a metal latch on each side of the memory module. The most popular type of SIMM is EDO (extended data out) memory.

- ◆ DIMMs can be inserted in any number. In other words, they do not have to be inserted in pairs. DIMMs are held in place by a supporting arm on each side of the module. As the DIMM is inserted vertically into the slot, the supporting arms should close around the module to hold it in place.

- ◆ SDRAM is currently the most popular type of memory. There are three types of SDRAM: regular SDRAM, DDR SDRAM (SDRAM II), and SyncLink (SLDRAM). Of the three, DDR SDRAM is the most popular. SLDRAM has become obsolete. SDRAM runs at the same speed as the system clock. DDR SDRAM runs twice as fast as regular SDRAM.

- ◆ SDRAM has two notches on the connector edge. DDR SDRAM only has one notch on the connector edge. For this reason, it is impossible to accidentally insert DDR SDRAM in a motherboard that does not support it (and vice-versa).

- ◆ RIMMs or a C-RIMM (Continuity RIMM) must fill every RIMM slot on a system board. The C-RIMM does not contain any memory, but provides electrical continuity throughout all socks. RIMMs are inserted and held in place in the same manner as DIMMs.

- ◆ RDRAM (also called Direct Rambus DRAM or Direct RDRAM) is a popular type of RIMM memory. It functions like a packet network and can run at speeds of up to 1200 MHz, depending upon the system bus speed. RDRAM's main competitor is DDR SDRAM.

- ◆ SODIMM memory is used in notebook computers and MICRODIMM memory is used on sub-compact computers.

- ◆ Some Pentium 4 motherboards can support either SDRAM or RDRAM modules.

- ◆ Newer system boards do not have Level 2 cache memory because L2 cache is now included inside the processor housing on a small circuit board or on the same die as the processor core.

OBJECTIVES ON THE JOB

Understanding the architecture of a system board and requirements in terms of SIMMs, DIMMs, RIMMs, SODIMMs, and MICRODIMMs is essential when a PC technician is upgrading and troubleshooting the system board and components.

PRACTICE TEST QUESTIONS

1. **What type of memory can a Pentium 4 motherboard support?**
   a. DDR SDRAM
   b. RDRAM
   c. Regular SDRAM
   d. All of the above

2. **Which type of memory needs to be installed in pairs?**
   a. SIMM
   b. DIMM
   c. RIMM
   d. None of the above

3. **Which type of memory requires that each slot be filled?**
   a. SIMM
   b. DIMM
   c. RIMM
   d. None of the above

4. **Which component is used to fill open slots on a motherboard that uses RIMMs?**
   a. D-RIMM
   b. C-RIMM
   c. SD_RIMM
   d. None of the above

5. **How do you not install RAM on a system board?**
   a. on COAST modules
   b. on individual chips on the system board
   c. on SIMMs
   d. on DIMMs

6. **Which of the following is currently the most popular type of memory?**
   a. DDR SDRAM
   b. SLDRAM
   c. RDRAM
   d. EDO RAM

7. **Where is Level 2 cache currently stored on newer computers?**
   a. on an external cache
   b. directly on the processor core die
   c. inside the processor housing on a circuit board
   d. b and c

4.3 Identify the most popular types of motherboards, their components, and their architecture (bus structures).

PROCESSOR SOCKETS: SLOT 1, SLOT 2, SLOT A, SOCKET A, SOCKET 7, SOCKET 8, SOCKET 423, SOCKET 478, AND SOCKET 370

UNDERSTANDING THE OBJECTIVE

Every system board has a slot or socket that is used to connect a CPU. Different manufacturers use different technologies to achieve performance gains.

WHAT YOU **REALLY** NEED TO KNOW

◆ Be able to identify the better known processors and the sockets or slots they use. Know the voltage requirements of these slots and sockets.

◆ These processors can run on system boards that run at 100 MHz and higher: Celeron, Pentium II and above, AMD-K6-2 and above, Intel Itanium, and Intel Xeon.

◆ Earlier sockets used a low insertion force (LIF) method, but current sockets use a zero insertion force (ZIF) mechanism to insert the CPU into the socket.

◆ Note the following:

Slot or Socket	Processor	Number of Pins	Voltage
Socket 7	Pentium MMX, some later Classic Pentiums, AMD K5, AMD K6, Cyrix M	321 pins (SPGA)	2.5 V to 3.3 V
Super Socket 7	AMD K6-2, AMD K6-III	321 pins (SPGA)	2.5 V to 3.3 V
Socket 8	Pentium Pro	387 pins (SPGA)	3.3 V
Socket 370 or PGA370 Socket	Pentium III FC-PGA, Celeron PPGA, Cyrix III	370 pins (SPGA)	1.5 V or 2 V
Slot 1 or SC242	Pentium II, Pentium III	242 pins in 2 rows	2.8 V and 3.3 V
Slot A	AMD Athlon	242 pins in 2 rows	1.5 V to 3.5 V
Socket A or Socket 462	AMD Athlon and Duron	462 pins, SPGA grid, rectangular shape	1.1 V to 1.85 V
Slot 2 or SC330	Pentium II Xeon, Pentium III Xeon	330 pins in 2 rows	1.5 V to 3.5 V
Socket 423	Pentium 4	423 pins, 39 × 39 SPGA grid	1.7 V to 1.75 V
Socket 478	Pentium 4	478 pins in a dense Micro PGA (mPGA)	1.7 V to 1.75 V

OBJECTIVES ON THE JOB

Understanding the architecture of a system board and its requirements and limitations in terms of processor speed and type is essential when a PC technician is upgrading and troubleshooting the system board and components.

PRACTICE TEST QUESTIONS

1. **What slot or socket does the Intel Pentium III use?**
    a. Socket 370
    b. Slot A
    c. Slot 1
    d. Either a or c

2. **How many pins does Socket 7 have?**
    a. 321
    b. 387
    c. 242
    d. 64

3. **What socket or slot does the Pentium Pro use?**
    a. Socket 7
    b. Super Socket 7
    c. Socket 8
    d. Slot 1

4. **Which processor uses 1.75 volts of power?**
    a. Pentium III Xeon
    b. the first Classic Pentiums
    c. AMD Athlon
    d. Socket 423

5. **What socket or slot does the Pentium Xeon use?**
    a. Slot 2
    b. Slot 1
    c. Socket A
    d. Slot A

6. **When is the Super Socket 7 used?**
    a. to hold the Pentium II Xeon processor
    b. on system boards that run at 100 MHz
    c. to hold the Pentium III processor
    d. to hold the Pentium Pro processor

7. **What is the difference between a SPGA grid and a PGA grid, as used by a CPU socket?**
    a. A PGA grid has more pins than a SPGA grid.
    b. A PGA grid is shaped like a rectangle, and a SPGA grid is shaped like a square.
    c. Pins in a SPGA grid are staggered, and pins in a PGA grid are in even rows.
    d. Pins in a PGA grid are staggered, and pins in a SPGA grid are in even rows.

4.3 Identify the most popular types of motherboards, their components, and their architecture (bus structures).

BUS ARCHITECTURE • ISA • PCI: PCI 32-BIT AND PCI 64-BIT • AGP: 2X, 4X, AND 8X (PRO) • USB (UNIVERSAL SERIAL BUS) • COMPONENTS: COMMUNICATION PORTS (SERIAL, USB, PARALLEL, IEEE 1394/FIREWIRE, AND INFRARED)

UNDERSTANDING THE OBJECTIVE

Know the different types of buses that can be found on a system board, their data bus width and speed, and the general purpose of each bus. Know the different types of communication ports and their general purposes.

WHAT YOU **REALLY** NEED TO KNOW

◆ Serial and parallel ports require system resources (IRQs and I/O addresses) and support popular legacy devices such as external modems and printers, respectively. These ports will eventually be replaced by USB ports.

◆ IEEE 1394/FireWire port is integrated into newer computers and supports high-bandwidth devices such as digital video.

◆ Infrared ports are integrated into some motherboards and support wireless devices such as mice, keyboards, and printers.

◆ The PCI bus is the fastest bus on the system board that can support peripheral devices.

◆ AGP was created to move video information off the increasingly saturated PCI bus and serves to isolate video data from I/O requests emanating from the rest of the computer (PCI devices, etc.).

◆ The USB ports connect to the USB bus that can support up to 127 devices daisy chained together. Several USB devices can connect to a USB hub.

◆ Original USB can transfer data at 1.5 Mbps or 12 Mbps. USB 2.0 (also called Hi-Speed USB) can transfer data at 480 Mbps.

Bus	Bus Speed in MHz	Address Lines	Data Width
System bus	66, 75, 100, 133, 200	32	64 bit
8-bit ISA	4.77	20	8 bit
16-bit ISA	8.33	24	16 bit
PCI 32-BIT	33	32	32 bit
PCI 64-BIT	66	64	64 bit
AGP 2X	66	NA	32 bit
AGP 4X	75	NA	32 bit
AGP 8X (Pro)	100	NA	32 bit
USB	3	Serial	Serial

OBJECTIVES ON THE JOB

When purchasing new devices for a system, the bus that the device will use is a critical part of the purchasing decision. In most cases, for peripheral devices, choose the PCI bus over the ISA bus because it is faster and easier to configure.

PRACTICE TEST QUESTIONS

1. **Which bus is primarily used on notebook computers?**
   a. 16-bit ISA
   b. PCI
   c. PC Card
   d. VESA

2. **Which bus only supports a video card?**
   a. AGP
   b. VESA
   c. PCI
   d. Both a and b

3. **Which bus is fastest?**
   a. EISA
   b. PCI
   c. ISA
   d. USB

4. **Which bus is no longer included on new system boards? (Choose all that apply.)**
   a. ISA
   b. PCI
   c. VESA
   d. USB

5. **Which bus can support either an 8-bit or 16-bit data path?**
   a. PCI
   b. AGP
   c. ISA
   d. VESA

6. **Which of the following is the most common width of the data path of the PCI bus?**
   a. 8 bits
   b. 16 bits
   c. 32 bits
   d. 64 bits

7. **Which bus runs in synchronization with the CPU?**
   a. ISA
   b. EISA
   c. USB
   d. PCI

Identify the most popular types of motherboards, their components, and their architecture (bus structures).

AMR (AUDIO MODEM RISER) SLOTS • CNR (COMMUNICATION NETWORK RISER) SLOTS • BASIC COMPATIBILITY GUIDELINES • IDE (ATA, ATAPI, ULTRA-DMA, EIDE) • SCSI (NARROW, WIDE, FAST, ULTRA, HVD, LVD (LOW VOLTAGE DIFFERENTIAL)) • CHIPSETS

UNDERSTANDING THE OBJECTIVE

When purchasing, upgrading, or troubleshooting motherboards and motherboard components, it is important to understand the basic compatibility guideline for each component.

WHAT YOU **REALLY** NEED TO KNOW

- ◆ An AMR (Audio Modem Riser) slot or CNR (Communication Network Riser) slot is integrated into inexpensive motherboards and supports a small modem card or networking riser card, respectively. Both slots can support an audio riser card.

- ◆ System boards today have several buses to accommodate slow and fast devices and different data bus widths and speeds. It is important to understand the basic compatibility guidelines that accompany each system.

- ◆ Basic compatibility guidelines are described in terms of form factors that describe the size, shape, and general configuration of a component. It's important to choose compatible form factors when upgrading or troubleshooting motherboards, power supplies, and cases.

- ◆ System boards today provide an IDE interface, which connects up to four IDE devices using two 40-pin IDE cables. ATA, ATAPI, Ultra-DMA, and EIDE are all standards that support various data transfer rates for IDE devices. The newer and more popular IDE standard is Ultra-DMA. It uses a special 40-pin IDE cable that provides additional ground lines to improve signal integrity. This standard supports hard drives on today's systems.

- ◆ When a system board has a SCSI interface, be aware of the different SCSI standards it supports. For example, a system might support Ultra2 SCSI and be backward compatible with single-ended SCSI devices.

- ◆ SCSI standards include 8-bit Narrow SCSI, 16-bit Wide SCSI, and variations of Fast SCSI and Ultra SCSI. The most popular SCSI standard includes variations on Ultra SCSI.

- ◆ Low voltage differential (LVD) signaling used by Ultra2 SCSI allows for faster data transfers and longer cable lengths up to 25 meters. High differential voltage (HDV) is an earlier obsolete signaling method that sometimes burned out hardware.

- ◆ A chipset is a set of chips that are integrated into the motherboard and control components such as the memory cache, external buses, and peripherals. Different chipsets support different bus speeds and processors. Chipset technology is always improving. The most popular chipset is often integrated into the newest, fastest motherboard.

OBJECTIVES ON THE JOB

If a SCSI interface is required and the system board does not support SCSI, use a SCSI host adapter in an expansion slot to provide the interface.

PRACTICE TEST QUESTIONS

1. What is the fastest and most popular IDE standard?
   a. ATA
   b. Ultra-DMS
   c. Ultra-DMA
   d. Wide SCSI

2. Which of the following slots are capable of supporting an audio riser card?
   a. AMR
   b. CNR
   c. PCI
   d. Both a and b

3. The SCSI standard that uses LVD is:
   a. Fast SCSI
   b. Ultra2 SCSI
   c. Regular SCSI
   d. Wide SCSI

4. What do basic compatibility guidelines typically describe?
   a. the size, shape, and general configuration of a component
   b. compatible form factors
   c. compatible motherboards and power supplies
   d. all of the above

5. Which SCSI standard is capable of supporting a 16-bit data bus?
   a. Wide SCSI
   b. Fast Wide SCSI
   c. Wide Ultra SCSI
   d. All of the above

6. Which of the following statements is true?
   a. A chipset can be upgraded on today's computers.
   b. A chipset cannot be upgraded on today's computers.
   c. A chipset can be updated on today's computers.
   d. None of the above.

7. Which company designs chipsets for Intel motherboards?
   a. RKCR
   b. Intel
   c. AMD
   d. All of the above

4.4   Identify the purpose of CMOS (Complementary Metal-Oxide Semiconductor) memory, what it contains, and how and when to change its parameters. Given a scenario involving CMOS, choose the appropriate course of action.

CMOS SETTINGS: DEFAULT SETTINGS, CPU SETTINGS, PRINTER PARALLEL PORT—UNI., BI-DIRECTIONAL, DISABLE/ENABLE, ECP, EPP, COM/SERIAL PORT— MEMORY ADDRESS, INTERRUPT REQUEST, DISABLE

UNDERSTANDING THE OBJECTIVE

One CMOS chip on the system board is known as CMOS and contains a small amount of RAM that is powered by a small battery when the PC is turned off. This RAM contains configuration information about the PC and user preferences.

WHAT YOU **REALLY** NEED TO KNOW

◆ If CMOS settings are set incorrectly, then your computer may not boot and load the operating system. An option named "Load default settings" will restore the original factory CMOS settings.

◆ CPU settings such as processor type and speed can be viewed in CMOS.

◆ Parallel ports are enabled and disabled in CMOS and can be set to uni-directional (also called output only), bi-directional, ECP, or EPP. ECP requires a DMA channel to work.

◆ Serial ports can be enabled and disabled in CMOS and configured to use certain IRQ and I/O memory addresses.

◆ If a serial port is not in use, the system resources (IRQ and I/O addresses) assigned to it should be available for other devices, however, for some systems, you must disable the port in CMOS in order to free these resources for another device.

OBJECTIVES ON THE JOB

Serial and parallel ports are enabled and disabled in CMOS, and system resources are assigned to them. Always check CMOS settings when troubleshooting problems with these ports.

Steps to access CMOS setup for most systems are listed below.

BIOS	Keys to Press During POST to Access Setup
AMI BIOS	Del
Award BIOS	Del
Older Phoenix BIOS	Ctrl+Alt+Esc or Ctrl+Alt+S
Newer Phoenix BIOS	F2 or F1
Dell computers using Phoenix BIOS	Ctrl+Alt+Enter
Older Compaq computers like the Deskpro 286 or 386	Place the Diagnostics disk in the disk drive, reboot your system, and choose Computer Setup on the menu.
Newer Compaq computers such as the ProLinea, Deskpro, Deskpro XL, Deskpro XE, or Presario	Press F10 while the cursor is in the upper–right corner of the screen, which happens during booting just after you hear two beeps.*
All other older computers	Use a setup program on the floppy disk that came with the PC.

* For Compaq computers, the CMOS setup program is stored on the hard drive in a small, non-DOS partition of about 3 MB. If this partition becomes corrupted, you must run setup from the floppy disk. If you cannot run setup by pressing F10 at startup, suspect a damaged partition or a virus taking up space in conventional memory.

PRACTICE TEST QUESTIONS

1. When troubleshooting a parallel port, you should verify that the port is enabled:
    a. by setting a jumper on the system board
    b. in CMOS setup
    c. using Windows Device Manager
    d. using a parameter in the OS kernel

2. Which setting for a parallel port gives the fastest data access time?
    a. standard
    b. bi-directional
    c. ECP
    d. EPP

3. When a parallel port is set to ECP, what resource is required?
    a. a second IRQ
    b. a DMA channel
    c. an ISA bus channel
    d. a second group of upper memory addresses

4. If the system is short of DMA channels, you can free one up by:
    a. changing the parallel port CMOS setting from EPP to ECP
    b. changing the parallel port CMOS setting from Bidirectional to ECP
    c. changing the parallel port CMOS setting from ECP to EPP or Bidirectional
    d. disabling the parallel port

5. If a serial port is not working, what should you verify?
    a. that the port is enabled in CMOS setup
    b. that the port is set to use a 50-pin cable
    c. that the port is set to use a DMA channel
    d. that the port switch on the back of the computer case is turned on

6. In CMOS setup, when a serial port is set to use IRQ 4 and I/O address 03F8, the port is configured as:
    a. COM1
    b. COM2
    c. COM3
    d. COM4

7. If a parallel port in CMOS setup is configured to use IRQ 5 and I/O address 0278, then the port is configured as:
    a. LPT1:
    b. LPT2:
    c. LPT3:
    d. PRINTER 1

4.4 Identify the purpose of CMOS (Complementary Metal-Oxide Semiconductor) memory, what it contains, and how and when to change its parameters. Given a scenario involving CMOS, choose the appropriate course of action.

CMOS SETTINGS: FLOPPY DRIVE—ENABLE/DISABLE DRIVE OR BOOT, SPEED, DENSITY, HARD DRIVE—SIZE AND DRIVE TYPE, MEMORY—SPEED, PARITY, NON-PARITY, BOOT SEQUENCE, DATE/TIME, PASSWORDS, PLUG AND PLAY BIOS, DISABLING ON-BOARD DEVICES, DISABLING VIRUS PROTECTION, POWER MANAGEMENT, AND INFRARED

UNDERSTANDING THE OBJECTIVE

CMOS settings affect floppy drives, hard drives, memory parity, the boot sequence, the date, the time, the power-on password, and how Plug and Play is used by the system.

WHAT YOU **REALLY** NEED TO KNOW

- ◆ The boot sequence can allow the system to boot from an IDE hard drive, SCSI hard drive, CD-ROM drive, Zip drive, floppy disk drive, or network device (sometimes using PXE technology), depending on the options supported by the system BIOS.
- ◆ Floppy drives are enabled and disabled in CMOS. The floppy drive type, speed, and density can be set in CMOS.
- ◆ Hard drive parameters are set in CMOS by auto detection or by manual entry. These parameters include size and drive type.
- ◆ The type of memory (parity or non-parity) is set in CMOS or is automatically detected by BIOS. Disable CMOS virus protection, if present. It should be handled by software installed in the OS.
- ◆ System date and time are set in CMOS, which are then read by the OS when it loads and are then passed to applications. If you are prompted to enter the date and time whenever you start your computer, you may need to replace the CMOS battery with a new one from Radio Shack.
- ◆ Onboard devices such as an integrated network interface card or audio card can be enabled or disabled from CMOS.
- ◆ Use CMOS setup to enable or disable a user password (to load OS) or supervisor password (used to access CMOS).
- ◆ If the password is forgotten, you can use a jumper on the system board to restore CMOS settings to default values, which will erase the forgotten password.
- ◆ Use CMOS setup to reserve an IRQ or DMA channel for a legacy device so Plug and Play will not assign the IRQ or DMA channel to a Plug and Play device.
- ◆ Power management settings for a PC, hard drive, and video can be disabled or enabled in CMOS. If power management is enabled, your computer can shut off after shutting down the operating system.
- ◆ An infrared port, if present, can be enabled or disabled in CMOS.

OBJECTIVES ON THE JOB

When troubleshooting problems with floppy drives, memory, the boot sequence, and so forth, check the settings in CMOS for accuracy. When installing a floppy drive, inform CMOS of the change. A power-on password can also be set in CMOS.

PRACTICE TEST QUESTIONS

1. **When a PC boots with the incorrect date or time, what is the likely cause?**
    a. The power supply is bad.
    b. The CMOS battery is weak.
    c. The hard drive is full.
    d. BIOS is corrupted.

2. **Which hard drive parameter is not set using CMOS setup?**
    a. the number of heads
    b. the storage capacity of the drive
    c. the number of cylinders
    d. the data access time

3. **Which of the following cannot be damaged by a virus?**
    a. data on a floppy disk
    b. CMOS
    c. the boot sector of the hard drive
    d. program files

4. **When installing a 3½ inch floppy drive to replace a 5¼ inch floppy drive, how does the system know to expect the new type of drive?**
    a. Jumpers are set on the system board.
    b. Startup BIOS will sense the new drive.
    c. You must first change the drive type in CMOS setup.
    d. You must first change the hardware parameters stored in the root directory of the hard drive.

5. **Which of the following hard drive parameters can be set in CMOS?**
    a. the number of cylinders
    b. the number of heads
    c. the number of sectors
    d. all of the above

6. **Boot sequence as set in CMOS is the order:**
    a. that hardware is checked by BIOS during the boot process
    b. the OS files load
    c. that drives are checked when searching for an OS
    d. that BIOS and drivers are loaded into memory during the boot process

7. **System date and time can be set:**
    a. by the operating system
    b. in CMOS setup
    c. by Microsoft Word
    d. both a and b

5.1 Identify printer technologies, interfaces, and options/upgrades.

TECHNOLOGIES INCLUDE: LASER, INK DISPERSION, DOT MATRIX, SOLID INK, THERMAL, AND DYE SUBLIMATION

UNDERSTANDING THE OBJECTIVE

You need to understand the basics of how the common printers work, how they are maintained, and which printer components are considered field-replaceable units.

WHAT YOU **REALLY** NEED TO KNOW

- The steps in laser printing are:
  1. Cleaning—The drum is cleaned of any residual toner and electrical charge.
  2. Conditioning—The drum is conditioned to contain a high electrical charge. The primary corona used in this step creates a very high negative charge.
  3. Writing—A laser beam discharges the high charge down to a lower charge, in those places where toner is to go.
  4. Developing—Toner is placed onto the drum where the charge has been reduced.
  5. Transferring—A strong electrical charge draws the toner off the drum onto the paper.
  6. Fusing—Heat and pressure are used to fuse the toner to the paper.
- The laser printer drum loses its high negative charge when the laser light hits it in the writing stage. The lightness and darkness of printing is controlled by the transfer corona.
- A dot matrix printer is an **impact printer**; the print head containing tiny pins hits the ribbon which hits the paper to produce a character.
- For ink dispersion (also called ink-jet) printers:
  - Ink-jet printers use an ink cartridge containing three colors (magenta, cyan, and yellow) in tubes. Tiny plates near the tubes heat up, causing the ink to boil and eject from the tubes. More plates carrying a magnetic charge direct the path of ink onto the paper to form the desired printed image.
- Solid ink printers use a solid stick of ink that is melted and then applied to the paper.
- Thermal printers use a wax-based ink that is heated and then melted onto the paper.
- Dye sublimation printers use a thermal print head to vaporize dye and transfer it from multi-colored film (cyan, magenta, yellow, and black) to the paper.

OBJECTIVES ON THE JOB

Supporting printers is a major part of the responsibilities of a PC technician. The first step in learning to support printers is to learn the basics of how they work.

PRACTICE TEST QUESTIONS

1. **In laser printing, the step between writing and transferring is:**
   - a. cleaning
   - b. conditioning
   - c. developing
   - d. fusing

2. **What component on a dot matrix printer forms each character?**
   - a. the ribbon
   - b. a laser beam
   - c. magnetic fields around tiny pins
   - d. pins on the print head

3. **On an ink-jet printer, what causes the ink to form characters and shapes on the paper?**
   - a. Each ink jet is directed using a highly charged fusing beam.
   - b. Each ink jet is directed using magnetized plates.
   - c. Each ink jet is directed using the heat from the charging plates.
   - d. Each ink jet is directed using tiny mechanical levels.

4. **In laser printing, which stage in the printing process forms the characters or shapes to be printed?**
   - a. writing
   - b. conditioning
   - c. transferring
   - d. fusing

5. **In laser printing, which stage puts the toner on the paper?**
   - a. writing
   - b. conditioning
   - c. transferring
   - d. fusing

6. **In laser printing, which is the last step?**
   - a. writing
   - b. fusing
   - c. developing
   - d. transferring

7. **In laser printing, what is the purpose of the laser beam?**
   - a. to cause the printer drum to loose its high negative charge
   - b. to cause the toner to stick to the paper
   - c. to cause the printer drum to heat up
   - d. to cause the printer drum to gain a high negative charge

INTERFACES INCLUDE: PARALLEL, NETWORK, SCSI, USB, INFRARED, SERIAL, IEEE 1394/FIREWIRE, AND WIRELESS

UNDERSTANDING THE OBJECTIVE

A printer can be connected directly to a PC (local printer) or a PC can access a printer that is shared on a network. A printer can also be connected directly to the network (network printer). When installing a printer using the OS, you tell the OS which connection is used as well as the printer configuration and type.

WHAT YOU **REALLY** NEED TO KNOW

◆ A local printer can be connected to a computer using a network connection, SCSI, IEEE 1394/FireWire, wireless, parallel, serial, infrared, or USB interface.

◆ The most popular types of printer interfaces are by way of a network connection, parallel port, or USB port.

◆ A local printer can be shared with others over a network. First, the PC must configure the printer to be shared across the network.

◆ A printer is made available to many on a network by one of the following three methods:

- The printer can be connected to a PC on the network, and the PC can then share the printer on the network.

- A network printer with embedded logic can manage network communication and be connected directly to the network and be assigned its own network address (IP address).

- A computer called a print server can control several printers connected to a network. (For example, HP Jet Direct is software that supports HP printers on a network.) Typically, printer drivers are stored on the print server and are automatically installed when the printer is setup on the desktop computer.

OBJECTIVES ON THE JOB

When servicing PCs on a network, be aware that the PC might support a printer that is shared on the network. Before the service is completed, verify that other users on the network still have access to the printer.

If there are problems printing when using a parallel port to connect to a printer, verify that the parallel port is enabled and configured correctly. In CMOS setup, choices for the parallel port mode might be Output Only, Bidirectional, ECP, and EPP. Because ECP mode uses a DMA channel, when the mode is set to ECP, an option for DMA channel might appear. When the mode is set to Output Only, the printer cannot communicate with the PC.

For fastest communication with the printer, select ECP. If problems arise, first try EPP, then Bidirectional. Only use Output Only if other options don't work. When using this option, disable bi-directional support for the printer using the Printer Properties dialog box in Windows 9x. If this method works when others don't, suspect the parallel printer cable. Verify that the cable is a bi-directional cable that complies with IEEE 1284 standards.

PRACTICE TEST QUESTIONS

1. **In what ways can a printer connect to a computer system?**
    a. by a parallel, serial, or power port
    b. by a parallel, serial, or floppy port
    c. by a parallel, serial, infrared, or USB port
    d. by a parallel, serial, infrared, USB, or mouse port

2. **If a printer is connected to a computer by way of a parallel cable and the computer is connected to a network, what must be done before others on the network can use this printer?**
    a. The computer must share the printer use file and print sharing.
    b. The printer must be connected to a network server.
    c. The printer must be converted to use a serial cable.
    d. The printer must be moved to a Windows NT computer.

3. **To access file and print sharing in Windows 9x, you should do which of the following?**
    a. Click Start, Programs, Control Panel, Network.
    b. Click Start, Settings, Control Panel, Network.
    c. Click Start, Settings, Printers, Sharing.
    d. Click Start, Settings, Network, Sharing.

4. **To share a printer over a network, you must:**
    a. Click Start, Settings, Printers, and select Sharing on the drop-down menu.
    b. Click Start, Settings, Printers, and select File and Print Sharing on the drop-down menu.
    c. Click Start, Settings, Control Panel, and select Sharing from the icons displayed.
    d. Double-click the Shared icon on the desktop.

5. **When sharing a printer over a network, you must:**
    a. disconnect the printer from the PC when you set up printer sharing
    b. give the shared printer a name
    c. use a modem to allow others on the network to use the printer
    d. keep the printer offline

6. **To use a shared printer on another PC, you must:**
    a. add the new printer to your list of installed printers
    b. be connected to the network when you install the printer
    c. know the name of the shared printer
    d. all of the above

7. **When troubleshooting problems with shared printers on a network, what is a good question to ask?**
    a. Is the printer online?
    b. Is the network printer on the remote PC configured correctly?
    c. Is there enough hard drive space available on the remote PC?
    d. All of the above.

OPTIONS/UPGRADES INCLUDE: MEMORY, HARD DRIVES, NICS, TRAYS AND FEEDERS, FINISHERS (E.G., STAPLING, ETC.), AND SCANNERS/FAX/COPIER

UNDERSTANDING THE OBJECTIVE

LaserJet printers can be upgraded and options can be added to improve performance and enhance usability. When purchasing or upgrading a printer, select a printer configuration that will match the needs of individuals who plan to use the printer.

WHAT YOU **REALLY** NEED TO KNOW

- ◆ Upgrading printer memory can help improve performance by increasing the speed at which large images print. For example, upgrading printer memory makes sense if you regularly print 5 MB or larger images.

- ◆ Many commercial printers such as the HP LaserJet 4100 use a hard drive to improve performance. The printer hard drive is similar to a hard drive used in a computer. The Cannon Imagerunner digital copier uses a hard drive to store copies so the original only has to be scanned a single time. This feature saves the copier from having to scan the original once per copy and therefore helps to reduce maintenance costs.

- ◆ Again, most commercial printers include the option to add a network interface card (NIC). The two most common NICs are 10 Mbps and 100 Mbps. LaserJet printers that are equipped with a NIC usually reflect the extra feature in their model name. For example, in the HP LaserJet 4100N, the N stands for a 100 Mbps NIC.

- ◆ Adding a paper tray or paper feeder can increase the amount of blank paper a printer can hold.

- ◆ Adding a finisher to a LaserJet printer can introduce features such as stapling, collating, and hole-punching.

- ◆ Home users and small businesses can take advantage of the low cost and flexibility available in a multi-function printer. Multi-function printers can often also scan, fax, and copy documents.

- ◆ Printers aimed at medium to large businesses have a larger duty cycle than most printers. A large duty cycle means that the printer is capable of handling large volumes of work on a monthly basis while printing at a faster rate (i.e. more pages per minute).

OBJECTIVES ON THE JOB

There are many options and upgrades available for improving and enhancing the performance of your printer. When purchasing an upgrade, make sure that the upgrade is compatible with your current printer and that it will meet the demands of its users. When buying a printer, ask plenty of questions about performance and the ability to upgrade components at a later time.

PRACTICE TEST QUESTIONS

1. Which printer listed below comes equipped with a NIC?
   a. HP LaserJet 4000
   b. HP LaserJet 4100N
   c. HP LaserJet 4100
   d. None of the above

2. Which option/upgrade will help increase performance when printing large images?
   a. memory
   b. NIC
   c. feeder
   d. finisher

3. Which option/upgrade will allow users to share a printer?
   a. memory
   b. NIC
   c. feeder
   d. finisher

4. Which option/upgrade may add the ability to collate and staple documents?
   a. memory
   b. NIC
   c. feeder
   d. finisher

5. Which option/upgrade will increase the amount of blank paper a printer can hold?
   a. memory
   b. NIC
   c. feeder
   d. finisher

6. What kind of printer offers the ability to scan documents?
   a. multi-function printer
   b. LaserJet printer
   c. ink-jet printer
   d. none of the above

7. Which of the following considerations should be taken when upgrading or choosing a printer?
   a. cost
   b. duty cycle
   c. needs of its users
   d. all of the above

5.2 Recognize common printer problems and techniques used to resolve them.

PRINTER DRIVERS • FIRMWARE UPDATES • CALIBRATIONS • PRINTING TEST PAGES • CONSUMABLES • ENVIRONMENT

UNDERSTANDING THE OBJECTIVE

Installing printer drivers and calibrating settings are common printer troubleshooting techniques. The first step to troubleshooting most printer problems is to attempt to print a test page.

WHAT YOU **REALLY** NEED TO KNOW

◆ When installing printer drivers, be sure to choose the set that matches your printer and operating system. Of all Microsoft's operating systems, Windows XP natively supports the largest number of printers and other devices.

◆ If you're experiencing a printing problem, try the following steps.

- Print a test page. In Windows, go to the printer control and right-click your printer. Then click Properties. Look for an option to print a test page.

- Download and install the latest set of printer drivers from the manufacturer's Web site.

- Check or replace the printer cable.

- Attach a new printer (same make and model) and try to print.

- If you're experiencing ink-jet print quality problems, you may need to calibrate the printer. Open the printer properties and look for a calibration section that will allow you to align the print cartridge.

- If you're experiencing LaserJet print quality problems, you may need to calibrate the printer. Refer to the user's manual for information on calibration print quality.

◆ It may be necessary to update firmware on LaserJet printers in order to improve reliability. Several security flaws have been discovered with HP LaserJet printer firmware. To update printer firmware, visit HP's Web site and follow the instructions for updating firmware.

◆ Printer consumables include paper, ink-jet cartridges, and toner cartridges. Replacement ink-jet and toner cartridges are expensive. Ink-jet cartridge refill kits are often useless because the print head on the cartridge wears down quickly and becomes unusable.

◆ Ink-jet, toner cartridges, and used printer paper should be recycled and never thrown in the trash. Some resellers offer a small amount of money in exchange for used cartridges.

OBJECTIVES ON THE JOB

Printer drivers can become corrupt with use, especially under Windows 9x, and may need to be reinstalled.

PRACTICE TEST QUESTIONS

1. Which of the following techniques are used to troubleshoot printer problems?
   a. Print a test page.
   b. Make sure printer is connected to computer.
   c. Reinstall the printer drivers.
   d. All of the above.

2. Which of the following items can be recycled?
   a. ink-jet cartridge
   b. toner cartridge
   c. paper
   d. all of the above

3. On which of the following devices should firmware be updated?
   a. ink-jet printers
   b. LaserJet printers
   c. dot matrix printers
   d. all of the above

4. How can a test page be printed under Windows XP?
   a. hold the printer button down
   b. under printer properties
   c. under Device Manager
   d. none of the above

5. Which of the following techniques are used to troubleshoot printing problems on a printer that cannot print?
   a. Turn printer on.
   b. Enable printer port in CMOS.
   c. Set printer port in CMOS to bi-directional.
   d. All of the above.

6. Which of the following techniques are used to troubleshoot a flashing cartridge light on an ink-jet printer that will not print?
   a. Replace the cartridge with a new cartridge.
   b. Reseat the cartridge.
   c. Recycle the print power.
   d. All of the above.

7. Which Microsoft operating system has built-in support for the largest number of printers?
   a. Window 98SE
   b. Windows 2000
   c. Windows XP
   d. All of the above

OBJECTIVES

5.2 Recognize common printer problems and techniques used to resolve them.

MEMORY • CONFIGURATION • NETWORK CONNECTIONS • CONNECTIONS

UNDERSTANDING THE OBJECTIVE

Memory and network errors are often the most common problems associated with medium to large business printers (including LaserJet printers). Most printers support the ability to print configuration information from the printer's control panel.

WHAT YOU **REALLY** NEED TO KNOW

◆ During normal use, an error message may be displayed on the printer itself and the printer may fail to work properly. If this occurs, the first thing to try is to recycle the printer's power (i.e. power off the printer and then turn the power on again). If the error message is still displayed, then consult the manufacturer's manual or Web site for additional information regarding the cause and solution of the error.

◆ If the error is related to a memory problem, the memory may need to be reseated (i.e. removed and reinserted into the memory sockets). LaserJet printers and other medium to large business printers usually hold one or more memory modules. To obtain the printer's configuration, consult the manufacturer's manual for directions on printing configuration information.

◆ Ink-jet and other home and small business printers usually do not have memory modules that can be reseated.

◆ The following steps explain how to reseat printer memory. Perform these steps only after you have determined that the displayed error message is related to printer memory.

- Refer to the printer's documentation for information on accessing the printer memory.
- Contact the manufacturer to determine if opening the printer will void the warranty. If it does not, then proceed with the following steps.
- Unplug the printer. Using a screwdriver, remove the screws holding onto the printer's memory panel.
- Remove the panel and remove the memory module(s).
- Using compressed air, blow all excess dust from the printer.
- Reseat the memory module(s) and re-attach the panel and screws.
- Plug in the printer and perform several printing tests.
- If the error message is displayed again, consider replacing the defective memory with new memory from the manufacturer.

◆ If a network printer fails to print or appears offline on a user's computer, check the network connection to ensure that the printer is still communicating properly over its connection (usually a twisted pair connection). If this fails to solve the problem, then recycle the printer's power. If this fails to solve the problem, then contact the network administrator.

OBJECTIVES ON THE JOB

A PC technician should be able to solve basic memory and network connection problems associated with LaserJet and other medium to large business printers.

PRACTICE TEST QUESTIONS

1. What types of network connections are usually found on a LaserJet printer?
   a. fiber-optic connection
   b. RJ-45 connection
   c. power connection
   d. all of the above

2. What's the first step in troubleshooting an error message that is displayed on the printer?
   a. Recycle the power.
   b. Refer to the printer documentation.
   c. Call the network administrator.
   d. None of the above.

3. Which types of printers listed below have memory modules that can be serviced?
   a. LaserJet printer
   b. ink-jet printer
   c. large format printer
   d. a and c

4. How should a PC technician obtain replacement memory?
   a. Contact the printer manufacturer.
   b. Insert EDO memory.
   c. You cannot obtain replacement memory.
   d. None of the above.

5. When troubleshooting a network printer issue, which of the following troubleshooting steps can be performed?
   a. Recycle the printer power.
   b. Replace the network connection with a known-good network connection.
   c. Reboot the computer.
   d. All of the above.

6. Which of the following maintenance tasks should be performed on a LaserJet printer?
   a. Blow all excess dust with compressed air.
   b. Replace power cord.
   c. Upgrade firmware as necessary.
   d. Both a and c.

7. How can a PC technician add printer information on the printer's configuration?
   a. Refer to the manufacturer's manual for instructions.
   b. Recycle the power.
   c. Add paper.
   d. None of the above.

5.2 Recognize common printer problems and techniques used to resolve them.

**PAPER FEED AND OUTPUT • ERRORS (PRINTED OR DISPLAYED) • PAPER JAM •
PRINT QUALITY • SAFETY PRECAUTIONS • PREVENTIVE MAINTENANCE**

UNDERSTANDING THE OBJECTIVE

Troubleshooting, maintaining, and servicing printers are skills needed by a PC technician. Know what errors and problems can occur and what to do about them.

WHAT YOU **REALLY** NEED TO KNOW

◆ Define **enhanced metafile format (EMF)** and **spooling** as used by Windows 9x, Windows 2000, and Windows XP. Most Windows printing is done using EMF spooling.

◆ When troubleshooting print problems, try disabling EMF conversion and disabling spooling of print jobs.

◆ When troubleshooting print problems, the source of the problem might be with bi-directional communication with the printer. From the Printer Properties dialog box, choose "Disable bidirectional support for this printer."

◆ When performing preventive maintenance on a dot matrix printer, never lubricate the print head pins; the ink on the ribbon serves as a lubricant for the pins.

◆ Dark spots on the paper indicate loose toner particles on a laser printer. The solution is to run extra paper through the printer.

◆ When servicing a laser printer, beware that the fuser assemblage can be hot to the touch. Also, remember to protect the toner cartridge from light as you work.

◆ A dot matrix print head can overheat which shortens the printer life.

◆ When troubleshooting problems with jammed paper in a printer, note the location of the leading edge of the jammed paper. It indicates where the jam begins and what component is causing the problem.

◆ If you can print a test page from the operating system (for Windows, double-click the Printer icon in the Control Panel to use the Printer Properties dialog box), then all is working correctly between the OS, the device drivers, the connectivity to the printer, and the printer itself.

◆ For a dot matrix printer, do the following:
  - If the head moves back and forth but nothing prints, suspect a problem with the ribbon.
  - Smudges on the paper can be caused by the ribbon being too tight.
  - Incomplete characters can be caused by broken print head pins.
  - If the printing is inconsistent, look for a problem with the ribbon advancing.

◆ For an ink-jet printer, poor print quality can sometimes be solved by cleaning the ink-jet nozzles by following the directions of the printer manufacturer. Or, try replacing the ink cartridge.

OBJECTIVES ON THE JOB

Troubleshooting problems with printers is a common task for a PC technician.

PRACTICE TEST QUESTIONS

1. **Into what format does Windows XP convert a print job file before printing?**
   a. a text document
   b. a Word document
   c. enhanced metafile
   d. spool job

2. **Spooling print jobs:**
   a. relieves an application from the delay of printing
   b. allows several print jobs to be placed into a queue
   c. is used by Windows 9x
   d. all of the above

3. **When troubleshooting a print problem, you can:**
   a. disable EMF conversion
   b. disable spooling of print jobs
   c. test the printer using a printer self test
   d. all of the above

4. **If there is a problem with the printer communicating with the computer, the problem can be solved by:**
   a. disconnecting the printer cable
   b. taking the printer offline
   c. disabling bi-directional support for this printer
   d. lubricating the print head pins

5. **When servicing a dot matrix printer, what device might be hot to the touch?**
   a. the print ribbon
   b. the print head
   c. the roller mechanism
   d. the paper carriage assembly

6. **When servicing a laser printer, which component might be hot to the touch?**
   a. the print head
   b. the paper drum
   c. the fuser assemblage
   d. the toner cartridge

7. **When troubleshooting a dot matrix printer, if the head moves back and forth but nothing prints, then suspect a problem with the:**
   a. pins on the print head
   b. paper feeder
   c. ribbon
   d. printer cable

6.1 Identify the common types of network cables, their characteristics and connectors.

COAXIAL: RG6, RG8, RG58, AND RG59 • BNC • AUI • PLENUM/PVC

UNDERSTANDING THE OBJECTIVE

Coaxial cable was first used commercially in the 1940s. It is very reliable, but has a limited data transmission rate. It is currently used in a wide variety of applications, including local area networks.

WHAT YOU **REALLY** NEED TO KNOW

◆ Coaxial cable consists of a center conductor wire surrounded by an insulator which is then surrounded by a braided outer conductor. The outer conductor serves as a grounded shield that minimizes electrical interference and is surrounded by a jacket made of extruded PVC (poly vinyl chloride).

◆ PVC cable (some forms of coaxial, twisted pair, and fiber-optic cable) cannot be used in plenum ceilings. A plenum ceiling is a ceiling which is open to one or more rooms or air ducts throughout a building. If a fire occurs and PVC cable is burned, it will emit large amounts of black toxic smoke and hydrochloric acid. More expensive plenum rated cable has a Teflon coating that requires a higher temperature in order to burn and emits fewer fumes than normal PVC cable.

◆ There are four types of coaxial cable.

   - RG59 coaxial cable is used for cable TV and VCR transmission.

   - RG6 coaxial cable has more shielding than RG59 and is used for satellite dish transmission and video applications such as security camera systems.

   - RG8 coaxial cable is used by ThickNet Ethernet.

   - RG58 coaxial cable is used by ThinNet Ethernet.

◆ The following table shows the types of coaxial cables that are used with Ethernet.

Cable System	Speed	Cables and Connectors	Max Cable Length
10Base2 (ThinNet)	10 Mbps	RG58 coaxial with a BNC connector	185 meters or 607 feet
10Base5 (ThickNet)	10 Mbps	RG8 coaxial with an AUI 15-pin D-shaped connector	500 meters or 1640 feet

◆ BNC (Bayone-Neill-Concelman) connectors come in three types: a T-connector, terminator, and barrel connector. A barrel connector is usually crimped onto a coaxial cable and multiple coaxial cables are then joined by way of T-connectors and may be ended with a terminator.

OBJECTIVES ON THE JOB

When running coaxial cable through a plenum (open ceiling), you must use plenum rated cable.

PRACTICE TEST QUESTIONS

1. Which of the following cable types is used in ThinNet Ethernet?
    a. RG58
    b. RG8
    c. RG28
    d. Both a and b

2. Which of the following cable types is used in ThickNet Ethernet?
    a. RG58
    b. RG8
    c. RG28
    d. Both a and b

3. Which of the following connector types is used in ThinNet Ethernet?
    a. BNC
    b. RJ-45
    c. AUI
    d. Both a and c

4. Which of the following connector types is used in ThickNet Ethernet?
    a. BNC
    b. RJ-45
    c. AUI
    d. Both a and c

5. Which type of coaxial cable should be used between closed walls?
    a. conventional coaxial cable
    b. regular coaxial cable
    c. Teflon coaxial cable
    d. a and b

6. Which type of coaxial cable should be used between open ceilings?
    a. conventional coaxial cable
    b. regular coaxial cable
    c. Teflon coaxial cable
    d. a and b

7. What is the maximum cable length of ThickNet Ethernet?
    a. 185 meters
    b. 500 meters
    c. 607 feet
    d. none of the above

6.1 Identify the common types of network cables, their characteristics and connectors.

UTP: CAT3, CAT5/E, AND CAT6 • STP • FIBER: SINGLE-MODE AND MULTI-MODE • RJ-45 • ST/SC • IDC/UDC

UNDERSTANDING THE OBJECTIVE

Twisted pair cable is fairly inexpensive and is used on many network and phone systems. Fiber cable offers high data transmission rates and is often used to connect servers or buildings.

WHAT YOU REALLY NEED TO KNOW

- ◆ Twisted pair consists of two independently insulated copper wires that have been twisted around each other. Each pair of wires has been twisted in order to reduce cross-talk and electromagnetic interference. In each pair, one wire transmits the signal while the other serves as a ground which absorbs interference.

- ◆ Twisted pair cable that is twisted tighter has a higher transmission rate and greater cost per foot. An RJ-45 connector (similar in appearance to a phone jack, but larger) is crimped onto the end of a twisted pair cable using a special tool.

- ◆ UTP (Unshielded Twisted Pair) consists of several pairs of twisted wires surround by a plastic encasement. STP (Shielded Twisted Pair) consists of several pairs of twisted wires encased in a grounding shield which is surrounded by a plastic encasement. UTP is most popular and is typically used in phone networks and local area networks. STP is used in environments with large amounts of electrical interference and in some local area networks.

- ◆ CAT3 is a popular type of UTP cable that is used on 10 Mbps Ethernet.

- ◆ CAT5, CAT5e, and CAT6 are also popular types of UTP cables that are used on 100 Mbps Ethernet (also called Fast Ethernet). CAT6 offers the best reliability by significantly reducing crosstalk.

Cable System	Speed	Cables/Connectors	Max Cable Length
10BaseT and 100BaseT (Twisted pair)	10 to 100 Mbps	UTP or STP uses an RJ-45 connector	100 meters or 328 feet
10BaseF, 10BaseFl, 100BaseFL, 100BaseFX, or 1000BaseFX	10 Mbps up to 1 Gbps	Fiber-optic cable uses an ST or SC fiber-optic connector	500 meters up to 2 km (6562 feet)

- ◆ Fiber-optic cable consists of a glass core or plastic fibers surrounded by several layers of protective insulation and a Teflon or PVC outer jacket. Single mode fiber-optic cable is thin, sometimes difficult to connect, offers the highest performance, and is most expensive. Multi-mode is the most popular type of fiber-optic cable.

- ◆ IDU and UDC connectors that are neither male nor female.

OBJECTIVES ON THE JOB

Know the most popular types of cables, their characteristics, and appropriate use in an enter-prise setting.

PRACTICE TEST QUESTIONS

1. Which type of fiber-optic cable connector is barrel-shaped like a BNC connector?
   a. ST
   b. SC
   c. IDC (IBM-type Data Connector)
   d. IDU (Universal Data Connector)

2. Which type of fiber-optic cable connector has a square face and is easier to connect in a confined space?
   a. ST
   b. SC
   c. IDC (IBM-type Data Connector)
   d. IDU (Universal Data Connector)

3. Which type of cable connector(s) is neither male nor female and is commonly found on IBM Type 1 cabling, a two-pair shielded cable?
   a. IDC (IBM-type Data Connector)
   b. IDU (Universal Data Connector)
   c. SC
   d. Both a and b

4. Which of the following UTP cabling offers the greatest amount of crosstalk reduction?
   a. CAT5
   b. CAT5e
   c. CAT6
   d. CAT20

5. Which fiber-optic cable system offers the highest bandwidth?
   a. 1000BaseFX
   b. 100BaseFX
   c. 100BaseFL
   d. all of the above

6. Which type of UTP cable should be used between open ceilings?
   a. conventional UTP cable
   b. CAT5 cable
   c. Teflon coated cable
   d. a and b

7. How many pairs of wire can an RJ-45 connector hold?
   a. 8
   b. 4
   c. 2
   d. none of the above

OBJECTIVES

6.2 Identify basic networking concepts including how a network works.

INSTALLING AND CONFIGURING NETWORK CARDS • ADDRESSING • BANDWIDTH • STATUS INDICATORS

UNDERSTANDING THE OBJECTIVE

Configuring a PCI network interface card (NIC) is much easier than configuring an ISA network interface card.

WHAT YOU **REALLY** NEED TO KNOW

◆ Sometimes, installing a network card involves unplugging the power to the computer, opening the computer case, and inserting a PCI network interface card (NIC) into an open PCI slot. Then, you supply device drivers if the operating system does not natively support the NIC. You can get drivers from the NIC manufacturer's Web site. Be sure to download the correct driver for your operating system. Of all Microsoft operating systems, Windows XP offers native support for the greatest number of NICs. Finally, install the network protocol appropriate for your network.

◆ If you're installing an ISA NIC on an older computer, you will have to manually configure it using Device Manager and may have to set jumpers on the NIC. An ISA device cannot share resources (IRQ, I/O address, and upper memory address) with any other device.

◆ When replacing a NIC on a PC, use a NIC that is identical to the one you are replacing. If you cannot match the NIC, then obtain drivers that support the new NIC and save them on a Zip disk or CD-ROM to be used during the installation process.

◆ A **media access control (MAC) address** or **adapter address** is a unique number that is hard-coded into a NIC and that is used to uniquely identify the NIC on the network.

◆ The most popular network for LANs is **Ethernet**, which can use coaxial and twisted pair wiring. It supports a bandwidth (or speed) of 10 to 1000 Mbps.

◆ Some NICs can operate at different bandwidths.

◆ Many NICs have status indicator LEDs next to the RJ-45 port. You can verify that it's working correctly if one light stays lit when the PC is connected to the network and another light flashes when data is being transmitted over the network.

◆ An Ethernet NIC, called a **combo card**, can support more than one cabling media by containing more than one transceiver on the card.

OBJECTIVES ON THE JOB

If you are experiencing network problems, do not assume that it may be a faulty NIC. Instead, reboot the computer and try again. If the problem still exists, check with other users on the same network. Finally, consider upgrading the NIC drivers.

PRACTICE TEST QUESTIONS

1. **Which type of NIC is easiest to configure?**
   - a. ISA NIC
   - b. PCI NIC
   - c. B.E.H. NIC
   - d. None of the above

2. **When replacing a NIC in a computer system, it is important to use an identical NIC because:**
   - a. Only one kind of NIC works on a particular network.
   - b. It is easier to fit the replacement NIC in the expansion slot.
   - c. The drivers for the NIC will not need replacing.
   - d. You cannot tell what kind of NIC will work on this network.

3. **A number permanently assigned to a NIC that uniquely identifies the computer to the network is:**
   - a. an IP address
   - b. a MAC address
   - c. a combo card address
   - d. a NIC Handle

4. **If you must install a different type of NIC than the one currently installed, what must you do?**
   - a. Verify that the new NIC uses the same type network cable.
   - b. Ask the network administration for the proper drivers for the new NIC or obtain them yourself.
   - c. Verify that network parameters are entered correctly.
   - d. All of the above.

5. **When the light on the back of the NIC is not lit solid, what can be the problem?**
   - a. the NIC, the network cable, or the hub
   - b. the NIC, the OS, or the hub
   - c. the NIC, the OS, or the application using the network
   - d. the OS, the user, or the application using the network

6. **What does the term bandwidth mean?**
   - a. a measure of the amount of data that can be transmitted over a system
   - b. data throughput
   - c. line speed
   - d. all of the above

7. **What type of NIC works on an Ethernet network and supports more than one cabling media?**
   - a. a dual NIC
   - b. a combo card
   - c. a NIC NIC
   - d. a double-NIC

OBJECTIVES

6.2 Identify basic networking concepts including how a network works.

PROTOCOLS: TCP/IP, IPX/SPX (NWLINK), APPLETALK, AND NETBEUI/NETBIOS • FULL-DUPLEX, HALF-DUPLEX • CABLING—TWISTED PAIR, COAXIAL, FIBER OPTIC, RS-232

UNDERSTANDING THE OBJECTIVE

TCP/IP is the most popular protocol used on networks. Each computer on a TCP/IP network is assigned a temporary IP address (called dynamic IP address) or a permanent IP address (called a static IP address) by the server.

WHAT YOU **REALLY** NEED TO KNOW

- ◆ Coaxial, twisted pair, and **fiber-optic** cables are all used in networks.
- ◆ RS-232 is a standard that controls serial cables.
- ◆ The most common LAN setup today is Ethernet 10BaseT star formation using UTP cabling with RJ-45 connectors.
- ◆ **Full-duplex** is communication in both directions simultaneously; **half-duplex** allows communication in only one direction at a time.
- ◆ Several networking protocols are supported by Windows. These include TCP/IP, IPX/SPX, AppleTalk, and NetBEUI.
- ◆ NetBEUI is the easiest protocol to configure. The only configuration that NetBEUI requires is to give the computer a NetBIOS name. The NetBIOS name is limited to 15 characters in Windows 9x. Windows 2000/XP uses host names which are limited to 63 characters. NetBEUI is a proprietary Microsoft protocol which is not routable. This means it cannot be used to communicate with other computers over the Internet.
- ◆ IPX/SPX is a NWLink networking protocol that was developed by Novell for its Netware file servers. Unlike NetBEUI, IPX/SPX is a routable protocol. NWLink is used along with Client Service for Netware to enable Windows computers to use file and print services from a Novell Netware server.
- ◆ AppleTalk is a networking protocol developed and used on the MAC OS.
- ◆ TCP/IP (Transmission Control Protocol/Internet Protocol) is the most common networking protocol used to connect computers on two or more networks. The IP component is responsible for moving a data packet between computers, to servers, and over the Internet based upon the IP address of the destination computer. The TCP component is responsible for verifying the correct delivery of data and can detect errors or lost data.

OBJECTIVES ON THE JOB

A PC technician should have a solid understanding of networking protocols and be able to troubleshoot network issues related to setting up, configuring, and maintaining a network.

PRACTICE TEST QUESTIONS

1. Which of the following network protocols are routable?
   a. TCP/IP
   b. NetBEUI
   c. IPX/PX
   d. Both a and c

2. Which of the following network protocols are non-routable?
   a. TCP/IP
   b. NetBEUI
   c. IPX/PX
   d. Both a and c

3. Which of the following network protocols is used to communicate with a Novell Netware file server?
   a. TCP/IP
   b. NetBEUI
   c. IPX/PX
   d. Both a and c

4. Which of the following is not a type of hardware protocol?
   a. Internet
   b. Ethernet
   c. Token Ring
   d. FDDI

5. Which standard is used to control serial cables?
   a. RS-232
   b. RS-232z
   c. RS-323
   d. None of the above

6. Full-duplex communication is communication in:
   a. two directions, but not at the same time
   b. two directions simultaneously
   c. only a single direction
   d. one direction at a time

7. Which of the following cabling is ideal for connecting servers or buildings on a local area network?
   a. coaxial
   b. twisted pair
   c. fiber-optic
   d. none of the above

OBJECTIVES

6.2 Identify basic networking concepts including how a network works.

NETWORKING MODELS: PEER-TO-PEER AND CLIENT/SERVER • INFRARED • WIRELESS

UNDERSTANDING THE OBJECTIVE

Two types of networking models are peer–to–peer and client/server. Wireless LAN technology can provide notebook computer users with a mobile method for accessing shared resources.

WHAT YOU **REALLY** NEED TO KNOW

◆ Peer-to-peer network systems allow users to share resources and files located on their computers with other connected users (and vice-versa). In this networking model, a centralized file server does not exist. Instead, all computers are equal and have the same ability to use shared resources on the network. This networking model includes ease of setup and a relative low cost. Users on a peer-to-peer network are part of a workgroup.

◆ Client/Server network systems allow users to access shared resources such as files and printers from a centralized file server. File services are often configured with extra security that requires users to provide a username and password for logging into a domain. Examples of servers include Windows 2000 server, Windows 2003 server, and Novell Netware server. Client/Server network systems are primarily used in medium to large local area networks. The advantages include access to centralized resources and easier management of clients. Users on a client/server network are part of a domain and may each be assigned an individual username and password.

◆ An infrared device (for example, an infrared printer) can access a network by way of a PC that has an infrared port. The device is installed on the PC and then shared with others on the network.

◆ Wireless LANs (WLAN) do not use cables to connect computers to a network. Instead, users typically install a wireless network card which allows for Wi-Fi (wireless fidelity) communication between their computer and a wireless access point (AP).

◆ Wireless networks are ideal for situations where it may be difficult to install networking cable.

◆ Antennae typically transmit RF signals in an omni-directional or directional pattern. Omni-directional signals provide the widest coverage by transmitting signal in a 360-degree horizontal direction (signals are not transmitted vertically). Directional transmission is often used for point-to-point links between buildings.

OBJECTIVES ON THE JOB

A PC technician should understand the advantages and disadvantages of using both peer–to–peer and client/server networking models and be able to setup, manage, and maintain both systems.

PRACTICE TEST QUESTIONS

1. **In which type of networking model do users logon to a domain?**
   a. peer-to-peer
   b. client/server
   c. infrared
   d. none of the above

2. **Which type of wireless LAN transmission technology is ideal for network communication between buildings?**
   a. directional transmission
   b. omni-directional transmission
   c. automatic transmission
   d. none of the above

3. **Which type of wireless LAN transmission technology is ideal for network communication within a building?**
   a. directional transmission
   b. omni-directional transmission
   c. automatic transmission
   d. none of the above

4. **In which type of networking model is a user part of a workgroup?**
   a. peer-to-peer
   b. client/server
   c. infrared
   d. none of the above

5. **Which type of networking model is best for configuring and managing settings on client computers?**
   a. peer-to-peer
   b. client/server
   c. infrared
   d. none of the above

6. **Which of the following statements is true about WLANs?**
   a. With omni-directional transmission, the signal strength becomes weaker as the user moves away from the AP.
   b. With omni-directional transmission, the signal strength becomes stronger as the user moves away from the AP.
   c. With omni-directional transmission, the signal strength remains the same as the user moves away from the AP.
   d. None of the above.

7. **What term refers to the process of marking (on sidewalks or buildings) a nearby wireless access point that may offer Internet access so that other individuals can access it?**
   a. wardialing
   b. chalking
   c. warchalking
   d. none of the above

6.3 Identify common technologies available for establishing Internet connectivity and their characteristics.

TECHNOLOGIES INCLUDE: LAN AND DSL • CHARACTERISTICS INCLUDE: DEFINITION, SPEED, AND CONNECTIONS

UNDERSTANDING THE OBJECTIVE

Several technologies exist that allow computers or computer networks in medium to large business enterprises to connect to the Internet. These technologies vary greatly in speed (bandwidth) and cost.

WHAT YOU **REALLY** NEED TO KNOW

◆ A local area network (LAN) is a group of computers and other equipment that can be setup to access information over the Internet. There are many technologies used to connect a LAN to the Internet. Please refer to the table below for more information.

LAN Technology	Max Bandwidth	Common Connection Uses
Fractional T1	# channels leased times 64 Kbps	Businesses that might grow into a T1
T1	1.544 Mbps	Can purchase multiple T1 lines
T3	45 Mbps	Enterprise environments
OC-1	52 Mbps	ISP to regional ISP
OC-3	155 Mbps	Internet or large enterprise backbone
OC-24	1.23 Gbps	Internet backbone using optical fiber
OC-256	13 Gbps	Major Internet backbone using optical fiber

◆ A DSL (Digital Subscriber Line) uses regular copper phone lines on a different frequency from voice to transmit and receive data. As a result, users can talk on the phone while accessing the Internet. DSL is always connected to the Internet. There are many forms of DSL.

DSL Technology	Max Bandwidth	Common Connection Uses
IDSL	128 Kbps	Home or small business
DSL Lite or G. Lite	384 Kbps upstream, 6 Mbps downstream	Less expensive then regular DSL
ADSL (Asymmetric)	640 Kbps up, 6.1 Mbps downstream	Home or small business
SDSL (Symmetric)	1.544 Mbps	Home or small business
HDSL (High-bit rate)	3 Mbps	Home or small business
VDSL (Very-high-rate)	55 Mbps over short distances	Under development

OBJECTIVES ON THE JOB

A PC Technician should have a basic understanding of technologies that can be used to connect a computer or computer network to the Internet. It is also important to understand the characteristics of each technology including the reliability, available bandwidth, cost, and appropriate use.

PRACTICE TEST QUESTIONS

1. What is the maximum bandwidth of IDSL?

    a. 128 Kbps

    b. 6 Mbps

    c. 1.544 Mbps

    d. 3 Mbps

2. What is the maximum downstream bandwidth of DSL Lite?

    a. 128 Kbps

    b. 6 Mbps

    c. 1.544 Mbps

    d. 3 Mbps

3. What is the maximum bandwidth of SDSL?

    a. 128 Kbps

    b. 6 Mbps

    c. 1.544 Mbps

    d. 3 Mbps

4. What is the maximum bandwidth of a T1 connection?

    a. 128 Kbps

    b. 6 Mbps

    c. 1.544 Mbps

    d. 3 Mbps

5. What is the maximum bandwidth of a T3 connection?

    a. 1.544 Mbps

    b. 6 Mbps

    c. 45 Mbps

    d. 52 Mbps

6. What is the maximum bandwidth of an OC-1 connection?

    a. 1.544 Mbps

    b. 6 Mbps

    c. 45 Mbps

    d. 52 Mbps

7. What kind of cabling does DSL typically use?

    a. copper phone line

    b. optic fiber

    c. coaxial

    d. none of the above

6.3 Identify common technologies available for establishing Internet connectivity and their characteristics.

TECHNOLOGIES INCLUDE: CABLE, ISDN, DIAL-UP, SATELLITE, AND WIRELESS

UNDERSTANDING THE OBJECTIVE

Several technologies exist that allow computers or computer networks at home or in small to medium businesses to connect to the Internet. These technologies vary greatly in speed (bandwidth), reliability, and cost.

WHAT YOU **REALLY** NEED TO KNOW

- ◆ A cable modem uses the same cable lines as cable TV, but at a different frequency from the cable television signal. Users can enjoy cable TV while accessing the Internet. A cable modem is always connected to the Internet and offers a bandwidth up to 5 Mbps.

- ◆ An ISDN (Integrated Services Digital Network) connection uses a standard phone line and is accessed by way of a dial-up connection. ISDN is an early version of DSL and was developed in the 1980s. It offers a bandwidth of up to 128 Kbps.

- ◆ A dial-up connection uses a modem and phone line to dial a phone number which connects the computer to an Internet Service Provider (ISP). It offers a bandwidth of up to 56 Kbps.

- ◆ A satellite access connection can provide users living in remote areas (where other forms of Internet connection are not available) with an Internet connection. Users sometimes connect to the Internet using a television satellite dish (for example, Direct TV) or a dedicated satellite dish. To use this technology, a clear view to the south is required since satellites typically orbit around the equator. Trees and bad weather can affect the bandwidth. Download speeds can be up to 560 Kbps.

- ◆ Wireless connection refers to any Internet connection that does not use cables. The 802.11b standard (most popular) uses a frequency around 2.4 GHz up to 100 meters and has a bandwidth of up to 11 Mbps. The 802.11a standard uses a frequency around 5.0 GHz up to 50 meters and has a bandwidth of up to 54 Mbps. The 802.11g standard uses a frequency around 2.4 GHz up to 100 meters and has a bandwidth that is slightly over 20 Mbps.

- ◆ Broadband technology refers to any type of networking technology that carries more than one type of transmission. Examples include cable modem, ISDN, DSL, and some satellite technology.

OBJECTIVES ON THE JOB

A PC technician should have a basic understanding of technologies that can be used to connect a computer or computer network to the Internet. It is also important to understand the characteristics of each technology including the reliability, available bandwidth, cost, and appropriate use.

PRACTICE TEST QUESTIONS

1. Which of the following are examples of broadband technology?
   a. cable modem
   b. ISDN
   c. DSL
   d. all of the above

2. What is the typical maximum bandwidth of a cable modem?
   a. 56 Kbps
   b. 128 Kbps
   c. 5 Mbps
   d. 560 Kbps

3. What is the typical maximum bandwidth of a dial-up modem?
   a. 56 Kbps
   b. 128 Kbps
   c. 5 Mbps
   d. 560 Kbps

4. What is the typical maximum bandwidth of an ISDN connection?
   a. 56 Kbps
   b. 128 Kbps
   c. 5 Mbps
   d. 560 Kbps

5. What is the typical maximum download bandwidth of a satellite connection?
   a. 56 Kbps
   b. 128 Kbps
   c. 5 Mbps
   d. 560 Kbps

6. Which wireless technology offers a bandwidth of up to 11 Mbps?
   a. 802.11a
   b. 802.11b
   c. 802.11g
   d. none of the above

7. Which wireless technology offers a bandwidth of up to 54 Mbps?
   a. 802.11a
   b. 802.11b
   c. 802.11g
   d. none of the above

A+ OS Technologies Exam Objectives

Descriptions of the A+ OS Technologies exam objective can be found on the CompTIA Web site at *www.comptia.org/certification/A/objectives.asp*.

	% OF EXAM
DOMAIN 1.0 OPERATING SYSTEM FUNDAMENTALS	**28%**
DOMAIN 2.0 INSTALLATION, CONFIGURATION, AND UPGRADING	**31%**
DOMAIN 3.0 DIAGNOSIS AND TROUBLESHOOTING	**25%**
DOMAIN 4.0 NETWORKS	**16%**

1.1 Identify the major desktop components and interfaces, and their functions. Differentiate the characteristics of Windows 9x/Me, Windows NT 4.0 Workstation, Windows 2000 Professional, and Windows XP.

CONTRASTS BETWEEN WINDOWS 9X/ME, WINDOWS NT 4.0 WORKSTATION, WINDOWS 2000 PROFESSIONAL, AND WINDOWS XP

UNDERSTANDING THE OBJECTIVE

Windows 2000 was built on Windows NT and is basically the next evolution of Windows NT 4.0 with the added user-friendly features of Windows 9x/ME. Windows 2000 is more reliable than Windows 9x/ME. Windows 9x/ME combines 16-bit and 32-bit OS components and supports legacy hardware and software that Windows 2000 does not support. Windows XP improves upon Windows 2000 and provides better backward-compatibility with Windows 98/ME. Windows XP is available in both Professional and Home editions.

WHAT YOU **REALLY** NEED TO KNOW

- ◆ Because of improved power management features; Windows 2000 and Windows XP are better choices for newer notebooks than Windows 9x/ME.
- ◆ Because of advanced security features, Windows 2000 and Windows XP Professional are better for the corporate and business environments.
- ◆ For the home environment, choose Windows 98/ME if legacy hardware support is required, otherwise choose Windows XP Home.
- ◆ Windows 9x/ME includes a DOS-based core and manages base, upper, and extended memory in fundamentally the same way as DOS. Windows 9x/ME uses both 16- and 32-bit coding, but Windows NT, 2000, and XP all use 32-bit code.
- ◆ Windows 9x/ME assigns virtual memory addresses to a page table. The VMM manages the page table by moving data in and out of the page table to RAM and virtual memory (a swap file).
- ◆ Windows NT and Windows 2000 server manage networks by assigning them to domains. The OS is the domain controller for the network.
- ◆ Windows 9x/ME installs applications, the DLLs for all applications are stored in a common folder, but Windows 2000/XP keeps an application's DLL files separate from other applications.
- ◆ Windows 9x/ME does not ask permission before it overwrites or deletes a critical system file, but Windows 2000/XP protects that from happening and thereby improves system reliability.
- ◆ Windows 2000 is a suite of operating systems. Windows 2000 Professional or Windows XP Professional are the choices for desktop and notebook computers.
- ◆ Windows 2000, Windows XP, and Windows 9x/ME all support Plug and Play, but Windows NT does not.
- ◆ Windows 9x/ME supports the FAT16 and FAT32 file systems while Windows NT, Windows 2000, and Windows XP add support for NTFS. Windows NT does not support FAT32.

OBJECTIVES ON THE JOB

Understanding differences and similarities among Windows 9x/ME, Windows 2000, and Windows XP helps you support these operating systems and their installed applications.

PRACTICE TEST QUESTIONS

1. Which operating system does not support the FAT32 file system?
    a. Windows 98
    b. Windows XP
    c. Windows 2000
    d. Windows NT

2. Which operating system does not support Plug and Play?
    a. Windows XP
    b. Windows 98
    c. Windows NT
    d. Windows 2000 Professional

3. Which operating system provides a feature to allow a user at home to connect a notebook computer to a network at his workplace using a virtual private network?
    a. Windows 2000
    b. Windows 95
    c. Windows 98
    d. All of the above

4. Which operating system does not offer the NTFS file system?
    a. Windows NT
    b. Windows XP Professional
    c. Windows 9x
    d. Windows 2000 Server

5. How does the Windows 95 Virtual Memory Manager assign memory addresses for applications to use?
    a. Addresses are assigned to a page table that points to RAM and virtual memory.
    b. Addresses are assigned to areas in RAM.
    c. Addresses are assigned to virtual memory, which can represent either a swap file or RAM.
    d. Addresses are assigned by the CPU, and VMM is not involved in the process.

6. Why would a user choose to use the NTFS file system on a notebook computer?
    a. The hard drive is very large.
    b. for added security over the FAT file system
    c. to allow the notebook to connect to the private network at his workplace
    d. to be able to use the Windows 2000 Active Directory on his network file server

7. Which operating system is best designed for small, inexpensive PCs where the user needs to run 16-bit application programs that require a graphical interface?
    a. Windows 98
    b. Windows 2000
    c. Windows XP
    d. UNIX

1.1 Identify the major desktop components and interfaces, and their functions. Differentiate the characteristics of Windows 9x/Me, Windows NT 4.0 Workstation, Windows 2000 Professional, and Windows XP.

MAJOR OPERATING SYSTEM COMPONENTS: REGISTRY, VIRTUAL MEMORY, AND FILE SYSTEM

UNDERSTANDING THE OBJECTIVE

Beginning with Windows 95, the registry became the central repository for all hardware, operating system, and application configuration information. The registry is a key component of Windows 9x/ME, Windows NT, Windows 2000, and Windows XP. Virtual memory is a file on the hard disk, referred to as a swap file or page file that the operating system uses to extend physical memory. The file system organizes your files on the disk in directories and subdirectories, and can provide features such as permissions, compression, and encryption.

WHAT YOU **REALLY** NEED TO KNOW

- The Windows 9x/ME registry is stored in two files: User.dat and System.dat, located in the Windows directory. In contrast, the Windows NT/2000/XP registry is stored in five files called hives, located in the \WINNT\SYSTEM32 directory.
- The **registry** is a hierarchical database organized as an upside-down tree. The tree is composed of branches called subtrees or major keys. Within each subtree are keys that may contain subkeys. Subkeys may also contain other subkeys. Keys and subkeys may also contain values which hold data. Values are the lowest level of the registry tree.
- Windows swap files, used for virtual memory, are normally stored in the root directory of the Windows installation drive. The swap file has the read-only, system, and hidden attributes set.
- The Windows NT, 2000, and XP swap file is named Pagefile.sys whereas the Windows 9x/ME swap file is called Win386.swp.
- In Windows 9x/ME, to view virtual memory settings, choose Start, Settings, Control Panel, System, Performance, and then Virtual Memory. In this dialog box, you should usually select the "Let Windows manage my virtual memory settings" option.
- In Windows 2000 and Windows XP, to view or change virtual memory settings, choose Start, Control Panel, System. Then click the Advanced tab and click the Settings button in the Performance section. Click the Advanced tab and click the Change button.
- Windows 9x/ME only supports the FAT16 and FAT32 file systems. FAT32 is required for hard drives larger than 2 GB and stores files more efficiently than FAT16.
- The NTFS file system is supported by Windows NT, 2000, and XP and provides features such as file and folder permissions, compression, and encryption.

OBJECTIVES ON THE JOB

The ability to troubleshoot problems related to the system registry and virtual memory is a critical skill for a PC technician. An understanding of the file system is critical when determining which file system to install.

PRACTICE TEST QUESTIONS

1. **The name of the temporary swap file in Windows 98 is:**
   a. Swap.fle
   b. Win386.swp
   c. 386spart.par
   d. Win.com

2. **Which statement about the Windows 95 methods of managing virtual memory is true?**
   a. The swap file is always a temporary version.
   b. The swap file is always stored in the root directory of the hard drive where Windows is installed.
   c. The name of the swap file is Swap.swp.
   d. The location of the swap file can be changed by the user.

3. **What is the name of the swap file in Windows XP?**
   a. Pagefile.sys
   b. Swapfile.swp
   c. Page.swp
   d. Win386.swp

4. **Which operating system does not use virtual memory?**
   a. Windows 2000
   b. DOS
   c. Windows XP
   d. Windows NT

5. **What are the two Windows 9x registry back-up files?**
   a. System.dat and User.dat
   b. Regedit.exe and Registry.sys
   c. Autoexec.bat and Config.sys
   d. System.da0 and User.da0

6. **What are the names of the Windows 9x registry files?**
   a. System.ini and Win.ini
   b. Win.com and Command.com
   c. System.dat and User.dat
   d. System.da0 and User.da0

7. **What file system offers permissions?**
   a. NTFS
   b. FAT16
   c. FAT32
   d. FAT12

1.1 Identify the major desktop components and interfaces, and their functions. Differentiate the characteristics of Windows 9x/Me, Windows NT 4.0 Workstation, Windows 2000 Professional, and Windows XP.

MAJOR OPERATING SYSTEM INTERFACES • WINDOWS EXPLORER, MY COMPUTER, AND CONTROL PANEL

UNDERSTANDING THE OBJECTIVE

Every operating system has tools to manage files and folders, view and use system resources, add and remove hardware and software, and perform other tasks. Windows 9x/ME, Windows 2000, and Windows XP provide three tools for most of these functions: Windows Explorer, My Computer, and Control Panel.

WHAT YOU **REALLY** NEED TO KNOW

- ◆ Use Control Panel to add and remove hardware and software and configure system resources. Be familiar with each icon or entry in Control Panel and know its primary purpose.
- ◆ My Computer is accessible from the desktop and from Windows Explorer. Use My Computer to view and access storage devices, Control Panel, Dial-Up Networking, and Network Neighborhood and other resources.
- ◆ The System Properties window can be accessed from Control Panel or by right-clicking My Computer and selecting Properties.
- ◆ Use either My Computer or Explorer to determine how much space is available on a hard drive.
- ◆ The following is a list of tasks and where to find them in Windows 2000, XP, and 98/ME.

Task	Windows 98/ME	Windows XP	Windows 2000
Add and delete users	Control Panel, Users	Control Panel, User Accounts	Control Panel, Users and Passwords
System and administrative tools	Start, Programs, Accessories, System Tools	Control Panel, Administrative Tools	Control Panel, Administrative Tools
MS-DOS command prompt	Start, Programs, MS-DOS prompt	Start, All Programs, Accessories, Command Prompt	Start, Programs, Accessories, Command Prompt
Configure a hardware device	Control Panel, System, Device	Control Panel, System, Hardware, Device Manager	Control Panel, System, Hardware, Device Manager
Dial-up connections and networking	Control Panel, Modems	Control Panel, Network Connections	Control Panel, Network and Dial-up Connections
Display options	Control Panel, Display	Control Panel, Display	Control Panel, Display
Install new hardware	Control Panel, Add New Hardware	Control Panel, Add Hardware	Control Panel, Add/Remove Hardware
Network configuration	Control Panel, Network	Control Panel, Network Connections	Control Panel, Network and Dial-up Connections
Set password	Control Panel, Passwords	Control Panel/ User Accounts	Control Panel/ Users and Passwords
Configure scanners and cameras	Not available	Control Panel, Scanners and Cameras	Control Panel, Scanners and Cameras
Configure UPS device	Control Panel, Power Management	Control Panel, Power Options	Control Panel, Power Options

OBJECTIVES ON THE JOB

A PC technician is expected to know how to use the major operating system components to service, maintain, and troubleshoot a computer system.

PRACTICE TEST QUESTIONS

1. **In Windows Explorer on Windows XP, how do you change the view option to see hidden files and folders?**
   a. Click the View menu and select All Files and Folders.
   b. Click the View menu and select Show Hidden Files.
   c. Click the Tools menu, select Folder Options and View tab, and click Show hidden files and folders.
   d. Click the Tools menu, select View tab, and click Show hidden files and folders.

2. **In Windows 98, to view your folders as a Web page you must:**
   a. Click the Tools menu, click Options, and then click "as Web Page".
   b. Right-click a folder and click View as Web Page.
   c. Click the View menu and click "as Web Page".
   d. You cannot view a folder as a Web page in Windows 98.

3. **Which icon in Windows 2000 Control Panel do you use to configure a modem for a dial-up connection to a network?**
   a. Network and Dial-up Connections
   b. Network
   c. Dial-Up Networking
   d. Add/Remove Hardware

4. **Which icon in Windows 98 Control Panel do you use to change the user's password?**
   a. Passwords and Users
   b. Passwords
   c. Network
   d. Add New Programs

5. **How do you change a password in Windows XP?**
   a. Control Panel, User Accounts
   b. Control Panel, Network
   c. Start, Programs, Accessories, Administrative Tools
   d. Start, Programs, Administrative Tools

6. **How can you determine how much space is available on a hard drive?**
   a. My Computer, Properties, System
   b. from Explorer, right-click the drive and select Properties
   c. from My Computer, right-click the drive and select Properties
   d. either b or c

7. **How do you access a command line prompt using Windows 98?**
   a. Start, Programs, Accessories, Command Prompt
   b. Control Panel, MS-DOS Prompt
   c. Start, Programs, MS-DOS Prompt
   d. Either b or c

1.1 Identify the major desktop components and interfaces, and their functions. Differentiate the characteristics of Windows 9x/Me, Windows NT 4.0 Workstation, Windows 2000 Professional, and Windows XP.

MAJOR OPERATING SYSTEM INTERFACES: COMPUTER MANAGEMENT CONSOLE, ACCESSORIES/SYSTEM TOOLS, AND COMMAND LINE

UNDERSTANDING THE OBJECTIVE

The Computer Management Console is a Windows 2000/Windows XP tool that provides problem solving and configuration utilities using a single user interface. The System Tools folder contains a number of useful tools for maintaining the disk, backing up data, and viewing system information among other tasks. The command line adds DOS-like command capabilities to the Windows graphical user interface.

WHAT YOU **REALLY** NEED TO KNOW

- The **Computer Management Console** is one of the pre-configured tools provided in Windows 2000/XP built from the Microsoft Management Console (MMC). This tool is accessed from Start, Control Panel, Administrative Tools, Computer Management.
- The Computer Management Console tools are divided into three sections: System Tools, Storage, and Services and Applications.
- The System Tools section of the Computer Management Console provides tools to view events, manage shared folders, manage users, monitor system performance, and manage devices.
- The Storage section of the Computer Management Console lets you manage removable storage, and defragment and manage disks.
- The Services and Applications section of the Computer Management Console contains tools to manage services, configure Windows Management Instrumentation (WMI), manage indexing, and configure the Internet Information Services (IIS).
- The System Tools folder is accessed from Start, Programs (All Programs on Windows XP), Accessories, System Tools.
- Some of the tasks performed from the System Tools folder include Backup, Disk Cleanup, Disk Defragmenter, Scheduled Tasks, System Information, and System Restore.
- Windows NT does not include a disk defragmenter tool nor a system information tool.
- A shortcut to accessing the command line in Windows NT, Windows 2000, and Windows XP is to click Start, Run, type cmd, and click OK.
- The command line provides a DOS-like interface for entering commands. Some useful programs that run from the Windows NT/2000/XP command line include Ipconfig.exe and Nslookup.exe. In addition most familiar DOS commands can be entered such as DIR, COPY, DEL, and RENAME.

OBJECTIVES ON THE JOB

A technician must be familiar with using a variety of troubleshooting and management tools. Related tools are indispensable for managing users, disks, events, and services. The command line interface provides a non-graphical suite of tools.

PRACTICE TEST QUESTIONS

1. **What is the name of the console building utility used in Windows 2000 and XP?**
   a. System Manager
   b. Program Management Interface
   c. Microsoft Management Console
   d. Graphical User Interface

2. **Which of the following is not a Computer Management Console tool category?**
   a. System Tools
   b. Files and Folders
   c. Storage
   d. Services and Applications

3. **What is the term given to individual tools installed in a management console?**
   a. plug-ins
   b. snap-ins
   c. applets
   d. tweak-ui

4. **Which of the following can be found in System Tools?**
   a. Passwords and Users
   b. Backup and System Information
   c. Network Connections and Device Manager
   d. Administrative Tools and User Accounts

5. **Where can System Tools be found in Windows XP?**
   a. Control Panel, System Tools
   b. Control Panel, Accessories, System Tools
   c. Start, All Programs, Accessories, System Tools
   d. Start, Programs, Administrative Tools, System Tools

6. **How do you close a command line window?**
   a. Quit
   b. Logout
   c. <CTL><ALT><DEL>
   d. Exit

7. **How do you access a command line prompt using Windows XP?**
   a. Start, All Programs, Accessories, Command Prompt
   b. Control Panel, MS-DOS Prompt
   c. Start, Run, and type Cmd.exe
   d. Either a or c

OBJECTIVES

1.1 Identify the major desktop components and interfaces, and their functions. Differentiate the characteristics of Windows 9x/Me, Windows NT 4.0 Workstation, Windows 2000 Professional, and Windows XP.

MAJOR OPERATING SYSTEM INTERFACES: NETWORK NEIGHBORHOOD/MY NETWORK PLACES, TASK BAR/SYSTRAY, START MENU, AND DEVICE MANAGER

UNDERSTANDING THE OBJECTIVE

Understanding the various components of the Windows desktop makes navigation of the operating system quick and easy. Network Neighborhood is used in Windows 9x/ME and Windows NT as a starting place to find network resources but this icon has been renamed to My Network Places in Windows 2000/XP. The taskbar and system tray provide fast access to running programs and system status whereas the start menu makes for quick navigation to applications and management programs. The Device Manager is used to troubleshoot devices and install or update drivers.

WHAT YOU **REALLY** NEED TO KNOW

- ◆ The Network Neighborhood and My Network Places icons only appear on the desktop if a network protocol and a client have been installed.
- ◆ In Windows XP, My Network Places never appears on the desktop unless the display properties are configured to display the icon.
- ◆ To display the My Network Places icon on the desktop, go to Control Panel, Display, and click the Desktop tab. Then click the Customize Desktop button and click the check box next to My Network Places.
- ◆ The taskbar normally sits at the bottom of the desktop but can be moved around if preferred. The taskbar shows which applications are currently running and can be used to quickly switch from one application to another.
- ◆ The taskbar can be configured in Windows XP by going to Control Panel, TaskBar and Start Menu. From there, Quick Launch can be enabled which allows easy access to frequently used programs.
- ◆ Typical icons found in the system tray include the clock and volume control. In addition, you may see network connection status icons in Windows 2000 and Windows XP.
- ◆ In Windows 2000 and Windows XP, Device Manager can be accessed by right-clicking My Computer and selecting Properties. From there, click the Hardware tab and click the Device Manager button.
- ◆ Device Manager shows a list of all hardware device types. Devices that have been disabled will have a red X on them. Devices that have a problem will have a yellow circle with an exclamation point. In Windows ME, a green question mark indicates a compatible driver is installed rather than a driver specific to that device.

OBJECTIVES ON THE JOB

Network Neighborhood and My Network Places, along with the taskbar, system tray, and Start menu, are among the most commonly used features of the Windows desktop. A technician must understand how to use these tools in order to access programs, discover other computers on the network, and view running tasks. Device Manager is the most frequently used tool to diagnose hardware problems or check driver status.

1. In Device Manager, a diamond icon with a short line through one side of it stands for?
   a. ISA bus
   b. USB device
   c. SCSI
   d. Video card

2. A yellow exclamation point through a device in Device Manager indicates:
   a. the device is disabled
   b. resources have been manually assigned
   c. there is a problem with the device
   d. the device is Plug and Play

3. Which of the following device properties can you not view in Device Manager?
   a. Device type
   b. Date installed
   c. IRQ
   d. I/O address

4. Which of the following is not a taskbar option in Windows 98?
   a. Always on top
   b. Show clock
   c. Auto hide
   d. Disabled

5. Which taskbar option is available in Windows XP, but not in Windows 98?
   a. Lock the taskbar
   b. Quick Launch
   c. Auto hide
   d. Always on top

6. In Windows XP, what do you do if you cannot see all of your system tray icons?
   a. Left-click the system tray and select Show all.
   b. Click the arrow on the left side of the system tray.
   c. Double-click the system tray.
   d. Right-click the system tray and select Show all.

7. If you have many windows open and you need to get to a desktop icon, how can you quickly access the desktop in Windows XP?
   a. Right-click the taskbar and click Minimize All Windows.
   b. Click the Start Menu and select Show the Desktop.
   c. Type <CTR><ALT><D>.
   d. Right-click the taskbar and select Show the Desktop.

1.2 Identify the names, locations, purposes, and contents of major system files.

WINDOWS 9X – SPECIFIC FILES: IO.SYS, MSDOS.SYS, AUTOEXEC.BAT, COMMAND.COM, CONFIG.SYS, AND WIN.COM

UNDERSTANDING THE OBJECTIVE

Windows 9x requires a core group of system files in order to boot. The three files required before Windows can load are Io.sys, Msdos.sys, and Command.com. If necessary, Config.sys is executed, followed by Autoexec.bat. Once these files are loaded, the core Windows file, Win.com is executed and Windows begins to load.

WHAT YOU **REALLY** NEED TO KNOW

◆ When the BIOS loads Windows 9x, the boot record program first searches for and loads Io.sys, a hidden file stored in the root directory of the boot device.

◆ Io.sys locates Msdos.sys and reads the configuration information found in that file. Msdos.sys contains parameters that affect the way Windows boots.

◆ If present, Config.sys is read next. Config.sys may contain commands that affect memory management and that load real-mode device drivers.

◆ Command.com is located and loaded next. Command.com is the program that provides the DOS command prompt and is used to manage I/O and interpret internal commands.

◆ Autoexec.bat, if found, is loaded by Command.com. Autoexec.bat may contain commands that specify programs and tasks to be run each time Windows boots.

◆ If, during boot up, the user chose to boot to a command prompt, the process is complete after Command.com executes Autoexec.bat. However, Win.com could be entered at the command prompt to start Windows at this point. If the user selected a normal Windows boot, Win.com would start automatically.

◆ While Config.sys and Autoexec.bat are extremely important files to the DOS operating system, Windows can run happily without these files. They are only necessary if the user requires the additional startup functionality they provide.

◆ Io.sys contains real mode input/output drivers that are required when booting to a command line and during the boot process before Windows is started.

◆ Msdos.sys is a text file that contains instructions about how Windows should boot. For example, the path to the Windows installation drive and directory are specified in this file, as is the option to tell Windows whether to run Scandisk.exe after an improper shutdown.

◆ Config.sys may contain commands such as DEVICE=CDROM.SYS which loads a real mode CD-ROM driver.

OBJECTIVES ON THE JOB

A PC technician is expected to know how the OS is loaded, how device drivers are referenced and loaded, and the differences between real–mode and protected–mode components of the OS. You must also know how to alter the Windows startup process when troubleshooting a problem. By eliminating elements of the startup, you can isolate the source of the problem.

PRACTICE TEST QUESTIONS

1. **Which of the following Windows 9x system files is a text file?**
   a. Io.sys
   b. Vmm32.vxd
   c. Msdos.sys
   d. Command.com

2. **To function properly under Windows 9x, a Plug and Play device requires:**
   a. that system BIOS be Plug and Play
   b. a 32-bit VxD driver
   c. that CMOS setup reserve the IRQ needed by the device
   d. that the device already be installed at the time Windows 9x is installed

3. **If Config.sys is present when Windows 9x loads:**
   a. it will be ignored because Windows 9x does not support Config.sys
   b. all device drivers listed in it are loaded except Himem.sys
   c. it will be executed even though Config.sys is not a required Windows 9x file
   d. none of the above

4. **How are device drivers loaded under Windows 9x?**
   a. from Config.sys
   b. from System.ini
   c. from the registry
   d. all of the above

5. **Which three files are required before Win.com can be loaded (pick three)?**
   a. Msdos.sys
   b. Config.sys
   c. Io.sys
   d. Command.com

6. **Which is the correct order of loading or execution?**
   a. BIOS, Msdos.sys, Io.sys
   b. Io.sys, Msdos.sys, Autoexec.bat
   c. BIOS, Io.sys, Msdos.sys
   d. BIOS, Config.sys, Io.sys

7. **Which file is an optional file for Windows 98 execution?**
   a. Msdos.sys
   b. Config.sys
   c. Io.sys
   d. Win.com

OBJECTIVES

1.2 Identify the names, locations, purposes, and contents of major system files.

WINDOWS 9X – SPECIFIC FILES: HIMEM.SYS, EMM386.EXE, SYSTEM.INI, AND WIN.INI

UNDERSTANDING THE OBJECTIVE

Some system files are essential and some are optional. Emm386.exe and Himem.sys are used to manage the hardware resource, memory. Himem.sys is required by Windows 9x, but Emm386.exe is optional. Most Windows configuration information is stored in the registry, but some can be stored in Win.ini and System.ini.

WHAT YOU **REALLY** NEED TO KNOW

- ◆ DOS does not let device drivers and applications access memory above 640K unless DOS extensions (Himem.sys and Emm386.exe) are executed to manage this memory.
- ◆ Himem.sys is used to make the high memory area available to load part of DOS, thereby saving conventional memory for applications.
- ◆ Himem.sys is a device driver that accesses and manages memory above 640K (upper memory and extended memory). Windows automatically loads Himem.sys, but for DOS, it must be loaded from Config.sys.
- ◆ Emm386.exe makes upper memory blocks (UMBs) available to legacy device drivers and other TSRs and can emulate expanded memory by causing some extended memory to act like expanded memory.
- ◆ Emm386.exe can emulate expanded memory, an older type of memory above 1 MB that is no longer used.
- ◆ The command in Config.sys for Emm386.exe to make UMBs available without creating emulated expanded memory is DEVICE=C:\DOS\Emm386.exe NOEMS.
- ◆ Emm386.exe is not automatically loaded by Windows 9x, therefore, if Emm386.exe is needed, it must be manually loaded from Config.sys.
- ◆ The System.ini file contains hardware settings and multitasking options for Windows.
- ◆ The [386Enh] section of System.ini loads protected mode drivers for older hardware. System.ini is largely maintained in Windows 9x for backward compatibility with older hardware.
- ◆ Win.ini, like System.ini, is largely maintained for compatibility with older applications that do not use the **Windows registry**. Win.ini contains user settings, printer and font information, file associations, and application settings.
- ◆ While device drivers and application settings can be specified in Win.ini and System.ini, the Windows registry files have taken on that function for most hardware and applications.
- ◆ Win.ini and System.ini are located in the \Windows directory and can be easily edited, along with other configuration files such as Autoexec.bat and Config.sys using the Systedit.exe command.

OBJECTIVES ON THE JOB

Understanding how PC operating systems manage memory is a necessary skill, particularly when working with older systems and applications. The Win.ini and System.ini configuration files, while quickly becoming extinct, are still used.

PRACTICE TEST QUESTIONS

1. **The purpose of Himem.sys is:**
   a. to allow access to extended memory
   b. to emulate expanded memory
   c. to load DOS high
   d. to create virtual memory

2. **The purpose of Emm386.exe is:**
   a. to allow access to extended memory
   b. to emulate expanded memory
   c. to allow programs to use upper memory blocks
   d. both b and c

3. **Where in memory are upper memory blocks located?**
   a. between 640K and 1024K
   b. above 1024K in extended memory
   c. below 640K
   d. in conventional memory

4. **Which of the following is true?**
   a. Emm386.exe must be loaded before Himem.sys.
   b. Emm386.exe is always loaded by Windows.
   c. Himem.sys is always loaded by Windows and can be loaded by Config.sys.
   d. Emm386.exe can be loaded by adding a line to Autoexec.bat.

5. **Which statement is true about Win.ini?**
   a. Win.ini is used for application and user preferences and is most like User.dat.
   b. Win.ini is used by DOS and Windows 95 only.
   c. Win.ini is executed by Command.com.
   d. Win.ini is a binary file and requires a special editor to modify it.

6. **What is the maximum file size for an .ini file?**
   a. 16K
   b. 32K
   c. 64K
   d. 1 MB

7. **Which section will you find in System.ini?**
   a. [Desktop]
   b. [Fonts]
   c. [Boot]
   d. [Windows]

1.2 Identify the names, locations, purposes, and contents of major system files.

WINDOWS 9X – SPECIFIC FILES: REGISTRY DATA FILES (SYSTEM.DAT AND USER.DAT)

UNDERSTANDING THE OBJECTIVE

Windows 9x stores most configuration information in the registry, a hierarchical database with a tree structure. The registry is most often changed when you use the Control Panel to modify settings or when you install hardware or software, but you can also manually edit the registry using the editor Regedit.exe. The registry is stored in two files in the \Windows folder.

WHAT YOU **REALLY** NEED TO KNOW

◆ The Windows 9x registry is stored in two files, System.dat and User.dat. The OS keeps a backup copy of each file under System.da0 and User.da0.

◆ During booting, if the OS cannot find the registry files, or if they are corrupt, it reverts to System.da0 and User.da0.

◆ During booting, if the OS detects a corrupted registry, it boots into Safe Mode and asks if you want to restore from backup. If you respond with Yes, it reverts to System.da0 and User.da0.

◆ To manually edit the registry, first back up the two files, System.dat and User.dat, and then type Regedit in the Run dialog box.

◆ Windows 98 includes Registry Checker that backs up, verifies, and recovers the registry. (From the Start menu, choose Programs, Accessories, System Tools, System Information, Tools, and then Registry Checker.)

◆ The registry keys contain subkeys, which contain values. The six major keys are listed below.

Key	Description
HKEY_CLASSES_ROOT	Contains information about file associations and OLE data. (This branch of the tree is a mirror of HKEY_LOCAL_MACHINE\ Software\Classes.)
HKEY_USERS	Includes user preferences, including desktop configuration and network connections.
HKEY_CURRENT_USER	If there is only one user of the system, this is a duplicate of HKEY_USERS, but for a multi-user system, this key contains information about the current user preferences.
HKEY_LOCAL_MACHINE	Contains information about hardware and installed software.
HKEY_CURRENT_CONFIG	Contains the same information in HKEY_LOCAL_MACHINE\ Config and has information about printers and display fonts.
HKEY_DYN_DATA	Keeps information about Windows performance and Plug and Play information.

OBJECTIVES ON THE JOB

A PC technician is expected to know how to recover from a corrupted or deleted registry and how to manually edit the registry.

PRACTICE TEST QUESTIONS

1. **What are the two Windows 9x registry back-up files?**
    a. System.dat and User.dat
    b. Regedit.exe and Registry.sys
    c. Autoexec.bat and Config.sys
    d. System.da0 and User.da0

2. **What program do you execute when you want to edit the Windows 95 registry?**
    a. System.dat
    b. sysedit.exe
    c. Regedit.exe
    d. Win.com

3. **Which registry key stores current information about hardware and installed software?**
    a. HKEY_USERS
    b. HKEY_CURRENT_USER
    c. HKEY_LOCAL_MACHINE
    d. HKEY_DYN_DATA

4. **How many major branches or keys are there in the Windows 9x registry?**
    a. 10
    b. 5
    c. 4
    d. 6

5. **What are the names of the Windows 9x registry files?**
    a. System.ini and Win.ini
    b. Win.com and Command.com
    c. System.dat and User.dat
    d. System.da0 and User.da0

6. **What is one reason that Windows 9x supports using System.ini and Win.ini during the boot process?**
    a. These files can support 16-bit programs that can't use the Windows registry.
    b. The only way Windows 95 can load Himem.sys is through System.ini.
    c. Windows 9x depends on real-mode device drivers to operate Plug and Play devices.
    d. None of the above; Windows 9x does not support System.ini and Win.ini.

7. **Most configuration information for Windows 9x is stored in:**
    a. System.ini and Win.ini
    b. the registry
    c. Vmm32.vxd
    d. none of the above

1.2 Identify the names, locations, purposes, and contents of major system files.

WINDOWS NT-BASED SPECIFIC FILES: BOOT.INI, NTLDR, NTDETECT.COM, NTBOOTDD.SYS, NTUSER.DAT, AND REGISTRY DATA FILES

UNDERSTANDING THE OBJECTIVE

The system files used by Windows NT are considerably different than those that are used by Windows 9x and DOS. Boot.ini, Ntldr, and Ntdetect are all critical NT boot files. Ntbootdd.sys is a necessary boot file when a SCSI disk is used as the boot disk instead of an IDE drive. Ntuser.dat is a registry file that provides user-specific configuration information and policies. The files described here also apply to Windows 2000 and XP.

WHAT YOU **REALLY** NEED TO KNOW

- ◆ The Boot.ini file is a text file that describes where the Windows NT system files are located. Boot.ini also is used by Ntldr to build a menu of available operating systems a user can choose from when the system contains multiple operating systems.
- ◆ Ntldr is the first Windows NT system file loaded after the BIOS loads the MBR. Ntldr then loads the Boot.ini file and displays a boot menu if specified. Ntldr is responsible for changing the processor mode to 32-bit mode and loading a file system.
- ◆ Ntdetect.com is loaded by Ntldr and basic hardware detection is done, such as detecting disk controllers.
- ◆ If a SCSI controller is used in the system, Ntbootdd.sys is needed to provide a basic SCSI device driver so the disk drive can be accessed to load additional boot files.
- ◆ An Ntuser.dat file is maintained for every user that logs onto the NT computer. The Ntuser.dat file is located in the *systemroot*\Profiles*username* folder in Windows NT and the *systemroot*\Documents and Settings*username* folder in Windows 2000/XP.
- ◆ Ntuser.dat contains all user-specific settings so that a user maintains such options as screen background and mouse settings every time that user logs in.
- ◆ The Ntuser.dat file makes up the HKEY_CURRENT_USER hive in the Windows NT registry.
- ◆ The NT registry consists of five major keys or subtrees: HKEY_LOCAL_MACHINE, HKEY_CLASSES_ROOT, HKEY_CURRENT_USER, HKEY_USERS, and HKEY_CURRENT_CONFIG.
- ◆ The **registry keys** are built from six primary files, called hives: SAM, SECURITY, SOFTWARE, SYSTEM, DEFAULT, and Ntuser.dat.

OBJECTIVES ON THE JOB

When Windows NT will not boot, a technician must be familiar with the primary files required for a successful startup. Knowing how to modify the Boot.ini file, or how to respond when Ntdetect.com cannot be located, can help a technician get a system up and running quickly.

PRACTICE TEST QUESTIONS

1. **Where is the Ntldr file located?**
   a. Root directory of the system partition
   b. \Winnt\System32 folder
   c. \Winnt folder
   d. \Winnt\Boot folder

2. **Which file is only used in the Windows NT boot process when a SCSI boot device is used?**
   a. Ntldr
   b. Scsi.sys
   c. Ntbootdd.sys
   d. Hal.dll

3. **Which of the following is a hidden text file?**
   a. Ntldr
   b. Boot.ini
   c. Ntdetect.com
   d. System.sys

4. **Which Windows NT file is responsible for most of the booting process?**
   a. Ntdetect.com
   b. Ntldr
   c. Boot.ini
   d. Io.sys

5. **What are the files called that hold the Windows NT registry?**
   a. registry files
   b. hives
   c. system files
   d. tree files

6. **Which program is the best one to use to edit the Windows NT registry?**
   a. Regedt32.exe
   b. Sysedit.exe
   c. Regedit.exe
   d. Word for Windows

7. **Which Windows NT registry key stores information about hardware and installed software and does not change when a new user logs on?**
   a. HKEY_USERS
   b. HKEY_CURRENT_USER
   c. HKEY_LOCAL_MACHINE
   d. HKEY_CLASSES_ROOT

Demonstrate the ability to use command-line functions and utilities to manage the operating system, including the proper syntax and switches.

COMMAND LINE FUNCTIONS AND UTILITIES INCLUDE: COMMAND/CMD, DIR, ATTRIB, VER, MEM, SCANDISK, DEFRAG, EDIT, XCOPY, COPY, AND FORMAT

UNDERSTANDING THE OBJECTIVE

The command line, while less important to PC users, is still a vital tool for technicians. The ability to navigate the file system, copy and edit files, and format disks, among other tasks, at the command line is a skill well worth knowing.

WHAT YOU **REALLY** NEED TO KNOW

◆ Windows 9x/ME uses Command.com to open a command-line interface. From the command line interface, one can run many utilities for file manipulation, disk management, and system information.

◆ Windows NT/2000 and Windows XP use Cmd.exe to open a command-line interface rather than Command.com.

◆ The following is a list of the command-line interface commands and common switches or parameters:

Command	Some Common Parameters or Switches
DIR	Displays a list of files and folders DIR/P – Displays one page at a time DIR I MORE – Displays one page or item at a time
ATTRIB	Displays or changes the read-only, archive, system, and hidden attributes of a file ATTRIB +H +R +S Filename.ext – Sets the hidden, read-only, and system attribute to a file
VER	Displays the version of the operating system loaded
MEM	Displays a report of memory MEM /C I MORE – A complete MEM report paged to screen
SCANDISK	Examines a hard drive for errors and repairs them if possible SCANDISK /A – Scans and repairs all drives in the system SCANDISK C: /P – Displays problems found but does not repair them
DEFRAG	Examines a hard drive for fragmented files and rewrites them in contiguous clusters DEFRAG C: /S:N – Arranges files in alphabetical order by filename
EDIT	Opens a full-screen text editor EDIT Filename.ext
XCOPY	Copies directories, their subdirectories, and files (not including hidden files) XCOPY A:*.* C:\DOS /S – Copies all files to DOS folder on hard drive including subdirectories
COPY	Same as XCOPY but does not include subdirectories
FORMAT	Formats a floppy disk or hard drive FORMAT C: /S – Formats a hard drive and writes system files on the drive, making it bootable

OBJECTIVES ON THE JOB

It is often necessary to use command-line programs when the Windows GUI will not operate or during initial system setup before you have Windows installed. Some administrators find that they can do certain tasks quicker using the command-line.

PRACTICE TEST QUESTIONS

1. Which command can make a file a hidden system file?
   a. SYS
   b. ATTRIB
   c. MEM
   d. VER

2. What is the purpose of the /C switch in the MEM command (MEM /C)?
   a. saves a memory report to drive C
   b. displays a complete report
   c. pages the report one screen at a time
   d. displays the current memory status

3. What command scans and repairs errors on a hard drive?
   a. SCANREG
   b. SCANDISK
   c. DEFRAG
   d. FORMAT C: /S

4. What is a text editor that can be used to edit a text file?
   a. EDIT
   b. WordPad
   c. NotePad
   d. All the above

5. Which command copies files including files in the subdirectories of the current folder?
   a. COPY
   b. TREE
   c. EDIT
   d. XCOPY

6. Which command will make a disk bootable after formatting it?
   a. FORMAT C: /T
   b. FORMAT C: /S
   c. FDISK C: /T
   d. FDISK C: /S

7. Which command can help speed up access to the files on a disk?
   a. FORMAT
   b. SCANREG
   c. DEFRAG
   d. DISKSPEED

OBJECTIVES

1.3 Demonstrate the ability to use command-line functions and utilities to manage the operating system, including the proper syntax and switches.

COMMAND LINE FUNCTIONS AND UTILITIES INCLUDE: FDISK, SETVER, SCANREG, MD/CD/RD, DELETE/RENAME, DELTREE, TYPE, ECHO, SET, AND PING

UNDERSTANDING THE OBJECTIVE

The command line utilities listed provide a variety of functionality from disk partition management and directory and file management to network testing. SCANREG can resolve problems related to the Windows registry.

WHAT YOU **REALLY** NEED TO KNOW

◆ The following is a list of more command-line interface commands and common switches or parameters:

Command	Some Common Parameters or Switches
FDISK	Hard drive partitioning program; view, create, and delete partitions FDISK /MBR to fix a corrupted MBR
SETVER	Fixes a problem with legacy DOS applications that require a certain version of DOS
SCANREG	Restores or repairs the registry using backups that Registry Checker creates each day ScanReg /Restore – Restores the registry from backup ScanReg /Fix – Repairs a corrupted registry ScanReg /Opt – Optimizes the registry by deleting unused entries
MD/CD/RD	Make directory, change directory, and remove directory MD path, CD [/D] path – changes drive (/D) and directory (Win 2000 and XP) RD /S path – /S option removes entire directory tree starting at path (Win 2000 and XP)
DEL	Deletes the specified file or files – same as ERASE DEL /F file specification – forces deletion of read-only files
RENAME	Renames the specified file(s) – same as REN REN file1 file2
DELTREE	Deletes all files and folders starting from specified folder – use RD /S in Windows 2000/XP DELTREE /Y path – deletes all files and folders starting from path suppressing all prompts
TYPE	Displays the contents of a text file to the screen
ECHO	Displays what follows to the screen. Mostly used in batch files. ECHO message, ECHO ON/OFF turns batch file command echoing on or off
SET	Sets the value of an environment variable, with no arguments displays environment variables SET TEMP=C:\TEMP – sets the temporary directory to C:\TEMP
PING	Sends an echo request message to a network host – used to test network connectivity PING – a ip-address – pings the specified address and resolves the host name

OBJECTIVES ON THE JOB

When disk problems occur or new disks must be installed, the FDISK utility can be used. File system navigation, and file and folder deletion are a frequent part of a technician's job. When the GUI cannot be used, files can be viewed using the TYPE command and batch files often use the ECHO and SET commands. PING is used to test network connectivity when installing new cables or new network cards.

PRACTICE TEST QUESTIONS

1. What command do you use if you receive an error about wrong DOS version?
   a. ATTRIB
   b. SETVER
   c. VERSION
   d. Command.com

2. Which program rewrites files in contiguous cluster chains?
   a. DEFRAG
   b. SCANDISK
   c. CHKDSK
   d. FDISK

3. What command can you use to correct a Windows startup problem?
   a. FDISK
   b. FORMAT a: /s
   c. SCANREG /fix
   d. DEL *.*

4. What command(s) do you use to show the contents of the Config.sys file (choose all that apply)?
   a. SHOW
   b. EDIT
   c. TYPE
   d. DISPLAY

5. What command did you use if you received the following output?
   `REPLY from 127.0.0.1: bytes=32 time<1ms TTL=128`
   a. TYPE localhost
   b. ECHO localhost
   c. REPLY localhost
   d. PING localhost

6. What does the following command do?
   `CD ..`
   a. change to your home directory
   b. change to the root directory
   c. change to the parent directory
   d. nothing, this is an invalid command

7. What command can you use to change your command line prompt (choose all that apply)?
   a. SET
   b. PROMPT
   c. PROMPTSET
   d. CP

OBJECTIVES

1.4 Identify basic concepts and procedures for creating, viewing, and managing disks, directories and files. This includes procedures for changing file attributes and the ramifications of those changes (for example, security issues).

DISKS: PARTITIONS (ACTIVE PARTITION, PRIMARY PARTITION, EXTENDED PARTITION, AND LOGICAL PARTITION) AND FILES SYSTEMS (FAT16, FAT32, NTFS4, AND NTFS5.X)

UNDERSTANDING THE OBJECTIVE

Part of installing a hard drive involves partitioning the drive and then formatting the drive which installs a file system. A primary partition can be active which means that the BIOS can boot an operating system from that partition. Once partitions are created, the partitions must be formatted to install the required file system.

WHAT YOU **REALLY** NEED TO KNOW

- ◆ The **partition table** at the very beginning of a hard drive (cylinder 0, track 0, sector 0) contains information about each partition on the drive, including what type of file system is used for the partition. The partition table also contains the master boot program called the boot strap loader.
- ◆ Disk drives installed in PCs can have a maximum of four partitions which can be a combination of primary and extended partitions, but only one extended partition is allowed. The FDISK program is limited to one primary DOS partition and one extended partition with logical drives. However, the Disk Manager in Windows NT/2000/XP can create up to four primary partitions or three primary and one extended partition.
- ◆ Extended partitions contain one or more logical partitions. An extended partition may have several logical partitions, and since each logical partition is assigned a drive letter, the practical maximum is until you run out of drive letters.
- ◆ DOS and Windows versions prior to Windows 95 OSR2 support only the FAT16 file system.
- ◆ Windows 95 OSR2, Windows 98, and Windows ME add support for the FAT32 file system. Windows NT/2000/XP support the NTFS file system. Both FAT32 and NTFS support small cluster sizes on large disks.
- ◆ Windows 2000 can access an NTFS volume (NTFS4) created with Windows NT 4.0 or 3.51. Windows NT 4.0 with Service Pack 5 can access a Windows 2000 NTFS volume (NTFS5).
- ◆ With FAT file systems, the file allocation table (FAT) contains an entry for each cluster of the logical drive.
- ◆ An OS sees a hard drive as a group of one or more logical drives, each of which has a root directory and FAT.
- ◆ The FAT16 file system supports drive sizes of up to 2 GB in DOS or Windows 9x and up to 4 GB in Windows NT/2000/XP whereas the FAT32 file system supports drives up to 32 GB.
- ◆ The NTFS file system is recommended for large drives and for systems requiring security and fault tolerance. NTFS supports drives up to 16 TB and supports permissions, compression, and encryption.
- ◆ The Disk Management utility is used to manage disks in Windows NT/2000/XP.

OBJECTIVES ON THE JOB

A PC technician must be able to install a hard drive. Partitioning, formatting, and installing software are essential steps in the process. A technician needs to know the file system to use and understand the consequences of each choice.

PRACTICE TEST QUESTIONS

1. **For very large hard drives, which file system provides the smallest cluster size?**
   a. FAT12
   b. FAT16
   c. FAT32
   d. Choices a, b, and c all yield the same cluster size.

2. **Where is the boot strap loader located?**
   a. near the FAT on drive C:
   b. in the partition table sector
   c. at the very end of the hard drive, after all data
   d. in drive D:

3. **The master boot program is located at:**
   a. cylinder 1, track 1, sector 1
   b. cylinder 1, track 0, sector 0
   c. cylinder 0, track 0, sector 1
   d. cylinder 0, track 0, sector 0

4. **What are the functions of FDISK?**
   a. It creates the partition table.
   b. It displays partition table information.
   c. It creates partitions and logical drives.
   d. All of the above.

5. **What file system is used by floppy disks?**
   a. FAT16
   b. FAT12
   c. FAT32
   d. FAT8

6. **Which file system is not supported by Windows NT?**
   a. FAT16
   b. FAT32
   c. NTFS
   d. None of the above; they are all supported by Windows NT.

7. **What is the first Microsoft OS to support FAT32?**
   a. Windows 95, Release 1 (Windows 95a)
   b. Windows NT
   c. DOS version 6.0
   d. Windows 95, Release 2 (Windows 95b)

1.4 Identify basic concepts and procedures for creating, viewing, and managing disks, directories and files. This includes procedures for changing file attributes and the ramifications of those changes (for example, security issues).

DIRECTORY STRUCTURES (ROOT DIRECTORY, SUBDIRECTORIES, ETC): CREATE FOLDERS, NAVIGATE THE DIRECTORY STRUCTURE, AND MAXIMUM DEPTH

UNDERSTANDING THE OBJECTIVE

The directory structure is composed of the root folder or directory, which may contain one or more files and subdirectories. Subdirectories, in turn, can contain files and other subdirectories. All directory structures have this structure.

WHAT YOU **REALLY** NEED TO KNOW

- ◆ The **root directory** is the top level of all file systems. The root directory is created whenever a disk partition is formatted with a file system.

- ◆ There is a limit of 512 file entries in the root directory of the FAT16 file system but no limit when using the FAT32 or NTFS file systems. Long filenames take up more directory entries because each filename occupies multiple directory entries.

- ◆ The root directory is represented by the slash ('\') character. When navigating a directory structure, you can specify either an absolute path which starts from the root of the file system or a relative path which starts from your current location in the file system.

- ◆ An example of using an absolute path in a command-line window: C:\MyDocs> CD \MyDocs\letters. An example of using a relative path: C:\MyDocs> CD letters.

- ◆ Each directory or folder has two special entries. The first is a single dot ('.') which represents the folder itself, and the second is two dots ('..') which represents the folder's parent directory. A parent directory is the folder in which the current directory is contained.

- ◆ A subdirectory is also know as a child directory.

- ◆ Creating folders can be accomplished at the command line using the MD or MKDIR command.

- ◆ To create folders in Windows, use Windows Explorer. Select the folder within which you want the new folder to be created, then right-click in the right-hand Explorer pane and select New/Folder.

- ◆ To navigate the directory structure using Windows Explorer, you can double-click a folder to open it to get to its subdirectories.

- ◆ The depth of the file system refers to how many levels of subdirectories exist below the root.

- ◆ DOS limits the directory depth to 8, but Windows can have the directory depth until the name of the full path to the last directory plus any files in that directory is no more than 256 characters in length; Windows limits the filename size to a total of 256 characters including the pathname to the file.

OBJECTIVES ON THE JOB

Finding files, creating folders, and navigating the directory are common tasks for any computer user. Proper use of folders makes organization of documents a much easier task than simply storing all files into a single folder on the disk.

PRACTICE TEST QUESTIONS

1. **What is the correct syntax to move to the C:\Docs folder?**
    a. C:\Docs\Reports> CD ..
    b. C:\Docs\Reports> CD Docs
    c. CD Docs\
    d. CD /Docs

2. **What is the maximum number of root directoy entries permitted in FAT32?**
    a. 512
    b. 1024
    c. 65535
    d. unlimited

3. **How do you create a folder in Windows Explorer?**
    a. select Folder/Options/Create
    b. right-click, select New/Folder
    c. left-click, select New/Folder
    d. select Edit/New Folder

4. **When creating a new folder on the root of your FAT16 file system, why might you receive the error: "Unable to create <"New Folder">. Make sure the disk is not full or read-only" even if you have plenty of space on the disk and it is not write-protected?**
    a. The NTFS permissions are set to Read Only.
    b. The "No New Folders" option has been set in Windows Explorer.
    c. You have exceeded the maximum number of directory entries.
    d. You need to change directory to the root first.

5. **In Windows Explorer, how do you navigate to the parent of the folder you are currently in?**
    a. Click the Up folder icon.
    b. Click the Back button.
    c. Right-click and select Up.
    d. Double-click the current folder.

6. **Which is the proper command to create the folder C:\MyDocs\Sheets?**
    a. C:\MyDocs> MD \Sheets
    b. C:\MyDocs> MD C:/Sheets
    c. C:\MyDocs> MKDIR Sheets
    d. C:\MyDocs> MAKDIR Sheets

7. **What command will change you to the directory C:\Reports?**
    a. C:\Docs> cd /Reports
    b. C:\Docs> cd ..\Reports
    c. C:\Docs> chdir Reports
    d. C:\Docs> chdir .\Reports

OBJECTIVES

1.4 Identify basic concepts and procedures for creating, viewing, and managing disks, directories and files. This includes procedures for changing file attributes and the ramifications of those changes (for example, security issues).

FILES: CREATING FILES, FILE NAMING CONVENTIONS (MOST COMMON EXTENSIONS, 8.3, MAXIMUM LENGTH)

UNDERSTANDING THE OBJECTIVE

This objective involves the conventions involved with creating and naming files and understanding the meaning of file extensions.

WHAT YOU **REALLY** NEED TO KNOW

◆ DOS files consist of two parts: a filename, which is required, and a file extension, which is optional but strongly recommended.

◆ DOS filenames must have one to eight characters with no spaces, periods, question marks, asterisks, or back-slashes in the filename. The file extension can have up to three characters.

◆ Windows 9x/ME and Windows NT/2000/XP use long filenames that can contain up to 255 characters. Both the long filename and an associated 8.3 filename are stored in the directory table so that older programs can access those files. Long filenames can contain spaces and periods.

◆ On a Windows 9x/ME system, when a long filename is created, Windows will create an 8.3 filename by using the first six characters of the long filename, adding the tilde ~ character, and then a number (starting with '1'). In the event of a duplicate, the number is incremented for each potential duplicate. In the event that more than 9 files begin with the same first six characters and have the same extension, the 8.3 filename is created by using the first five characters of the long filename, adding a tilde, and a two-digit number starting with ten.

◆ On a Windows NT/2000/XP system, the procedure for creating the 8.3 filename is the same except that when more than four files with the first six characters in common are created, the first two characters of the name are used followed by four random characters plus '~1'.

◆ The extension of a file tells Windows which application to use when opening that file. For example, Word will open a file that has a .doc extension and a file with a .txt extension is considered a text file and will be opened by Notepad.

◆ Files with an extension of .exe or .com are considered binary program files that can be executed by double-clicking the filename in Windows Explorer or by typing the filename at the command prompt.

◆ Files with the .bat extension are considered batch files, which are text files that contain command line commands that can be executed in a batch.

◆ Other important file extensions include .sys (system file or device driver), .ini (system or application configuration or initialization file), .cab (a Windows cabinet file that is used to store many compressed files), and .hlp (a Windows help file).

◆ The extensions that are recognized by a Windows XP system can be viewed and configured in Windows Explorer.

OBJECTIVES ON THE JOB

Understanding how Windows deals with filenames is critical when trying to locate files for a particular application or when using older software to view files created with long filenames.

PRACTICE TEST QUESTIONS

1. In DOS, what is the combined maximum number of characters a filename and file extension can have?
   a. 8
   b. 3
   c. 11
   d. 255

2. A file named My Long File Document in Windows 95 will be displayed in DOS as:
   a. Mylong~1
   b. Mylong.fle
   c. Mylongfiledocument.txt
   d. My long1

3. What is a valid file extension for DOS?
   a. TXT
   b. T?T
   c. T*
   d. *

4. What is the maximum number of characters allowed in a Windows 95 filename?
   a. 8
   b. 255
   c. 1024
   d. 256

5. What happens if you double-click a file with a .com extension?
   a. The program Command.com will open the file.
   b. The file is opened with Notepad.
   c. The file is loaded into memory and executed.
   d. A batch file is run.

6. How can you change Windows XP so that double-clicking a file named Readme.txt will open the EDIT program instead of Notepad?
   a. Change the filename extension to .edt.
   b. Open the files properties and check the box next to Use Edit to Open.
   c. In Windows Explorer, go to Tool/Folder Options and edit the .txt entry in the File Types tab.
   d. You cannot make this change.

7. In Windows 9x, if you have 10 long filenames in the same directory that start with Abcdef and have a .doc extension, what will the 8.3 filename of the 10th file be?
   a. Abcde~10.doc
   b. Abcdef~10.doc
   c. Abcd~10.doc
   d. Abcdef-1.doc

1.4 Identify basic concepts and procedures for creating, viewing, and managing disks, directories and files. This includes procedures for changing file attributes and the ramifications of those changes (for example, security issues).

FILES: FILE ATTRIBUTES - READ ONLY, HIDDEN, SYSTEM, AND ARCHIVE ATTRIBUTES, FILE COMPRESSION, FILE ENCRYPTION, FILE PERMISSIONS, AND FILE TYPES (TEXT VS BINARY FILE)

UNDERSTANDING THE OBJECTIVE

File attributes and permissions define how a file can be used or accessed on the system.

WHAT YOU **REALLY** NEED TO KNOW

- ◆ Using the FAT file system, the attributes are stored in an 8-bit byte called the attribute byte.
- ◆ File attributes in the FAT16 and FAT32 file system are hidden, system, archive, and read-only. NTFS4 adds an attribute for compress and NTFS5 adds another for encrypt.
- ◆ By default Windows Explorer cannot view files with the hidden or system attribute set.
- ◆ Windows Explorer can be set to view hidden files by going to Tools/Folder Options and the View tab and then selecting the Show hidden files and folders radio button. To view system files, uncheck the Hide protected operating system files check box.
- ◆ The archive bit is used by the DOS BACKUP command or other third-party backup software to know to back up the file because it has changed since the last backup. If the archive bit is set to on, the backup software knows that the file has been created or modified since the last backup and includes the file during a backup procedure.
- ◆ To help protect a file from damage by the user, set the file attributes of the file to hidden, read-only.
- ◆ In Windows 9x, before you can edit Msdos.sys, make the file available for editing by removing the hidden, system, and read-only attributes.
- ◆ To view the attributes of a file in Windows, right-click the file and select Properties.
- ◆ The compress attribute, available in Windows NT, 2000, and XP, instructs the file system to compress the file on the disk.
- ◆ The encrypt attribute, available in Windows 2000 and XP, tells the system to encrypt the file on the disk. By default, only the creator of the file can decrypt the file and see its contents.
- ◆ Permissions can be set on a file or folder on an NTFS file system. Permissions include Read, Write, and Full Control.
- ◆ Files can contain binary data or text data or both. Files with only text (printable characters) can be viewed by programs such as Notepad or Edit. Binary files require special applications to open and view them or may be program files.

OBJECTIVES ON THE JOB

A PC technician is expected to understand the meaning and purpose of each of the file attributes and use commands in DOS and Windows to change these attributes as appropriate.

PRACTICE TEST QUESTIONS

1. **What command can make a file read-only?**
   a. READONLY
   b. ATTRIB
   c. COPY
   d. DIR

2. **Which of the following is a hidden file?**
   a. Win.com
   b. Autoexec.bat
   c. System.dat
   d. Regedit.exe

3. **What is the result of the ATTRIB -R Myfile.txt command?**
   a. The file Myfile.txt cannot be edited.
   b. The file Myfile.txt can be edited.
   c. The file Myfile.txt is erased.
   d. The file Myfile.txt is not affected.

4. **What is the command to hide Autoexec.bat?**
   a. ATTRIB +H Autoexec.bat
   b. HIDE Autoexec.bat
   c. UNERASE Autoexec.bat
   d. ATTRIB -H Autoexec.bat

5. **What in Windows 95 performs a function similar to the ATTRIB command in DOS?**
   a. Regedit
   b. ScanDisk
   c. a file's Properties dialog box
   d. a PIF file

6. **What file attribute does the DOS BACKUP command use to determine if the file is to be backed up?**
   a. the hidden status of the file
   b. the read-only status of the file
   c. the archive bit of the file
   d. none of the above; BACKUP backs up all files it finds

7. **What file system has an encrypt file attribute?**
   a. FAT32
   b. NTFS5
   c. NTFS4
   d. FAT12

1.5 Identify the major operating system utilities, their purpose, location, and available switches.

DISK MANAGEMENT TOOLS: DEFRAG.EXE, FDISK.EXE, BACKUP/RESTORE UTILITY (MSBACKUP, NTBACKUP, ETC), SCANDISK, CHKDSK, DISK CLEANUP, AND FORMAT

UNDERSTANDING THE OBJECTIVE

The Windows utilities listed above are used to manage and troubleshoot the file system on a hard drive. Fdisk.exe and FORMAT are used to create partitions and file systems. ScanDisk and CHKDSK are used to fix file system problems, while DEFRAG and DISK CLEANUP are used to optimize the file system.

WHAT YOU **REALLY** NEED TO KNOW

- After prolonged use, a file system becomes fragmented. When files are stored and later deleted, the file system stores files in a non-contiguous manner making access to those files slower and making the file system less reliable. Defrag.exe resolves that problem by re-organizing the disk so that files are stored contiguously.

- FDISK is used to view and modify the partition table. FDISK is usually used to initially set up a disk in preparation for the installation of a file system. FDISK can also recover a damaged master boot record by using the /MBR switch. For example: FDISK /MBR copies the backup MBR to the sector 0 of the hard drive.

- The BACKUP and RESTORE functions provided by MSBACKUP (Windows 9x/ME) and NTBACKUP (Windows NT, Windows 2000, and XP) create backups of disks or individual files so they can be restored.

- To access the backup utility in Windows, go to Start/Programs/Accessories/System Tools and select Backup. The backup programs can also be accessed using Start/Run and typing MSBACKUP or NTBACKUP depending on the operating system in use.

- You can backup an entire drive or select files and folders to backup. The Windows registry can also be backed up. There are a number of options available with the backup utilities that can be accessed by choosing Tools/Options while in the backup program advanced mode.

- ScanDisk (in Windows 9x/ME) fixes file system problems such as cross-linked clusters, lost clusters, and lost allocation units. When Windows 9x/ME is shutdown improperly, ScanDisk usually runs automatically at next boot. This behavior can be changed by editing the Msdos.sys file on C:\.

- CHKDSK is an older utility used in DOS but it is also used in Windows NT/2000/XP because ScanDisk is not available with those operating systems. CHDKSK performs similar tasks as ScanDisk.

- The Disk Cleanup utility is used to delete unnecessary files such as files in the recycle bin, temporary files, and Internet Explorer cache files.

- Format is used to install a file system. Format can also make a disk bootable by using the /s switch which transfers system files and writes to the MBR. The /FS switch is used to specify which file system to install (FAT16, FAT32, NTFS), and the /Q option is used to perform a quick format on a partition that has already been formatted before. To see all of the options available, use FORMAT /?.

OBJECTIVES ON THE JOB

The use of disk management utilities is an essential part of any technician's job. If a user complains about sporadic system lockups, sometimes running ScanDisk or CHKDSK can resolve the problem.

PRACTICE TEST QUESTIONS

1. You are building a computer to run Windows 9x and you have just installed a new hard drive. What must you do to make Windows boot from the hard disk? (select all that apply)
   a. Run FDISK to create a primary partition.
   b. Run FDISK to create a logical drive in the extended partition.
   c. Run FORMAT to install the NTFS file system.
   d. Run FDISK to make a primary partition active.

2. You have had your Windows ME computer for about six months and you notice that is takes longer for applications to load and for files to be accessed. What utility may help this problem?
   a. FDISK
   b. DEFRAG
   c. FORMAT
   d. SPEEDUP

3. You want to convert your FAT16 file system to FAT32. What utility should you run before converting?
   a. FDISK
   b. FORMAT
   c. CHKCONVERT
   d. MSBACKUP

4. A user complains that they receive a disk error when trying to access a file from the hard drive. What utility may help this problem?
   a. FDISK
   b. FORMAT
   c. CHKDSK
   d. CLEANUP

5. When you try to install a new application, you receive the error that there is not enough disk space to continue. What can you try to resolve the problem?
   a. Backup all files, format the disk and restore all files.
   b. Run Disk Cleanup.
   c. Run FORMAT /MBR.
   d. Run FDISK, delete the partition, and reformat using NTFS.

6. You are running Windows XP and you receive a disk error, what should you do?
   a. Reboot and run ScanDisk.
   b. In Explorer, right-click the disk and select FIXDISK.
   c. In Explorer, right-click the disk, select Properties, click the Tools tab, and click Check Now.
   d. Power off the system and then reboot so ScanDisk will run automatically.

7. You are running Windows NT and find that disk access has slowed over time, what should you do?
   a. Run DEFRAG.
   b. Use a third-party tool to defragment the disk.
   c. Run FORMAT /MBR.
   d. Run ScanDisk.

1.5 Identify the major operating system utilities, their purpose, location, and available switches.

SYSTEM MANAGEMENT TOOLS: DEVICE MANAGER, SYSTEM MANAGER, COMPUTER MANAGER, MSCONFIG.EXE, REGEDIT.EXE (VIEW INFORMATION/BACKUP REGISTRY), AND REGEDT32.EXE

UNDERSTANDING THE OBJECTIVE

The operating system utilities help troubleshoot problems with both hardware and software. Use Device Manager, System Manager, and Computer Manager to resolve system resource conflicts and monitor system performance. Use MSCONFIG and the registry editors to troubleshoot startup and system problems.

WHAT YOU **REALLY** NEED TO KNOW

- ◆ Device Manager is a Windows utility that lets you view, enable, display, and set parameters for hardware devices.
- ◆ In Windows 9x, if you suspect a resource conflict, use Device Manager to report the I/O addresses, DMA channels, IRQs, and upper memory addresses currently in use and to report conflicts with these resources.
- ◆ In **Device Manager**, recognize these symbols: Open diamond with a bar, red X, yellow exclamation point, and blue "I" on a white field.
- ◆ Computer Management is a Windows 2000 and XP tool that consolidates several tools to manage the local PC or other computers on the network. To access the Manager, click Start, Programs, Administrative Tools, Computer Management. Some Manager tools include Event Viewer, System information, Disk Defragmenter, and Device Manager.
- ◆ Msconfig.exe is a Windows utility that allows you to temporarily modify the system configuration to troubleshoot problems.
- ◆ Regedit.exe and Regedt32.exe are two registry editors. For Windows NT or Windows 2000/XP, use Regedt32.exe to edit the registry or backup or restore registry keys.
- ◆ To view, change, or update device drivers, double-click the device and select the Driver tab.
- ◆ Device Manager can be used to modify hardware profiles. To enable or disable a device in the current profile, select the device and from the General tab click the box next to Disable in this hardware profile.
- ◆ MSCONFIG can be used to change which programs run at startup and make changes to the major system files such as Config.sys, Autoexec.bat, Win.ini, and System.ini.
- ◆ To backup a key in Regedit or Regedt32, select the key, right-click and select Export. You will be asked where to save the key and the name you wish to give it. To restore a saved key, double-click the file in Windows Explorer. Saved registry keys have the extension .reg.

OBJECTIVES ON THE JOB

Advanced troubleshooting tools must be used with care. Whenever possible, make a backup of the system or the affected files before making changes with these utilities. Take special care when using the registry editors and know how to restore a saved registry in case Windows does not boot.

PRACTICE TEST QUESTIONS

1. **In Device Manager, a red X through a device icon indicates:**
    a. The device is working using 16-bit drivers.
    b. The device is not Plug and Play.
    c. Device Manager changed the manual settings to its own default settings.
    d. The device has been disabled.

2. **To manually assign resources to an installed device, you should:**
    a. Use MSCONFIG to edit the [Driver] section for that device.
    b. From Device Manager, uncheck the Use Automatic Settings box.
    c. From Device Manager, uncheck the Plug and Play box.
    d. Use REGEDIT to modify the device settings.

3. **Using Windows 98, how do you see a list of the I/O addresses currently used by the system?**
    a. Control Panel, System, Hardware Profiles
    b. Control Panel, System, Device Manager, Computer, Properties
    c. Control Panel, System, Device Manager, View devices by connection
    d. Control Panel, System, Performance, Virtual Memory

4. **You are running Windows XP and want to check the free space and status of your disk drives. What tool can you use?**
    a. Device Manager
    b. MSCONFIG
    c. Computer Manager
    d. System Manager

5. **Which icon represents SCSI in Device Manager?**
    a. a red X
    b. a yellow S
    c. an open diamond with a bar through it
    d. an S with a circle around it

6. **Which of the following is not a major registry key in Windows 98?**
    a. HKEY_USERS
    b. HKEY_LOCAL_USER
    c. HKEY_CURRENT_CONFIG
    d. HKEY_DYN_DATA

7. **To backup a registry key, you should:**
    a. In REGEDIT, select the key, and then choose Registry/Export Registry File.
    b. Using Windows Explorer, find the key folder and copy it to a new location.
    c. Using REGEDIT, select the key, right-click, and choose Backup Key.
    d. Using REGEDT32, go to File/Save Registry Key.

1.5 Identify the major operating system utilities, their purpose, location, and available switches.

SYSTEM MANAGEMENT TOOLS: SYSEDIT.EXE, SCANREG, COMMAND/CMD, EVENT VIEWER, AND TASK MANAGER

UNDERSTANDING THE OBJECTIVE

Event Viewer and Task Manager are Windows NT/2000/XP utilities that help with system monitoring and troubleshooting. SYSEDIT is an editing tool for modifying .ini files. SCANREG is used to fix and backup the registry and is run from Command.com in Windows 9x/ME but is not available in Windows NT/2000/XP.

WHAT YOU **REALLY** NEED TO KNOW

- ◆ Use the Sysedit.exe text editor in the \Windows\System folder to edit these and other text files: Autoexec.bat, Config.sys, Win.ini, System.ini, and Protocol.ini. Sysedit is also available in Windows 2000 and XP but is seldom used to edit these configuration files.
- ◆ Run SCANREG to restore or repair a corrupted Windows 9x registry. The utility can use a backup copy of the registry created earlier by Registry Checker. Common switches include: /FIX to repair the registry, /BACKUP to backup the registry, and /RESTORE to restore from a backup.
- ◆ Command.com and Cmd.exe provide a command-line interface for Windows. In Windows 9x/ME Command.com is located in the root of the boot drive and in the \Windows directory. In Windows NT/2000/XP, Cmd.exe is used to provide a command prompt. Cmd.exe is located in \WINNT\SYSTEM32.
- ◆ Common switches used with CMD and COMMAND include /C *command* which executes *command* and exits, and /K *command* which executes command and continues running.
- ◆ Windows NT/2000/XP also have a Command.com which acts just like Command.com in Windows 9x but the use of Cmd.exe is more commonly used for administrative tasks.
- ◆ The Event Viewer is a Windows NT/2000/XP utility that displays the system log files. There is a Security log, an Application log, and a System log. These logs can be consulted to view problems.
- ◆ The **Security log** is used to view messages created when auditing has been enabled. For example, auditing of failed logon attempts can be viewed. The audit message shows from which station the logon attempt occurred.
- ◆ Event Viewer is accessed by Start/Administrative Tools/Event Viewer or Start/Run and typing eventvwr.
- ◆ The Task Manager shows running applications and processes, plus provides performance statistics. Task Manager is run by right-clicking the taskbar and selecting Task Manager, or by typing <CTL><ALT><DEL> and choosing the Task Manager button.
- ◆ Task Manager can be used to terminate an unresponsive program and to view CPU and memory usage. Task Manager is available on Windows NT/2000/XP.

OBJECTIVES ON THE JOB

If a system becomes very sluggish, Task Manager can be used to view which application is using most of the CPU time and the application can be terminated if necessary. If the system displays an error indicating that a service failed to start upon boot up, Event Viewer can be used for more information.

PRACTICE TEST QUESTIONS

1. **Which files can be edited using SYSEDIT? (choose all that apply)**
   a. Config.sys
   b. Io.sys
   c. Boot.ini
   d. Autoexec.bat

2. **What task can you do with SCANREG?**
   a. delete the registry
   b. save a registry key
   c. restore the registry
   d. edit the registry

3. **What is the correct way to fix the registry?**
   a. click the SCANREG icon in Accessories
   b. C:\> SCANREG User.dat /FIX
   c. C:\> SCANREG /FIX
   d. C:\> SCANREG /F /ALL

4. **Which of the following are Event Viewer log files? (choose all that apply)**
   a. Security
   b. System
   c. Error
   d. Performance

5. **To erase the messages in the System log file, you should:**
   a. Select the System log and choose File/Erase.
   b. Select the System log, right-click, and choose Clear all Events.
   c. Select the System log and choose Action/Delete Messages.
   d. You cannot erase log file messages.

6. **Which are Task Manager tabs? (choose all that apply)**
   a. Memory
   b. System
   c. Applications
   d. Networking

7. **How do you terminate an application with Task Manager?**
   a. From the Processes tab, select the application and choose Stop Task.
   b. From the Applications tab, select the application and choose End Task.
   c. From the Processes tab, right-click the application and choose Kill.
   d. From the Applications tab, select the application and click File/End Task.

OBJECTIVES

1.5 Identify the major operating system utilities, their purpose, location, and available switches.

FILE MANAGEMENT TOOLS: ATTRIB.EXE, EXTRACT.EXE, EDIT.COM, AND WINDOWS EXPLORER

UNDERSTANDING THE OBJECTIVE

The Windows utilities are used to view, modify, and manage files and folders. Attrib.exe and Windows Explorer can be used to change and view file attributes. Edit is a command-line editor used for text file editing and Extract is used to manage Windows cabinet files.

WHAT YOU **REALLY** NEED TO KNOW

◆ Use Attrib.exe to display and change file attributes. Attrib.exe can be used to change and view only the Read Only, Archive, Hidden, and System attributes. Windows Explorer must be used to modify and view the NTFS attributes Compress and Encrypt.

◆ Use Extract.exe to manage cabinet files. Use *Extract /E cabinet filename* to extract a particular file from a .cab file.

◆ Extract.exe is useful for repairing a corrupted Windows system file. To make adding Windows components after installation easier, copy the cab files from the installation CD to a directory on the hard drive. Use Extract.exe /? to see all of the options for this program.

◆ Edit.com is a 16-bit real-mode text editor that can be used in DOS mode. Edit.com is very useful for editing system files at a command prompt.

◆ Windows Explorer is used to view the file system, run applications, and view system information. Explorer can be run by right-clicking My Computer and selecting Explore or by going to Start/Run and typing Explorer.

◆ The Folder Options selection can be reached in Windows 9x/ME by selecting View from the menu bar and selecting Folder Options. In Windows 2000/XP, select Tools from the menu bar and select Folder Options.

◆ In Windows 9x, Control Panel is found in My Computer but in Windows 2000/XP, you must use the Explorer Folder Options to enable Control Panel in My Computer.

◆ You can change how items are opened (single-click or double-click) by going to the Folder Options/Custom Settings from the General tab in Windows 9x or just the General Tab in Windows 2000/XP.

◆ To open a new Explorer window, right-click a drive or folder in Explorer and choose Explore. In Windows 2000/XP, you can use Explorer to view graphic images as thumbnails; in Windows 9x, folders can be viewed as a Web page.

◆ To search for files in Windows 2000/XP, right-click the file and choose Search. In Windows 9x, right-click and choose Find. You can search by filename or by key words.

◆ To view or change the attributes of a file using Explorer, right-click the file and choose Properties.

OBJECTIVES ON THE JOB

Being able to find and view files, as well as modify those files is critical to any computer technician. For example, in order to solve a Windows 2000 boot problem that involves the Boot.ini file, you may need to use Edit.com to edit the file.

PRACTICE TEST QUESTIONS

1. **Your desktop is obscured by open windows of running applications and you need to open Windows Explorer. What is a quick way to get to an Explorer window?**
   a. Choose File from your application menu and click Run Explorer.
   b. Right-click the Start button and click Explore.
   c. Type <ALT><E>.
   d. Both b and c.

2. **Windows NT will not boot and you suspect the Boot.ini file. You boot from a bootable floppy and run Edit.com but you cannot save the file. What should you do before running Edit.com?**
   a. EXTRACT /E win.cab Boot.ini
   b. CHKDSK C:
   c. ATTRIB –r Boot.ini
   d. ATTRIB +r Boot.ini

3. **From Windows Explorer, how can you select several files that are listed consecutively?**
   a. Select the first file, then while holding the <CTRL> key, choose the last file.
   b. Select the first file, then while holding the <ALT> key, choose the last file.
   c. Select the first file, then while holding the <SHIFT> key, choose the last file.
   d. Select the first file, then while holding the <ENDL> key, choose the last file.

4. **How do you view all of the .exe files in a folder so that they are listed consecutively?**
   a. Choose View/Arrange Icons by and select Name.
   b. Choose View/Arrange Icons by and select Extension.
   c. Choose View/Arrange Icons by and select All EXE.
   d. Right-click in the right-hand pane and choose Arrange Icons by/Type.

5. **You are in Windows Explorer viewing the root of the C: drive in Windows 9x. You cannot see the Msdos.sys file. How do you explain this?**
   a. Windows 9x does not have a Msdos.sys file.
   b. Msdos.sys is a hidden and system file.
   c. Msdos.sys is a read only file.
   d. Msdos.sys is located in the C:\WINDOWS directory.

6. **You just created a file called ReadMe.txt with Notepad but when you view it in Windows Explorer, it just says ReadMe. How can this be resolved?**
   a. You forgot the extension. Right-click the file and rename it.
   b. Choose Tools/Folder Options/View and uncheck Hide extensions for known file types.
   c. Choose Tools/Folder Options/File Types and add an entry for the .TXT extension.
   d. Open the file with Edit.com and save it again.

7. **You are running Windows XP and you want to find a file that is a letter to Dr. Abrams, how might you do this?**
   a. Click the Start menu and select Search, type Letters in the box Search for files or folders named:.
   b. Click the Start menu and select Find, type Letters in the box Search for files or folders named:.
   c. Click the Start menu and select Search, type Dr. Abrams in the box Containing text:.
   d. From a command line, type Search Dr. Abrams.

2.1 Identify the procedures for installing Windows 9x/Me, Windows NT 4.0 Workstation, Windows 2000 Professional, and Windows XP, and bringing the operating system to a basic operational level.

VERIFY HARDWARE COMPATIBILITY AND MINIMUM REQUIREMENTS • DETERMINE OS INSTALLATION OPTIONS: INSTALLATION TYPE (TYPICAL, CUSTOM, OTHER), NETWORK CONFIGURATION, FILE SYSTEM TYPE, AND DUAL BOOT SUPPORT

UNDERSTANDING THE OBJECTIVE

Installation procedures may differ depending upon the operating system version, status of the target computer, and options that are required for a particular environment. You'll need to choose the type of installation, what type of networking is required, the file system needed, and whether this operating system will co-exist with another operating system (dual boot).

WHAT YOU **REALLY** NEED TO KNOW

- ◆ Before an installation begins, the system must be checked out for hardware compatibility with the new operating system. Windows 95 requires a minimum 486DX at 25 MHz, Windows 98 requires a 66 MHz 486DX and Windows ME requires at least a Pentium 150 MHz. You should also know the minimum RAM and free hard disk space requirements for these OSs.
- ◆ Microsoft publishes a hardware compatibility list (HCL) for Windows NT/2000/XP. This list of known compatible hardware devices is on the installation CD for these operating systems but Microsoft's Web site should be consulted because the most current information is maintained there.
- ◆ Windows 2000 Pro and Windows XP Pro require a minimum of a Pentium 133 and Pentium 233 respectively, and 64 MB of RAM. Whereas Windows NT 4.0 has more modest requirements of any Pentium-class processor plus 16 MB RAM.
- ◆ The Windows 9x installation has four choices: Typical, Portable, Compact, and Custom. Typical is for a standard workstation installation, portable is for a laptop installation, compact will do a minimal installation, and custom lets the installer choose the components.
- ◆ Windows 2000/XP has two options during the installation of networking components: Typical or Custom. Typical network installation will install the Client for Microsoft Networks, File and Print Sharing, and the TCP/IP protocol along with the driver for your network card. A Custom network configuration permits the installer to delete or add components.
- ◆ Before installing Windows 9x you must partition the drive. Partitions over 2 GB will automatically use FAT32 but you can choose FAT32 even for smaller partitions. Windows NT 4.0 has the choice of either FAT16 or NTFS, but partitions over 4 GB will require NTFS. And Windows 2000/XP permits either FAT16, FAT32, or NTFS.
- ◆ In a dual-boot configuration with Windows 9x and Windows NT/2000/XP, it is best to install Windows 9x first and Windows NT/2000/XP next. Windows NT/2000/XP will detect the Windows 9x installation and build a menu choice in Boot.ini so that the user may choose when the system boots. Note that you cannot dual-boot with Windows NT and Windows 9x when Windows 9x uses FAT32.

OBJECTIVES ON THE JOB

Whether a computer is being upgraded to a new version, or a new installation is required on a new computer, knowing how to complete an installation is a valuable skill.

PRACTICE TEST QUESTIONS

1. **Which of the following is not a Windows 9x setup type?**
   a. Portable
   b. Compact
   c. Standard
   d. Typical

2. **What are the options for setting up Windows XP networking? (pick all that apply)**
   a. Custom
   b. Portable
   c. Typical
   d. Compatible

3. **Which file system is recommended on Windows NT for the most secure installation?**
   a. NTFS
   b. FAT32
   c. FAT16
   d. HPFS

4. **When dual-booting with Windows XP, what file is used to build the boot menu?**
   a. Menu.txt
   b. Menu.ini
   c. Boot.ini
   d. Bootmenu.ini

5. **What file system should you use with Windows 2000 if you wish to have a dual-boot with Windows 98 such that Windows 98 can access the Windows 2000 partition?**
   a. FAT12
   b. HPFS
   c. NTFS version 4
   d. FAT32

6. **When installing Windows XP from a bootable floppy and a CD-ROM, what command do you use to start the installation?**
   a. Winnt32.exe
   b. Winnt.exe
   c. Setup.exe
   d. Install.exe

7. **What command can you run to check if a computer is ready to install a Windows XP upgrade?**
   a. Checkup.exe
   b. Hcl.com
   c. winnt32 /checkupgradeonly
   d. setup /checkupgradeonly

OBJECTIVES

2.1 Identify the procedures for installing Windows 9x/Me, Windows NT 4.0 Workstation, Windows 2000 Professional, and Windows XP, and bringing the operating system to a basic operational level.

DISK PREPARATION ORDER (CONCEPTUAL DISK PREPARATION): START THE INSTALLATION, PARTITION, AND FORMAT DRIVE • RUN APPROPRIATE SET UP UTILITY: SETUP AND WINNT

UNDERSTANDING THE OBJECTIVE

Windows 9x and Windows NT/2000/XP are often installed from a CD-ROM drive, although Windows NT/2000/XP can easily be installed over a network. Part of installation is partitioning and formatting the hard drive, installing device drivers for all hardware, and configuring the system to meet user needs.

WHAT YOU **REALLY** NEED TO KNOW

- ◆ The Windows NT setup program is called Winnt.exe. There is no Setup.exe in Windows NT. Windows 2000 and XP have a Setup.exe program that runs if the CD is started using Autorun or if you boot from CD. Setup.exe calls Winnt32.exe. Winnt.exe must be used if starting setup from a DOS boot disk.

- ◆ Switches that can be added to the Windows 9x Setup command are Setup /D (don't use the existing version of Windows), Setup /IC (perform a clean boot—use this option if you suspect corrupted drivers are stalling the installation) and Setup /IN (do not set up the network).

- ◆ The Windows 9x FDISK command can create up to two partitions on the drive: one primary and one extended. The partition table is written at the very beginning of the hard drive and is 512 bytes (1 sector) long.

- ◆ A logical drive or volume is assigned a drive letter by FDISK. The drive must then be formatted before the logical drive or volume can be used. An extended partition can contain several logical drives.

- ◆ The primary partition contains only one logical drive (drive C:) and is called the active partition because it is bootable, and should be at least 150 MB for it to hold Windows 9x.

- ◆ The beginning of the partition table contains the master boot record (MBR) that BIOS executes when booting from the drive.

- ◆ Use FAT32 instead of FAT16 on the hard drive to eliminate as much slack as possible. Of course, this does not apply to Windows NT as Windows NT does not support FAT32. When using Windows NT/2000/XP, you may want to consider formatting with NTFS for better security but keep in mind that DOS and Windows 9x cannot access an NTFS partition.

- ◆ During the Windows 2000/XP installation, you will be asked to choose the partition to install to. You may use an existing partition or delete and recreate a partition or create a new partition from free space. At this time, you select the file system you wish to have the drive formatted with.

OBJECTIVES ON THE JOB

Knowing how to run the setup program is critical for OS installation. If you cannot boot from the installation CD, you must know how to boot from a floppy that has CD drivers installed and then run the correct setup program.

PRACTICE TEST QUESTIONS

1. What command do you use to eliminate the partition table as the source of a problem with a hard drive?
    a. FORMAT
    b. DISPLAY
    c. FDISK
    d. PARTITION

2. Which Windows setup option should you use when installing Windows 98 on a notebook?
    a. Typical
    b. Portable
    c. Notebook
    d. Custom

3. What is the command to begin installing Windows 9x?
    a. Install
    b. Setup
    c. Start
    d. Makeboot

4. After partitioning the hard drive using FDISK, the next step is to:
    a. low-level format the drive
    b. use the SYS C: command to make the hard drive bootable
    c. use FORMAT to format each logical drive
    d. enter the drive parameters in CMOS setup

5. When the FORMAT program is formatting the drive, how are bad sectors handled?
    a. FORMAT tests each sector and marks the sector as bad.
    b. FORMAT does not distinguish bad sectors from good sectors, but uses all just the same way.
    c. FORMAT reads bad sector information left on the sector by the low-level format program and records the sector as bad in the FAT.
    d. FORMAT reads bad sector information from the partition table and records that information in the FAT.

6. How many partitions can a hard drive have using Windows 9x?
    a. one primary and one extended partition
    b. one primary and up to three extended partitions
    c. one primary and up to two extended partitions
    d. two primary and one extended partition

7. How many logical drives can the primary partition contain?
    a. 1 to 8
    b. only 1
    c. 1 or 2
    d. none

2.1 Identify the procedures for installing Windows 9x/Me, Windows NT 4.0 Workstation, Windows 2000 Professional, and Windows XP, and bringing the operating system to a basic operational level.

INSTALLATION METHODS: BOOTABLE CD, BOOT FLOPPY, NETWORK INSTALLATION, AND DRIVE IMAGING • DEVICE DRIVER CONFIGURATION: LOAD DEFAULT DRIVERS AND FIND UPDATED DRIVERS

UNDERSTANDING THE OBJECTIVE

New computers with no disk installed will normally use a bootable CD but other options include using a boot floppy, installing from the network and using drive imaging which copies the hard disk image of a successful installation from one computer and copies it to another computer's hard disk.

WHAT YOU **REALLY** NEED TO KNOW

- Installing from a bootable CD is often the easiest method to install an OS but remember that you must have a CD-ROM drive that supports booting (most do) and a BIOS that can be set to boot from CD.
- If you cannot boot from CD, you need a boot floppy that loads CD-ROM drivers. Perhaps the easiest way to accomplish this is to create a Windows 9x startup disk.
- If you have many computers to install and not enough CDs or not all computers have CD drives, you can perform a network installation.
- To install from a network, either the computer must have an OS already installed that has network support or you must have a bootable floppy or CD that has network support installed. In either case, you boot the system, locate the shared folder on the network that contains the installation files and run the appropriate setup program.
- During installation, Windows will detect your hardware and install default drivers for the hardware it detects. It is a good idea to use the Windows Update utility after installation to install any new drivers that have been posted on the Microsoft Web site.
- If your hardware came with an installation disk, you can update the default drivers by using Device Manager. In Windows 2000/XP, right-click the device and select Update driver. In Windows 9x, right-click the device, select Properties, and select Update Driver from the Driver tab.
- When many similar computers must be installed with an OS, perhaps the most efficient method is to install the OS on one computer, configure all settings, install any common applications, and then create an image of the drive. That image can then be copied to all other computers that need the installation. Several programs are available to copy disk images including Norton Ghost, and PowerQuest's Drive Image.

OBJECTIVES ON THE JOB

A PC technician must know which method of installation to choose for the particular environment. A bootable CD is usually fine for just one or two computer installations but when there are several or dozens of computers to install, a network installation or a drive image may be the optimal install method.

PRACTICE TEST QUESTIONS

1. **What should you check if you cannot boot from the bootable Windows XP CD?**
   a. Make sure you did not put the CD in a CD burner.
   b. The CD must be inserted after the POST.
   c. Check the BIOS to be sure CD booting is enabled.
   d. Hit <CTRL><SHIFT> while starting the computer.

2. **What program should you have on your floppy disk when booting to floppy before running the setup program on the CD?**
   a. Format.com
   b. Install.exe
   c. Bootup.com
   d. Mscdex.exe

3. **What folder should you copy from the installation CD to a network server before doing a network installation for Windows 2000?**
   a. Windows
   b. Windows-NT
   c. I386
   d. Winnt

4. **After you install Windows 2000, you check Device Manager and find that your network card has an exclamation point symbol on it. To resolve this, you should:**
   a. Delete the device in Device Manager and reboot.
   b. Right-click the device and select Re-install.
   c. Double-click the device, go to the Update tab and select Driver.
   d. Nothing, there is no problem with the device.

5. **You have just finished installing Windows XP Professional. When you see the desktop, you notice that the colors are washed out and the icons are very big. You check the display settings and find that they are set to 640x480 resolution at 16 colors. You know your graphic card supports higher resolutions but you cannot change the settings. What is the most likely problem?**
   a. No problem, Windows XP cannot be run at higher resolutions.
   b. Your video card is probably damaged, replace it.
   c. You are using a PCI card and XP requires an AGP card.
   d. The standard VGA driver is installed—you need to install the correct driver.

6. **You boot to a floppy disk and begin the Windows 2000 installation from CD. The setup program complains that Himem.sys is required and is missing. What do you do?**
   a. Get a copy of Himem.sys and run it by typing Himem.sys at the command prompt.
   b. Edit the Config.sys file and add the line Device=A:\himem.sys.
   c. Edit the Autoexec.bat file and add the line Device=A:\himem.sys.
   d. Add Himem.sys to the Msdos.sys file.

7. **You need to create a set of startup floppy disks to install Windows NT 4.0, what command do you use from the installation CD?**
   a. makefloppy
   b. setup /f
   c. winnt /ox
   d. winnt /b

2.1 Identify the procedures for installing Windows 9x/Me, Windows NT 4.0 Workstation, Windows 2000 Professional, and Windows XP, and bringing the operating system to a basic operational level.

RESTORE USER DATA FILES (IF APPLICABLE) • IDENTIFY COMMON SYMPTOMS AND PROBLEMS

UNDERSTANDING THE OBJECTIVE

When a computer is upgraded with a new OS from a clean install, the disk is frequently wiped clean and all new applications are installed. In this case it is important to restore the original data files. In installations, it is important to know what can go wrong and how to resolve the problem.

WHAT YOU **REALLY** NEED TO KNOW

- ◆ Transferring user data and configuration files is a process that is painstaking when the new OS is Windows 9x, NT, or Windows 2000. You must know where all the data files and configuration files are stored and copy them to a server, a Zip drive, or a similar device and then you must copy them back to the location where the newly installed applications expect to find them.

- ◆ Because of the inherent difficulties with transferring user information from one OS to another, Microsoft created the **User State Migration Tool** in Windows XP to make the process much easier. A Wizard that runs the tool is called Files and Settings Transfer Wizard and can be found in Start/All Programs/Accessories/System Tools.

- ◆ The User State Migration Tool can transfer user files and settings from Windows 9x or Windows NT/2000/XP to a Windows XP computer. The Wizard is run in two locations: first on the new computer with Windows XP, and then on the old computer. Finally, you return to the new computer to transfer the files.

- ◆ There are two command line programs for using the User State Migration Tool: Scanstate copies the user information to a removable disk or server and Loadstate copies the saved information to the new computer with Windows XP.

- ◆ After installing Windows, you should go to Device Manager and see if any devices did not install correctly. A device that has an exclamation point on it indicates that there is a problem. Delete any non-functioning devices from Device Manager and reboot. The hardware detection wizard will recognize the device at boot up and you will be able to see what the problem is or install a new driver.

- ◆ Sometimes devices are not recognized correctly and will show up in Device Manager in a category called Other Devices. These devices will have a yellow question mark next to them. Try the same steps as outlined in the previous bullet to resolve the problem.

- ◆ Video cards are a frequent source of driver problem. If your video card is not recognized, either the standard VGA driver has been installed or you will not be able to view the video. In the latter case, start the computer in Safe Mode and install the manufacturer's video driver.

OBJECTIVES ON THE JOB

Knowing how to transfer user files and settings is a skill that user's will appreciate in a technician. In addition, if you want to avoid long nights, know how to resolve installation problems.

PRACTICE TEST QUESTIONS

1. What is the command line program to copy user data to a disk for later transfer to a new XP installation?
   a. loadstate
   b. scanstate
   c. userscan
   d. userload

2. What is the name of the tool for saving user preferences and data?
   a. System State Migration Tool
   b. User Preferences Backup
   c. User State Migration Tool
   d. System Preferences Backup

3. Where will you find devices in Device Manager that the installation program did not recognize?
   a. Unknown Devices
   b. Other Devices
   c. Problem Devices
   d. Device Ignored

4. You have just finished your installation of Windows 95 but when the computer restarts, you get an error that says "Invalid system disk: replace and press any key." What is the most likely cause of this?
   a. The MBR on the hard disk is corrupted.
   b. There is a floppy disk in the drive.
   c. The CD-ROM is corrupted.
   d. Boot.ini is damaged.

5. After you complete the Windows 2000 installation, your system reboots and you get the Windows 2000 setup program. What should you do?
   a. Change the BIOS settings to boot from the hard disk first.
   b. Remove the floppy disk.
   c. Reinstall Windows 2000.
   d. Reboot and try again.

6. What kind of data will not be migrated by the Files and Settings Transfer Wizard?
   a. Windows application settings
   b. Office documents
   c. MS-DOS application settings
   d. Mail settings

7. You have just completed a dual-boot installation of Windows XP and Windows 98 but every time the system starts, Windows XP is started after a few seconds if you don't choose Windows 98 from the menu. You prefer to have Windows 98 started automatically. How can you accomplish this?
   a. In Windows XP, go to Start/All Programs/Accessories/System Tools and choose BootMenu.
   b. In Windows 98, go to Start/Programs/Accessories/System Tools and choose BootMenu.
   c. In Windows XP, go to the System control panel, select the Advanced tab and click Settings under Startup and Recovery.
   d. In Windows 98, go to the System control panel, select the Advanced tab and click Settings under Startup and Recovery.

OBJECTIVES

2.2 Identify steps to perform an operating system upgrade from Windows 9.x/ME, Windows NT 4.0 Workstation, Windows 2000 Professional, and Windows XP. Given an upgrade scenario, choose the appropriate next steps.

UPGRADE PATHS AVAILABLE • DETERMINE CORRECT UPGRADE STARTUP UTILITY (E.G. WINNT32 VS WINNT)

UNDERSTANDING THE OBJECTIVE

When upgrading from one Windows operating system to another, an important decision is whether you will overwrite the existing OS (clean install) or if you will upgrade the existing OS (upgrade). If you choose to upgrade, the system configuration, device drivers, and applications will carry forward to the new installation. If you do a clean install, you must start fresh and install all device drivers and applications from the ground up. Perform a clean install if the existing OS is corrupted.

WHAT YOU **REALLY** NEED TO KNOW

- Before upgrading from Windows 9x to Windows NT or Windows 2000, check that all hardware and applications on the system are compatible, as Windows NT and Windows 2000 do not support all legacy hardware and software.

- To upgrade from Windows 9x to Windows 2000, insert the Windows 2000 CD in the drive. If your PC does not automatically recognize the CD, click Start, Run, and enter this command: D:\i386\winnt32.exe. Select the option to upgrade on the opening menu.

- To perform a **clean install** of Windows 2000 when Windows 9x is the current OS, on the opening Windows 2000 setup menu, select the option, "Install a new copy of Windows 2000 (Clean Install)."

- When upgrading from Windows NT to Windows 2000, be aware that the NTFS file system on Windows 2000 (NTFS5) is not compatible with the NTFS file system used by Windows NT (NTFS4). For that reason, using a dual boot between Windows NT and Windows 2000 is not recommended.

- For a dual boot system, use a file system that is compatible with both operating systems. Windows 2000 requires that a second OS be installed in a different partition than the one holding Windows 2000.

- When installing Windows 9x from a CD, CD-ROM drivers must be available. The Windows 9x upgrade expects the CD-ROM drivers to already be loaded. You can load these from the DOS bootable disk in real mode.

- During a Windows 9x installation, Setup records information in the following log files: Setuplog.txt records how far Setup got in the installation, Detlog.txt records hardware detected, Detcrash.log is a binary file that helps Setup recover from a failed installation due to a hardware problem, Netlog.txt records problems with network setup, and Bootlog.txt records problems during the boot.

- Executable files that perform the Windows 9x installation are Setup.exe, Winit.exe, and Grpconv.exe. Windows 98 and Windows 2000 have an upgrade CD and a new install CD. The cost for each is different. An upgrade CD requires that a previous OS be installed.

OBJECTIVES ON THE JOB

Installing an operating system is a typical task expected of a PC technician. Know how to do this in a variety of situations.

PRACTICE TEST QUESTIONS

1. **During a Windows 98 upgrade, Vmm32.vxd is built specifically for this PC. Why is that so?**
   a. because each PC has a different serial number that is recorded in this file
   b. because Vmm32.vxd contains the serial number for this specific Windows 98 license
   c. because Vmm32.vxd contains drivers for devices specific to this hardware system
   d. because Vmm32.vxd contains user preferences specific for this installation

2. **What is the purpose of the Windows 95 Setup option "Portable"?**
   a. The installation can be ported from one computer platform to another.
   b. The installation is for notebook computers and includes utilities for remote computing.
   c. The installation requires minimum user interaction.
   d. This minimum installation requires little hard drive space.

3. **To create a dual boot between Windows 2000 and Windows 98, which file system should be used?**
   a. NTFS
   b. FAT16
   c. FAT32
   d. FAT12

4. **The name of the setup program to install Windows NT is:**
   a. Setup.com
   b. Setup.exe
   c. Winnt.exe
   d. Install.exe

5. **Which operating system requires it be the only OS installed on a partition?**
   a. Windows 95
   b. Windows 98
   c. Windows NT
   d. Windows 2000

6. **What is the purpose of the program Mscdex.exe?**
   a. It is used as an installation support program when installing Windows 95.
   b. It is a DOS extension that supports CD-ROM drives.
   c. It is a universal CD-ROM driver that works with any CD-ROM.
   d. It is part of the Windows 95 kernel.

7. **What are the four options for a Windows NT installation?**
   a. Typical, Portable, Express, Custom
   b. Typical, Portable, Compact, Custom
   c. Typical, Compact, Express, Custom
   d. Typical, Express, Custom, Extensive

2.2 Identify steps to perform an operating system upgrade from Windows 9.x/ME, Windows NT 4.0 Workstation, Windows 2000 Professional, and Windows XP. Given an upgrade scenario, choose the appropriate next steps.

VERIFY HARDWARE COMPATIBILITY AND MINIMUM REQUIREMENTS • VERIFY APPLICATION COMPATIBILITY • APPLY OS SERVICE PACKS, PATCHES, AND UPDATES • INSTALL ADDITIONAL WINDOWS COMPONENTS

UNDERSTANDING THE OBJECTIVE

Before upgrading to a new OS, it is wise to check that the hardware meets the minimum system requirements for that OS. After installation is complete, the first thing to do is check for service packs, patches, and updates on the OS vendor Web site. These will help make the system more stable and will protect from security holes.

WHAT YOU **REALLY** NEED TO KNOW

- ◆ Before upgrading to Windows 2000 or Windows XP, you should run an upgrade analyzer. You can do this by running x:\i386\winnt32 /checkupgradeonly where x is the CD-ROM drive. This program will run a report and verify which hardware is incompatible and which applications may need to be reinstalled.
- ◆ If you are upgrading from Windows NT to Windows 2000 or XP, you should be aware that antivirus software and third-party network software should be removed before upgrading.
- ◆ Upgrading from Windows 9x to Windows NT is not permitted and upgrading from Windows 9x to Windows 2000 or XP, while possible may have problems due to registry incompatibilities. It is best to do a clean install when upgrading from Windows 9x.
- ◆ Not all software that was installed in Windows 9x will run correctly after upgrading to Windows 2000 or XP. This is due to the fact that some applications may rely on APIs specific to Windows 98.
- ◆ If you are upgrading from Windows 9x to Windows 2000/XP and wish to utilize the NTFS file system, you can convert to NTFS using the *convert c:\ /fs:ntfs* command.
- ◆ After upgrading, use the Windows Update program to get the latest service packs and patches as well as driver updates for the new OS. In Windows XP, go to Start/Help and Support and then choose "Keep your computer up to date with Windows Update" under Pick a Task. In Windows 2000, go to Start/Windows Update.
- ◆ After the installation, you may want additional Windows components installed. To do this go to Start/Control Panel/Add Remove Programs and then select Add/Remove Windows Components.
- ◆ To turn Windows 2000 or Windows XP into a Web server, use Add/Remove Windows Components and install Internet Information Services (IIS).
- ◆ To allow Unix computers to print to printers on the Windows 2000 or XP computer, you can add Unix Print Services from Add/Remove Windows Components.

OBJECTIVES ON THE JOB

Just as it is important for a technician to know the tasks needed to complete before an installation, it is just as important to know what to do after a successful installation. Failing to install service packs and patches leaves the computer open to failures due to bugs and security holes.

PRACTICE TEST QUESTIONS

1. Which is the correct command to analyze a computer before performing a Windows 2000 or XP upgrade?
   a. winnt /analyze
   b. winnt32 /analyze
   c. winnt32 /checkupgradeonly
   d. winnt /checkupgradeonly

2. You have just upgraded to Windows 2000 from Windows 95 and you want to defragment your disk. When you try to run your third-party defragmentation program, you receive an error. What is the most likely reason for this?
   a. Your disk is not fragmented.
   b. Your disk is too fragmented.
   c. The program accesses hardware directly.
   d. The program is corrupted.

3. You want to upgrade from Windows 95 OSR2 computer to Windows NT. Your primary partition is 6GB and your extended partition is 8GB. Before starting you reformat both partitions. Windows NT will not install. What is the likely problem?
   a. Your Windows NT installation disks are corrupt.
   b. Windows NT detected the previous Windows 95 installation and will not permit the upgrade.
   c. The BIOS needs to be updated.
   d. The drives are formatted FAT32.

4. How do you run the Windows Update program from Windows XP?
   a. Start/Run and type Update
   b. Start/Help and Support and click the Windows Update link
   c. Start/Program/Accessories/System Tools/Windows Update
   d. Both b and c

5. From Windows 2000, how do you run the Windows Update program?
   a. Start/Windows Update
   b. Start/Help and Support and click the Windows Update link
   c. Start/Program/Accessories/System Tools/Windows Update
   d. Both a and c

6. You want to do a clean install upgrade from Windows 95 to Windows XP and you have a DOS-based program that you want to continue to run. The manufacturer says the program will run in Windows XP fine. Once the installation is complete, you don't see the icon to run the program. What do you do?
   a. Call the manufacturer for technical support.
   b. Create a shortcut to the executable file on the desktop.
   c. Delete the application and reinstall it.
   d. Reinstall Windows XP and select "Migrate DOS Programs."

7. You are running Windows NT 4.0 with Service Pack 4. You just installed some new networking components and now none of the networking is working. What might solve this problem?
   a. Remove the new networking components.
   b. Reinstall Windows NT.
   c. Run Windows Update.
   d. Reinstall Service Pack 4.

2.3 Identify the basic system boot sequences and boot methods, including the steps to create an emergency boot disk with utilities installed for Windows 9x/Me, Windows NT 4.0 Workstation, Windows 2000 Professional, and Windows XP.

BOOT SEQUENCE: FILES REQUIRED TO BOOT AND BOOT STEPS (9.X, NT-BASED) • ALTERNATIVE BOOT METHODS: LAST KNOWN GOOD CONFIGURATION, COMMAND PROMPT MODE, BOOTING TO A SYSTEM RESTORE POINT, RECOVERY CONSOLE, BOOT.INI SWITCHES, AND DUAL BOOT

UNDERSTANDING THE OBJECTIVE

Know the files required to boot each OS and the part each of these files plays in the boot process. Also, you must know the troubleshooting boot modes in case the OS does not boot.

WHAT YOU **REALLY** NEED TO KNOW

- ◆ These files are needed in this order for a DOS boot: Io.sys, Msdos.sys, Config.sys (optional), Command.com, and Autoexec.bat (optional).
- ◆ To step through the Config.sys and Autoexec.bat files one line at a time during a DOS boot press F8 when DOS begins to boot. To bypass the Config.sys and Autoexec.bat files, press F5 when DOS begins to boot.
- ◆ These are the files required in the Windows 9x boot sequence up to the point that Windows 9x switches to protected mode: Io.sys, which checks the contents of Config.sys (optional), Msdos.sys, Command.com, Autoexec.bat (optional), Win.com, and Vmm32.vxd.
- ◆ To boot into Windows 9x Safe Mode, hit the F5 key during boot up; to get a boot menu, press the F8 key. From the boot menu, you can select a normal, logged, safe mode, step-by-step, command prompt, or safe mode command prompt boot method.
- ◆ Files needed to boot Windows NT, Windows 2000, and Windows XP:
  - Ntldr—NT loader is the first file started by the PC BIOS after it completes the POST
  - Boot.ini—text file with boot switches; tells Ntldr where the Windows system files are located
  - Bootsect.dos—only used when the system has a dual boot with Windows 9x
  - Ntdetect.com—detects hardware and loads drivers; started by Ntldr
  - Ntbootdd.sys—only needed when booting from a SCSI device
  - Ntoskrnl.exe and Hal.dll—kernel components; started by Ntldr; now Ntoskrnl takes control
- ◆ Hitting F8 during Windows 2000/XP boot displays a boot menu. The Last Known Good Configuration option will attempt to start the computer with a copy of the registry that was used the last time the system booted successfully. VGA mode will start Windows with a standard VGA driver.
- ◆ A System Restore Point is created when major changes are made such as the addition of new components or large applications are installed. This utility saves registry settings and some system files. If you boot into Safe Mode, Windows XP asks if you want to do a System Restore or you can perform one manually.
- ◆ Recovery console can be run by booting to the Windows 2000/XP installation CD and selecting R to repair and then C to go to the Recovery Console.

OBJECTIVES ON THE JOB

A PC technician is expected to understand and be able to troubleshoot the process of loading an OS.

PRACTICE TEST QUESTIONS

1. Which Windows 2000 system file is required to boot only when booting from a SCSI device?
   a. Ntldr
   b. Ntdetect.com
   c. Ntbootdd.sys
   d. Ntoskrnl.exe

2. What is the correct boot sequence using DOS?
   a. Io.sys, Config.sys, Msdos.sys
   b. Io.sys, Msdos.sys, Config.sys
   c. Io.sys, Autoexec.bat, Config.sys
   d. Autoexec.bat, Config.sys, Command.com

3. Which Windows 9x component is responsible for loading static device drivers?
   a. Kernel32.dll
   b. Vmm32.vxd
   c. Io.sys
   d. Gdi.exe

4. Which Windows 2000 component is part of the kernel?
   a. Ntldr
   b. Boot.ini
   c. Hal.dll
   d. System

5. Where can installed device drivers be listed so they are loaded when Windows 98 loads?
   a. the registry
   b. System.ini
   c. Config.sys
   d. all the above

6. What are the three core components of Windows 9x?
   a. Kernel, GDI, Windows Explorer
   b. Kernel, GDI, User
   c. Command.com, Io.sys, and Msdos.sys
   d. Win.com, the registry, and Windows Explorer

7. What switch can you add to a Boot.ini entry to force a standard VGA driver to be loaded instead of the specific driver for your video card?
   a. /SOS
   b. /DEBUGMODE
   c. /VGA
   d. /BASEVIDEO

2.3 Identify the basic system boot sequences and boot methods, including the steps to create an emergency boot disk with utilities installed for Windows 9x/Me, Windows NT 4.0 Workstation, Windows 2000 Professional, and Windows XP.

ALTERNATIVE BOOT METHODS: USING A STARTUP DISK AND SAFE/VGA-ONLY MODE • CREATING EMERGENCY DISKS WITH OS UTILITIES • CREATING EMERGENCY REPAIR DISK (ERD)

UNDERSTANDING THE OBJECTIVE

An emergency boot disk is essential in a troubleshooting situation. The boot disk must be created before the problem occurs and is specific to the operating system installed. In addition, you must know how to use the troubleshooting boot methods.

WHAT YOU **REALLY** NEED TO KNOW

◆ When installing a new OS, make **emergency startup disks** when prompted to do so. These disks can later be used to recover from a failed installation.

◆ A startup disk contains the software necessary to boot the OS. For Windows 9x, go to Control Panel and select Add/Remove Programs and select the Startup Disk tab. This boot floppy will contain CD-ROM drivers.

◆ Files on a Windows 9x emergency startup disk differ depending on the version of Windows installed. A typical group of files on the disk include Attrib.exe, Chkdsk.exe, Edit.com, Fc.exe, Fdisk.exe, Format.com, Mem.exe, More.com, Mscdex.exe, Msd.exe, Scandisk.exe, Setver.exe, Sys.com, and Xcopy.exe. Know the purpose of each file.

◆ The Windows 98 emergency startup disk contains a cabinet file, Extract.exe (a utility program needed to manage the cabinet file), and drivers necessary to access a CD-ROM drive.

◆ Windows 9x will automatically boot to Safe Mode when a previous boot attempt did not succeed, or you can manually go to safe mode by hitting F5 or F8 when Windows begins to boot. Safe Mode does not execute registry entries, Config.sys, Autoexec.bat, or the [Boot] and [386Enh] sections of System.ini. Network support is disabled in Safe Mode unless you choose Safe Mode with Networking from the F8 boot menu.

◆ Safe mode Command Prompt Only will not execute the Windows GUI and will not run the commands in Config.sys and Autoexec.bat.

◆ Windows NT has three disks that together can boot a system. Create these disks using this command entered in the Run dialog box: D:\i386\winnt32.exe /ox, where D: is the CD-ROM drive with the Windows NT CD.

◆ Create an emergency repair disk (ERD) for Windows NT using this command: C:\Winnt\System32\rdisk.exe /s. For Windows 2000, use the Backup program and go to the Tools menu or the Welcome tab. The ERD contains information specific to the system configuration. Update the disk after you have installed new hardware. The disk contains a backup of the registry. Windows XP replaces the ERD with the Automated System Recovery.

◆ Windows 2000 uses four disks to boot from floppies. Create the four disks using this command: D:\bootdisk\makeboot.exe A:, where D: is the CD-ROM drive containing the Windows 2000 CD. There are not floppy boot disk options for Windows XP.

OBJECTIVES ON THE JOB

A PC technician should never be without an emergency startup disk. Be sure to run a current version of antivirus software against the disk before using it on a customer's PC to be certain you don't spread a virus while troubleshooting.

PRACTICE TEST QUESTIONS

1. **To create an emergency startup disk in Windows 95:**
   a. use the System icon in Control Panel
   b. use the Add/Remove Programs icon in Control Panel
   c. use the Utilities icon in Control Panel
   d. use Explorer

2. **To go directly to Safe Mode when booting Windows 9x, press:**
   a. F8
   b. F1
   c. <CTRL><SHIFT>
   d. F5

3. **The Mscdex.exe file on the Windows 9x startup disk is used for:**
   a. system debugging
   b. providing access to the CD-ROM drive
   c. executing Microsoft Change Directory
   d. running an advanced Windows editor

4. **What command is used to manage cabinet files?**
   a. Fc.exe
   b. Edit.com
   c. Setup.exe
   d. Extract.exe

5. **What is the program used by Windows 2000 to create a set of startup disks?**
   a. Startup.exe
   b. Makeboot.exe
   c. Winnt32.exe
   d. Rdisk.exe

6. **What troubleshooting feature is available in Windows 2000 and Windows NT but not in Windows XP?**
   a. Recovery Console
   b. Automated System Recovery
   c. Emergency Repair Disk
   d. Scanreg

7. **What boot mode disables networking support?**
   a. Safe Mode
   b. Safe Mode Command Prompt Only
   c. Command Prompt Only
   d. All of the the above

2.4 Identify procedures for installing/adding a device, including loading, adding, and configuring device drivers, and required software.

DEVICE DRIVER INSTALLATION: PLUG AND PLAY (PNP) AND NON-PNP DEVICES, INSTALL AND CONFIGURE DEVICE DRIVERS, AND INSTALL DIFFERENT DEVICE DRIVERS

UNDERSTANDING THE OBJECTIVE

Plug and Play helps automate the process of installing new hardware devices. The OS, the system BIOS, and the device must all support Plug and Play.

WHAT YOU **REALLY** NEED TO KNOW

- ◆ Windows 9x , Windows 2000, and Windows XP support **Plug and Play**, but Windows NT does not.
- ◆ Most system BIOS produced after 1994 support Plug and Play.
- ◆ A device that is Plug and Play compliant includes text such as "Windows 98 Ready" on the box or in the documentation.
- ◆ To install a device driver when a new hardware device is installed, choose Start, Settings, Control Panel, and Add New Hardware. Often, this step is unusual because Windows Plug and Play will usually detect a Plug and Play device when the system boots after installing new hardware, but if the system does not detect the device or the device is not Plug and Play, follow those steps.
- ◆ To change a device driver for a device, open the Properties dialog box for the device in Device Manager and select Drive, and then Update Driver. The Update Device Driver Wizard steps you through the process. In Windows XP, you can simply right-click the device and select Update Driver.
- ◆ During the Windows 9x load process, Vmm32.vxd creates virtual machines, loads static Virtual Device Drivers (VxD drivers) named in the Windows registry and System.ini and shifts the OS to protected mode.
- ◆ Static VxDs are device drivers that remain in memory while Windows 9x is running.
- ◆ Dynamic VxDs are 32-bit protected mode device drivers that Plug and Play devices require.
- ◆ The following is a summary of the two kinds of device drivers in Windows 9x and when and how to use them:

	16-bit Device Drivers	32-bit Device Drivers
Operating Mode	Real mode	Protected mode
Use of memory	May use upper memory addresses	Stored in extended memory
How loaded	Loaded by a DEVICE= line in Config.sys at startup	Automatically loaded by Windows 9x
How changed	Edit the Config.sys file	From Device Manager, select the device and use Properties, Device tab
How to identify the type	In Device Manager, look for an exclamation point beside the device name	Look for no exclamation point beside the device name in Device Manager. Also, "32" is typically included in the driver filename.
When to use this type	Use a 16-bit driver under Windows only when a 32-bit driver is not available	When you can, always use 32-bit drivers. They are faster.

OBJECTIVES ON THE JOB

When upgrading to Windows 9x from DOS, make every effort to convert all 16-bit drivers to 32-bit versions. If Windows 9x does not support a device, check the device manufacturer Web site for a 32-bit version of the driver.

PRACTICE TEST QUESTIONS

1. **Which operating system supports Plug and Play?**
   a. DOS
   b. Windows NT
   c. Windows XP
   d. UNIX

2. **In order for a system to be fully Plug and Play compliant, what must be true?**
   a. The BIOS, operating system, and devices must be Plug and Play.
   b. The operating system and devices must be Plug and Play.
   c. The operating system, device drivers, and devices must be Plug and Play.
   d. The operating system and application software must be Plug and Play.

3. **A 16-bit device driver is loaded from:**
   a. Config.sys
   b. the registry
   c. Plug and Play configuration information in Device Manager
   d. Autoexec.bat

4. **One advantage a 32-bit driver has over a 16-bit driver is that the 32-bit driver:**
   a. can easily be disabled by commenting out the line in Config.sys
   b. can be stored in upper memory
   c. can be stored in extended memory
   d. does not require as much memory

5. **Using Windows 9x, where do you look to find the name of a 32-bit device driver used by a device?**
   a. the Properties dialog box for the device under Device Manager
   b. the device driver name in System.ini
   c. the device driver name in the Windows 95 registry
   d. in Config.sys for the driver name

6. **You have just installed a new sound card in your Pentium 4 system that runs Windows NT. When your system boots, you find that the sound card was not recognized by the system. What is the likely problem?**
   a. The sound card is not Plug and Play compatible.
   b. The BIOS is not Plug and Play compatible.
   c. There is no virtual device driver.
   d. Windows NT is not Plug and Play compatible.

7. **You cannot locate your CD-ROM drive in My Computer but you can access the driver letter assigned to the CD-ROM. What is the likely reason for this?**
   a. My Computer is corrupted and must be refreshed.
   b. A Real Mode CD-ROM driver was installed from Config.sys.
   c. A 32-bit CD-ROM driver was installed from Config.sys.
   d. The Mscdex.exe program is not loaded.

2.4 Identify procedures for installing/adding a device, including loading, adding, and configuring device drivers, and required software.

DEVICE DRIVER INSTALLATION: MANUALLY INSTALL A DEVICE DRIVER, SEARCH THE INTERNET FOR UPDATED DEVICE DRIVERS, AND USING UNSIGNED DRIVERS (DRIVER SIGNING)

UNDERSTANDING THE OBJECTIVE

Sometimes a driver must be manually installed either because the system or device is not Plug and Play, or the Plug and Play feature failed for some reason. Also, device drivers that come with Windows or that are packaged with a device are frequently old and must be updated through an Internet download and finally, Windows has developed a procedure called driver signing that indicates whether a driver has been tested with the OS or not.

WHAT YOU **REALLY** NEED TO KNOW

◆ If a device is not recognized by Windows after it is installed, you may need to manually install the driver. This may entail using the Add Hardware Wizard found in Control Panel, or running a setup program provided by the manufacturer of the device.

◆ To manually install a device driver, run the Add Hardware Wizard from Control Panel. When you run the Wizard, it searches for new hardware. If the hardware is not found, you can select to Add a new Hardware Device and manually select the hardware you wish to install. You will need a floppy disk or CD-ROM with the driver on it if you cannot find the driver from the manufacturer's list presented by the wizard.

◆ If you need to update a driver because the current driver is not compatible or has problems, the best place to look is on the Internet. Manufacturers usually post the most updated driver for their products on their Web site.

◆ If you download a new driver from the Internet, make a note of where you saved it. Usually the drivers will be stored in a compressed format and you will need to run a package such as WinZip to uncompress the files. Or the drivers may be in an .exe file that is self-uncompressing. In any case, after the driver is uncompressed, use the Update Driver wizard from Device Manager and specify the driver location when prompted.

◆ If a device never installed properly, sometimes the best method to update the driver is to delete the device from Device Manager and reboot the system. When the Found New Hardware wizard begins, you can choose to provide a driver manually and specify the driver location.

◆ If a driver is signed, the driver has been tested for compatibility with Windows and contains a digital signature. An unsigned driver may still work properly but it is best to periodically check for a new driver that is signed to avoid system stability problems. Windows Update will check for new drivers or you can check with the Manufacturer's Web site.

◆ If you install a hardware device that does not have a digital signature, you can either continue with the installation or choose not to install the driver. If you do not install the driver, you should remove the device until you have a digitally signed driver so that Windows does not find the device each time the system boots.

OBJECTIVES ON THE JOB

Maintaining current device drivers is a critical task for a technician. Outdated drivers can cause intermittent system problems that are hard to track down. Using digitally signed drivers provides a comfort level that the driver is reliable.

PRACTICE TEST QUESTIONS

1. Manual installation of a driver can occur using:
   a. floppy disk
   b. CD-ROM
   c. hard disk
   d. all of the above

2. What does it mean if you manually install a driver and a message pops up and says that the driver does not have a digital signature from Microsoft?
   a. The driver will not work.
   b. The driver probably has a virus.
   c. The driver may work but has not been tested for compatibility.
   d. The driver is fine and has been tested for compatibility.

3. If a driver is not Plug and Play compatible and has been manually installed through System.ini, the driver is referred to as a:
   a. Digitally signed driver
   b. Legacy driver
   c. Incompatible driver
   d. Protected mode driver

4. How can drivers be installed manually in Windows 9x?
   a. add New Hardware
   b. Config.sys
   c. System.ini
   d. all of the above

5. The way to install a driver using Config.sys is:
   a. Use a Protected Mode driver and include the line DEVICE=drivername.
   b. Use a Protected Mode driver and include the line DRIVER=drivername.
   c. Use a Real Mode driver and include the line DEVICE=drivername.
   d. Use a Real Mode driver and include the line DRIVER=drivername.

6. When you manually update a driver in Windows XP using Device Manager, which of the following are choices? (choose all that apply)
   a. Search removable media
   b. Search the Internet
   c. Don't Search. I will choose the driver to install.
   d. Search URL

7. You have just discovered that a new driver is available for your video card. You are running Windows XP. How should you install the new driver?
   a. Download the driver and copy it over the old one.
   b. Reboot the system to Maintenance Mode and install the new driver.
   c. Right-click the device in Device Manager and select Update Driver.
   d. Reinstall Windows and select Custom Install—have a floppy disk ready with the new driver.

OBJECTIVES

2.4 Identify procedures for installing/adding a device, including loading, adding, and configuring device drivers, and required software.

INSTALL ADDITIONAL WINDOWS COMPONENTS • DETERMINE IF PERMISSIONS ARE ADEQUATE FOR PERFORMING THE TASK

UNDERSTANDING THE OBJECTIVE

After a successful Windows installation, you may need to install additional Windows components to provide added functionality, or you may choose to remove Windows components. In Windows 9x, any user can install drivers and software but Windows NT/2000/XP requires that the user have administrator rights to perform these tasks.

WHAT YOU **REALLY** NEED TO KNOW

◆ To install or remove Windows 2000 or Windows XP components, go to Control Panel/Add or Remove Programs and then select Add/Remove Windows Components.

◆ To install or remove Windows 9x components, go to Control Panel/Add/Remove Programs, and select the Windows Setup tab.

◆ In the Add/Remove Windows Components Wizard, you will see a list of components to choose from. Component categories that have a white box are not installed, categories that have a check in a white box are installed, and categories that have a check in a gray box are partially installed.

◆ To see the individual components that can be selected for each category, select the category and click the Details button. There, you can check individual components for a category.

◆ To delete a Windows component, use the Add/Remove Windows Components Wizard and uncheck the box next to the component. If there is more than one component for a category, click Details and uncheck individual components if desired.

◆ Not all tasks in Windows can be performed by regular users. Windows NT/2000/XP requires that a user belong to the Administrator group to perform tasks that involve changing Windows components, or changing device drivers.

◆ A user that belongs to the Power Users group can install applications but cannot change device drivers or add or remove devices.

◆ A user that belongs to the Users group cannot install applications or perform any other task related to hardware, device drivers, or Windows components.

OBJECTIVES ON THE JOB

A computer technician must know how to make necessary changes in the Windows operating environment in order to fulfill the needs of users. Therefore, it is critical that a technician who is expected to troubleshoot, diagnose, and resolve problems, has adequate permissions to do so on each computer for which he or she is responsible.

PRACTICE TEST QUESTIONS

1. **A user calls you at lunch the day after you upgrade his computer from Windows 95 to Windows 98 and complains that he cannot find the Solitaire game. How can you resolve his problem?**
   a. Tell him the Games folder moved to the Start/Programs/Entertainment folder.
   b. Take the Windows 98 installation CD and reinstall Windows 98 with the All Components option selected.
   c. Go to Add/Remove Programs/Windows Setup tab and choose the Accessories category, hit Details and click the Games checkbox.
   d. Tell him Games have been removed from Windows 98.

2. **You are running Windows XP and want to install FTP services which are located in the IIS category of Add/Remove Windows Components. You see that the box next to IIS is already checked but you cannot find the FTP service on your computer. What can be the problem?**
   a. FTP is not part of the IIS services category.
   b. The checkbox is gray, indicating not all components in the IIS category are installed.
   c. You don't have privileges to install FTP services.
   d. You must reboot your computer to access FTP services.

3. **A user running Windows 2000 calls you because his sound card is not working. When you get to his computer, you go to the Device Manager, choose the device properties and go to the Driver tab so you can update the driver, but you don't find an Update Driver button. What is the problem?**
   a. Sound cards don't use drivers.
   b. You have to log on to the computer with Administrative privileges.
   c. The Update Driver button is not located on the Driver tab.
   d. The device is probably damaged.

4. **How can you install the Indexing Service in Windows XP?**
   a. go to Add or Remove Programs, select Add/Remove Windows Components
   b. go to Add/Remove Programs, select the Windows Setup tab
   c. run Indsetup from Start/Run
   d. the Indexing Service is only found on Windows 2000 Server

5. **You try to install the Paint program in Windows XP but cannot run the Add/Remove Windows Components Wizard. What should you do?**
   a. Paint cannot be installed from Add/Remove Windows Components.
   b. Paint is always installed in Windows and therefore should not have to be installed.
   c. You should log on with a different user account.
   d. Windows XP does not have that wizard.

6. **You want to install a new spreadsheet program on your computer, where should you go?**
   a. Add or Remove Programs/Add/Remove Windows Components
   b. Add or Remove Programs/Add New Programs
   c. Start/Run and type C:\Windows\Install
   d. Add or Remove Programs/Change or Remove Programs

7. **In Windows XP, how can you easily change the default Java virtual machine?**
   a. Start/Run and type chgdefaults
   b. right-click the JVM and select Use as Default
   c. Add or Remove Programs/Set Program Access and Defaults
   d. you cannot change the default Java virtual machine

2.5 Identify procedures necessary to optimize the operating system and major operating system subsystems.

VIRTUAL MEMORY MANAGEMENT • DISK DEFRAGMENTATION • FILES AND BUFFERS • CACHES • TEMPORARY FILE MANAGEMENT

UNDERSTANDING THE OBJECTIVE

Once the OS is installed, a technician's job is not complete. Very often, there are additional tasks to perform in order to optimize system performance such as adjusting virtual memory, defragmenting disks, and optimizing caches and buffers.

WHAT YOU **REALLY** NEED TO KNOW

- ◆ In Windows 9x, you access the Virtual Memory Manager from the System control panel and then select the Performance tab and click the Virtual Memory button.
- ◆ Windows 9x offers three primary settings for virtual memory: Let Windows manage my virtual memory settings, Let me specify my own virtual memory settings, and Disable virtual memory. The first option is recommended because incorrect settings could seriously degrade system performance.
- ◆ If you specify your own virtual memory settings, you can specify a permanent size for the swap file which will prevent Windows from resizing the file which can impact performance. You can also specify the location of the swap file which you may choose to do in order to free up disk space on the C: drive.
- ◆ To specify a permanent swap file that will not change in size, set the minimum and maximum file size to the same value which should be about 2.5 times the amount of physical memory you have.
- ◆ To manage virtual memory in Windows 2000, go to the System control panel, select the Advanced tab and click the Performance Options button. In Windows XP, click the Settings button in the Performance section of the Advanced tab of the System control panel.
- ◆ You can specify more than one location for the paging file in Windows NT/2000/XP. It is usually a good idea to place the paging file on a separate disk from the Windows system files if possible to increase performance.
- ◆ If available, place the Windows NT/2000/XP paging file on a disk stripe set to get optimal performance from your virtual memory.
- ◆ Be aware that Windows must have at least 5 MB of free hard disk space to operate properly so do not create a paging file so big that you go below that amount. If you are running out of disk space on the volume that the paging file is, you can move the paging file to another disk or partition.
- ◆ File fragmentation slows access to files on the hard drive because the drive heads must move more to read and write all of the fragments.
- ◆ The number of files and buffers can be specified in Config.sys for DOS or Windows 9x. The FILES=n command specifies the number of open files possible and BUFFERS=n specifies the number of memory areas reserved for transferring data between devices.
- ◆ A cache is a dynamic, usually high-speed storage area for data that is being transferred from one place to another. Hard disks use cache memory to speed the access to files. Cache is not something you can usually adjust as Windows 9x and Windows 2000/XP have disk caching built in. DOS uses SMARTDrive for disk caching, which is loaded by Autoexec.bat.

OBJECTIVES ON THE JOB

Optimizing the system is a frequent task for technicians, particularly when working with older systems with slower processors and less memory. Usually, the default settings are okay when a system is new but the settings may require tweaking as the system ages.

PRACTICE TEST QUESTIONS

1. **Virtual memory: (select all that apply)**
   a. cannot be changed
   b. enhances system performance
   c. is a new feature in Windows 2000 and Windows XP
   d. uses hard drive space to augment physical memory

2. **In Windows 9x, the swap file is called:**
   a. Pagefile.sys
   b. Swap.386
   c. Win386.swp
   d. Win.swp

3. **The swap file for Windows 2000 is located by default at:**
   a. C:\WINNT\Pagefile.sys
   b. C:\WINNT\SYSTEM32\Win2k.swp
   c. C:\Win2k.swp
   d. C:\Pagefile.sys

4. **The options for specifying the paging file in Windows XP include: (select all that apply)**
   a. No paging file
   b. Custom size
   c. System managed size
   d. Set for optimum performance

5. **The best place to put the Windows XP paging file for performance is:**
   a. on the same partition that the system boots from
   b. on a different partition but the same disk
   c. on a different disk
   d. on a server

6. **You get an error when you run a DOS database program that says "Too Many Open Files," what can you do?**
   a. Change the BUFFERS= command in Config.sys.
   b. Change the BUFFERS= command in Autoexec.bat.
   c. Change the FILES= command in Autoexec.bat.
   d. Change the FILES= command in Config.sys.

7. **The optimum size of the paging file in Windows 9x for best performance is:**
   a. 2.5 times physical RAM
   b. 100 MB
   c. 2.5 MB
   d. .5 times physical RAM

3.1 Recognize and interpret the meaning of common error codes and startup messages from the boot sequence, and identify steps to correct the problems.

COMMON ERROR MESSAGES AND CODES: BOOT FAILURE AND ERRORS (INVALID BOOT DISK, INACCESSIBLE BOOT DEVICE, MISSING NTLDR, AND BAD OR MISSING COMMAND INTERPRETER)

UNDERSTANDING THE OBJECTIVE

When an OS does not boot, very often an error message can help point the way to what went wrong. Startup errors can be caused by a number of things from having a disk in the floppy drive to inadvertently deleted or corrupted files.

WHAT YOU **REALLY** NEED TO KNOW

- ◆ The "Invalid system disk" message can occur from the system trying to boot from an unbootable floppy disk or from a hard drive that has not been made bootable.

- ◆ To restore system boot files on a DOS or Windows 9x computer, boot to a floppy disk that has the SYS command and type SYS C:. This will restore the Io.sys, Msdos.sys, and Command.com files and write the master boot record.

- ◆ An "Inaccessible Boot Device" message can occur when trying to install Windows NT/2000/XP, and the mass storage controller you are using is not on the HCL or is not recognized. This problem can be resolved by pressing F6 during setup and supplying the appropriate driver.

- ◆ The "Bad or missing command interpreter" error message can be fixed by copying Command.com to the root of the boot disk (usually the C: drive). Config.sys can specify an alternate location for Command.com using the COMSPEC command. Check Config.sys and make sure Command.com is in the specified path.

- ◆ The error message Missing Ntldr can be caused by a couple of things. If you have a disk in the floppy drive that was formatted with Windows NT/2000/XP, the boot record on the disk specifies that Ntldr should be loaded. Unless Ntldr is on the floppy disk, the message will appear.

- ◆ Missing Ntldr can also occur when trying to boot Widows NT/2000/XP from the hard disk and Ntldr has been deleted or corrupted. If your active partition is formatted with FAT16 or FAT32, you can boot to a floppy and copy Ntldr to the hard disk. If the partition is formatted NTFS, you can boot to the Windows installation CD and choose to Repair an installation or use Recovery Console to copy the Ntldr file.

- ◆ A typo in the Boot.ini file that specifies where the Windows system files are located can cause Ntldr to report that it cannot locate the Windows kernel file.

- ◆ To create a Windows NT/2000/XP boot disk, copy the following files to a floppy that was formatted with the operating system you are trying to boot: Boot.ini, Ntldr, Ntdetect.com. If your system fails to boot because any of these files become corrupted on your C: drive, you can insert this floppy and your system will boot fine as long as no other files are damaged.

OBJECTIVES ON THE JOB

A technician is frequently called upon to resolve boot errors. A corrupt MBR or missing boot files can be fixed with the SYS command or by running the Repair installation on a Windows NT/2000/XP installation CD.

PRACTICE TEST QUESTIONS

1. How can you resolve the error "Invalid sytem disk"?
   a. copy Command.com to the appropriate directory
   b. repartition the disk and make it active
   c. SYS C:
   d. copy a new Win.com file to the c:\windows directory

2. You are trying to boot to Windows 2000 and receive an error that Ntldr is missing. You have another computer that has Windows 2000 installed and you copy Ntldr to a boot floppy. After you have booted to the floppy you type the command: a:\> copy ntldr C:\ntldr and you get the error message "Invalid drive specification." What is wrong?
   a. Windows 2000 is on the D: drive.
   b. The C: drive is formatted NTFS.
   c. The file is read only.
   d. You don't have permissions to copy the file.

3. You receive the message "Bad or missing command interpreter" and you verify that C:\command.com is there. You copy a new Command.com to c:\ just in case the existing file is corrupted but you get the same error message when you try to reboot. What could be the problem?
   a. The problem is not with Command.com.
   b. The COMSPEC command specifies Command.com to be in the C:\WINDOWS directory.
   c. You need to change the attributes of Command.com to Hidden and System.
   d. None of the above.

4. When is a good time to use Recovery Console? (choose all that apply)
   a. The Ntoskrnl.exe file is missing or corrupt.
   b. The Io.sys file is missing or corrupt.
   c. The Hal.dll file is missing or corrupt.
   d. The Ntldr file is missing or corrupt.

5. How do you run the Recovery Console?
   a. Start/Run and type rconsole
   b. boot to CD, type R and then C
   c. boot to a DOS floppy with the Rc.exe program and type RC
   d. hit <CTRL><ALT><R>

6. What do you need if you get the error "Inaccessible Disk" when installing Windows XP?
   a. a new hard drive
   b. a new installation CD
   c. a floppy with the right driver
   d. more memory

7. Your Windows XP installation gives you an error that the Ntldr file is missing so you insert the installation CD to repair the installation but when you restart the computer, you receive the same error message. What can you do?
   a. Your CD is probably corrupted; try a different CD.
   b. You need to reformat your hard drive.
   c. Boot to a DOS floppy first.
   d. Change the BIOS to boot from CD first.

3.1 Recognize and interpret the meaning of common error codes and startup messages from the boot sequence, and identify steps to correct the problems.

COMMON ERROR MESSAGES AND CODES: STARTUP MESSAGES (ERROR IN CONFIG.SYS LINE XX, HIMEM.SYS NOT LOADED, MISSING OR CORRUPT HIMEM.SYS, AND DEVICE/SERVICE HAS FAILED TO START) AND A DEVICE REFERENCED IN SYSTEM.INI, WIN.INI, REGISTRY IS NOT FOUND

UNDERSTANDING THE OBJECTIVE

Errors when loading Windows 9x can be caused by missing or corrupt program files, errors in command lines stored in Autoexec.bat and Config.sys, wrong program files present, or wrong paths to these program files.

WHAT YOU **REALLY** NEED TO KNOW

- ◆ Press Shift+F8 at startup to step through commands in Config.sys and Autoexec.bat.
- ◆ Himem.sys is loaded from Config.sys with the DEVICE= command under DOS.
- ◆ Himem.sys is automatically loaded by Windows 9x and is a required component.
- ◆ Errors in Config.sys can be caused by missing or corrupt device drivers or errors in the command line to load a driver.
- ◆ System.ini can be used to load device drivers in Windows 9x and Win.ini is sometimes used to start applications. In troubleshooting, use a semicolon to disable a command line in System.ini or Win.ini.
- ◆ Registry entries are used to start drivers, services, and programs at startup. The Msconfig.exe utility can be used to disable services, drivers, and programs started at system boot that are referenced by the registry, System.ini and Win.ini.
- ◆ Know these errors:

Error	Meaning of Error Message and What to Do
Incorrect DOS version	You are attempting to use a DOS command file that belongs to a different version of DOS than the one now running. Use the DOS software from the same version you are running.
Invalid drive specification	The PC is unable to find a hard drive or a floppy drive that setup tells it to expect. The hard drive may have a corrupted partition table.
Invalid or missing Command.com	This may be caused by a nonbooting disk in drive A, or a deleted Command.com on drive C. Remove the disk and boot from the hard drive or replace Command.com.
Not ready reading drive A:	The disk in drive A is missing, unformatted, or corrupted. Try another disk.

OBJECTIVES ON THE JOB

When troubleshooting problems with loading an OS, the problem might be with the command being executed, the program file it refers to, or the path or location of the program file. A PC technician should know how to interpret associated error messages, investigate and research the problem, and arrive at a solution.

PRACTICE TEST QUESTIONS

1. **What is the purpose of the Windows 98 command WIN.COM /D:F?**
   a. to cause Windows 98 to boot from a floppy disk
   b. to load Windows 98 without 32-bit disk access
   c. to load Windows 98 and create a new Bootlog.txt file
   d. to load Windows 98 into Safe Mode

2. **When does Windows 98 create the Bootlog.txt file?**
   a. during the Windows 98 installation process
   b. when loading Windows from the command prompt using the Win.com/B switch
   c. when booting into Safe Mode
   d. all of the above

3. **Which statement about VxDs is true?**
   a. A static VxD is loaded when a device needs it and unloads when the device is no longer being used.
   b. A dynamic VxD is loaded when a device needs it and unloads when the device is no longer being used.
   c. Dynamic VxDs are loaded from System.ini.
   d. Plug and Play uses only static VxDs.

4. **To temporarily disable a command in Config.sys, you should:**
   a. delete the command line from the Config.sys file
   b. put a semicolon at the beginning of the command line
   c. put REM at the beginning of the command line
   d. rename Config.sys

5. **Using Windows 9x, from where can device drivers be loaded?**
   a. System.ini, Win.ini, the registry, and Vmm32.vxd
   b. only from the registry
   c. Config.sys, the registry, System.ini, Vmm32.vxd
   d. only from Vmm32.vxd

6. **How can you load Windows 2000 bypassing entries in System.ini and Win.ini?**
   a. Press F8 during the load process.
   b. Disable these files using MSCONFIG.
   c. Disable these files using the System icon in Control Panel.
   d. Make an entry at the beginning of each file saying the file is to be skipped.

7. **Which of the following Windows 9x files is built specifically for the current system?**
   a. Vmm32.vxd
   b. Himem.sys
   c. Win.com
   d. Command.com

OBJECTIVES

3.1 Recognize and interpret the meaning of common error codes and startup messages from the boot sequence, and identify steps to correct the problems.

COMMON ERROR MESSAGES AND CODES: EVENT VIEWER – EVENT LOG IS FULL, FAILURE TO START GUI, WINDOWS PROTECTION ERROR, USER-MODIFIED SETTINGS CAUSE IMPROPER OPERATION AT STARTUP, AND REGISTRY CORRUPTION

UNDERSTANDING THE OBJECTIVE

Unfortunately, there are countless ways that an operating system can fail to boot or boot with error messages. Components such as the event viewer and the registry are possible sources of errors, as is the startup of the GUI, and erroneous user settings.

WHAT YOU **REALLY** NEED TO KNOW

- ◆ The event viewer is a utility in Windows NT/2000/XP that logs system and security events. If these logs become full, an error stating that the event log is full will be displayed.
- ◆ To clear the event logs, open Event Viewer from Administrative Tools, and right-click one of the three logs and select Clear All Events. To change the way the event log behaves when it is full, right-click the log and select Properties. From there you can change the event log size, set it to automatically overwrite old events, or require a manual clearing of events.
- ◆ If the Windows GUI for Windows 9x does not start, you can usually boot to a DOS prompt and from there, solve the problem in many cases. Or, if the system will start in Safe Mode, that may be a better option.
- ◆ If the Windows GUI in Windows NT/2000/XP does not start, there is no DOS prompt to boot to so your options are usually one of the Safe Modes, Last known-good configuration, or, in Windows 2000/XP, the Recovery Console. Windows NT/2000 also can use the Emergency Recovery Disk set after booting to CD.
- ◆ A **Windows Protection Error** is usually caused when Windows fails to load a VxD. This can happen if a real-mode driver is in conflict with VxD, the registry is damaged, virus infection of key boot files, Windows attempts to load a protected-mode driver specified in System.ini that is already loaded, and a host of other reasons.
- ◆ To resolve a Windows Protection Error, boot to Safe Mode and run MSCONFIG and try disabling various startup components such as Win.ini and System.ini until you find which file causes the problem. If Safe Mode will not boot, boot to Safe Mode with Command Prompt and restore the registry using an Emergency Boot Disk or scanreg /restore.
- ◆ If the registry is corrupted in Windows 95, the backup files System.da0 and User.da0 are automatically used. If those backups are no good, you can use files from a manual backup and if all else fails, you can copy the file called System.1st from the root directory to the Windows directory.
- ◆ Windows 98/ME keeps five days of registry backups which can be restored using scanreg /restore.
- ◆ If the Windows 2000/XP registry is corrupt, use System Console to restore it from a system state backup.

OBJECTIVES ON THE JOB

Many people give up trying to solve the really difficult startup problems, such as the Windows Protection Errors, but if you know how to resolve the tough problems, your skills will be indispensable.

PRACTICE TEST QUESTIONS

1. **What is the name of the file from which the System.dat was created when Windows 9x was first installed?**
   a. Registry.ini
   b. System.1st
   c. System.da0
   d. Registry.da0

2. **How often does Registry Checker back up the registry and how many backups does it keep?**
   a. once a week, 5
   b. once per boot, 10
   c. once a day, 5
   d. never, this must be done manually

3. **You get a Windows Protection Error on startup and you cannot boot to Safe Mode, what do you do?**
   a. Run Setup.exe from the Windows installation CD.
   b. Boot to CD and run Recovery Console.
   c. Boot to a Safe Mode Command Prompt and delete Win386.swp.
   d. Boot to a Safe Mode Command Prompt and run scanreg /restore.

4. **What are the five registry files you can restore in Windows 2000/XP if they become corrupt?**
   a. Default, Sam, Security, Software, System
   b. User, Sam, Security, Software, System
   c. Default, Sam, Security, User, System
   d. User, Sam, Security, Hardware, System

5. **You have determined that your Boot.ini files are corrupt, so you run Recovery Console. Which of the following commands can you run from Recovery Console to try to fix the problem?**
   a. Fixboot c:
   b. Copy A:\boot.ini C:\boot.ini
   c. Fixmbr
   d. Recover Boot.ini and Boot.bak

6. **Which of the following cannot be used to solve a Windows NT boot problem?**
   a. scanreg
   b. Recovery Console
   c. System Restore
   d. all of the above

7. **Which of the following are possible reasons for a Windows Protection Error?**
   a. driver conflict
   b. missing Io.sys
   c. bad hard disk
   d. bad entry in Startup.ini

3.1 Recognize and interpret the meaning of common error codes and startup messages from the boot sequence, and identify steps to correct the problems.

USING THE CORRECT UTILITIES: DR. WATSON, BOOT DISK, AND EVENT VIEWER

UNDERSTANDING THE OBJECTIVE

When problems strike, a technician needs to know what tools are available to diagnose and correct problems. Dr. Watson provides information on application errors, and Event Viewer keeps a log of system, security, and application events that can provide clues as to what caused a particular problem.

WHAT YOU **REALLY** NEED TO KNOW

- ◆ Use Dr. Watson to solve problems with applications. Start Dr. Watson, reproduce the error, and then look in the log files created by Dr. Watson for information about the error.
- ◆ To start Dr. Watson, click Start, Programs, Accessories, System Tools, System Information. In the System Information window, click Tools, and click Dr. Watson.
- ◆ Log files created by Dr. Watson are named \Windows\Drwatson\WatsonXX.wlg where XX is an incrementing number.
- ◆ Use the three Windows NT boot disks to boot the system when it fails to boot from the hard drive.
- ◆ Create a Windows 9x boot disk from the Startup Disk tab in Add/Remove Programs or create a boot floppy by formatting the floppy using the format a: /s command.
- ◆ The Windows NT Emergency Repair Disk (ERD) contains information specific to the system including a copy of the registry. Keep the disk current.
- ◆ Boot from the three Windows NT boot disks and, from the setup menu that appears, select the option to repair a damaged installation.
- ◆ Event Viewer is a log of failed events. Using Windows NT, to access it, click Start, Programs, Administrative Tools, Event Viewer. Icons in the event list are: I (event completed successfully), Exclamation point (possible future problem), and Stop Sign (failed event).
- ◆ In Windows NT, use the Log menu to save Event Viewer information to a log file, open a previously saved log file, and clear all events from the current log.
- ◆ Using Windows 2000, to access the Event Viewer from the Control Panel, select the Administrative Tools icon and then select Event Viewer.
- ◆ Windows 2000 uses the Action menu for the same functions as the Log menu in the Windows NT Event Viewer.
- ◆ There are three Event Viewer logs: Application, System, and Security. The System log contains messages from Windows services and critical operating system components. The Application log contains messages from installed software and some Windows services such as DNS, and the Security log contains messages generated as a result of security audits.

OBJECTIVES ON THE JOB

Know that a boot disk can get a system up and running so that repairs to critical files can be made. Dr. Watson and Event Viewer help when applications or services do not work correctly.

PRACTICE TEST QUESTIONS

1. **Where are the log files created by Dr. Watson stored?**
   a. in the root directory of the hard drive
   b. in the \Windows\System folder
   c. in the \Windows\Drwatson folder
   d. in the \Windows\Temp folder

2. **How do you start Dr. Watson?**
   a. click Start, Programs, Accessories, System Tools, System Information
   b. click Start, Programs, Accessories, Dr. Watson
   c. click Start, Settings, Control Panel, Dr. Watson

3. **What are the log files in Event Viewer? (choose all that apply)**
   a. Application
   b. Services
   c. System
   d. Security

4. **Which is true about Event Viewer?**
   a. It can only be accessed from Recovery Console.
   b. It always overwrites events when it gets too big.
   c. It contains both error messages and informational messages.
   d. It is only available with Windows 98.

5. **To create a Windows 9x boot disk, you should:**
   a. Format a floppy and copy Win.com to the floppy.
   b. Format a floppy using the option to transfer system files.
   c. Copy Io.sys, Msdos.sys, and Command.com to a blank floppy.
   d. Format a a floppy and copy Ntldr, Ntdetect, and Boot.ini to the floppy.

6. **An exclamation point sign in an Event Viewer log file indicates:**
   a. system has crashed
   b. a service has failed
   c. possible problem
   d. operation completed

7. **To view a message in Event Viewer, you should:**
   a. Double-click the event.
   b. Right-click the event and select Edit.
   c. Open the file Eventlog.txt with Notepad.
   d. Open the file Eventview.log with Notepad.

3.2 Recognize when to use common diagnostic utilities and tools. Given a diagnostic scenario involving one of these utilities or tools, select the appropriate steps needed to resolve the problem.

STARTUP DISKS: REQUIRED FILES FOR A BOOT DISK AND BOOT DISK WITH CD-ROM SUPPORT

UNDERSTANDING THE OBJECTIVE

What files are needed to make a disk bootable for an operating system? This question is important so a computer can be started even if the operating system on the hard disk will not boot or if you are installing an OS from scratch. Since most operating systems are installed using a CD, the boot disk should have CD-ROM support so the CD-drive can be accessed.

WHAT YOU **REALLY** NEED TO KNOW

- ◆ A simple DOS/Window 9x boot floppy can be created by just formatting a floppy disk and choosing to transfer system files. Whichever OS you format with, it is those system files that will be transferred.

- ◆ To create a boot floppy from Windows 9x, insert a floppy in the drive, select the A: drive from Explorer or My Computer, right-click, and select Format. Check the box next to Copy System Files.

- ◆ You can also use the FORMAT A: /S command to format a floppy and transfer system files, or, if a floppy is already formatted, the SYS A: command will transfer the system files and make the disk bootable.

- ◆ The above procedures will create a bootable disk, giving you access to the command line but unless your hard drive is accessible and has the utilities you need installed, you should add some files to the boot floppy.

- ◆ The following is a list of files and utilities you should have available on your boot floppy. This is not an exhaustive list but should be enough for many situations:

  - XCOPY: to copy files and directories
  - EDIT: to edit configuration files
  - FDISK: to view and modify the partition table
  - FORMAT: to format the disk
  - Config.sys: to load drivers at startup

  - Himem.sys: for extended memory support
  - A CD-ROM driver
  - Mscdex.exe: to assign a drive letter to the CD-ROM
  - ATTRIB: to set or reset attributes on files
  - SCANREG: to resolve registry problems

- ◆ The Windows NT/2000/XP boot disk requires a floppy that is formatted with one of those operating systems plus Ntldr, Ntdetect.com, and Boot.ini. The Boot.ini should be a copy of the Boot.ini on the hard disk. Note that this disk only works if the operating system files on the hard disk are okay.

OBJECTIVES ON THE JOB

Knowing what files to put on a boot disk and how to best use the boot disk to recover from problems is critical to resolve boot problems.

PRACTICE TEST QUESTIONS

1. Your Windows 2000 system will not boot because of a corrupted Boot.ini file. You do not have a Windows 2000 boot disk for that system, but you do have a Windows 9x boot disk. The C: drive is partitioned with FAT32. What should be on your boot disk to help you out?
   a. Attrib.exe
   b. Edit.com
   c. Xcopy.exe
   d. Fdisk.exe

2. How do you format a Windows XP floppy so that it is bootable?
   a. FORMAT A: /S
   b. FORMAT A: /B
   c. FORMAT A:
   d. FORMAT A: /T

3. Which file is needed on a Windows XP boot floppy if the hard disk is a SCSI drive?
   a. Bootsect.dos
   b. Scsidrv.sys
   c. Ntbootdd.sys
   d. Bootdrv.scs

4. Which file is needed if you want to access the CD-ROM drive after booting to a floppy?
   a. Format.com
   b. Cdrom.drv
   c. Fdisk.exe
   d. Mscdex.exe

5. What line is necessary in Config.sys to provide CD-ROM support?
   a. DEVICE=cd-driver.sys
   b. LOAD=cd-driver.sys
   c. DRIVER=cd-driver.sys
   d. RUN=cd-driver.sys

6. You suspect there is a problem with the Msdos.sys file in Windows 98. What file can help you fix the problem?
   a. Debug.exe
   b. Msconfig.exe
   c. Dosedit.com
   d. Edit.com

7. You installed a dual-boot with Windows 98 and Windows 2000 but you have decided to remove the Windows 2000 installation which was on a different partition from Windows 98. You delete the partition but find that the Windows 2000 boot loader still runs when the computer boots. What can you do?
   a. Boot to Safe Mode and run Uninst2000.
   b. Boot to a Windows boot floppy and run SYS C:.
   c. Reinstall Windows 2000 and choose Remove Boot Loader when prompted.
   d. You must delete all partitions and reformat.

3.2 Recognize when to use common diagnostic utilities and tools. Given a diagnostic scenario involving one of these utilities or tools, select the appropriate steps needed to resolve the problem.

STARTUP MODES: SAFE MODE, SAFE MODE WITH COMMAND PROMPT, SAFE MODE WITH NETWORKING, STEP-BY-STEP/SINGLE STEP MODE, AND AUTOMATIC SKIP DRIVER (ASD.EXE)

UNDERSTANDING THE OBJECTIVE

Problems with loading an operating system are communicated to the user as error messages on screen or the system may simply lock up. Safe Mode is only one of several options Windows 9x and Windows 2000/XP offer to help resolve problems when loading the OS. The Automatic Skip Driver agent will skip drivers that prevent Windows from loading.

WHAT YOU **REALLY** NEED TO KNOW

- ◆ When Windows encounters problems with loading the OS, it might enter **Safe Mode** or it might offer the Startup menu from which you can select Safe Mode.
- ◆ Here's what to expect when you select each option on the Windows 9x Startup menu:
  - **Normal** In Msdos.sys, if BootGUI=1, then this option starts Windows 9x. If BootGUI=0, then this option will boot to the DOS 7.0 or DOS 7.1 prompt. Either way, the commands in Autoexec.bat and Config.sys are executed.
  - **Logged (\Bootlog.txt)** Same as Normal, except Windows 9x tracks the load and startup activities and logs them to this file.
  - **Safe Mode** Windows loads with a minimum configuration.
  - **Safe mode with Network Support** Network drivers are loaded when booting into Safe Mode.
  - **Step-by-Step Confirmation** The option asks for confirmation before executing each command in Io.sys, Config.sys, and Autoexec.bat.
  - **Command Prompt Only** Also called DOS mode. Executes Config.sys and Autoexec.bat.
  - **Safe mode Command Prompt Only** Does not execute the commands in Autoexec.bat or Config.sys. You will be given a DOS prompt. Type WIN to load Windows 9x.
  - **Previous Version of MS-DOS** Loads a previous version of DOS if one is present. This is the same as pressing F4 when the message "Starting Windows 95/98" displays.
- ◆ Once in Safe Mode in Windows 9x or Windows 2000/XP, the following may help resolve a problem:
  - Reboot the system; sometimes this is all that's needed; run antivirus software to check for a virus.
  - If the Safe Recovery dialog box appears, select Use Safe Recovery to let Windows attempt a solution.
  - Disable any devices just installed; undo any receive configuration changes.
  - Run ScanDisk and Defrag; for Windows 98, run System File Checker, Automatic Skip Driver Agent, System Configuration Utility.

OBJECTIVES ON THE JOB

Understanding and using Safe Mode and the other options on the Windows 9x Startup menu or the Windows 2000/XP Advanced Options Menu are important skills to have when troubleshooting problems with the OS.

PRACTICE TEST QUESTIONS

1. **What is the source of the error message "MS-DOS compatibility mode"?**
   a. Windows is using real mode device drivers to access the hard drive.
   b. You are using DOS mode. To load Windows, type WIN at the DOS prompt.
   c. Windows has booted into Safe Mode.
   d. Windows is running a DOS application.

2. **What is the source of the error message "Invalid VxD dynamic link call from IFSMGR" and what do you do to solve the problem?**
   a. The registry is corrupted. Restore the registry files from backup.
   b. Msdos.sys is corrupted. Restore the file from a backup.
   c. The boot sector is corrupted. Format the hard drive and reinstall Windows 95.
   d. The partition table is corrupted. Use FDISK to create a new table.

3. **What is one of the first things you should do after booting into Safe Mode?**
   a. Run antivirus software.
   b. Reinstall Windows.
   c. Use RECOVER to restore the system files.
   d. Use SYS C: to restore the system files.

4. **What happens if the Win.com file is missing from the Windows 9x load?**
   a. Windows will create a new Win.com file and continue to load.
   b. An error message displays and Windows 9x continues to load.
   c. Windows will automatically boot into Safe Mode.
   d. An error message displays and the load stops.

5. **What troubleshooting tool can you try if a device causes your computer to hang during startup?**
   a. Devscan.exe
   b. Fixdriver.com
   c. Scandev.exe
   d. Asd.exe

6. **Which statement about booting Windows 9x into Safe Mode is not true?**
   a. A minimum configuration is used so that the problem is not masked by a complex load.
   b. The registry is rebuilt at the beginning of loading in Safe Mode.
   c. Entries in the registry, Config.sys, Autoexec.bat, and most of System.ini are not executed.
   d. Standard VGA drivers are loaded.

7. **What is one way to access Safe Mode under Windows 2000?**
   a. Press F1 during startup.
   b. Press F8 and select Safe Mode from the Advanced Options Menu.
   c. Press F3 during startup.
   d. Select Safe Mode from the taskbar tray.

3.2 Recognize when to use common diagnostic utilities and tools. Given a diagnostic scenario involving one of these utilities or tools, select the appropriate steps needed to resolve the problem.

DIAGNOSTIC TOOLS, UTILITIES AND RESOURCES: USER/INSTALLATION MANUALS, INTERNET/WEB RESOURCES, TRAINING MATERIALS, TASK MANAGER, AND DR. WATSON

UNDERSTANDING THE OBJECTIVE

Some information sources include printed manuals and training documents or Web resources. Some sources are from the computer itself, such as the Task Manager or Dr. Watson.

WHAT YOU **REALLY** NEED TO KNOW

- ◆ Printed manuals for hardware and software are becoming a thing of the past but some manufacturer's still include some printed documentation with their products. More likely, documentation will be on a CD in the form of a PDF document or HTML document. These have an added advantage over printed material in that you can use electronic searches to find error messages or key words.
- ◆ Training materials such as this book are invaluable sources of information about standard hardware and common software problems. To most easily find what you are looking for, use the book index.
- ◆ The Web is sometimes the only place you can find information about specific problems. Using a manufacturer's knowledgebase to research problems can be a lifesaver, saving perhaps hours of troubleshooting.
- ◆ Use keyword searches on a manufacturer's knowledgebase or FAQ using specific error messages or error codes to quickly find the meaning and often times a solution to an error.
- ◆ Numerous Web sites and newsgroups are dedicated to training and troubleshooting. The use of a general search engine such as Google or Dogpile frequently can yield results when a manufacturer's site fails to.
- ◆ Task Manager is a Windows NT/2000/XP utility that shows running applications and processes and the resources they are using. To access Task Manager, right-click the Taskbar and select Task Manager, or hit <CTRL><ALT><DEL> and select Task Manager from the menu displayed.
- ◆ Task Manager has four tabs: Applications, Processes, Performance, and Networking. The Applications tab shows currently loaded applications and their status. If a task is not responding, the status will reflect that.
- ◆ To see the CPU and memory resources for a loaded application, right-click the application name in the Task Manager Application tab and select Go To Process.
- ◆ The Processes tab shows the process name, the name of the user that started the process, the percentage of CPU time the process is using and the amount of memory allocated to the process.
- ◆ To end a process that is using excessive CPU time, select the process from the Processes tab and click the End Process button. Note that ending some processes can cause instability in the system. Be wary of ending processes that are started by SYSTEM.
- ◆ When no other processes need the CPU, a special process called System Idle receives all of the CPU time.

OBJECTIVES ON THE JOB

Knowing which resource to use and how and when to use it is a skill all good technicians possess. To view information about current system status and to stop misbehaving processes, use Task Manager. Dr. Watson can provide detailed information about why an application terminated unexpectedly.

PRACTICE TEST QUESTIONS

1. In Windows XP, to view a list of running processes and the amount of CPU they are using, you should:
   a. go to Start/Run and type drwtsn32
   b. right-click the taskbar and select Task Manager
   c. go to Start/All Programs/Accessories/System Tools/System Information
   d. both b and c

2. To start Dr. Watson in Windows 98, you should:
   a. Start/Run and type drwtsn32
   b. Start/Run and type drwtsn
   c. Start/Run and type drwatson
   d. Start/Administrative Tools/Dr Watson

3. You are running a program that freezes often and displays an error about Illegal Operation. How can you view detailed information about the errors occurring in the application?
   a. System Information
   b. Scanreg
   c. Msinfo
   d. Dr. Watson

4. Which of the following is not a tab in Windows XP Task Manager?
   a. Services
   b. Applications
   c. Networking
   d. Performance

5. You run Task Manager and notice that a process called System Idle is taking 99 percent of the CPU time, what should you do?
   a. select the process and hit the End Process button
   b. select the process and hit the Kill Process button
   c. nothing
   d. reboot the computer

6. You notice a lot of disk activity when you have several applications loaded even though those applications are not accessing files on the disk. You suspect you may be making heavy use of virtual memory. How can you determine if this is the case?
   a. Run Dr. Watson and view the Processes tab.
   b. Run Task Manager and view the Performance tab.
   c. Run the System control panel, choose the Advanced tab, and view the Performance settings.
   d. Use Explorer to view the size of Pagefile.sys on the C: drive.

7. Every time you try to run Microsoft Word, you receive a specific error message. You have been unable to resolve the problem yourself. What is the best thing to try next?
   a. Reinstall Microsoft Word.
   b. Reboot the computer.
   c. Do a search for the error on the Microsoft Knowledgebase.
   d. Use Task Manager to view the Application status.

3.2 Recognize when to use common diagnostic utilities and tools. Given a diagnostic scenario involving one of these utilities or tools, select the appropriate steps needed to resolve the problem.

DIAGNOSTIC TOOLS, UTILITIES AND RESOURCES: BOOT DISK, EVENT VIEWER, DEVICE MANAGER, WINMSD, MSD, RECOVERY CD, AND CONFIGSAFE

UNDERSTANDING THE OBJECTIVE

The proper use of utilities to troubleshoot and resolve problems is a key PC technician skill. Know how and when to use a boot disk, Event Viewer, Device Manager, MSD and WinMSD. In addition, some manufacturers provide a recovery CD to restore your hard disk to a known state, and ConfigSafe from imagineLAN allows you to restore your system configuration to a previous status.

WHAT YOU **REALLY** NEED TO KNOW

- ◆ Every system should have a related boot disk with the necessary files to boot the computer and access the CD-ROM in the event the OS on the hard disk will not boot. If the system is bootable from the hard disk, there are usually other, better troubleshooting tools you can use.
- ◆ Event Viewer should be frequently checked for service, security, or application problems. The log files should be set to overwrite old messages or the logs should be checked and cleared when necessary. Use Event Viewer when services don't start or terminate and when auditing is enabled to verify security.
- ◆ Device Manager is the tool to use when a device is not working. The status of the device can be determined, the driver can be updated and used resources can be viewed and configured. When necessary, a device can be disabled if it is causing a conflict, or deleted and reinstalled.
- ◆ MSD, while an aging utility, is still useful in Windows 9x and DOS systems. MSD can show BIOS information, resources in use, and other basic system information. It is most useful on a boot floppy to diagnose resource conflicts or view other system information when the system will not boot to run Device Manager.
- ◆ WinMSD is a utility for Windows NT that provides a report of the system configuration. To create a report to a file use the command WinMSD /a/f.
- ◆ The WinMSD command is also available in Windows 2000 and Windows XP but this just runs the System Information utility found in the System Tools folder of Accessories.
- ◆ Some computer manufacturers supply a Recovery CD with their systems that contains all of the software and drivers that are preloaded on the computer when it is shipped. Use this CD to reinstall the OS, applications, or to completely restore the hard disk to the state is was in when the computer first arrived.
- ◆ ConfigSafe is a utility for Windows 9x, Windows 2000 and Windows XP. ConfigSafe takes a snapshot of vital system information at a particular moment so that the computer can be restored to that state later, if necessary.
- ◆ ConfigSafe saves Win.ini, System.ini, Autoexec.bat, Config.sys, the Desktop, and the registry. In addition, system changes and drive configurations are also recorded.

OBJECTIVES ON THE JOB

When a system is not working correctly, Device Manager and MSD can resolve resource conflicts or provide other useful system information. A Recovery CD and ConfigSafe help restore the system to an earlier known operating state.

PRACTICE TEST QUESTIONS

1. To find out information about device resource usage, you should use: (choose all that apply)
   a. MSD
   b. WinMSD
   c. Device Manager
   d. Task Manager

2. The use of a boot disk is usually only necessary when:
   a. You get application errors.
   b. A service won't start.
   c. The OS won't boot.
   d. Networking is not operational.

3. In Windows 2000, to view a summary of DMA channels in use, you should:
   a. run Device Manager, select View/Resources by Connection
   b. run Device Manager, select View/Devices by Connection
   c. run WinMSD, select View/Devices by Connection
   d. run WinMSD, select View/Resources by Connection

4. To get a report of resource usage and system information in Windows NT, you should:
   a. run MSINFO
   b. run System Information
   c. run WinMSD
   d. run Device Manager

5. You boot your Windows XP computer and receive a message that a service failed to start. Where do you go to get additional information?
   a. Dr. Watson
   b. Event Viewer
   c. System Information
   d. Task Manager

6. You have been unable to resolve a problem that started after you installed a new application. You have uninstalled the application but the problem persists. You believe the problem is related to the registry and some configuration files. What tool is most likely to solve this problem?
   a. Dr. Watston
   b. Boot disk
   c. ConfigSafe
   d. Device Manager

7. You cannot boot the Windows GUI and you think there may be a resource conflict. What tool can help you determine if a resource conflict exists?
   a. Boot disk with MSD
   b. Boot disk with Dr. Watson
   c. WinMSD
   d. Device Manager

OBJECTIVES

3.2 Recognize when to use common diagnostic utilities and tools. Given a diagnostic scenario involving one of these utilities or tools, select the appropriate steps needed to resolve the problem.

ELICITING PROBLEM SYMPTOMS FROM CUSTOMERS • HAVING CUSTOMER REPRODUCE ERROR AS PART OF THE DIAGNOSTIC PROCESS • IDENTIFYING RECENT CHANGES TO THE COMPUTER ENVIRONMENT FROM THE USER

UNDERSTANDING THE OBJECTIVE

Whether you support PCs on the phone, on-site, or in a shop, you need a plan to follow when you approach a service call. One mistake PC technicians often make is assuming they already understand what the problem is without thoroughly interviewing the customer. Know how to approach a customer, to communicate, and to ask questions to investigate the source of the problem before you turn your attention to the computer system.

WHAT YOU **REALLY** NEED TO KNOW

- ◆ Let the customer explain the problem in his or her own way. Take notes, and then interview the customer about the problem so you understand it thoroughly.
- ◆ Have the customer reproduce the problem and carefully note each step taken and its results. This process gives you clues about the problem and about the technical proficiency of the customer, which helps you know how to communicate with the customer.
- ◆ When interacting with a customer, display confidence that you are competent and can solve the problem. Keep a professional and confident attitude. Don't talk down to the customer or disparage the customer's choice of hardware or software. If you have made a mistake or must pass the problem on to someone with more expertise, be honest.
- ◆ Protect the confidentiality of the customer's data on the PC.
- ◆ Here are some helpful questions to ask the user when trying to discover the source of the problem:
  - When did the problem start? Were there any error messages or unusual displays on the screen?
  - What programs or software were you using?
  - Did you move your computer system recently?
  - Has there been a recent thunderstorm or electrical problem?
  - Have you made any hardware changes? Did you recently install any new software?
  - Did you recently change any software configuration setups?
  - Has someone else been using your computer recently? When was the last time you ran antivirus software?

OBJECTIVES ON THE JOB

A PC technician is expected to be able to give good service. Part of providing good service is being a good communicator. By effectively interviewing the customer before you begin work on a PC, you can quickly discover valuable information that can save you hours of time that might have been required without the customer's assistance.

PRACTICE TEST QUESTIONS

1. **What is something you can do to promote good communication?**
   a. Be silent until the customer is finished describing the problem.
   b. Take notes as the customer describes the problem.
   c. Begin work while the customer is talking.
   d. Both a and b.

2. **What is something you should do while talking with a customer?**
   a. Ask the customer when the problem began.
   b. Ask the customer to reproduce the problem.
   c. Never admit you have made a mistake.
   d. Both a and b.

3. **What is one question to ask a customer?**
   a. Why did you buy this brand of PC anyway?
   b. Did you recently install any new software?
   c. Why can't you even understand my question?
   d. How much did you pay for this equipment?

4. **What are some things you need to know from the customer?**
   a. Is the PC still under warranty?
   b. Has the PC been moved recently?
   c. Has there been a lightning storm recently?
   d. All of the above.

5. **What is the first thing you should do when you arrive at a customer's site?**
   a. Shut the PC down and perform a cold start.
   b. Fill out the necessary paperwork about the visit.
   c. Interview the customer.
   d. Attempt to reproduce the problem.

6. **What do you do if you make a mistake while attempting to repair a PC?**
   a. Hide it from your boss.
   b. Be honest where appropriate.
   c. Resign from your job.
   d. Hide it from the customer.

7. **When interviewing a customer, why is it important to know if the PC has been near a lightning storm recently?**
   a. The problem might be caused by electrical damage.
   b. There still might be ozone in the atmosphere.
   c. The customer needs to know to purchase a line conditioner.
   d. You can eliminate the power supply as a source of the problem.

3.3 Recognize common operational and usability problems and determine how to resolve them.

TROUBLESHOOTING WINDOWS-SPECIFIC PRINTING PROBLEMS: PRINT SPOOL IS STALLED, INCORRECT/INCOMPATIBLE DRIVER FOR PRINT, AND INCORRECT PARAMETER

UNDERSTANDING THE OBJECTIVE

Problems with printing can be caused by the printer, the connection from the printer to the computer, the computer hardware, operating system, printer driver, application attempting to print, the network (for network printers), and the printer parameters. The first step in solving a printer problem is narrowing down the problem to one of these sources. The error messages listed in this objective have to do with problems with the operating system.

WHAT YOU **REALLY** NEED TO KNOW

- ◆ To remove print jobs from the Windows 9x printer queue (spool), access the Printer dialog box and select Purge Print Documents from the Printer menu. For Windows 2000, the menu option in the Printer menu is Cancel All Documents.
- ◆ Successfully printing a self-test page using controls on the printer eliminates the printer as the source of a printing problem.
- ◆ Successfully printing an operating system test page eliminates all but the application attempting to print as a source of a printing problem.
- ◆ A printer self-test page often shows the amount of memory installed in a printer.
- ◆ Remove and reinstall a printer that is having problems that appear to be operating-system related. To remove a printer, right-click the printer icon in the Printer window and then click Delete on the shortcut menu.
- ◆ Verify printer properties. For DOS applications, verify the printer is configured to capture DOS application printing to LPT1.
- ◆ Try lowering the resolution. In the Printer Properties dialog box, try disabling the Check Port State Before Printing option.
- ◆ Try disabling printer spooling. In the Printer Properties dialog box, select Print Directly to the Printer.
- ◆ To eliminate bi-directional communication with the printer, in the Printer Properties dialog box, select the Disable bi-directional support for this printer option.
- ◆ Using Device Manager, examine the properties of LPT1 (I/O addresses are 0378–037B and IRQ is 7) and verify that Device Manager reports "No conflicts."
- ◆ Sometimes an outdated or incorrect printer driver will cause incorrectly formatted printer output or simply no output at all. Check the printer driver. In Windows XP, go to the printer Properties Advanced tab and verify the correct driver is installed. In the event the driver is corrupt, replace it.
- ◆ In Windows NT/2000/XP, printing problems can sometimes be resolved by stopping and restarting the print spooler. A stalled print spooler will no longer send documents to the print device. Access the Services control panel and look for the Print Spooler service. Stop the service and then start the service.

OBJECTIVES ON THE JOB

A PC technician is expected to be able to narrow down the source of a printing problem and, once the source is identified, use a variety of techniques and procedures to solve the problem.

PRACTICE TEST QUESTIONS

1. **If you can print a test page from the Windows 98 Print window, what is the most likely source of a user's continuing print problem?**
   a. the printer cable
   b. the printer
   c. the printer device driver
   d. the application

2. **You cannot print from an application or the Windows 98 Print window. What do you do first?**
   a. Exchange the printer for one you know is working.
   b. Uninstall and reinstall the printer drivers.
   c. Check that the printer is turned on and is online.
   d. Disable the parallel port in CMOS setup.

3. **You are unable to print and several jobs are in the print queue. How do you clear the queue?**
   a. Turn the printer off and back on.
   b. In the Printer window, select Printer on the menu bar, and then select Purge Print Documents.
   c. In the Printer window, select Printer on the menu bar, and then select Empty Printer Queue.
   d. From Device Manager, disable and then enable the printer.

4. **How do you uninstall a printer's device drivers?**
   a. From Device Manager, select the printer and then click Delete.
   b. From Device Manager, right-click the printer and select Uninstall.
   c. In the Printer window, right-click the printer and select Delete.
   d. In the Control Panel window, select Printer on the menu bar, and then select Delete.

5. **What is one source of a problem that would prevent Windows 98 from printing?**
   a. An application is not installed correctly.
   b. The hard drive does not have enough available space.
   c. Command.com is missing or corrupted.
   d. Either b or c.

6. **If you can print from a DOS prompt, but cannot print from Windows, what is the next thing you should do?**
   a. uninstall and reinstall the Windows printer drivers
   b. disable Windows printer spooling
   c. replace the printer cable
   d. tell the user to only print from a DOS prompt

7. **How can you access the Print Spooler service in Windows XP?**
   a. Start/Control Panel/Services
   b. Start/Control Panlel/Administrative Tools/Services
   c. Start/Run and type srvmgr
   d. Start/All Programs/Accessories/Print Spooler

3.3 Recognize common operational and usability problems and determine how to resolve them.

OTHER COMMON PROBLEMS: GENERAL PROTECTION FAULTS, BLUESCREEN ERROR (BSOD), ILLEGAL OPERATION, INVALID WORKING DIRECTORY, SYSTEM LOCK UP, OPTION (SOUND CARD, MODEM, INPUT DEVICE) WILL NOT FUNCTION, APPLICATION WILL NOT START OR LOAD, AND APPLICATIONS DON'T INSTALL

UNDERSTANDING THE OBJECTIVE

Problems like the ones listed above generally occur after the OS has loaded successfully and when you are loading or using application software. Problems with application software can be caused by the application itself and conflict with other applications. GPFs are generally caused by errors in the software or the OS, by a virus, or by two applications attempting to use the same memory space.

WHAT YOU **REALLY** NEED TO KNOW

◆ In Windows 9x, when an application is installed, it may write .dll files to the Windows\System folder that can overwrite the .dll file of another installed application, which can cause a problem with the other application.

◆ Some problems with options are caused by insufficient memory because an application is using too much of a memory heap. Close some applications and/or install more RAM.

◆ When an application begins to consistently give errors, try uninstalling and reinstalling the application. In the Control Panel window, double-click the Add/Remove Program icon.

◆ The error message, "Bad command or file not found" is the result of the OS not being able to locate the specified program file. The program file may be in a different directory from the one specified in the path portion of the command line or in the list of paths in the last PATH command executed.

◆ If an application continues to give errors after you have reinstalled it, try verifying Windows system files or reinstalling Windows.

◆ Some errors reported by the OS that have to do with applications can be caused by a virus. Run a current version of antivirus software.

◆ When solving problems with applications, run Defrag and ScanDisk and verify that there is enough extra space on the hard drive for an application to store its temporary files while running.

◆ "Illegal operation" errors are often caused by application bugs or a virus. These errors can sometimes lead to a system lock up in which the system stops responding. It is best to reboot Windows after an illegal operation.

◆ When an application fails to install correctly, use Dr. Watson to help isolate the problem. Also check the Web site of the application manufacturer for information about the problem.

◆ The infamous blue screen of death is usually a STOP error in Windows NT/2000/XP, which is a system crash. There are numerous causes for the blue screen: bad or incorrect drivers, viruses, disk corruption, BIOS incompatibilities, and hardware problems, among others. Debug information is written to a Memory.dmp file.

OBJECTIVES ON THE JOB

Solving problems with application software is an expected and common task for a PC technician. Know that other software, the hardware, the operating system, or the application itself can be the cause of the problem.

PRACTICE TEST QUESTIONS

1. **When an application fails to load, what should you do first?**
   a. Close all other applications and try again.
   b. Uninstall and reinstall the application.
   c. Reboot and try again.
   d. Add more memory.

2. **How can you change the icon of a shortcut object on the desktop?**
   a. Right-click the icon, select Properties, select the Shortcut tab, and then click Change Icon.
   b. Right-click the icon, and then select Change Icon.
   c. Click the icon, and then select Change Icon.
   d. Edit the registry entry for this shortcut.

3. **You are running several applications and one of them locks up. What do you do?**
   a. Reboot the PC.
   b. Turn off the PC and turn it back on.
   c. Press Ctrl+Alt+Del and then end the task.
   d. Click Start on the taskbar, click Shutdown, and then click End Task.

4. **An application cannot access a device. How can you know if the device is installed properly?**
   a. From Device Manager, select the device and click Properties.
   b. Look for an X next to the device name in Device Manager.
   c. Try to use the device using another application.
   d. All of the above.

5. **In implementing Plug and Play, the bus enumerator inventories the resources required by devices on the bus. Which bus does Windows 95 not support?**
   a. SCSI
   b. IDE
   c. MCA
   d. ISA

6. **What is the generic name given to a Windows 2000 STOP error?**
   a. System down
   b. Application error
   c. Blue screen of death
   d. Black screen

7. **An application gives an "illegal operations" error. What is one possible cause?**
   a. The application has a bug.
   b. The application is infected with a virus.
   c. Windows has corrupted system files.
   d. All of the above.

3.3 Recognize common operational and usability problems and determine how to resolve them.

OTHER COMMON PROBLEMS: CANNOT LOG ON TO NETWORK (OPTION – NIC NOT FUNCTIONING) AND NETWORK CONNECTION

UNDERSTANDING THE OBJECTIVE

Problems logging onto a network or establishing a network connection can have a variety of sources. Begin with the easy to check and work your way up to the more difficult problems and resolutions. Many times a simple reboot is all that is required to reestablish a failed network connection.

WHAT YOU **REALLY** NEED TO KNOW

- ◆ Approach problems connecting to a TCP/IP network systematically. Try these things:
  - Verify the user name and password. Try using the Administrator logon.
  - Verify that the PC has a physical connection to the hub by looking for a light on the network card.
  - Try to ping another PC on the LAN.
  - Verify the PC has received an IP address from the DHCP server.
  - Check Network Neighborhood for Windows 9x or My Network Places for Windows 2000 to verify the PC can view resources on the network.
  - Uninstall and reinstall TCP/IP and then reboot.
  - Check physical connections.
  - Try a cold reboot.
  - Scan for viruses.
  - Suspect corrupted NIC drivers. Uninstall and reinstall the drivers.
  - Verify that other computers on the LAN can access the network.
  - Determine what does work. Can you connect successfully through a different port on the hub?
  - Replace the network cable.
  - Replace the NIC.

OBJECTIVES ON THE JOB

Solving problems within a network requires patience and perseverance. Many times what didn't work will begin to work after a few retries with no apparent changes. Try several reboots. Go over the same things several times. Don't overlook that the problem can be a failed NIC, network cable, or hub port.

PRACTICE TEST QUESTIONS

1. **How can you know a PC has a physical connection to an Ethernet hub?**
   a. Look for resources listed in Network Neighborhood.
   b. Look for a light on the NIC.
   c. Look for a light on the hub.
   d. Either b or c.

2. **How can you verify using Windows 2000 that a PC has good communication over the network?**
   a. Look for network resources listed in My Network Places.
   b. Look for network resources listed in Network Neighborhood.
   c. Check for a blinking light on the back of the network card.
   d. Attempt to print to a network printer.

3. **How can you verify that your computer can communicate with another computer on the TCP/IP network?**
   a. Use the Ping utility.
   b. Use the Winipcfg utility.
   c. Use the Router utility.
   d. Reinstall TCP/IP.

4. **What is a possible cause of a failure to connect to the network?**
   a. a virus
   b. a failed network card
   c. corrupted Windows system files
   d. all of the above

5. **You cannot connect to a network even after a reboot. What is the next thing to do?**
   a. Replace the NIC.
   b. Move the PC to another network port off the hub.
   c. Verify network settings.
   d. Replace the network cable.

6. **You can print to a network printer but cannot see another host on the network that should be listed in Network Neighborhood. What might be the cause?**
   a. The network card has failed.
   b. TCP/IP is not installed correctly.
   c. The other PC is not online.
   d. File and print sharing is not enabled.

7. **How do you share a folder on the network?**
   a. Using Windows Explorer, right-click the folder name and select Sharing.
   b. Using Windows Explorer, select the folder and click Sharing on the Explorer menu.
   c. Drag and drop the folder into Network Neighborhood.
   d. Open Network Neighborhood, select the folder and click Sharing on the menu.

OBJECTIVES

3.3 Recognize common operational and usability problems and determine how to resolve them.

VIRUSES AND VIRUS TYPES: WHAT THEY ARE, TSR (TERMINATE STAY RESIDENT) PROGRAMS AND VIRUS, SOURCES (FLOPPY, EMAILS, ETC.), AND HOW TO DETERMINE PRESENCE

UNDERSTANDING THE OBJECTIVE

Viruses are common with today's computer systems. Computer infestations are generally classified as viruses, worms, or Trojan horses. The best line of defense against infestations is to use common sense to not expose the system to a virus, to back up important data in the event of a failure caused by a virus, and to use antivirus software to detect and remove viruses.

WHAT YOU **REALLY** NEED TO KNOW

◆ A **boot sector virus** hides in the boot sector program on a hard drive or diskette. A **file virus** hides in a program file. A **multipartite virus** can hide in either a boot sector program or a program file.

◆ A **macro virus** hides in a **macro** that is part of a word processing document, spreadsheet, or similar file.

◆ A virus cannot hide in text or regular data files that don't contain macros.

◆ Symptoms of a virus include system performance slows, disk access is excessive, unusual error messages appear, files mysteriously disappear and appear, unusual reduction in disk space, the system locks up, devices are not available, number of bad sectors on a hard drive continue to increase, and strange graphics appear.

◆ Use **antivirus (AV) software** to detect and remove viruses. Keep the software current as new viruses are discovered daily.

◆ **Polymorphic, encrypting,** and **stealth viruses** have different methods of cloaking themselves from detection by antivirus software.

◆ A virus hoax is a letter or e-mail warning about a nonexistent virus that is itself a pest because it overloads network traffic.

◆ The BIOS in some computer systems has antivirus protection that can be enabled in CMOS setup. This protection prevents the partition-table master boot program (MBR) from being altered.

◆ Know the symptoms of a virus and have antivirus software available and use it during a troubleshooting session.

◆ Always scan your bootable disks for a virus before using them on a customer's system.

◆ More viruses are received through e-mail attachments than by any other single means. Never open an e-mail attachment from someone you don't trust without first scanning the file for a virus.

◆ Antivirus software includes Norton AntiVirus, Dr. Solomon's Software, McAfee VirusScan, eSafe, F-PROT, and Command AntiVirus.

◆ Keep antivirus software current by downloading data files about viruses and upgrades to the antivirus software from the antivirus software Web site.

◆ Some viruses that are attached to executable programs remain in memory even after the program is closed—these are Terminate and Stay Resident viruses. The virus can then attach itself to other programs when they are loaded and wreak havoc with your system until you reboot.

OBJECTIVES ON THE JOB

Be proactive when protecting your own and your customers' systems against viruses. Use antivirus software regularly. If a system supports it, set up a scheduled task so that the OS executes the software automatically at certain times, such as when the PC boots.

PRACTICE TEST QUESTIONS

1. **How does a boot sector virus differ from a file virus?**
   a. the payload they deliver
   b. where they hide
   c. how long they can stay in memory
   d. how many times they can replicate

2. **How does a virus typically spread over e-mail?**
   a. in the software that provides the e-mail service
   b. in the software downloaded from the ISP
   c. in the boot sector of floppy disks used to attach files to e-mail messages
   d. in files attached to e-mail messages

3. **What is a macro virus?**
   a. a virus that replicates itself multiple times before unloading from memory
   b. a virus that destroys the hard drive
   c. a virus that hides in scripts or other short programs embedded in document files
   d. a virus that uses two different ways to hide: in files and in boot sectors of the hard drive

4. **What can you do to protect against a virus?**
   a. Use antivirus software.
   b. Never use pirated software.
   c. Make regular backups.
   d. All of the above.

5. **What is one thing that a virus cannot do?**
   a. erase all data on a hard drive
   b. damage the partition table
   c. damage the boot strap loader program
   d. damage the controller card of the hard drive

6. **What is the purpose of virus protection in CMOS setup?**
   a. It prevents someone from accidentally making changes to CMOS setup.
   b. It prevents the partition table from being altered.
   c. It prevents someone from uninstalling antivirus software.
   d. It prevents macro files from entering a system.

7. **What is a symptom of a virus being present or having done damage?**
   a. The PC will not boot.
   b. You cannot access the CD-ROM drive.
   c. The system performance is slow.
   d. All of the above.

4.1 Identify the networking capabilities of Windows. Given configuration parameters, configure the operating system to connect to a network.

CONFIGURE PROTOCOLS: TCP/IP (GATEWAY, SUBNET MASK, DNS (AND DOMAIN SUFFIX), WINS, STATIC ADDRESS ASSIGNMENT, AND AUTOMATIC ADDRESS ASSIGNMENT (APIPA, DHCP))

UNDERSTANDING THE OBJECTIVE

Most offices today are networked, even if there are only a few computers. Understand how to configure TCP/IP, the most popular protocol. There are two primary methods of assigning IP configuration: static and automatic. Automatic addressing can use DHCP or Automatic Private IP Adressing (APIPA).

WHAT YOU **REALLY** NEED TO KNOW

◆ TCP/IP is the protocol of the Internet and almost all networks today use this protocol suite. To configure IP settings you must specify an IP address and a subnet mask at minimum.

◆ An IP address consist of four numbers separated by a period, with each number between the value of 0 and 255.

◆ If one network is connected to another network, or the Internet, through a router, a default gateway must be configured so that the computers on each network can communicate.

◆ A DNS server looks up host and domain names (e.g., *www.course.com*) and returns the IP address assigned to that server. IP configurations that access the Internet need a primary and secondary DNS server address configured so Internet resources can be accessed using names rather than IP addresses.

◆ Windows Internet Naming Service (WINS) is used in a Windows network. WINS resolves computer names on the network to IP addresses.

◆ The Domain Suffix is the domain name that is automatically added to a host name if no domain is specified. More than one Domain Suffix can be configured and the domains will be searched in the order specified.

◆ To use static IP address configuration, a technician must go to each computer in the network and assign a unique IP address, a subnet mask and usually a default gateway and DNS server addresses. In addition, a WINS server address may also be defined.

◆ Automatic addressing includes Dynamic Host Configuration Protocol (DHCP) in which a DHCP server listens for requests for an IP address and sends the IP address configuration to the client making the request.

◆ APIPA is used starting with Windows 98. If no DHCP server is found, the Windows client selects an IP address with the format 169.254.x.x, where x.x are random numbers between 0 and 255. This way, a Windows client configures its own IP address but note that no Default Gateway or DNS servers can be assigned this way.

OBJECTIVES ON THE JOB

When first setting up a network, a common problem is an incorrect TCP/IP configuration. If static addressing is used, the technician must be cautious of typos—one transposed set of numbers can cause networking to fail. If DHCP addressing is used, the technician must configure each host to use DHCP and the DHCP server must be properly configured to provide IP address, subnet mask, default gateway, and DNS server.

PRACTICE TEST QUESTIONS

1. You are configuring static addressing on a Windows computer. You have to change to the Gateway tab to install the Default Gateway. What operating system are you using?
   a. Windows 98
   b. Windows 3.1
   c. Windows NT
   d. Windows XP

2. A user complains that he cannot access the Internet with his Windows computer. You check his computer and find that you can access the company Web server using the IP address but not the name. Where should you go to fix this?
   a. Control Panel/Network and then Identification tab
   b. Control Panel/Network TCP/IP Properties and then DNS Configuration tab
   c. Control Panel/Network TCP/IP Properties and then IP Address tab
   d. Control Panel/Network TCP/IP Properties and then Advanced tab

3. You are a consultant for a small business and they want you to tell them how the IP address is configured. You run IPCONFIG on several machines and find that their IP addresses all start with 169.254. How is the IP address configured?
   a. using a DHCP server
   b. using an APIPA server
   c. using a class C static address
   d. using Automatic Private IP Addressing

4. A technician you work with explains to you that he just configured the IP address settings on a customer's computer but it still does not connect to the network. When asked, he tells you he configured the IP address, Default Gateway, and DNS Server. What should he do?
   a. Remove the DNS server address.
   b. Change the Default Gateway.
   c. Configure the Subnet Mask.
   d. Uninstall TCP/IP and reinstall it.

5. A user can access hosts on the the Internet fine but is unable to locate other Windows computers in the corporate network. What might resolve the problem?
   a. Configure the Default Gateway.
   b. Configure the WINS server address.
   c. Change the IP address.
   d. Change the Subnet Mask.

6. How do you configure IP address settings in Windows XP?
   a. Control Panel/Network Connections and select IP Settings
   b. Control Panel/Network select Properties and then double-click Internet Protocol
   c. Control Panel/Network Connections then choose TCP/IP from the Advanced menu
   d. Control Panel/Network Connections then select the connection and double-click Internet Protocol

7. What does DHCP mean?
   a. Direct Host Connection Protocol
   b. Dynamic Host Configuration Protocol
   c. Direct Host Computer Process
   d. Dynamic Host Creation Process

4.1 Identify the networking capabilities of Windows. Given configuration parameters, configure the operating system to connect to a network.

CONFIGURE PROTOCOLS: IPX/SPX (NWLINK), APPLETALK, AND NETBEUI/NETBIOS

UNDERSTANDING THE OBJECTIVE

While TCP/IP is the dominant protocol in networks today, you will still need to know how to configure the Novell protocol IPX/SPX, and for networks with Macintosh computers, AppleTalk is still frequently used. NetBEUI/NetBIOS has few configuration parameters so it is popular for small Windows networks that do not access the Internet.

WHAT YOU **REALLY** NEED TO KNOW

◆ For Windows computers to communicate with NetWare servers running IPX/SPX, that protocol must be installed on the Windows client.

◆ In Windows NT/2000/XP, IPX/SPX is referred to as NWLink. To install the IPX/SPX protocol in Windows 9x, go to the Network control panel, click Add, then select Protocol and hit the Add button and choose Microsoft in the left-hand window and IPX/SPX-compatible Protocol in the right-hand window.

◆ To configure IPX/SPX, select the protocol in the network properties dialog box and click Properties. If required in your network, you may need to enter a network address in the IPX/SPX properties and a Frame Type. Normally IPX/SPX requires no configuration changes because the Windows client gets settings from the NetWare server.

◆ If IPX/SPX is used only on Windows clients, you must enable the NetBIOS over IPX/SPX protocol so that Windows computer names can be resolved.

◆ The AppleTalk protocol cannot be configured on Windows clients but can be configured on Windows NT or Windows 2000 servers to support Macintosh clients running AppleTalk.

◆ The NetBEUI protocol is simple and fast but is limited in its capabilities with large networks. NetBEUI requires no configuration but cannot be routed so it cannot be used in a network that uses a router to communicate between LANs.

◆ NetBEUI uses NetBIOS names to identify computers on a Windows network.

◆ While Windows can run several protocols at the same time, it is best to only run the protocols that must be run in order to communicate. For example, there is little need to run both TCP/IP and NetBEUI unless some computers on the network only support NetBEUI.

◆ IPX/SPX is a Novell proprietary protocol and was the predominant network protocol used on NetWare servers through NetWare 4.1. Novell changed to using TCP/IP as the default protocol starting with NetWare 5.0.

OBJECTIVES ON THE JOB

Keep in mind, whenever possible, it is probably best to change to TCP/IP so that Internet access is possible. Also, it is very likely that IPX/SPX, AppleTalk, and NetBEUI will no longer be supported in the future. Note that Microsoft has discontinued NetBEUI support in Windows XP but for backward compatibility, it can be installed from the XP installation CD.

PRACTICE TEST QUESTIONS

1. What protocol is the default protocol used on a NetWare 4 server?
   - a. TCP/IP
   - b. NetBEUI
   - c. IPX/SPX
   - d. NWConnect

2. Which protocol is native to Windows computers and is a good choice for small networks not requiring Internet access?
   - a. TCP/IP
   - b. NetBEUI
   - c. IPX/SPX
   - d. NWConnect

3. How do Windows computers running NetBEUI name computers?
   - a. DNS
   - b. WINS
   - c. NetBIOS
   - d. NetNAME

4. With which protocol might you need to configure a frame type?
   - a. NetBEUI
   - b. NWLink
   - c. TCP/IP
   - d. DLC

5. What protocol is used by Macintosh computers?
   - a. DLC
   - b. NWLink
   - c. AppleTalk
   - d. MacLink

6. How do you add the NWLink protocol in Windows XP?
   - a. Click Install in the Local Area Connection Properties dialog box.
   - b. Click Protocols in the Local Area Connection Properties dialog box.
   - c. Click Install in the Advanced menu of the Network control panel.
   - d. Click Protocols in the Advaned menu of the Network control panel.

7. Which protocol is not supported in Windows 2000 clients?
   - a. TCP/IP
   - b. IPX/SPX
   - c. AppleTalk
   - d. NetBEUI

4.1 Identify the networking capabilities of Windows. Given configuration parameters, configure the operating system to connect to a network.

CONFIGURE CLIENT OPTIONS: MICROSOFT AND NOVELL • VERIFY THE CONFIGURATION

UNDERSTANDING THE OBJECTIVE

A network client allows a computer to access resources on a server. To access Windows resources, a Microsoft Windows client is required, and to access Novell resources, a Novell client is required.

WHAT YOU **REALLY** NEED TO KNOW

◆ The name of the client to connect to Windows network shares is called Client for Microsoft Networks. In Windows 98, Windows 2000, and Windows XP, this client is installed by default.

◆ In Windows NT, the Microsoft client is called the Workstation Service.

◆ To access resources on a Novell NetWare network from a Windows 9x client, you need either the Microsoft Client for NetWare Networks or the Novell Client. The Novell Client integrates better with NetWare servers but you will need to download it from the Novell Web site.

◆ In Windows NT/2000/XP, the Microsoft client for NetWare networks is called the Client Service for NetWare.

◆ To configure Windows 9x to log in to a Windows NT or Windows 2000 domain, the Client for Microsoft Networks must be configured.

◆ To configure the Client for Microsoft Networks, double-click the client in the Network control panel and select the check box to log on to Windows NT domain. Fill in the domain name under Windows NT domain.

◆ To specify a domain to log on to with Windows XP, go to System Properties, select the Computer Name tab and click either the Network ID button to run a wizard or the Change button to enter the information manually.

◆ To specify a domain to log on to with Windows 2000, go to System Properties, select the Network Identification tab and click either the Network ID button to run a wizard or the Properties button to enter the information manually.

◆ To verify a correct Windows network configuration, try to access a Windows resource on the local network by using either Network Neighborhood (My Network Places in Windows 2000/XP) or by going to Start/Run and typing *servername* where servername is the name of the computer whose resource you wish to access. If a Window opens showing a list of shared resources, your configuration is correct.

◆ To verify TCP/IP settings, try to ping your DNS servers. If that does not work, try to ping your default gateway and finally, try to ping yourself (127.0.0.1).

◆ Use IPCONFIG /ALL from the command line to view TCP/IP settings in Windows 98, Windows 2000, and Windows XP. For Windows 95, use the GUI utility Winipcfg, which is also available in Windows 98.

OBJECTIVES ON THE JOB

A technician must know how to install and configure network clients and verify the correct operation and configuration of network settings.

PRACTICE TEST QUESTIONS

1. **What is the name of the Windows 2000 client supplied by Microsoft that allows access to a NetWare server?**
   a. Microsoft Client for Novell
   b. Windows NetWare Client
   c. Client Service for NetWare
   d. Novell Client32

2. **You are running a Windows 98 computer and you want the computer to log on to a Windows domain upon start up, what must you do?**
   a. Configure the Client for Microsoft Networks to log on to a domain and enter the domain name.
   b. Install the Client for Windows Domains.
   c. Windows 98 will automatically detect a Windows domain and prompt for a log in name.
   d. Select Log in at Windows Startup in the Network control panel.

3. **What must you do for Windows 2000 to log on to a Windows domain?**
   a. Go to the Client for Microsoft Networks properties and check log on to Windows NT domain.
   b. Join a domain in System Properties.
   c. Windows 2000 will automatically detect a Windows domain and prompt for a log in name.
   d. Add the Domain client protocol.

4. **You are trying to make Windows 98 log into a NetWare 3.2 server named NW-SERV1. You have the Client for NetWare Networks installed but it is not working correctly, what can you try to solve the problem?**
   a. Configure the client to join the Novell Directory Service.
   b. Configure the NetWare server to recognize the workstation.
   c. From the Client for NetWare Networks properties, make NW-SERV1 the Preferred server.
   d. Reinstall the client.

5. **You don't see the Windows server called DB1 in Network Neighborhood, how can you try to connect to that server?**
   a. Install the Active Directory client.
   b. Start/Run and type \\DB1.
   c. Ping the server with the /connect option.
   d. Configure the Client for Microsoft Network with a Preferred server called DB1.

6. **You want to verify that your network connection and IP configuration are okay, what can you do?**
   a. ping 127.0.0.1
   b. ping localhost
   c. ping the DNS server
   d. ping 255.255.255.255

7. **To view all of your network connection IP settings plus the configured DNS server and DHCP server, what can you do? You are running Windows XP.**
   a. Go to the TCP/IP Properties in Network Control Panel.
   b. Type IPCONFIG /ALL from a command prompt.
   c. Type WINIPCFG /DETAIL from a command prompt.
   d. Type IPCONFIG –DETAIL from a command prompt.

4.1 Identify the networking capabilities of Windows. Given configuration parameters, configure the operating system to connect to a network.

UNDERSTAND THE USE OF THE FOLLOWING TOOLS: IPCONFIG.EXE, WINIPCFG.EXE, PING, TRACERT.EXE, AND NSLOOKUP.EXE

UNDERSTANDING THE OBJECTIVE

Ipconfig.exe and Winipcfg.exe are utilities used to view TCP/IP configuration settings. Ping, Tracert.exe and Nslookup.exe are all troubleshooting tools to verify connectivity, router operation, and DNS operations.

WHAT YOU **REALLY** NEED TO KNOW

◆ TCP/IP has a suite of utility programs designed to help troubleshoot problems with network communication. The utility programs that are automatically installed when TCP/IP is installed under Windows 9x and Windows 2000/XP are listed below:
- **ARP** manages the IP-to-Ethernet address translation tables that are used to find MAC addresses of a host and other configuration information.
- **Ipconfig** displays the IP address of the host and other configuration information (not in Windows 95).
- **FTP** transfers files over a network.
- **Nbtstat** displays current information about TCP/IP and NetBIOS when both are used on the same network.
- **Netstat** displays information about current TCP/IP connections.
- **Ping** verifies there is a connection on a network between two hosts.
- **Route** allows you to manually control network routing tables.
- **Telnet** provides a console session for a UNIX or Windows 2000 computer so you can enter console commands over the network.
- **Tracert** traces and displays the route from the host to a remote destination.
- **Winipcfg** displays IP address and other configuration information (only in Windows 9x).

The following are only in Windows 2000 and Windows XP:
- **Finger** displays information about a user on a specified system.
- **Hostname** displays the name of the current computer.
- **Lpq** displays status of a print queue.
- **Lpr** is used to print a file to a computer running an LPD server (print service).
- **Nslookup** shows information about the Domain Name System (DNS) name server on a network.
- **Rcp** is used to copy files between a Windows 2000 computer and a UNIX computer.
- **Rexec** and **Rsh** run commands on remote computers.
- **Tftp** transfers files between two computers.

OBJECTIVES ON THE JOB

A PC technician is expected to help support PCs on a network and the Internet. A technician should be familiar with all these utilities and be comfortable using the more critical ones including Ping, Winipcfg, Ipconfig, and Tracert.

PRACTICE TEST QUESTIONS

1. Which utility can you use to verify DNS information?
   a. Netstat
   b. Nslookup
   c. Hostname
   d. DNSinfo

2. What utility can you use to see the path a packet takes between your computer and *www.course.com*?
   a. Ping *www.course.com*
   b. Route *www.course.com*
   c. Tracert *www.course.com*
   d. Netstat *www.course.com*

3. Your computer was unable to reach a DHCP server when it first booted but you have solved the problem. How can you make your computer try to get an IP address from the DHCP server?
   a. DHCP /retry
   b. Netstat DHCP
   c. Ipconfig /renew
   d. Winipcfg /retry

4. Which TCP/IP utility is used to verify that two computers are connected over a network?
   a. FTP
   b. Ping
   c. Ipconfig
   d. Winipcfg

5. Which TCP/IP utility is a part of Windows 9x TCP/IP but is not included with Windows 2000 TCP/IP?
   a. Winipcfg
   b. Ipconfig
   c. Ping
   d. Route

6. What is Telnet?
   a. a service that allows a user to connect to a remote computer with a command line interface
   b. a service that allows files to be transmitted over the Internet from an FTP server
   c. a service that sends HTML documents over the Internet
   d. a service that allows a user to map a network drive to a network resource shared by someone else on the network

7. You want to view the MAC address of a computer on the network that you just pinged. How can you do this?
   a. Netstat -M
   b. Tracert /all
   c. Arp -a
   d. Ipconfig ip-address-of-remote-computer

4.1 Identify the networking capabilities of Windows. Given configuration parameters, configure the operating system to connect to a network.

SHARE RESOURCES (UNDERSTAND THE CAPABILITIES/LIMITATIONS WITH EACH OS VERSION) • SETTING PERMISSIONS TO SHARED RESOURCES

UNDERSTANDING THE OBJECTIVE

A shared disk drive is seen as a network drive on a PC that accesses the drive of another computer. When a printer is connected to a PC by way of a parallel or serial cable or infrared port in a network environment, that PC can share that printer with others on the network. Shared resources are available to others on the network, and, in Windows 9x, can be viewed in Network Neighborhood, and, in Windows 2000, can be viewed in My Network Places. Files and folders can be shared using Windows Explorer and can be password protected.

WHAT YOU **REALLY** NEED TO KNOW

◆ Using Windows 9x, to install file and printer sharing for Microsoft Networks, in the Control Panel, double-click the Network icon, click the Configuration tab, and then click the File and printer sharing for Microsoft Networks button.

◆ If the Network Neighborhood icon appears on the desktop, then Client for Microsoft Networks is installed. Double-click this icon to view and access resources on the network.

◆ To share a file or folder with others on the network using Windows 9x, right-click the file or folder name in Windows Explorer, and select Sharing from the shortcut menu. You must then give the folder or drive a name that will be used by others on the network to access this resource. Enter a password for added security.

◆ A shared drive or folder is displayed in Windows Explorer with a hand underneath the folder or drive icon.

◆ To map a network drive to a remote computer in Windows Explorer, click Tools on the menu bar, and then click Map Network Drive. Enter the host computer name preceded by two backslashes.

◆ To share a printer to others on the network, right-click the printer name in the Printer window and select Sharing from the shortcut menu. Give the printer a name, which will later appear to other users in the Network Neighborhood window on their desktop.

◆ Windows 9x has limited security available for network shares. Two passwords can be set: a read-only password and a full control password.

◆ Windows NT/2000/XP allow permissions to be set based upon individual users or groups. The sharing permissions are Read, Change, and Full Control.

◆ Windows NT Workstation, Windows 2000 Professional, and Windows XP Professional only permit 10 simultaneous connections for the purposes of sharing resources.

◆ Windows 9x does not have limitations on connections but more than 10 connections is impractical because Windows 9x is not optimized for file sharing activities.

OBJECTIVES ON THE JOB

In a business environment, it is a common practice to share printers, disk drives on file servers, and files on users' PCs. A PC technician's job has grown in today's networked environment to include frequent network configuration tasks.

PRACTICE TEST QUESTIONS

1. **What are the sharing permissions in Windows 2000?**
   a. Read, Write, Change
   b. Read, List, Full Control
   c. Read, Change, Full Control
   d. Read, Change, Delete

2. **Which is installed by default on Windows 2000 but not on Windows 9x?**
   a. TCP/IP
   b. File and Print Sharing for Microsoft Networks
   c. Client for Microsoft Networks
   d. Both b and c

3. **How do you install file and printer sharing for Microsoft Networks?**
   a. Control Panel, Network, Configuration, Add, Services
   b. Control Panel, Add/Remove Programs, Windows Setup
   c. Control Panel, Add New Hardware
   d. Control Panel, System Properties, Device Manager

4. **How do you share a file or folder with others on the network?**
   a. In Explorer, select the object, then use Network on the menu.
   b. In Explorer, right-click the object and select Sharing.
   c. In Network Neighborhood, right-click the object and select Sharing.
   d. Right-click the item displayed on the desktop, point to Properties, and then click Sharing.

5. **Using Windows 9x, how do you map a drive letter to a network resource?**
   a. In Explorer, select Tools, Map Network Drive.
   b. In Network Neighborhood, right-click the object and select Map Network Drive.
   c. In My Computer, right-click the object and select Map Network Drive.
   d. Either a or b.

6. **When you share a printer with others on the network, what is required?**
   a. The shared printer must be given a name.
   b. The shared printer must use a parallel cable rather than a serial cable.
   c. The shared printer must be a special network printer.
   d. The network protocol used must be NetBEUI.

7. **When using Windows Explorer, how can you tell that an object is network shared?**
   a. There is a blue "N" beside the object.
   b. There is a hand underneath the object.
   c. The object name is written in blue and underlined.
   d. All of the above.

4.1 Identify the networking capabilities of Windows. Given configuration parameters, configure the operating system to connect to a network.

NETWORK TYPE AND NETWORK CARD

UNDERSTANDING THE OBJECTIVE

The three most common local area network architectures used today are Ethernet, Token Ring, and FDDI. (Ethernet is by far the most popular of the three.) Each type requires its own network interface card (NIC), which must also match the type of network cabling used. The NIC requires that device drivers be installed under the OS.

WHAT YOU **REALLY** NEED TO KNOW

- ◆ Windows 95 supports Ethernet, Token Ring, and ARCnet networking cards; Windows 98 supports ATM, Ethernet, Token Ring, FDDI, IrDA, and ARCnet networking cards. Windows 2000/XP supports Ethernet, Token Ring, cable modem, DSL, FDDI, ATM, IrDA, wireless, T1, and Frame Relay.
- ◆ To view how a NIC is configured by Windows 9x, open the Control Panel, double-click the Network icon, and then click the Configuration tab. Right-click the network card and then click Properties on the shortcut menu.
- ◆ Windows 9x includes drivers for many network cards from many manufacturers, and you can also install drivers provided by the manufacturer.
- ◆ Windows 95 supports networks from four manufacturers: Banyan, Microsoft, Novell, and SunSoft. Windows 98 supports networks from three manufacturers: Banyan, Microsoft, and Novell.

OBJECTIVES ON THE JOB

On the job, when installing device drivers for a network card or installing the software to connect to a network, work under the supervision of the network administrator who is responsible for the overall configuration and security of the network.

Item	Ethernet	Token Ring	FDDI
Logical topology or shape	Bus	Single ring	Dual ring
Physical topology or shape	Star or bus	Ring or star	Ring
Media	Twisted pair, coaxial, or fiber-optic cable	Twisted pair, fiber-optic cable	Primarily fiber-optic
Standard bandwidth	10 Mbps or 100 Mbps	4 or 16 Mbps	100 Mbps to 200 Mbps
How token is released	Not applicable	After receive	After transmit
Advantages	Of the three networks, Ethernet is the least expensive, simplest, and most popular solution	Token Ring operates more reliably under heavy traffic than does Ethernet, but can be difficult to troubleshoot	FDDI is much faster than Token Ring and regular Ethernet and faster than 100BaseT (fast Ethernet)

PRACTICE TEST QUESTIONS

1. **What type of networks does Windows 95 support?**
   a. Ethernet, Token Ring, and FDDI
   b. Ethernet, Token Ring, and ARCnet
   c. Ethernet, Token Ring, and IrDA
   d. Token Ring, FDDI, and ARCnet

2. **You have a network card that has a port that looks like a large phone jack. What type of NIC is it?**
   a. an Ethernet card using a BNC connection
   b. an Ethernet card using a RJ-45 connection
   c. a Token Ring card
   d. a Banyan card

3. **Which is the most popular network architecture for a LAN?**
   a. FDDI
   b. Token Ring
   c. ATM
   d. Ethernet

4. **What is the most common topology used by Ethernet?**
   a. twisted pair
   b. TCP/IP
   c. star
   d. RJ-45

5. **Which type of network is not supported by Windows 98?**
   a. DecNet
   b. IPX/SPX
   c. TCP/IP
   d. NetBEUI

6. **Before data can be sent over a network, what happens to it?**
   a. It is put in packets with a header and trailer.
   b. It is segmented into 64-bit segments.
   c. It is converted into 16-bit bytes that are ready for parallel transmission.
   d. It is converted into ASCII form.

7. **Windows 98 has built-in support for what type of networking?**
   a. ATM
   b. peer-to-peer
   c. wide area
   d. SCSI

4.2 Identify the basic Internet protocols and terminologies. Identify procedures for establishing Internet connectivity. In a given scenario, configure the operating system to connect to and use Internet resources.

PROTOCOLS AND TERMINOLOGIES: ISP, TCP/IP, HTTPS, SSL, TELNET, AND DNS

UNDERSTANDING THE OBJECTIVE

The Internet has become ubiquitous in today's businesses and homes, so it is crucial that a PC technician understands the terminology and can perform basic configuration tasks related to Internet access. The technician must also know the types of applications and protocols used on the Internet, particularly as they apply to security (e.g., HTTPS and SSL).

WHAT YOU **REALLY** NEED TO KNOW

◆ An ISP is an Internet Service Provider. These are usually private companies that provide home and business users with an on-ramp to the Internet. Common types of connections to ISPs include dial-up networking, cable modem, ISDN, and DSL.

◆ TCP/IP is the protocol suite that is used for all communications on the Internet. Many protocols make up this suite including HTTP/HTTPS, SSL, Telnet and DNS.

◆ HTTP is hypertext transfer protocol. This is the protocol used to transfer Web pages from a Web server to a Web browser. HTTPS is similar to HTTP except that the 'S' on the end denotes security.

◆ Often, a browser automatically switches from HTTP to HTTPS when a link takes the browser to a secure site. In Internet Explorer, you can tell you are connected via HTTPS by the closed padlock icon in the status bar at the bottom of the IE window.

◆ SSL means secure socket layer and it is the underlying protocol that is used by HTTPS for security. With SSL, data is encrypted so that it cannot be easily intercepted and read.

◆ Telnet is a protocol used to communicate using a command line interface to a remote computer. This could be a Unix or Linux computer or even a Windows 2000 server. Telnet use in Windows 2000 is normally limited to occasional management tasks that can be performed at the command line.

◆ The Telnet client software is usually installed on any computer that runs TCP/IP but the server software usually must be configured on the Linux/Unix computer or Windows server.

◆ The DNS protocol means Domain Name Service. DNS client software is installed on computers that run TCP/IP but the DNS server must be specified in the TCP/IP configuration. DNS translates Internet host and domain names to IP addresses and in Windows 2000 domains, largely replaces WINS and NetBIOS for computer name resolution.

◆ To configure DNS settings in Windows 2000/XP, open the TCP/IP properties for the network connection you wish to configure and fill in the Primary and Secondary (if available) DNS server addresses. Two addresses are given for fault tolerance in case one server fails.

OBJECTIVES ON THE JOB

The PC technician must understand how to use the various Internet protocols and in some cases, how to configure these protocols.

PRACTICE TEST QUESTIONS

1. If a home computer user wants to access the Internet, who should be contacted?
   - a. the local phone company
   - b. an Internet service contractor
   - c. an installation service professional
   - d. an Internet service provider

2. To be sure your Web transaction is secure, the protocol field of the URL should be:
   - a. HTTP
   - b. SSL
   - c. HTTPS
   - d. FTP

3. SSL keeps transactions safe by which method?
   - a. requiring a password
   - b. encrypting data
   - c. using a private line
   - d. using a type 3 data transfer

4. Jane complains that she can access all of the computers in the company network but cannot access her favorite Web site, *www.bargains4u.com*. What can you check to troubleshoot the problem?
   - a. Jane's hostname
   - b. Jane's IP address
   - c. Jane's DHCP server
   - d. Jane's DNS server

5. Which protocol suite is the protocol of the Internet?
   - a. TC/ISP
   - b. Transmission Control Protocol/Internet Protocol
   - c. Transport Communication Protocol/Internet Protocol
   - d. Internetwork Packet Exchange Protocol

6. Which of the following is not a communication method for connecting to the Internet through an ISP?
   - a. DLC
   - b. DSL
   - c. ISDN
   - d. Dial-Up

7. You want to connect to the Internet through an ISP using dial-up networking, what must you have available to do so?
   - a. a T1 line to your house
   - b. a WAN circuit
   - c. a phone line and a modem
   - d. a cable modem

4.2 Identify the basic Internet protocols and terminologies. Identify procedures for establishing Internet connectivity. In a given scenario, configure the operating system to connect to and use Internet resources.

PROTOCOLS AND TERMINOLOGIES: E-MAIL (POP, SMTP, IMAP), HTML, HTTP, AND FTP

UNDERSTANDING THE OBJECTIVE

The Internet is a transportation service for many services, each using their own protocols. One of these protocols, **HTTP**, is used to pass documents to Web browsers over the World Wide Web originating from Web servers which are identified by IP addresses or domain names. These documents are often written so that text in the document can have an embedded link to other text or other documents. These documents are called hypertext files and are written using **HTML**. E-mail and FTP are two popular network services that use the Internet. FTP is used to transfer files across a network that supports TCP/IP.

WHAT YOU **REALLY** NEED TO KNOW

◆ The Internet is a group of networks that can be used by network services including Web browsers, chat rooms, e-mail, and FTP.

◆ Protocols at the Application layer of the OSI model, such as HTTP, FTP, POP, IMAP, and SMTP, use sockets or **NetBIOS** to establish communication with lower-level protocols. HTTP, FTP, POP, and SMTP all use the sockets method.

◆ For FTP to work, FTP software must be running at both the host and the client. The host runs FTP server and the client runs FTP client.

◆ For e-mail, a PC client establishes a session with a server to receive e-mail using the POP or IMAP protocol and send e-mail using the SMTP protocol. POP means post office protocol and IMAP means Internet Message Access Protocol.

◆ IMAP is a newer protocol than POP but is less frequently used. An advantage of IMAP is that only message headers such as From/To/Subject are initially sent to the E-mail client. Only when the user chooses to read the message is the message body transferred.

◆ Web browsers use HTTP protocol.

◆ HTML documents have an HTML file extension or an HTM file extension.

◆ A Web site is identified by its **IP address**, but a **domain name** can be substituted for the IP address when addressing the Web site.

◆ The protocol, domain name, and a path or filename are collectively called a **URL**, as in *http://www.course.com/pcrepair*. In this URL, *http* is the protocol used, the domain name is *www.course.com* and *pcrepair* is the name of a file on this Web site.

◆ Internet Corporation for Assigned Names and Numbers (ICANN) oversees the process of assigning IP addresses and domain names. A company that can register IP addresses and domain names is called a registrar.

◆ Valid endings for domain names include .com (commercial use), .edu (education), .gov (government), .org (nonprofit institutions), and .net (Internet provider).

OBJECTIVES ON THE JOB

A PC technician needs to understand how domain names and URLs are written and used.

PRACTICE TEST QUESTIONS

1. When a user wishes to send mail, the message is transferred to a server before going on to its destination. What protocol is used to transfer the message from the E-mail client to the server?

   a. POP
   b. SMTP
   c. IPX
   d. IMAP

2. What protocol is used to transfer a file from a Web server to a Web browser?

   a. HTML
   b. SMTP
   c. HTTP
   d. URL

3. What is FTP?

   a. a service that allows a user to enter UNIX commands in a UNIX window on a personal computer
   b. a service that allows files to be transmitted over a network to or from a remote computer
   c. a service that sends HTML documents over the Internet
   d. a service that allows a user to map a network drive to a network resource shared by someone else on the network

4. What organization tracks domain names and IP addresses?

   a. ICANN
   b. Microsoft
   c. IBM
   d. National Science Foundation

5. What is a URL?

   a. a uniform resource locator consisting of a protocol, a host name, and a domain name
   b. a unified return location consisting of a protocol, a host name, and a document title
   c. a uniform resource locator consisting of a user name, a host name, and a domain name
   d. a unified resource logistic consisting of a protocol, a host name, and a document title

6. What protocol is used to transfer mail from the mail server to the mail client?

   a. SMTP
   b. POP
   c. Presentation Office Protocol
   d. HTTPS

7. What protocol will you use to transfer a 2 MB binary file from a server to your workstation?

   a. HTML
   b. HTTPS
   c. UDP
   d. FTP

4.2 Identify the basic Internet protocols and terminologies. Identify procedures for establishing Internet connectivity. In a given scenario, configure the operating system to connect to and use Internet resources.

CONNECTIVITY TECHNOLOGIES: DIAL-UP NETWORKING, DSL NETWORKING, ISDN NETWORKING, CABLE, SATELLITE, WIRELESS, AND LAN

UNDERSTANDING THE OBJECTIVE

An Internet Service Provider (ISP) provides access to the Internet for businesses and personal use. Users can access the ISP by any of several methods, including a dedicated circuit, ISDN line, or regular analog phone line. Today's Internet user demands faster access through technologies such as DSL, Cable, and Satellite. Wireless LANs are a burgeoning technology, particularly for small offices and home networks.

WHAT YOU REALLY NEED TO KNOW

- ◆ When connecting to an ISP and then to the Internet using dial-up access, data is packaged using TCP/IP for Internet traffic, but is also packaged in a line protocol for travel over phone lines to the ISP.
- ◆ Two line protocols are **Serial Line Internet Protocol (SLIP)** and **Point-to-Point Protocol (PPP)**. The older SLIP has been replaced by the faster PPP.
- ◆ Windows 9x supports **Dial-Up Networking (DUN)** so that the modem acts like a network card when calling an ISP or other entry point into a network.
- ◆ DSL and cable technologies provide fast, always-on connectivity to the Internet—typically as much as 50 times faster than dial-up.
- ◆ ISDN is still used in some areas but DSL and cable are the primary high-speed technologies for home access. ISDN is often used by businesses as a backup technology if their primary connection goes down.
- ◆ Both DSL and ISDN can work over standard phone lines provided the location is not too far away from the telephone company switching office.
- ◆ Satellite Internet access is becoming popular, especially in areas that do not have cable access or DSL. However, the user must usually be in a line of site with the ISP satellites.
- ◆ Wireless LANs are becoming very popular, especially in situations where running wire is impractical or undesirable such as older buildings or in homes and small offices. The dominant wireless LAN technology is 802.11 with subcategories 802.11b, 802.11a, and 802.11g. 802.11b runs at 11 Mbps and 802.11a and 802.11g both run at speeds up to 54 Mbps.

OBJECTIVES ON THE JOB

A PC technician may be called upon to install and configure Internet access. Knowing the technologies available and their strengths and weaknesses will help when deciding which technology to use. Dial–up networking (DUN) is still very common, even with the faster technologies available. DUN's biggest strength is low cost, but the slow speed makes it unsuitable for most business uses. But DUN can be finicky to set up and configure for optimal transfer speeds.

PRACTICE TEST QUESTIONS

1. When configuring a PC to use a modem to an ISP to connect to the Internet, what line protocol is most likely to be used today?
   - a. PPP
   - b. SLIP
   - c. TCP/IP
   - d. none of the above

2. Which technology can use standard phone lines? (choose all that apply)
   - a. ISP
   - b. DSL
   - c. Cable
   - d. ISDN

3. What LAN technology might you choose in a home network that allows you to carry a laptop from room to room and remain connected?
   - a. DSL
   - b. 802.11b
   - c. ISDN
   - d. 10BaseT

4. When an IP address is assigned to a PC each time it logs onto a network, this is called:
   - a. the Internet
   - b. TCP/IP addressing
   - c. dynamic IP addressing
   - d. static IP addressing

5. Which high-speed technology for Internet access is appropriate where there is no cable television and the location is a very long distance from the phone company?
   - a. 802.11a
   - b. Satellite
   - c. DSL
   - d. Dial-up

6. What technology permits two 64K B channels which can be combined for a 128K connection?
   - a. Dial-up
   - b. Satellite
   - c. Wireless
   - d. ISDN

7. When using DUN, what is the highest speed connection possible?
   - a. 1 Mbps
   - b. 33 Kbps
   - c. 56 Kbps
   - d. 192 Kbps

4.2 Identify the basic Internet protocols and terminologies. Identify procedures for establishing Internet connectivity. In a given scenario, configure the operating system to connect to and use Internet resources.

INSTALLING AND CONFIGURING BROWSERS: ENABLE/DISABLE SCRIPT SUPPORT, CONFIGURE PROXY SETTINGS, AND CONFIGURE SECURITY SETTINGS • FIREWALL PROTECTION UNDER WINDOWS XP

UNDERSTANDING THE OBJECTIVE

A primary concern for Internet users is security. Scripts are small programs that can be run by a Web browser over the Internet, causing potential harm to your system or transferring a virus. Browsers and operating systems are equipped with technologies to prevent undesirable access to your computer. These include Web proxies, firewalls, and the ability to turn certain browser features on and off.

WHAT YOU **REALLY** NEED TO KNOW

- ◆ Internet scripting was developed to add interactivity and additional functionality to Web browsing. These scripting languages include JavaScript, Jscript, Perl, and more. Unfortunately, crackers can use scripting for malicious purposes such as transporting viruses or getting crucial information off your computer.
- ◆ To disable scripting in Internet Explorer 6, go to Tools/Internet Options and select the Security tab. You can choose a Security Zone or just select Internet for all sites not listed in other zones, and then choose Custom Level.
- ◆ A proxy is a computer that acts on another's behalf in making Internet requests. When proxy settings are enabled, the Web browser contacts the proxy server with a Web site request and the proxy server forwards that request, thereby insulating the client from direct interaction with the Internet.
- ◆ To configure proxy settings on Internet Explorer, go to Tools/Internet Options and select the Connections tab. Click Settings and check the box under Proxy settings.
- ◆ To configure all security settings, go to Tools\Internet Options and select the Security tab. From here you can create different levels of security for zones that consist of lists of Web sites.
- ◆ Windows XP provides an Internet Connection Firewall. A firewall is a device or program that scans Internet packets as they are transferred. Packets that meet certain criteria are filtered or discarded so that they cannot cause harm to the system or network.
- ◆ To enable the Internet Connection Firewall, go to the Properties of your Internet connection, click the Advanced tab, and check the box next to Internet Connection Firewall.
- ◆ To configure Internet Connection Firewall, enable the firewall and then click the Settings button. By default, all services are disabled but you can click the check box next to any service you wish to make available to outside users.

OBJECTIVES ON THE JOB

A PC technician may not be required to know all of the ins and outs of network configuration but because a network connection, particularly a connection to the Internet, is part of almost every PC installation today, the technician must know the basics of configuring browsers and connections. Security know-how is a must so that a user's PC and a company's network is protected.

PRACTICE TEST QUESTIONS

1. **Where can you configure scripting support in Internet Explorer?**
   a. Tools/Security and then choose Scripting
   b. Tools/Internet Options/Security tab
   c. Options/Settings/Security tab
   d. File/Options/Scripting

2. **Which of the following is not a type of script?**
   a. ActiveX controls
   b. Java applets
   c. Microsoft application scripts
   d. Perl

3. **What type of device acts as an intermediary between a Web client and a Web server?**
   a. Firewall
   b. File and Print server
   c. Active host
   d. Proxy

4. **What device or program can filter out undesirable packets from reaching a host or network?**
   a. Firewall
   b. File and Print server
   c. Active host
   d. Proxy

5. **How can you configure Windows XP Internet Firewall Connection to only allow Web server packets into the network?**
   a. Configure proxy settings from Internet Explorer.
   b. Configure ICW and check the Web Server check box.
   c. Go to Start/Run and type icw-setup.
   d. You cannot do this.

6. **Which is true about the Internet Connection Firewall?**
   a. It is enabled by default.
   b. Once enabled, it blocks only FTP and HTTP services by default.
   c. Once enabled, it blocks all Web services by default.
   d. It only blocks outgoing packets.

7. **Which of the following can you configure on IE 6? (choose all that apply)**
   a. Proxy settings
   b. Undesirable content filtering
   c. Firewall settings
   d. SSL settings

PAGE 2

Objective 1.1	Identify the names, purpose, and characteristics, of system modules. Recognize these modules by sight or definition.	Motherboard Ports

Practice Test Questions

1. Which statement about the motherboard is false?
   Correct answer: d

2. In the drawing at the right, item 1 is a(n):
   Correct answer: a

3. In the drawing at the right, item 2 is a(n):
   Correct answer: c

4. In the drawing at the right, item 3 is a(n):
   Correct answer: c

5. In the drawing at the right, item 4 is a(n):
   Correct answer: c

6. A FRU that is installed on the motherboard is:
   Correct answer: a

7. Timing on the motherboard is controlled by the:
   Correct answer: d

PAGE 4

Objective 1.1	Identify the names, purpose, and characteristics, of system modules. Recognize these modules by sight or definition.	Firmware

Practice Test Questions

1. When the PC loses setup information each time it is booted, a possible cause of this problem is:
   Correct answer: b

2. The system date and time can be set using:
   Correct answer: d

3. One reason you might flash ROM is to:
   Correct answer: a

4. Plug and Play is a feature of:
   Correct answer: d

5. How do you access CMOS to view settings and make changes?
   Correct answer: a

6. The program to change CMOS can be stored:
   Correct answer: d

7. The type of ROM BIOS that can be changed without exchanging the chip is called:
   Correct answer: c

PAGE 6

Objective 1.1	Identify the names, purpose, and characteristics, of system modules. Recognize these modules by sight or definition.	Power supply

Practice Test Questions

1. Which power supply provides 3 volts of DC current to a motherboard?
   Correct answer: c

2. What is the relationship between power, current, and voltage?
   Correct answer: b

3. What is the unit of measure for the capacitance of a capacitor?
   Correct answer: d

4. Which statement is true about the power from an ATX power supply to a motherboard?
   Correct answer: b

5. Which statement is true about a power supply?
   Correct answer: a

6. The voltage used by a floppy disk drive is:
   Correct answer: c

7. An AT motherboard uses which voltages?
   Correct answer: a

PAGE 8

Objective 1.1	Identify the names, purpose, and characteristics, of system modules. Recognize these modules by sight or definition.	Processor/CPU

Practice Test Questions

1. Running a motherboard at a higher speed than that suggested by the manufacturer is called:
   Correct answer: b

2. What does the CPU do?
   Correct answer: b

3. Which CPU technology is used to improve software multitasking performance?
   Correct answer: d

4. If the CPU is running at 300 MHz and the system bus is running at 100 MHz, then the multiplier is:
   Correct answer: c

5. Typical speeds for today's system bus are:
   Correct answer: b

6. RISC stands for:
   Correct answer: a

7. A memory cache stored on the CPU microchip is called:
   Correct answer: a

PAGE 10

Objective 1.1	Identify the names, purpose, and characteristics, of system modules. Recognize these modules by sight or definition.	Memory Display devices

Practice Test Questions

1. Another name for reserved memory is:
   Correct answer: d

2. Which type of monitor provides the highest quality performance?
   Correct answer: c

3. A parity error is most likely caused by what device?
   Correct answer: b

4. Which device is not considered a field replaceable unit?
   Correct answer: d

5. Which DOS device driver is used to gain access to extended memory?
   Correct answer: b

6. Space on the hard drive that is used as though it were RAM is called:
   Correct answer: d

7. Which memory module is used to hold memory cache on the motherboard?
   Correct answer: c

PAGE 12

Objective 1.1	Identify the names, purpose, and characteristics, of system modules. Recognize these modules by sight or definition.	Storage devices

Practice Test Questions

1. What is the purpose of ATAPI standards?
   Correct answer: b

2. What is a Jaz drive?
   Correct answer: a

3. Which statement is true about an IDE hard drive and a SCSI hard drive?
   Correct answer: b

4. How can you change the boot priority of a system?
   Correct answer: c

5. What is boot priority?
   Correct answer: b

6. Which statement is true about Zip drives and Jaz drives?

Correct answer: c

7. Which statement is true about secondary storage?

Correct answer: b

PAGE 14

Objective 1.1	Identify the names, purpose, and characteristics, of system modules. Recognize these modules by sight or definition.	Adapter cards Cases Riser cards

Practice Test Questions

1. Low-profile cases use which motherboard form factors?

   Correct answer: d

2. In which direction do adapter cards run when used in conjunction with a riser card?

   Correct answer: a

3. Which types of adapter cards may have BIOS that run before POST?

   Correct answer: b

4. The modem command to hang up the phone is:

   Correct answer: b

5. An external modem connects to:

   Correct answer: c

6. Which of the following is NOT an adapter card?

   Correct answer: b

7. Which adapter card uses a 15-pin 3 row port?

   Correct answer: c

PAGE 16

Objective 1.2	Identify basic procedures for adding and removing field-replaceable modules for desktop systems. Given a replacement scenario, choose the appropriate sequences.	Motherboard

Practice Test Questions

1. The purpose of a standoff is to:

   Correct answer: a

2. Which of the following devices are considered FRUs?

   Correct answer: d

3. Before replacing a dead motherboard, one thing you should do is:

   Correct answer: d

4. What is one thing that might cause damage to a motherboard as you service a PC?

   Correct answer: a

5. When installing AT power supply connections to a motherboard, what should you remember?
   Correct answer: b

6. When installing a motherboard, which is installed first?
   Correct answer: b

7. When exchanging a motherboard, why is it important to remove other components?
   Correct answer: d

PAGE 18

Objective 1.2	Identify basic procedures for adding and removing field-replaceable modules for desktop systems. Given a replacement scenario, choose the appropriate sequences.	Storage device: FDD HDD CD/CDRW DVD/DVDRW Tape drive Removable storage

Practice Test Questions

1. If a system has two IDE hard drives that each have primary and extended partitions with one logical drive in each partition, what is the drive letter assigned to the primary partition of the second hard drive?
   Correct answer: b

2. After performing a low-level format of a hard drive, what is the next step in the installation process?
   Correct answer: b

3. What kind of cable is a 34-pin data cable?
   Correct answer: d

4. How many pins does an IDE data cable have?
   Correct answer: c

5. When a CD-ROM drive and an IDE hard drive are sharing the same data cable:
   Correct answer: a

6. A port on the back of a PC has 50 pins. What type port is it?
   Correct answer: b

7. Which IRQ does the primary IDE channel use?
   Correct answer: c

Objective 1.2	Identify basic procedures for adding and removing field–replaceable modules for desktop systems. Given a replacement scenario, choose the appropriate sequences.	Power supply: AC adapter and AT/ATX Display device Input devices: Keyboard, mouse/ pointer devices, and touch screen

Practice Test Questions

1. The ESD bracelet is designed to protect:
   Correct answer: a

2. If a monitor does not power on, what should you check?
   Correct answer: d

3. Before exchanging a power supply, you should:
   Correct answer: d

4. If the cable connector on a keyboard does not fit the keyboard port on the system board, then:
   Correct answer: b

5. If the mouse port on a system board does not work, then:
   Correct answer: d

6. What ports can a mouse use?
   Correct answer: d

7. How does a keyboard get its power?
   Correct answer: a

Objective 1.2	Identify basic procedures for adding and removing field-replaceable modules for desktop systems. Given a replacement scenario, choose the appropriate sequences.	Cooling systems: Fans, heat sinks, and liquid cooling Processor/CPU Memory

Practice Test Questions

1. A system has two SIMMs installed and two SIMM slots are still open. Which is correct?
   Correct answer: c

2. A system has four DIMM slots and one DIMM installed. Which statement is correct?
   Correct answer: a

3. Which statement is true about RAM on a system board?

Correct answer: c

4. After installing memory and booting the system, the memory does not count up correctly. The most likely problem is:

Correct answer: b

5. How many pins are there on a DIMM?

Correct answer: d

6. Without the system board documentation, how can you tell if a DIMM is the correct type of memory for a system board?

Correct answer: b

7. Why does a Pentium system require that SIMMs be installed in pairs?

Correct answer: a

PAGE 24

Objective 1.2	Identify basic procedures for adding and removing field-replaceable modules for desktop systems. Given a replacement scenario, choose the appropriate sequences.	Adapters: Sound card, video card, SCSI, IEEE 1394/FireWire, and USB

Practice Test Questions

1. The fastest port used for video boards today is:

Correct answer: c

2. What is the difference in an AGP slot and an AGP Pro slot on a system board?

Correct answer: b

3. What is one thing you can do to speed up a sluggish system that is graphic intensive?

Correct answer: a

4. AGP 4X is defined by the AGP 2.0 specification. The 4X refers to:

Correct answer: a

5. What bus is no longer found on system boards today?

Correct answer: d

6. The video system does not work. What is the first thing you check?

Correct answer: a

7. What is the name of the string identifier that is used to match a specific hardware device with its installation software?

Correct answer: a

PAGE 26

Objective 1.2	Identify basic procedures for adding and removing field-replaceable modules for desktop systems. Given a replacement scenario, choose the appropriate sequences.	Adapters: Network Interface Card (NIC), modem, and wireless

Practice Test Questions

1. Which of the following techniques are useful for troubleshooting modem problems?
   Correct answer: d

2. What is the most common cause of modem failure?
   Correct answer: b

3. What is one thing you can do to speed up sluggish bandwidth on a wireless network?
   Correct answer: b

4. What is the most common type of network cable used today?
   Correct answer: b

5. Which bus can be used to install a modem?
   Correct answer: d

6. How can users be authenticated on a wireless network?
   Correct answer: b

7. How can you tell that the network card is connected to and communicating with other network equipment on the network?
   Correct answer: d

PAGE 28

Objective 1.3	Identify basic procedures for adding and removing field-replaceable modules for portable systems. Given a replacement scenario, choose the appropriate sequences.	Storage devices: FDD, HDD, CD/CDRW, DVD/DVDRW, and removable storage Memory

Practice Test Questions

1. Which of the following devices is considered a field replaceable unit on a notebook computer?
   Correct answer: d

2. Which types of technology are often bundled together into a single drive?
   Correct answer: b

3. To hot-swap an external storage device, which statement must be true?
   Correct answer: b

4. What kind of memory do notebook computers use?
   Correct answer: a

5. Which operating system provides the most comprehensive support for hot-swapping devices?
   Correct answer: d

6. Which of the following steps should be followed, given the following scenario? Upgrade notebook memory.
   Correct answer: d

7. Which hardware or software listed below is typically proprietary to the make and model of the notebook computer?
   Correct answer: d

Objective 1.3	Identify basic procedures for adding and removing field-replaceable modules for portable systems. Given a replacement scenario, choose the appropriate sequences.	PCMCIA/Mini PCI Adapters: Network interface card (NIC), modem, SCSI, IEEE 1394/FireWire, USB, and storage (memory and hard drive)

Practice Test Questions

1. Which of the following operating systems support USB 2.0 via a Microsoft patch or service pack?

   Correct answer: d

2. Which of the following techniques is useful in troubleshooting issues with a PCMCIA card?

   Correct answer: d

3. To hot-swap an external storage device, which statement must be true?

   Correct answer: b

4. If a notebook does not have an internal modem included in the hardware, how is a modem typically added to the system?

   Correct answer: c

5. What is the Windows XP feature that allows you to share an Internet connection between two computers?

   Correct answer: c

6. Which of the following operating systems support USB 1.0?

   Correct answer: d

7. What is important to first determine before servicing or upgrading a notebook computer?

   Correct answer: a

Objective 1.3	Identify basic procedures for adding and removing field-replaceable modules for portable systems. Given a replacement scenario, choose the appropriate sequences.	Power sources: AC adapter, DC adapter, and battery LCD panel

Practice Test Questions

1. Which type of battery is most often shipped with state-of-the-art notebook computers?
   Correct answer: b

2. Which types of notebook batteries typically experienced memory problems?
   Correct answer: c

3. Which of the following is true concerning LCD panels?
   Correct answer: d

4. Which of the following technologies produce a sharper image?
   Correct answer: a

5. Which of the following can be used to power a notebook computer?
   Correct answer: d

6. What is the danger in using the AC adapter too much to power a notebook?
   Correct answer: d

7. Which of the following steps should you take if an LCD panel is cracked?
   Correct answer: d

PAGE 34

Objective 1.3	Identify basic procedures for adding and removing field-replaceable modules for portable systems. Given a replacement scenario, choose the appropriate sequences.	Docking station/Port replicators Input devices: Keyboard, mouse/pointer devices, and touch screen Wireless: Adapter/ Controller and antennae

Practice Test Questions

1. Which Intel processor is integrating support for wireless LANs?
   Correct answer: c

2. How should an antenna that transmits an omni-directional be physically positioned?
   Correct answer: a

3. How can a PCI card be added to a notebook computer?
   Correct answer: b

4. What do access points use to transmit RF signals to wireless cards in notebook computers?
   Correct answer: a

5. Which operating provides the most comprehensive support for wireless network cards?
   Correct answer: d

6. Which notebook hardware listed below is considered a field-replaceable unit?
   Correct answer: d

7. Which hardware or software listed below is typically proprietary to the make and model of the notebook computer?
   Correct answer: d

Objective 1.4	Identify typical IRQs, DMAs, and I/O addresses, and procedures for altering these settings when installing and configuring devices. Choose the appropriate installation or configuration steps in a given scenario.	Legacy devices (e.g., ISA sound card) Specialized devices (e.g., CAD/CAM) Multimedia devices

Practice Test Questions

1. Which of the following statements is true?
   Correct answer: b

2. Which of the following IRQs is typically available:
   Correct answer: d

3. In this scenario, choose a common technique for modify resource settings (either on the computer or device itself) for a common device such as a sound card.
   Correct answer: d

4. The purpose of an IRQ is to:
   Correct answer: b

5. The purpose of an I/O address is to:
   Correct answer: a

6. Which IRQ can a device using an 8-bit ISA bus NOT use?
   Correct answer: d

7. On the 16-bit ISA bus, IRQ 2 is used to cascade to the higher IRQs, so its position on the ISA bus is taken by which IRQ?
   Correct answer: c

Objective 1.4	Identify typical IRQs, DMAs, and I/O addresses, and procedures for altering these settings when installing and configuring devices. Choose the appropriate installation or configuration steps in a given scenario.	Internal modems Floppy drive controllers Hard drive controllers NICs

Practice Test Questions

1. A disk drive can access primary memory without involving the CPU by using a(n):
   Correct answer: c

2. IRQ 14 is reserved for:
   Correct answer: d

3. IRQ 15 is reserved for:
   Correct answer: c

4. IRQ 4 is reserved for:
   Correct answer: d

5. Give the following scenario, which of the following steps should you take to solve the problem? An ISA modem is conflicting.
Correct answer: d

6. IRQ 9 is reserved for:
Correct answer: a

7. Which of the following statements are true?
Correct answer: a

PAGE 40

Objective 1.4	Identify typical IRQs, DMAs, and I/O addresses, and procedures for altering these settings when installing and configuring devices. Choose the appropriate installation or configuration steps in a given scenario.	I/O ports: Serial, parallel, USB ports, IEEE 1394/FireWire, and infrared

Practice Test Questions

1. IRQ 5 is reserved for:
Correct answer: b

2. IRQ 3 is reserved for:
Correct answer: a

3. In this scenario, choose a common technique to modify resource settings (either on the computer or device itself) for a common device such as an IEEE 1394/FireWire card.
Correct answer: d

4. IRQ 9 is reserved for:
Correct answer: c

5. Give the following scenario, which of the following steps should you take to solve the problem? Under Windows 2000/XP, a USB device is not being detected after being plugged into a USB port.
Correct answer: d

6. Which of the following operating systems have offered native support for USB ports?
Correct answer: d

7. Which of the following operating systems have offered native support for FireWire ports?
Correct answer: a

PAGE 42

Objective 1.5	Identify the names, purposes, and performance characteristics, of standardized/common peripheral ports, associated cabling, and their connectors. Recognize ports, cabling, and connectors, by sight.	Port types: Serial, parallel, USB ports, IEEE 1394/FireWire, and infrared

Practice Test Questions

1. Serial ports can support:
   Correct answer: c

2. A normal printer port is also known as a(n) ____ port.
   Correct answer: a

3. EPP and ____ ports can transmit data in both directions.
   Correct answer: d

4. A USB cable has only ____ wires.
   Correct answer: c

5. The maximum usable length of a parallel cable is ____ meters.
   Correct answer: a

6. The maximum usable length of a USB 1.0 cable is ____ meters.
   Correct answer: c

7. The maximum usable length of an IEEE cable is ____ meters.
   Correct answer: c

PAGE 44

Objective 1.5	Identify the names, purposes, and performance characteristics, of standardized/common peripheral ports, associated cabling, and their connectors. Recognize ports, cabling, and connectors, by sight.	Cable types: Serial (straight through vs. null modem), parallel, and USB Connector types: Serial (DB-9, DB-25, RJ-11, and RJ-45), parallel (DB-25 and Centronics (mini, 36)), PS2/mini-din, USB, and IEEE 1394

Practice Test Questions

1. A 25-pin female port on the back of your computer is most likely to be a:
   Correct answer: a

2. What component controls serial port communication?
   Correct answer: c

3. Which port provides the faster data transmission speeds?
   Correct answer: d

4. Which port cannot support a printer?
   Correct answer: d

5. Which port provides the fastest data transmission rate for a printer?
   Correct answer: b

6. Which device can use a DMA channel?
   Correct answer: b

7. Which device uses a 9-pin data cable?
   Correct answer: b

Objective 1.6	Identify proper procedures for installing and configuring common IDE devices. Choose the appropriate installation or configuration sequences in given scenarios. Recognize the associated cables.	IDE interface types: EIDE, ATA/ATAPI, serial ATA, and PIO RAID (0, 1, 5) Master/Slave/Cable select Devices per channel Primary/Secondary Cable orientation/ requirements

Practice Test Questions

1. When installing a second IDE device on an IDE channel, you must:
   Correct answer: c

2. How many EIDE devices can be installed in a system?
   Correct answer: c

3. A system has a single IDE device installed on the primary IDE channel, and a new IDE device is installed on the secondary IDE channel. The new device does not work. What might be a cause of the problem?
   Correct answer: c

4. Which RAID level is used to write the same data to two hard drives?
   Correct answer: b

5. Two IDE devices share a data cable. Which statement is true?
   Correct answer: c

6. When connecting a floppy drive data cable to a system board connection, how do you know the correct orientation of the cable to the connection?
   Correct answer: b

7. A CD-ROM drive that uses an IDE interface to the system board is following what specifications?
   Correct answer: b

Objective 1.7	Identify proper procedures for installing and configuring common SCSI devices. Choose the appropriate installation or configuration sequences in given scenarios. Recognize the associated cables.	SCSI interface types: Narrow, fast, wide, ultra-wide, LVD, and HVD Raid (0, 1, 5)

Practice Test Questions

1. SCSI-2 can support how many devices?
   Correct answer: c

2. The data path of Wide Ultra SCSI is:
   Correct answer: c

3. Which is the fastest SCSI standard?
   Correct answer: d

4. Which of the following is a difference between a single-ended SCSI cable and a differential SCSI cable?
   Correct answer: d

5. What is true about SCSI termination?
   Correct answer: a

6. Which major SCSI standard does not include a standard for 16-bit data transmission?
   Correct answer: a

7. How many pins does a Narrow SCSI data cable have?
   Correct answer: a

PAGE 50

Objective 1.7	Identify proper procedures for installing and configuring common SCSI devices. Choose the appropriate installation or configuration sequences in given scenarios. Recognize the associated cables.	Internal versus External SCSI IDs: Jumper block/DIP switch settings (binary equivalents) and resolving ID conflicts Cabling: Length, type, and termination requirements (active, passive, auto)

Practice Test Questions

1. A SCSI ID is set on a SCSI device using three jumpers. If the ID is set to 6, what will be the jumper settings?
   Correct answer: a

2. Which statement about a SCSI configuration is true?
   Correct answer: d

3. Two SCSI hard drives are installed on the same SCSI bus. Which statement is true?
   Correct answer: d

4. How many devices can be used on a single SCSI bus, including the host adapter?
   Correct answer: b

5. A SCSI CD-ROM drive is installed on an existing SCSI bus in a system. Which statement is true?
   Correct answer: a

6. How can a SCSI ID be set on a SCSI device?
   Correct answer: d

7. A SCSI bus has three SCSI devices and a host adapter. Which device(s) can communicate with the CPU?
   Correct answer: a

274   SOLUTIONS FOR CORE PRACTICE TESTS

PAGE 52

Objective 1.8	Identify proper procedures for installing and configuring common peripheral devices. Choose the appropriate installation or configuration sequences in given scenarios.	Modems and Transceivers (dial-up, cable, DSL, ISDN) Monitors

Practice Test Questions

1. An external modem will most likely use which port on a PC?
   Correct answer: a

2. Video cards are normally installed in which bus expansion slot?
   Correct answer: d

3. A VESA bus expansion slot:
   Correct answer: b

4. The AGP expansion slot:
   Correct answer: a

5. What IRQ does an external modem use?
   Correct answer: a

6. Which device does not require an IRQ?
   Correct answer: c

7. Describe the port typically used by a monitor on today's systems.
   Correct answer: b

PAGE 54

Objective 1.8	Identify proper procedures for installing and configuring common peripheral devices. Choose the appropriate installation or configuration sequences in given scenarios.	External storage Digital cameras PDAs Wireless access points

Practice Test Questions

1. After physically installing a floppy drive, the next step is to:
   Correct answer: b

2. You attach a Palm Pilot to the serial port on your computer and would like to synchronize files between your computer and PDA. How can this be accomplished?
   Correct answer: b

3. An IDE Zip drive data cable has how many pins?
   Correct answer: d

4. You install an internal CD-R drive on a computer that already has an internal CD-ROM drive. To which IDE ribbon should the CD-R drive be connected in order to optimize performance?
   Correct answer: b

5. You install a floppy drive and reboot the PC. The drive light on the floppy drive stays lit and the system hangs. What is the most likely source of the problem?

Correct answer: a

6. You have installed an IDE CD-ROM drive as the only device using the secondary IDE channel, and the drive is not recognized by the system. What is likely to be wrong?

Correct answer: b

7. You have installed an external Zip drive using a second parallel port in a system, and you cannot get the system to recognize the drive. What is likely to be wrong?

Correct answer: d

PAGE 56

Objective 1.8	Identify proper procedures for installing and configuring common peripheral devices. Choose the appropriate installation or configuration sequences in given scenarios.	Infrared devices Printers UPS (Uninterruptible Power Supply) and suppressors

Practice Test Questions

1. Which of the following techniques can be used to troubleshoot printing problems on an ink-jet printer?

Correct answer: d

2. When does a parallel port require a DMA channel?

Correct answer: b

3. You use an UPS to supply power to your Windows XP computer and would like to enable the UPS to automatically shutdown the computer in the event of a power failure. What should you do?

Correct answer: d

4. You install a printer, but the PC cannot communicate with the printer. What is one thing to check?

Correct answer: d

5. Surge suppressors can protect which of the following devices?

Correct answer: d

6. What port on the back of a computer allows you to use a keyboard or other input device without a connecting cord to the computer?

Correct answer: d

7. Which of the following techniques can be used to troubleshoot problems with infrared devices?

Correct answer: d

Objective 1.9	Identify procedures to optimize PC operations in specific situations. Predict the effects of specific procedures under given scenarios.	Cooling systems: Liquid, air, heat sink, and thermal compound Memory Additional processors

Practice Test Questions

1. Given the following scenario, predict the outcome. You upgrade the memory to 256 MB of PC100 RAM on a computer with a system bus of 133MHz.
   Correct answer: a

2. Given the following scenario, predict the outcome. You over-clock your CPU by 25 percent.
   Correct answer: d

3. Given the following scenario, predict the outcome. You add a second processor to a file server without adding a fan.
   Correct answer: a

4. Given the following scenario, predict the outcome. After installing Windows XP, you add a second processor to your computer.
   Correct answer: b

5. What is the minimum amount of memory for Windows XP, as recommended by Microsoft?
   Correct answer: a

6. What is the best practice when choosing memory for an upgrade?
   Correct answer: b

7. Given the following scenario, predict the outcome. Your computer keeps freezing and you suspect that it may be caused by faulty memory. Which of the following techniques are useful in troubleshooting this problem?
   Correct answer: d

Objective 1.9	Identify procedures to optimize PC operations in specific situations. Predict the effects of specific procedures under given scenarios.	Disk subsystem enhancements: Hard drives, controller cards (e.g., RAID, ATA-100, etc.), and cables NICs Specialized video cards

Practice Test Questions

1. Given the following scenario, predict the outcome. You add a graphics accelerator card to your computer.
   Correct answer: d

2. Which of the following is false?
   Correct answer: a

3. Which of the following is not a standard for IDE drives?
   Correct answer: d

4. How many pins are in an 80 wire IDE cable?
   Correct answer: b

5. Given the following scenario, predict the outcome. The integrated NIC has failed. How can you replace the NIC?
   Correct answer: d

6. Where is the hard drive controller located on newer computers?
   Correct answer: c

7. Given the following scenario, predict the outcome. Video processing is slow. What can be done to increase performance?
   Correct answer: d

PAGE 62

Objective 1.10	Determine the issues that must be considered when upgrading a PC. In a given scenario, determine when and how to upgrade system components.	CPU Processor speed and compatibility Memory Memory capacity and characteristics Motherboards Cache in relationship to motherboards Bus types and characteristics

Practice Test Questions

1. Given the following scenario, determine how to upgrade system components. Which of the following steps is important in upgrading a motherboard?
   Correct answer: d

2. Cache memory is usually installed on a system board in increments of:
   Correct answer: b

3. What is a reasonable amount of cache memory on a system board?
   Correct answer: c

4. L2 cache memory can exist in a system as:
   Correct answer: d

5. What is the purpose of installing additional cache memory?
   Correct answer: b

6. Why do newer system boards not have cache memory installed?

Correct answer: a

7. What can result if there is not enough RAM installed in a system?

Correct answer: d

PAGE 64

Objective 1.10	Determine the issues that must be considered when upgrading a PC. In a given scenario, determine when and how to upgrade system components.	Power supply output capacity Hard drives Hard drive capacity and characteristics Adapter cards Drivers for legacy devices

Practice Test Questions

1. Given the following scenario, determine when to upgrade system components. Which of the following problems may be related to a faulty power supply?

Correct answer: d

2. Which storage device provides the fastest access time for large multimedia files?

Correct answer: c

3. Given the following scenario, determine when to upgrade system components. Which of the following problems may be related to a faulty hard drive?

Correct answer: d

4. Given the following scenario, determine how to upgrade system components.

After upgrading to Windows XP an ISA device card no longer functions correctly.

Correct answer: d

5. Given the following scenario, determine how to upgrade system components. You would like to replace a faulty hard drive. Which of the following steps are necessary to perform this task?

Correct answer: d

6. What type of IDE cable is necessary to support hard drives on newer computers?

Correct answer: b

7. What size hard drive is supported under Windows XP if it is formatted FAT32?

Correct answer: d

PAGE 66

Objective 1.10	Determine the issues that must be considered when upgrading a PC. In a given scenario, determine when and how to upgrade system components.	BIOS System/Firmware limitations

Practice Test Questions

1. The major advantage of using Flash ROM is:
   Correct answer: a

2. One reason to upgrade a BIOS is to:
   Correct answer: a

3. You can find an upgrade for BIOS in:
   Correct answer: c

4. How often does a PC technician perform a BIOS upgrade on a system?
   Correct answer: a

5. To identify the BIOS manufacturer and model look:
   Correct answer: a

6. When upgrading the BIOS, the most likely way to get the BIOS upgrade is to:
   Correct answer: b

7. When upgrading BIOS, what should you remember?
   Correct answer: c

PAGE 68

Objective 1.10	Determine the issues that must be considered when upgrading a PC. In a given scenario, determine when and how to upgrade system components.	Laptop power sources: Lithium ion, NiMH, and fuel cell PCMCIA Type I, II, III cards

Practice Test Questions

1. Given the following scenario, determine how to upgrade system components. Which of the following steps is important in replacing a dead notebook battery?
   Correct answer: d

2. Which PC Card is the thickest?
   Correct answer: d

3. Which type of PC Card is typically used for a modem?
   Correct answer: b

4. Hot-swapping refers to:
   Correct answer: a

5. Given the following scenario, determine how to upgrade system components. Which of the following steps is important in upgrading a Lithium Ion battery with a fuel cell?
   Correct answer: d

6. A power-saving feature of a notebook computer that turns the power off after a period of inactivity is:
   Correct answer: b

7. Which bus technology is CardBus based on?
   Correct answer: c

Objective 2.1	Recognize common problems associated with each module and their symptoms, and identify steps to isolate and troubleshoot the problems. Given a problem situation, interpret the symptoms and infer the most likely cause.	I/O ports and cables: Serial, parallel, USB ports, IEEE 1394/FireWire, infrared, and SCSI

Practice Test Questions

1. How many bits of data are transmitted over a parallel port at one time?
   Correct answer: b

2. Which IRQ does the parallel port LPT1 typically use?
   Correct answer: b

3. What standard should a parallel printer cable meet?
   Correct answer: b

4. Given the problem situation, interpret the symptoms and infer the most likely cause. A SCSI port resource is not listed under Device Manager.
   Correct answer: a

5. Given the problem situation, interpret the symptoms and infer the most likely cause. A serial device has stopped communicating with the computer.
   Correct answer: c

6. Given the problem situation, interpret the symptoms and infer the most likely cause. A USB device is not detected when it is attached to the computer.
   Correct answer: a

7. Given the problem situation, interpret the symptoms and infer the most likely cause. An infrared device has stopped communicating with the computer.
   Correct answer: c

PAGE 72

Objective 2.1	Recognize common problems associated with each module and their symptoms, and identify steps to isolate and troubleshoot the problems. Given a problem situation, interpret the symptoms and infer the most likely cause.	Motherboards: CMOS/BIOS settings and post audible/visual error codes

Practice Test Questions

1. A PC continuously reboots itself. What is the most likely cause of the problem?
   Correct answer: a

2. POST error codes in the 1700 range indicate a problem with:
   Correct answer: a

3. One long continuous beep or several steady long beeps most likely indicate a problem with:
   Correct answer: d

4. You want to install a large hard drive on a system whose BIOS does not support large drives and you cannot upgrade the BIOS. What is the best solution?
   Correct answer: b

5. An error message, "Parity error," displays and the system hangs. The source of the problem is:
   Correct answer: a

6. When a PC boots, the screen is blank and you hear a single beep. What is most likely to be the problem?
   Correct answer: c

7. When a PC boots, the screen is blank and you hear several beeps. What is most likely to be the problem?
   Correct answer: d

PAGE 74

Objective 2.1	Recognize common problems associated with each module and their symptoms, and identify steps to isolate and troubleshoot the problems. Given a problem situation, interpret the symptoms and infer the most likely cause.	Peripherals Input devices: Keyboard, mouse/pointer devices, and touch screen

Practice Test Questions

1. If a peripheral stops working, what's one of the first things to check?
   Correct answer: a

2. What is one check you can make to be certain a printer is communicating properly with a computer?
   Correct answer: a

3. If a keyboard fails intermittently, what might be a source of the problem?
   Correct answer: c

4. Video does not work. What are the things you should replace and the order you should replace them?
   Correct answer: a

5. What standard should a parallel printer cable meet?
   Correct answer: b

6. When a printer does not work, what are some things you can check?
   Correct answer: d

7. You've just powered the computer on and receive a keyboard stuck error message. What is the first thing you should do?
   Correct answer: a

PAGE 76

Objective 2.1	Recognize common problems associated with each module and their symptoms, and identify steps to isolate and troubleshoot the problems. Given a problem situation, interpret the symptoms and infer the most likely cause.	Computer case: Power supply, slot covers, and front cover alignment

Practice Test Questions

1. The device inside a power supply that retains a charge even after power is disconnected is a:
   Correct answer: a

2. Covering empty slots on the back of a PC case with slot covers helps to:
   Correct answer: a

3. A power supply uses which IRQ?
   Correct answer: d

4. The IDE hard drive does not spin up when the PC is turned on. What is most likely to be the problem?
   Correct answer: b

5. A PC repeatedly reboots. You replace the power supply with one you know is good. What do you do next?
   Correct answer: a

6. Which beep codes could indicate that there is a problem with the power supply?
   Correct answer: c

7. The computer system appears dead, with no lights on the front panel, nothing on the screen, and no beeps. What do you check first?
   Correct answer: c

PAGE 78

Objective 2.1	Recognize common problems associated with each module and their symptoms, and identify steps to isolate and troubleshoot the problems. Given a problem situation, interpret the symptoms and infer the most likely cause.	Storage devices and cables: FDD, HDD, CD/CDRW, DVD/DVDRW, tape drive, and removable storage

Practice Test Questions

1. How is a real-mode device driver for a CD-ROM drive loaded?
   Correct answer: a

2. The DOS extension that manages a CD-ROM drive is:
   Correct answer: b

3. What could cause the error message, "General failure reading drive A, Abort, Retry Fail?"
   Correct answer: b

4. Possible sources of problems with reading a floppy disk include:
   Correct answer: d

5. The user reports that a floppy drive reads the first disk inserted into the drive after a reboot but does not read subsequent disks. What might be the problem?
   Correct answer: d

6. Which utility manages a CD-ROM drive for DOS?
   Correct answer: c

7. Why is Mscdex.exe not used with Windows 9x?
   Correct answer: b

PAGE 80

Objective 2.1	Recognize common problems associated with each module and their symptoms, and identify steps to isolate and troubleshoot the problems. Given a problem situation, interpret the symptoms and infer the most likely cause.	Cooling systems: Fans, heat sinks, liquid cooling, and temperature sensors Processor/CPU Memory

Practice Test Questions

1. A Windows XP PC continuously reboots itself. What can you do to view a specific error message?
   Correct answer: b

2. A computer keeps hanging or freezing for no apparent reason. Which of the following should you do to troubleshoot the problem?
   Correct answer: a

3. Which of the following utilities can be used to test RAM?
   Correct answer: b

4. Which of the following can be installed to monitor the inside temperature of your computer?
   Correct answer: a

5. An error message, "Parity error," displays and the system hangs. The source of the problem is:
   Correct answer: a

6. Which of the following components is crucial to maintaining the properly temperature inside your computer?
   Correct answer: d

7. Which of the following tasks falls under the category of proper maintenance of your computer?
   Correct answer: a

| Objective 2.1 | Recognize common problems associated with each module and their symptoms, and identify steps to isolate and troubleshoot the problems. Given a problem situation, interpret the symptoms and infer the most likely cause. | Display device Adapters: Network Interface Card (NIC), sound card, video card, modem, SCSI, IEEE 1394/FireWire, and USB |

Practice Test Questions

1. If nothing is showing on the monitor screen, the first thing to do is:
   Correct answer: a

2. If the LED light on the monitor is lit but the screen is blank, what is NOT a source of the problem?
   Correct answer: d

3. What IRQ does a sound card typically use?
   Correct answer: b

4. Your modem was working fine until you installed a sound card; now neither the modem nor the sound card work. What is likely the problem?
   Correct answer: b

5. What IRQ does a monitor use?
   Correct answer: d

6. ESD is least likely to cause damage to what device?
   Correct answer: b

7. Which of the following is typically an input and output device?
   Correct answer: b

| Objective 2.1 | Recognize common problems associated with each module and their symptoms, and identify steps to isolate and troubleshoot the problems. Given a problem situation, interpret the symptoms and infer the most likely cause. | Portable Systems: PCMCIA, batteries, docking stations/port replicators, and portable unique storage |

Practice Test Questions

1. Given the problem situation, interpret the symptoms and infer the most likely cause. You are unable to write to a 100 MB Zip disk using your 750 MB Zip drive.
   Correct answer: c

2. Given the problem situation, interpret the symptoms and infer the most likely cause. A used notebook battery will not hold a charge.
   Correct answer: a

3. Given the problem situation, interpret the symptoms and infer the most likely cause. A CD-R disc cannot be read in the notebook's CD-R drive.
   Correct answer: a

4. Given the problem situation, interpret the symptoms and infer the most likely cause. A CDRW disc cannot be read in the notebook's CD-R drive.
   Correct answer: c

5. A PCMCIA card is not detected after replacing another PCMCIA card on a running notebook computer. Given the situation, interpret the symptoms and infer the most likely cause.
   Correct answer: a

6. Given the problem situation, interpret the symptoms and infer the most likely cause. When you try to undock/eject your Windows XP computer by pressing the Undock/Eject button on your docking station, the computer does NOT undock. You receive a message similar to: "Problem Undocking from docking station. You cannot eject your computer because you do not have sufficient security privileges to do so."
   Correct answer: a

7. Given the problem situation, interpret the symptoms and infer the most likely cause. The Windows 98 computer freezes when you attempt to write a large file to a 100 MB Zip disk using your 250 MB Zip drive.
   Correct answer: c

PAGE 86

Objective 2.2	Identify basic troubleshooting procedures and tools, and how to elicit problem symptoms from customers. Justify asking particular questions in a given scenario.	Troubleshooting/ isolation/problem determination procedures Determining whether a hardware or software problem

Practice Test Questions

1. You install a second IDE hard drive in a system using the same IDE primary channel used by the first drive. When you boot up, the first drive works but the system fails to recognize the new drive. What is the most likely cause of the problem?
   Correct answer: c

2. A POST error code in the 6000 range indicates a problem with:
   Correct answer: d

3. POST is done when the computer is:
   Correct answer: c

4. POST is performed by:
   Correct answer: a

5. When you use a floppy drive cable with a twist, the order of connections on the data cable supporting two floppy drives is:
   Correct answer: b

6. A system appears dead but you notice that the small green light on the front of the monitor is on. What can you safely assume?
   Correct answer: b

7. You replace a system board because the old board is dead. You turn on the PC. It boots up correctly but hangs, dies, and refuses to reboot. What is most likely the source of the problem?
   Correct answer: b

PAGE 88

Objective 2.2	Identify basic troubleshooting procedures and tools, and how to elicit problem symptoms from customers. Justify asking particular questions in a given scenario.	Gathering information from user: Customer environment, symptoms/error codes, and situation when the problem occurred

Practice Test Questions

1. What question might you ask a user to help you locate a problem?
   Correct answer: d

2. How can the customer help you identify the source of an intermittent problem?
   Correct answer: c

3. Which of the following questions is not appropriate to ask the user to help you locate the source of a problem?
   Correct answer: c

4. You are late for an appointment with a customer. What should you do when you arrive?
   Correct answer: a

5. A hard drive has failed but you think you can fix it if you reformat the drive. What should you do first?
   Correct answer: a

6. What should you always do at a customer site?

Correct answer: c

7. When you first arrive at the customer's site, what is the first thing you should do?

Correct answer: b

PAGE 90

Objective 3.1	Identify the various types of preventive maintenance measures, products and procedures and when and how to use them.	Liquid cleaning compounds Types of materials to clean contacts and connections Non-static vacuums (chasis, power supplies, fans) Cleaning monitors Cleaning removable media devices Ventilation, dust and moisture control on the PC hardware interior

Practice Test Questions

1. Which product should be used to clean fingerprints and dirt off a keyboard?

Correct answer: b

2. Which product should be used to clean a notebook computer's LCD screen?

Correct answer: d

3. Which of the following is most likely to do damage to data stored on a removable disk such as a floppy disk or Zip disk?

Correct answer: d

4. Why is dust inside a computer case considered dangerous?

Correct answer: c

5. The best way to remove dust from inside a computer case is to:

Correct answer: b

6. Preventive maintenance on a mouse includes:

Correct answer: b

7. What should you use to clean a monitor screen?

Correct answer: d

PAGE 92

Objective 3.1	Identify the various types of preventive maintenance measures, products and procedures and when and how to use them.	Hard disk maintenance (defragging, ScanDisk, CHKDSK) Verifying UPS (Uninterruptible Power Supply) and suppressors

Practice Test Questions

1. During a power outage, what should you do before the power is restored?
   Correct answer: a

2. Which device helps prevent power surges to computer equipment?
   Correct answer: b

3. Which device prevents interruptions to power to computer equipment?
   Correct answer: a

4. How can computer equipment be completely protected from damage during an electrical storm?
   Correct answer: c

5. What question do you ask to determine if power is getting to a computer?
   Correct answer: a

6. You're working at your computer and a thunderstorm begins. What do you do?
   Correct answer: d

7. What utility is useful in reorganizing the way data is stored on your hard drive so it can be accessed more quickly?
   Correct answer: a

PAGE 94

Objective 3.2	Identify various safety measures and procedures, and when/how to use them.	ESD (Electrostatic Discharge) precautions and procedures: What ESD can do, how it may be apparent, or hidden, common ESD protection devices, and situations that could present a danger or hazard

Practice Test Questions

1. Damage from ESD can be caused by:
   Correct answer: d

2. To avoid damage from ESD as you work on a computer, you should:
   Correct answer: b

3. An ESD wrist strap contains a:
   Correct answer: c

4. What is the best ground to use when working on a computer?
   Correct answer: a

5. Which situation poses the worst possible potential danger from ESD?
   Correct answer: c

6. ESD is:
   Correct answer: a

7. A human cannot feel ESD unless it reaches a charge of ____ volts
   Correct answer: b

PAGE 96

Objective 3.2	Identify various safety measures and procedures, and when/how to use them.	Potential hazards and proper safety procedures relating to: High–voltage equipment, power supply, and CRTs

Practice Test Questions

1. If the fan inside a power supply stops working, what should you do?
   Correct answer: b

2. When servicing a laser printer, why is it important to first unplug the printer?
   Correct answer: d

3. Why do you *not* wear an ESD bracelet while servicing a monitor?
   Correct answer: c

4. A device that retains a high charge even after disconnected from power is:

Correct answer: d

5. The electrical component that retains a charge after the power is turned off is:
   Correct answer: c

6. When troubleshooting a monitor, one task a PC technician who is not trained to work inside the monitor can safely do is:
   Correct answer: d

7. The best way to ground an ESD bracelet when servicing a power supply is to:
   Correct answer: d

PAGE 98

Objective 3.3	Identify environmental protection measures and procedures, and when/how to use them.	Special disposal procedures that comply with environmental guidelines: Batteries, CRTs, chemical solvents and cans, and MSDS (Material Safety Data Sheet)

Practice Test Questions

1. Which of the following statements are true?
   Correct answer: d

2. Which component requires that you follow EPA environmental guidelines for disposal?
   Correct answer: b

3. How do you recycle an alkaline battery?
   Correct answer: c

4. To know how to properly dispose of a can of contact cleaner, what do you do?
   Correct answer: b

5. How do you dispose of a CMOS battery?
   Correct answer: d

6. Before disposing of a CRT, what must you do?
   Correct answer: c

7. When disposing of an entire computer system, which components need special attention?
   Correct answer: a

PAGE 100

Objective 4.1	Distinguish between the popular CPU chips in terms of their basic characteristics.	Popular CPU chips (Pentium class compatible) Speeds (actual vs. advertised) Cache level I, II, III

Practice Test Questions

1. Which processor is the most powerful?
   Correct answer: a

2. Which processor is comparable to Intel's Itanium CPU?
   Correct answer: c

3. How wide is the data path of the Pentium CPU?
   Correct answer: c

4. How much L1 cache is there in a Pentium II CPU?
   Correct answer: b

5. The Pentium II typically uses what clock bus speed?
   Correct answer: b

6. Which processor has L3 cache?
   Correct answer: c

7. Which processor does not have L2 cache included inside the processor housing?
   Correct answer: c

PAGE 102

Objective 4.1	Distinguish between the popular CPU chips in terms of their basic characteristics.	Voltage Sockets/slots VRM(s)

Practice Test Questions

1. Which connector is used by Intel Xeon processors?

   Correct answer: b

2. Which processor form factor fits into Socket 370?

   Correct answer: c

3. Which processor uses 5 volts?

   Correct answer: b

4. How much voltage does the Itanium processor require?

5. How many pins are used by the Intel Xeon processor?

   Correct answer: a

6. Which slot or socket is *not* used by Intel processors?

   Correct answer: d

7. How many pins are used by the Intel Pentium 4 processor?

   Correct answer: a

Correct answer: b

PAGE 104

Objective 4.2	Identify the types of RAM (Random Access Memory), form factors, and operational characteristics. Determine banking and speed requirements under given scenarios.	Types: EDO RAM (Extended Data Output RAM), DRAM (Dynamic Random Access Memory), SRAM (Static RAM),VRAM (Video RAM), SDRAM (Synchronous Dynamic RAM), DDR (Double Data Rate), and RAMBUS

Practice Test Questions

1. Which type of memory is fastest?
   Correct answer: b

2. Which type of memory runs in sync with the system clock?
   Correct answer: b

3. Which type of memory is especially designed to work on a video card?
   Correct answer: c

4. Which type of memory uses a narrow 16–bit data path?
   Correct answer: a

5. The connection inside a SEC between the CPU and the L2 cache is called the:
   Correct answer: c

6. Why must DRAM be refreshed?
   Correct answer: c

7. The Pentium II backside bus is:
   Correct answer: b

Objective 4.2	Identify the types of RAM (Random Access Memory), form factors, and operational characteristics. Determine banking and speed requirements under given scenarios.	Form factors (including pin count): SIMM (Single In-line Memory Module), DIMM (Dual In-line Memory Module), SODIMM (Small outline DIMM), MICRODIMM, and RIMM (Rambus Inline Memory Module)

Practice Test Questions

1. Which type of memory is seen on newer computers?

   Correct answer: a

2. Which type of memory is best suited for sub-notebook computers?

   Correct answer: d

3. What is the current maximum bus speed that DDR SDRAM supports?

   Correct answer: b

4. Which type of memory uses a 64-bit data path?

   Correct answer: d

5. How many pins are found on RIMMs?

   Correct answer: d

6. How many pins are found on MICRODIMMs?

   Correct answer: a

7. Which of the following is true about RIMM technology?

   Correct answer: d

Objective 4.2	Identify the types of RAM (Random Access Memory), form factors, and operational characteristics. Determine banking and speed requirements under given scenarios.	Operational characteristics: Memory chips (8-bit, 16-bit, and 32-bit), Parity chips versus non-parity chips, ECC vs. non-ECC, and single-sided vs. double-sided

Practice Test Questions

1. Which of the following is a common width of a memory module data bus?
   Correct answer: d

2. Which type of memory has an error-checking technology that cannot repair the error when it is detected?
   Correct answer: c

3. Which type of memory has an error-checking technology that can repair the error when it is detected?
   Correct answer: a

4. Which type of memory has an error-checking technology that can detect multiple-bit errors?
   Correct answer: a

5. If a system contains 64 MB of RAM in two banks of 2 SIMMs each, how much memory is on one SIMM?
   Correct answer: a

6. Which of the following statements is true?
   Correct answer: a

7. Which of the following statements is true?
   Correct answer: a

PAGE 110

Objective 4.3	Identify the most popular types of motherboards, their components, and their architecture (bus structures).	Types of motherboards: AT and ATX

Practice Test Questions

1. The AT power supply connects to the system board with:
   Correct answer: a

2. The ATX power supply connects to the system board with:
   Correct answer: b

3. Which type of motherboard is used in low-profile desktop computers?
   Correct answer: d

4. What is one advantage that the ATX system board has over the AT system board?
   Correct answer: a

5. Which statement is true concerning the style of system board?
   Correct answer: b

6. Which type of system board is required for a 500 MHz Pentium II that is using Slot 1?
   Correct answer: c

7. Which type of system board measures 22 cm × 33 cm?
   Correct answer: b

Objective 4.3	Identify the most popular types of motherboards, their components, and their architecture (bus structures).	Memory: SIMM, DIMM, RIMM, SODIMM, and MICRODIMM External cache memory (Level 2)

Practice Test Questions

1. What type of memory can a Pentium 4 motherboard support?
   Correct answer: d

2. Which type of memory needs to be installed in pairs?
   Correct answer: a

3. Which type of memory requires that each slot be filled?
   Correct answer: c

4. Which component is used to fill open slots on a motherboard that uses RIMMs?
   Correct answer: b

5. How do you not install RAM on a system board?
   Correct answer: b

6. Which of the following is currently the most popular type of memory?
   Correct answer: a

7. Where is Level 2 cache currently stored on newer computers?
   Correct answer: d

Objective 4.3	Identify the most popular types of motherboards, their components, and their architecture (bus structures).	Processor sockets: Slot 1, Slot 2, Slot A, Socket A, Socket 7, Socket 8, Socket 423, Socket 478, and Socket 370

Practice Test Questions

1. What slot or socket does the Intel Pentium III use?
   Correct answer: d

2. How many pins does Socket 7 have?
   Correct answer: a

3. What socket or slot does the Pentium Pro use?
   Correct answer: c

4. Which processor uses 1.75 volts of power?
   Correct answer: d

5. What socket or slot does the Pentium
   Xeon use?
   Correct answer: a

6. When is the Super Socket 7 used?
   Correct answer: b

7. What is the difference between a
   SPGA grid and a PGA grid, as used by
   a CPU socket?
   Correct answer: c

PAGE 116

Objective 4.3	Identify the most popular types of motherboards, their components, and their architecture (bus structures).	Bus Architecture ISA PCI: PCI 32-bit and PCI 64-bit AGP: 2X, 4X, and 8X (Pro) USB (Universal Serial Bus) Components: Communication ports (Serial, USB, parallel, IEEE 1394/FireWire, and infrared)

Practice Test Questions

1. Which bus is primarily used on notebook
   computers?
   Correct answer: c

2. Which bus only supports a video card?
   Correct answer: d

3. Which bus is fastest?
   Correct answer: b

4. Which bus is no longer included on new
   system boards?
   Correct answer: a and c

5. Which bus can support either an 8-bit or
   16-bit data path?
   Correct answer: c

6. Which of the following is the most
   common width of the data path of the
   PCI bus?
   Correct answer: c

7. Which bus runs in synchronization with
   the CPU?
   Correct answer: d

Objective 4.3	Identify the most popular types of motherboards, their components, and their architecture (bus structures).	AMR (audio modem riser) slots CNR (communication network riser) slots Basic compatibility guidelines IDE (ATA, ATAPI, ULTRA-DMA, EIDE) SCSI (Narrow, Wide, Fast, Ultra, HVD, LVD (Low Voltage Differential)) Chipsets

Practice Test Questions

1. What the fastest and most popular IDE standard?
   Correct answer: c

2. Which of the following slots are capable of supporting an audio riser card?
   Correct answer: d

3. The SCSI standard that uses LVD is:
   Correct answer: b

4. What do basic compatibility guidelines typically describe?
   Correct answer: d

5. Which SCSI standard is capable of supporting 16-bit data bus?
   Correct answer: d

6. Which of the following statements is true?
   Correct answer: b

7. Which company designs chipset for Intel motherboards?
   Correct answer: b

Objective 4.4	Identify the purpose of CMOS (Complementary Metal-Oxide Semiconductor) memory, what it contains, and how and when to change its parameters. Given a scenario involving CMOS, choose the appropriate course of action.	CMOS Settings: Default settings, CPU settings, printer parallel port—Uni., bi-directional, disable/enable, ECP, EPP, COM/serial port—memory address, interrupt request, disable

Practice Test Questions

1. When troubleshooting a parallel port, you should verify that the port is enabled:

   Correct answer: b

2. Which setting for a parallel port gives the fastest data access time?

   Correct answer: c

3. When a parallel port is set to ECP, what resource is required?

   Correct answer: b

4. If the system is short of DMA channels, you can free one up by:

   Correct answer: c

5. If a serial port is not working, what should you verify?

   Correct answer: a

6. In CMOS setup, when a serial port is set to use IRQ 4 and I/O address 03F8, the port is configured as:

   Correct answer: a

7. If a parallel port in CMOS setup is configured to use IRQ 5 and I/O address 0278, then the port is configured as:

   Correct answer: b

PAGE 122

Objective 4.4	Identify the purpose of CMOS (Complementary Metal–Oxide Semiconductor) memory, what it contains, and how and when to change its parameters. Given a scenario involving CMOS, choose the appropriate course of action.	CMOS Settings: Floppy drive— enable/disable drive or boot, speed, density, hard drive—size and drive type, memory—speed, parity, non-parity, boot sequence, date/time, passwords, Plug and Play BIOS, disabling on-board devices, disabling virus protection, power management, and infrared

Practice Test Questions

1. When a PC boots with the incorrect date or time, what is the likely cause?

   Correct answer: b

2. Which hard drive parameter is not set using CMOS setup?

   Correct answer: d

3. Which of the following cannot be damaged by a virus?

   Correct answer: b

4. When installing a 3½ inch floppy drive to replace a 5¼ inch floppy drive, how does the system know to expect the new type of drive?

   Correct answer: c

5. Which of the following hard drive parameters can be set in CMOS?
   Correct answer: d

6. Boot sequence as set in CMOS is the order:
   Correct answer: c

7. System date and time can be set:
   Correct answer: d

PAGE 124

Objective 5.1	Identify printer technologies, interfaces, and options/upgrades.	Technologies include: Laser, ink dispersion, dot matrix, solid ink, thermal, and dye sublimation

Practice Test Questions

1. In laser printing, the step between writing and transferring is:
   Correct answer: c

2. What component on a dot matrix printer forms each character?
   Correct answer: d

3. On an ink-jet printer, what causes the ink to form characters and shapes on the paper?
   Correct answer: b

4. In laser printing, which stage in the printing process forms the characters or shapes to be printed?
   Correct answer: a

5. In laser printing, which stage puts the toner on the paper?
   Correct answer: c

6. In laser printing, which is the last step?
   Correct answer: b

7. In laser printing, what is the purpose of the laser beam?
   Correct answer: a

PAGE 126

Objective 5.1	Identify printer technologies, interfaces, and options/upgrades.	Interfaces include: Parallel, network, SCSI, USB, infrared, serial, IEEE 1394/FireWire, and wireless

Practice Test Questions

1. In what ways can a printer connect to a computer system?
   Correct answer: c

2. If a printer is connected to a computer by way of a parallel cable and the computer is connected to a network, what must be done before others on the network can use this printer?
   Correct answer: a

3. To access file and print sharing in Windows 9x, you should do which of the following?
   Correct answer: b

4. To share a printer over a network, you must:
   Correct answer: a

5. When sharing a printer over a network, you must:
   Correct answer: b

6. To use a shared printer on another PC, you must:
   Correct answer: d

7. When troubleshooting problems with shared printers on a network, what is a good question to ask?
   Correct answer: d

PAGE 128

Objective 5.1	Identify printer technologies, interfaces, and options/upgrades.	Options/Upgrades include: Memory, hard drives, NICs, trays and feeders, finishers (e.g., stapling, etc.), and scanners/fax/copier

Practice Test Questions

1. Which printer listed below comes equipped with a NIC?
   Correct answer: b

2. Which option/upgrade will help increase performance when print large images?
   Correct answer: a

3. Which option/upgrade will allow users to share a printer?
   Correct answer: b

4. Which option/upgrade may add the ability to collate and staple documents?
   Correct answer: d

5. Which option/upgrade will increase the amount of blank paper a printer can hold?
   Correct answer: c

6. What kind of printer offers the ability to scan documents?
   Correct answer: a

7. Which of the following considerations should be taken when upgrading or choosing a printer?
   Correct answer: d

PAGE 130

Objective 5.2	Recognize common printer problems and techniques used to resolve them.	Printer drivers Firmware updates Calibrations Printing test pages Consumables Environment

Practice Test Questions

1. Which of the following techniques are used to troubleshoot printer problems?
   Correct answer: d

2. Which of the following items can be recycled?
   Correct answer: d

3. On which of the following devices should firmware be updated?
   Correct answer: b

4. How can a test page be printed under Windows XP?
   Correct answer: b

5. Which of the following techniques are used to troubleshoot printing problems on a printer that cannot print?
   Correct answer: d

6. Which of the following techniques are used to troubleshoot a flashing cartridge light on an ink-jet printer that will not print?
   Correct answer: d

7. Which Microsoft operating system has built-in support for the largest number of printers?
   Correct answer: c

PAGE 132

Objective 5.2	Recognize common printer problems and techniques used to resolve them.	Memory Configuration Network connections Connections

Practice Test Questions

1. What types of network connections are usually found on a LaserJet printer?
   Correct answer: b

2. What's the first step in troubleshooting an error message that is displayed on the printer?
   Correct answer: a

3. Which types of printers listed below have memory modules that can be serviced?
   Correct answer: d

4. How should a PC technician obtain replacement memory?
   Correct answer: a

5. When troubleshooting a network printer issue, which of the following troubleshooting steps can be performed?
   Correct answer: d

6. Which of the following maintenance tasks should be performed on a LaserJet printer?
   Correct answer: d

7. How can a PC technician printer information on the printer's configuration?
   Correct answer: a

PAGE 134

Objective 5.2	Recognize common printer problems and techniques used to resolve them.	Paper feed and output Errors (printed or displayed) Paper jam Print quality Safety precautions Preventive maintenance

Practice Test Questions

1. Into what format does Windows XP convert a print job file before printing?
   Correct answer: c

2. Spooling print jobs:
   Correct answer: d

3. When troubleshooting a print problem, you can:
   Correct answer: d

4. If there is a problem with the printer communicating with the computer, the problem can be solved by:
   Correct answer: c

5. When servicing a dot matrix printer, what device might be hot to the touch?
   Correct answer: b

6. When servicing a laser printer, which component might be hot to the touch?
Correct answer: c

7. When troubleshooting a dot matrix printer, if the head moves back and forth but nothing prints, then suspect a problem with the:
Correct answer: c

PAGE 136

Objective 6.1	Identify the common types of network cables, their characteristics and connectors.	Coaxial: RG6, RG8, RG58, and RG59 BNC AUI Plenum/PVC

Practice Test Questions

1. Which of the following cable types is used in ThinNet Ethernet?
Correct answer: a

2. Which of the following cable types is used in ThickNet Ethernet?
Correct answer: b

3. Which of the following connector types is used in ThinNet Ethernet?
Correct answer: a

4. Which of the following connector types is used in ThickNet Ethernet?
Correct answer: c

5. Which type of coaxial cable should be used between closed walls?
Correct answer: d

6. Which type of coaxial cable should be used between open ceilings?
Correct answer: c

7. What is the maximum cable length of ThickNet Ethernet?
Correct answer: b

PAGE 138

Objective 6.1	Identify the common types of network cables, their characteristics and connectors.	UTP: CAT3, CAT5/e, and CAT6 STP Fiber: Single-mode and multi-mode RJ-45 ST/SC IDC/UDC

Practice Test Questions

1. Which type fiber-optic cable connector is barrel-shaped like a BNC connector?
   Correct answer: a

2. Which type fiber-optic cable connector has a square face and is easier to connect in a confined space?
   Correct answer: b

3. Which type cable connector(s) is neither male nor female and is commonly found on IBM Type 1 cabling, a two-pair shielded cable?
   Correct answer: d

4. Which of the following UTP cabling offers the greatest amount of crosstalk reduction?
   Correct answer: c

5. Which fiber-optic cable system offers than highest bandwidth?
   Correct answer: a

6. Which type of UTP cable should be used between open ceilings?
   Correct answer: c

7. How many pairs of wire can an RJ-45 connector hold?
   Correct answer: b

PAGE 140

Objective 6.2	Identify basic networking concepts including how a network works.	Installing and configuring network cards Addressing Bandwidth Status indicators

Practice Test Questions

1. Which type of NIC is easiest to configure?
   Correct answer: b

2. When replacing a NIC in a computer system, it is important to use an identical NIC because:
   Correct answer: c

3. A number permanently assigned to a NIC that uniquely identifies the computer to the network is:
   Correct answer: b

4. If you must install a different type of NIC than the one currently installed, what must you do?
   Correct answer: d

5. When the light on the back of the NIC is not lit solid, what can be the problem?
   Correct answer: a

6. What does the term bandwidth mean?
   Correct answer: d

7. What type of NIC works on an Ethernet network and supports more than one cabling media?
   Correct answer: b

PAGE 142

Objective 6.2	Identify basic networking concepts including how a network works.	Protocols: TCP/IP, IPX/SPX (NWLINK), AppleTalk, and NetBEUI/NetBIOS Full-duplex, half-duplex Cabling—twisted pair, coaxial, fiber optic, RS-232

Practice Test Questions

1. Which of the following network protocols are routable?
   Correct answer: d

2. Which of the following network protocols are non-routable?
   Correct answer: b

3. Which of the following network protocols is used to communicate with a Novell Netware file server?
   Correct answer: c

4. Which of the following is not a type of hardware protocol?
   Correct answer: a

5. Which standard is used to control serial cables?
   Correct answer: a

6. Full-duplex communication is communication in:
   Correct answer: b

7. Which of the following cabling is ideal for connecting servers or buildings on a local area network?
   Correct answer: c

Objective 6.2	Identify basic networking concepts including how a network works.	Networking models: Peer-to-peer and client/server Infrared Wireless

Practice Test Questions

1. In which type of networking model do users logon to a domain?

   Correct answer: b

2. Which type of wireless LAN transmission technology is ideal for network communication between buildings?

   Correct answer: a

3. Which type of wireless LAN transmission technology is ideal for network communication within a building?

   Correct answer: b

4. In which type of networking model is a user part of a workgroup?

   Correct answer: a

5. Which type of networking model is best for configuring and managing settings on client computers?

   Correct answer: b

6. Which of the following statements is true about WLANs?

   Correct answer: a

7. What term refers to the process of marking (on sidewalks or buildings) a nearby wireless access point that may offer Internet access so that other individuals can access it?

   Correct answer: c

Objective 6.3	Identify common technologies available for establishing Internet connectivity and their characteristics.	Technologies include: LAN and DSL Characteristics include: Definition, speed, and connections

Practice Test Questions

1. What is the maximum bandwidth of IDSL?
   Correct answer: a

2. What is the maximum downstream bandwidth of DSL Lite?
   Correct answer: b

3. What is the maximum bandwidth of SDSL?
   Correct answer: c

4. What is the maximum bandwidth of a T1 connection?
   Correct answer: c

5. What is the maximum bandwidth of a T3 connection?
   Correct answer: c

6. What is the maximum bandwidth of an OC-1 connection?
   Correct answer: d

7. What kind of cabling does DSL typically use?
   Correct answer: a

PAGE 148

Objective 6.3	Identify common technologies available for establishing Internet connectivity and their characteristics.	Technologies include: Cable, ISDN, dial-up, satellite, and wireless

Practice Test Questions

1. Which of the following are examples of broadband technology?
   Correct answer: d

2. What is the typical maximum bandwidth of a cable modem?
   Correct answer: c

3. What is the typical maximum bandwidth of a dial-up modem?
   Correct answer: a

4. What is the typical maximum bandwidth of an ISDN connection?
   Correct answer: b

5. What is the typical maximum download bandwidth of a satellite connection?
   Correct answer: d

6. Which wireless technology offers a bandwidth of up to 11 Mbps?
   Correct answer: b

7. Which wireless technology offers a bandwidth of up to 54 Mbps?
   Correct answer: a

PAGE 152

Objective 1.1	Identify the major desktop components and interfaces, and their functions. Differentiate the characteristics of Windows 9x/Me, Windows NT 4.0 Workstation, Windows 2000 Professional, and Windows XP.	Contrasts between Windows 9x/Me, Windows NT 4.0 Workstation, Windows 2000 Professional, and Windows XP

Practice Test Questions

1. Which operating system does not support the FAT32 file system?
   Correct answer: d

2. Which operating system does not support Plug and Play?
   Correct answer: c

3. Which operating system provides a feature to allow a user at home to connect a notebook computer to a network at his workplace using a virtual private network?
   Correct answer: a

4. Which operating system does not offer the NTFS file system?
   Correct answer: c

5. How does the Windows 95 Virtual Memory Manager assign memory addresses for applications to use?
   Correct answer: a

6. Why would a user choose to use the NTFS file system on a notebook computer?
   Correct answer: b

7. Which operating system is best designed for small, inexpensive PCs where the user needs to run 16-bit application programs that require a graphical interface?
   Correct answer: a

PAGE 154

Objective 1.1	Identify the major desktop components and interfaces, and their functions. Differentiate the characteristics of Windows 9x/Me, Windows NT 4.0, Workstation, Windows 2000 Professional, and Windows XP.	Major Operating System Components: Registry, virtual memory, and file system

Practice Test Questions

1. The name of the temporary swap file in Windows 98 is:

   Correct answer: a

2. Which statement about the Windows 95 methods of managing virtual memory is true?

   Correct answer: d

3. What is the name of the swap file in Windows XP?

   Correct answer: a

4. Which operating system does not use virtual memory?

   Correct answer: b

5. What are the two Windows 9x registry back-up files?

   Correct answer: a

6. What are the names of the Windows 9x registry files?

   Correct answer: d

7. What file system offers permissions?

   Correct answer: a

PAGE 156

Objective 1.1	Identify the major desktop components and interfaces, and their functions. Differentiate the characteristics of Windows 9x/Me, Windows NT 4.0, Workstation, Windows 2000 Professional, and Windows XP.	Major Operating System Interfaces Windows Explorer, My Computer, and Control Panel

Practice Test Questions

1. In Windows Explorer on Windows XP, how do you change the view option to see hidden files and folders?

   Correct answer: c

2. In Windows 98, to view your folders as a Web page you must:

   Correct answer: c

3. Which icon in Windows 2000 Control Panel do you use to configure a modem for a dial-up connection to a network?

   Correct answer: a

4. Which icon in Windows 98 Control Panel do you use to change the user's password?

   Correct answer: b

5. How do you change a password in Windows XP?

   Correct answer: a

6. How can you determine how much space is available on a hard drive?

   Correct answer: d

7. How do you access a command line prompt using Windows 98?

   Correct answer: c

PAGE 158

Objective 1.1	Identify the major desktop components and interfaces, and their functions. Differentiate the characteristics of Windows 9x/Me, Windows NT 4.0 Workstation, Windows 2000 Professional, and Windows XP.	Major Operating System Interfaces: Computer Management Console, Accessories/ System Tools, and Command line

Practice Test Questions

1. What is the name of the console building utility used in Windows 2000 and XP?
   Correct answer: c

2. Which of the following is not a Computer Management Console tool category?
   Correct answer: b

3. What is the term given to individual tools installed in a management console?
   Correct answer: b

4. Which of the following can be found in System Tools?
   Correct answer: b

5. Where can System Tools be found in Windows XP?
   Correct answer: c

6. How do you close a command line window?
   Correct answer: d

7. How do you access a command line prompt using Windows XP?
   Correct answer: d

PAGE 160

Objective 1.1	Identify the major desktop components and interfaces, and their functions. Differentiate the characteristics of Windows 9x/Me, Windows NT 4.0 Workstation, Windows 2000 Professional, and Windows XP.	Major Operating System Interfaces: Network Neighborhood/My Network Places, Task Bar/Systray, Start Menu, and Device Manager

Practice Test Questions

1. In Device Manager, a diamond icon with a short line through one side of it stands for?
   Correct answer: c

2. A yellow exclamation point through a device in Device Manager indicates:
   Correct answer: c

3. Which of the following device properties can you not view in Device Manager?
   Correct answer: b

4. Which of the following is not a taskbar option in Windows 98?
   Correct answer: d

5. Which taskbar option is available in Windows XP, but not in Windows 98?

Correct answer: a

6. In Windows XP, what do you do if you cannot see all of your system tray icons?

Correct answer: b

7. If you have many windows open and you need to get to a desktop icon, how can you quickly access the desktop in Windows XP?

Correct answer: d

PAGE 162

Objective 1.2	Identify the names, locations, purposes, and contents of major system files.	Windows 9x –specific files: Io.sys, Msdos.sys, Autoexec.bat, Command.com, Config.sys, Win.com

Practice Test Questions

1. Which of the following Windows 9x system files is a text file?

Correct answer: c

2. To function properly under Windows 9x, a Plug and Play device requires:

Correct answer: b

3. If Config.sys is present when Windows 9x loads:

Correct answer: c

4. How are device drivers loaded under Windows 9x?

Correct answer: d

5. Which three files are required before Win.com can be loaded (pick three)?

Correct answer: a, c, d

6. Which is the correct order of loading or execution?

Correct answer: c

7. Which file is an optional file for Windows 98 execution?

Correct answer: b

PAGE 164

Objective 1.2	Identify the names, locations, purposes, and contents of major system files.	Windows 9x –specific files: Himem.sys, Emm386.exe, System.ini, and Win.ini

Practice Test Questions

1. The purpose of Himem.sys is:

Correct answer: a

2. The purpose of Emm386.exe is:

Correct answer: d

3. Where in memory are upper memory blocks located?

Correct answer: a

4. Which of the following is true?
   Correct answer: c

5. Which statement is true about Win.ini?
   Correct answer: a

6. What is the maximum file size for an .ini file?
   Correct answer: c

7. Which section will you find in System.ini?
   Correct answer: c

PAGE 166

Objective 1.2	Identify the names, locations, purposes, and contents of major system files.	Windows 9x – specific files: registry data files (System.dat and User.dat)

Practice Test Questions

1. What are the two Windows 9x registry back-up files?
   Correct answer: f

2. What program do you execute when you want to edit the Windows 95 registry?
   Correct answer: c

3. Which registry key stores current information about hardware and installed software?
   Correct answer: c

4. How many major branches or keys are there in the Windows 9x registry?
   Correct answer: d

5. What are the names of the Windows 9x registry files?
   Correct answer: c

6. What is one reason that Windows 9x supports using System.ini and Win.ini during the boot process?
   Correct answer: a

7. Most configuration information for Windows 9x is stored in:
   Correct answer: b

PAGE 168

Objective 1.2	Identify the names, locations, purposes, and contents of major system files.	Windows NT-Based Specific Files: Boot.ini, Ntldr, Ntdetect.com, Ntbootdd.sys, Ntuser.dat, and Registry Data Files

Practice Test Questions

1. Where is the Ntldr file located?
   Correct answer: a

2. Which file is only used in the Windows NT boot process when a SCSI boot device is used?
   Correct answer: c

3. Which of the following is a hidden text file?
   Correct answer: b

4. Which Windows NT file is responsible for most of the booting process?
   Correct answer: b

5. What are the files called that hold the Windows NT registry?
   Correct answer: b

6. Which program is the best one to use to edit the Windows NT registry?
   Correct answer: a

7. Which Windows NT registry key stores information about hardware and installed software and does not change when a new user logs on?
   Correct answer: c

PAGE 170

Objective 1.3	Demonstrate the ability to use command–line functions and utilities to manage the operating system, including the proper syntax and switches.	Command Line Functions and Utilities Include: Command/ CMD, DIR, ATTRIB, VER, MEM, SCANDISK, DEFRAG, EDIT, XCOPY, COPY, FORMAT

Practice Test Questions

1. Which command can make a file a hidden system file?
   Correct answer: b

2. What is the purpose of the /C switch in the MEM command (MEM /C)?
   Correct answer: b

3. What command scans and repairs errors on a hard drive?
   Correct answer: a

4. What is a text editor that can be used to edit a text file?
   Correct answer: d

5. Which command copies files including files in the subdirectories of the current folder?
   Correct answer: d

6. Which command will make a disk bootable after formatting it?
   Correct answer: b

7. Which command can help speed up access to the files on a disk?
   Correct answer: c

PAGE 172

Objective 1.3	Demonstrate the ability to use command-line functions and utilities to manage the operating system, including the proper syntax and switches.	Command Line Functions and Utilities Include: FDISK, SETVER, SCANREG, MD/CD/RD, Delete/Rename, DELTREE, TYPE, ECHO, SET, and PING

Practice Test Questions

1. What command do you use if you receive an error about wrong DOS version?
   Correct answer: b

2. Which program rewrites files in contiguous cluster chains?
   Correct answer: a

3. What command can you use to correct a Windows startup problem?
   Correct answer: c

4. What command(s) do you use to show the contents of the Config.sys file (choose all that apply)?
   Correct answer: b, c

5. What command did you use if you received the following output?
   REPLY from 127.0.0.1: bytes=32 time<1ms TTL=128
   Correct answer: d

6. What does the following command do?
   CD ..
   Correct answer: c

7. What command can you use to change your command line prompt (choose all that apply)?
   Correct answer: a, b

PAGE 174

Objective 1.4	Identify basic concepts and procedures for creating, viewing, and managing disks, directories and files. This includes procedures for changing file attributes and the ramifications of those changes (for example, security issues).	Disks: Partitions (Active partition, primary partition, extended partition, and logical partition) and Files Systems (FAT16, FAT32, NTFS4, and NTFS5.X)

Practice Test Questions

1. For very large hard drives, which file system provides the smallest cluster size?
   Correct answer: c

2. Where is the boot strap loader located?
   Correct answer: b

3. The master boot program is located at:
   Correct answer: d

4. What are the functions of FDISK?
   Correct answer: d

5. What file system is used by floppy disks?
   Correct answer: b

6. Which file system is not supported by Windows NT?
   Correct answer: b

7. What is the first Microsoft OS to support FAT32?
   Correct answer: d

PAGE 176

Objective 1.4	Identify basic concepts and procedures for creating, viewing, and managing disks, directories and files. This includes procedures for changing file attributes and the ramifications of those changes (for example, security issues).	Directory Structures (Root Directory, Subdirectories, etc): Create folders, navigate the directory structure, and maximum depth

Practice Test Questions

1. What is the correct syntax to move to the C:\Docs folder?
   Correct answer: a

2. What is the maximum number of root directoy entries permitted in FAT32?
   Correct answer: d

3. How do you create a folder in Windows Explorer?
   Correct answer: b

4. When creating a new folder on the root of your FAT16 file system, why might you receive the error: "Unable to create <"New Folder">. Make sure the disk is not full or read-only" even if you have plenty of space on the disk and it is not write-protected?
   Correct answer: c

5. In Windows Explorer, how do you navigate to the parent of the folder you are currently in?
   Correct answer: a

6. Which is the proper command to create the folder C:\MyDocs\Sheets?
   Correct answer: c

7. What command will change you to the directory C:\Reports?
   Correct answer: b

Objective 1.4	Identify basic concepts and procedures for creating, viewing, and managing disks, directories and files. This includes procedures for changing file attributes and the ramifications of those changes (for example, security issues).	Files: Creating files, file naming conventions (most common extensions, 8.3, maximum length)

Practice Test Questions

1. In DOS, what is the combined maximum number of characters a filename and file extension can have?
   Correct answer: c

2. A file named My Long File Document in Windows 95 will be displayed in DOS as:
   Correct answer: a

3. What is a valid file extension for DOS?
   Correct answer: a

4. What is the maximum number of characters allowed in a Windows 95 filename?
   Correct answer: b

5. What happens if you double-click a file with a .com extension?
   Correct answer: c

6. How can you change Windows XP so that double-clicking a file named Readme.txt will open the EDIT program instead of Notepad?
   Correct answer: c

7. In Windows 9x, if you have 10 long filenames in the same directory that start with Abcdef and have a .doc extension, what will the 8.3 filename of the 10th file be?
   Correct answer: a

PAGE 180

Objective 1.4	Identify basic concepts and procedures for creating, viewing, and managing disks, directories and files. This includes procedures for changing file attributes and the ramifications of those changes (for example, security issues).	File Attributes – Read Only, Hidden, System, and Archive Attributes, File Compression, File Encryption, File Permissions, and File Types (Text vs Binary File)

Practice Test Questions

1. What command can make a file read-only?
   Correct answer: b

2. Which of the following is a hidden file?
   Correct answer: c

3. What is the result of the ATTRIB -R Myfile.txt command?
   Correct answer: b

4. What is the command to hide Autoexec.bat?
   a Correct answer: a

5. What in Windows 95 performs a function similar to the ATTRIB command in DOS?
   Correct answer: c

6. What file attribute does the DOS BACKUP command use to determine if the file is to be backed up?
   Correct answer: c

7. What file system has an encrypt file attribute?
   Correct answer: b

PAGE 182

Objective 1.5	Identify the major operating system utilities, their purpose, location, and available switches.	Disk Management Tools: Defrag.exe, Fdisk.exe, Backup/ Restore Utility (MSbackup, NTbackup, etc), ScanDisk, CHKDSK, Disk Cleanup, and Format

Practice Test Questions

1. You are building a computer to run Windows 9x and you have just installed a new hard drive. What must you do to make Windows boot from the hard disk? (select all that apply)
   Correct answer: a, d

2. You have had your Windows ME computer for about six months and you notice that is takes longer for applications to load and for files to be accessed. What utility may help this problem?
   Correct answer: b

3. You want to convert your FAT16 file system to FAT32. What utility should you run before converting?
   Correct answer: d

4. A user complains that they receive a disk error when trying to access a file from the hard drive. What utility may help this problem?
   Correct answer: c

5. When you try to install a new application, you receive the error that there is not enough disk space to continue. What can you try to resolve the problem?
   Correct answer: b

6. You are running Windows XP and you receive a disk error, what should you do?
   Correct answer: c

7. You are running Windows NT and find that disk access has slowed over time, what should you do?
   Correct answer: b

PAGE 184

Objective 1.5	Identify the major operating system utilities, their purpose, location, and available switches.	System Management Tools: Device Manager, System Manager, Computer Manager, Msconfig.exe, Regedit.exe (View information/Backup registry), and Regedt32.exe

Practice Test Questions

1. In Device Manager, a red X through a device icon indicates:
   Correct answer: d

2. To manually assign resources to an installed device, you should:
   Correct answer: b

3. Using Windows 98, how do you see a list of the I/O addresses currently used by the system?
   Correct answer: b

4. You are running Windows XP and want to check the free space and status of your disk drives. What tool can you use?
   Correct answer: c

5. Which icon represents SCSI in Device Manager?
   Correct answer: c

6. Which of the following is not a major registry key in Windows 98?
   Correct answer: b

7. To backup a registry key, you should:
   Correct answer: a

PAGE 186

Objective 1.5	Identify the major operating system utilities, their purpose, location, and available switches.	System Management Tools: Sysedit.exe, SCANREG, COMMAND/CMD, Event Viewer, and Task Manager

Practice Test Questions

1. Which files can be edited using SYSEDIT? (choose all that apply)
   Correct answer: a, d

2. What task can you do with SCANREG?
   Correct answer: c

3. What is the correct way to fix the registry?
   Correct answer: c

4. Which of the following are Event Viewer log files? (choose all that apply)
   Correct answer: a, b

5. To erase the messages in the System log file, you should:
   Correct answer: b

6. Which are Task Manager tabs? (choose all that apply)
   Correct answer: c, d

7. How do you terminate an application with Task Manager?
   Correct answer: b

PAGE 188

Objective 1.5	Identify the major operating system utilities, their purpose, location, and available switches.	File Management Tools: Attrib.exe, Extract.exe, Edit.com, and Windows Explorer

Practice Test Questions

1. Your desktop is obscured by open windows of running applications and you need to open Windows Explorer. What is a quick way to get to an Explorer window?
   Correct answer: b

2. Windows NT will not boot and you suspect the Boot.ini file. You boot from a bootable floppy and run Edit.com but you cannot save the file. What should you do before running Edit.com?
   Correct answer: c

3. From Windows Explorer, how can you select several files that are listed consecutively?
   Correct answer: c

4. How do you view all of the .exe files in a folder so that they are listed consecutively?
   Correct answer: d

5. You are in Windows Explorer viewing the root of the C: drive in Windows 9x. You cannot see the Msdos.sys file. How do you explain this?
   Correct answer: b

6. You just created a file called ReadMe.txt with Notepad but when you view it in Windows Explorer, it just says ReadMe. How can this be resolved?
   Correct answer: b

7. You are running Windows XP and you want to find a file that is a letter to Dr. Abrams, how might you do this?
   Correct answer: c

Objective 2.1	Identify the procedures for installing Windows 9x/Me, Windows NT 4.0 Workstation, Windows 2000 Professional, and, Windows XP and bringing the operating system to a basic operational level.	Verify Hardware Compatibility and Minimum Requirements Determine OS Installation Options: Installation Type (typical, custom, other), Network Configuration, File System Type, and Dual Boot Support

Practice Test Questions

1. Which of the following is not a Windows 9x setup type?
   Correct answer: c

2. What are the options for setting up Windows XP networking? (pick all that apply)
   Correct answer: a, c

3. Which file system is recommended on Windows NT for the most secure installation?
   Correct answer: a

4. When dual-booting with Windows XP, what file is used to build the boot menu?
   Correct answer: c

5. What file system should you use with Windows 2000 if you wish to have a dual-boot with Windows 98 such that Windows 98 can access the Windows 2000 partition?
   Correct answer: d

6. When installing Windows XP from a bootable floppy and a CD-ROM, what command do you use to start the installation?
   Correct answer: b

7. What command can you run to check if a computer is ready to install a Windows XP upgrade?
   Correct answer: c

Objective 2.1	Identify the procedures for installing Windows 9x/Me, Windows NT 4.0 Workstation, Windows 2000 Professional, and Windows XP, and bringing the operating system to a basic operational level.	Disk Preparation Order (conceptual disk preperation: Start the installation, partition, and format drive run appropriate set up Utility: Setup and Winnt

Practice Test Questions

1. What command do you use to eliminate the partition table as the source of a problem with a hard drive?

   Correct answer: c

2. Which Windows setup option should you use when installing Windows 98 on a notebook?

   Correct answer: b

3. What is the command to begin installing Windows 9x?

   Correct answer: b

4. After partitioning the hard drive using FDISK, the next step is to:

   Correct answer: c

5. When the FORMAT program is formatting the drive, how are bad sectors handled?

   Correct answer: c

6. How many partitions can a hard drive have using Windows 9x?

   Correct answer: a

7. How many logical drives can the primary partition contain?

   Correct answer: b

PAGE 194

Objective 2.1	Identify the procedures for installing Windows 9x/Me, Windows NT 4.0 Workstation, Windows 2000 Professional, and, Windows XP and bringing the operating system to a basic operational level.	Installation Methods: Bootable CD, boot floppy, network installation, and drive imaging Device Driver Configuration: Load default drivers and find updated drivers

Practice Test Questions

1. What should you check if you cannot boot from the bootable Windows XP CD?

   Correct answer: a

2. What program should you have on your floppy disk when booting to floppy before running the setup program on the CD?

   Correct answer: d

3. What folder should you copy from the installation CD to a network server before doing a network installation for Windows 2000?

   Correct answer: c

4. After you install Windows 2000, you check Device Manager and find that your network card has an exclamation point symbol on it. To resolve this, you should:

   Correct answer: a

5. You have just finished installing Windows XP Professional. When you see the desktop, you notice that the colors are washed out and the icons are very big. You check the display settings and find that they are set to 640x480 resolution at 16 colors. You know your graphic card

supports higher resolutions but you cannot change the settings. What is the most likely problem?

Correct answer: d

6. You boot to a floppy disk and begin the Windows 2000 installation from CD. The setup program complains that Himem.sys is required and is missing. What do you do?

Correct answer: b

7. You need to create a set of startup floppy disks to install Windows NT 4.0, what command do you use from the installation CD?

Correct answer: c

PAGE 196

Objective 2.1	Identify the procedures for installing Windows 9x/Me, Windows NT 4.0 Workstation, Windows 2000 Professional, and Windows XP, and bringing the operating system to a basic operational level.	Restore User Data Files (If Applicable) Identify Common Symptoms and Problems

Practice Test Questions

1. What is the command line program to copy user data to a disk for later transfer to a new XP installation?

Correct answer: b

2. What is the name of the tool for saving user preferences and data?

Correct answer: c

3. Where will you find devices in Device Manager that the installation program did not recognize?

Correct answer: b

4. You have just finished your installation of Windows 95 but when the computer restarts, you get an error that says "Invalid system disk: replace and press any key." What is the most likely cause of this?

Correct answer: b

5. After you complete the Windows 2000 installation, your system reboots and you get the Windows 2000 setup program. What should you do?

Correct answer: a

6. What kind of data will not be migrated by the Files and Settings Transfer Wizard?

Correct answer: c

7. You have just completed a dual-boot installation of Windows XP and Windows 98 but every time the system starts, Windows XP is started after a few seconds if you don't choose Windows 98 from the menu. You prefer to have Windows 98 started automatically. How can you accomplish this?

Correct answer: c

PAGE 198

Objective 2.2	Identify steps to perform an operating system upgrade from Windows 9.x/ME, Windows NT 4.0 Workstation, Windows 2000 Professional, and Windows XP. Given an upgrade scenario, choose the appropriate next steps.	Upgrade Paths Available Determine Correct Upgrade Startup Utility (e.g. WINNT32 vs WINNT)

Practice Test Questions

1. During a Windows 98 upgrade, Vmm32.vxd is built specifically for this PC. Why is that so?
   Correct answer: c

2. What is the purpose of the Windows 95 Setup option "Portable"?
   Correct answer: b.

3. To create a dual boot between Windows 2000 and Windows 98, which file system should be used?
   Correct answer: b

4. The name of the setup program to install Windows NT is:
   Correct answer: c

5. Which operating system requires it be the only OS installed on a partition?
   Correct answer: c

6. What is the purpose of the program Mscdex.exe?
   Correct answer: a

7. What are the four options for a Windows NT installation?
   Correct answer: b

PAGE 200

Objective 2.2	Identify steps to perform an operating system upgrade from Windows 9.x/ME, Windows NT 4.0 Workstation, Windows 2000 Professional, and Windows XP. Given an upgrade scenario, choose the appropriate next steps.	Verify Hardware Compatibility and Minimum Requirements Verify Application Compatibility Apply OS service packs, patches, and updates Install Additional Windows Components

Practice Test Questions

1. Which is the correct command to analyze a computer before performing a Windows 2000 or XP upgrade?

   Correct answer: c

2. You have just upgraded to Windows 2000 from Windows 95 and you want to defragment your disk. When you try to run your third-party defragmentation program, you receive an error. What is the most likely reason for this?

   Correct answer: c

3. You want to upgrade from Windows 95 OSR2 computer to Windows NT. Your primary partition is 6GB and your extended partition is 8GB. Before starting you reformat both partitions. Windows NT will not install. What is the likely problem?

   Correct answer: d

4. How do you run the Windows Update program from Windows XP?

   Correct answer: b

5. From Windows 2000, how do you run the Windows Update program?

   Correct answer: a

6. You want to do a clean install upgrade from Windows 95 to Windows XP and you have a DOS-based program that you want to continue to run. The manufacturer says the program will run in Windows XP fine. Once the installation is complete, you don't see the icon to run the program. What do you do?

   Correct answer: b

7. You are running Windows NT 4.0 with Service Pack 4. You just installed some new networking components and now none of the networking is working. What might solve this problem?

   Correct answer: d

PAGE 202

Objective 2.3	Identify the basic system boot sequences and boot methods, including the steps to create an emergency boot disk with utilities installed for Windows 9x/Me, Windows NT 4.0 Workstation, Windows 2000 Professional, and Windows XP.	Boot Sequence: Files required to boot and boot steps (9.x, NT-based) Alternative Boot Methods: Last known good configuration, command prompt mode, booting to a system restore point, recovery console, Boot.ini switches, and dual boot

Practice Test Questions

1. Which Windows 2000 system file is required to boot only when booting from a SCSI device?

   Correct answer: c

2. What is the correct boot sequence using DOS?

   Correct answer: b

3. Which Windows 9x component is responsible for loading static device drivers?

   Correct answer: b

4. Which Windows 2000 component is part of the kernel?

   Correct answer: c

5. Where can installed device drivers be listed so they are loaded when Windows 98 loads?

   Correct answer: d

6. What are the three core components of Windows 9x?

   Correct answer: b

7. What switch can you add to a Boot.ini entry to force a standard VGA driver to be loaded instead of the specific driver for your video card?

   Correct answer: d

PAGE 204

Objective 2.3	Identify the basic system boot sequences and boot methods, including the steps to create an emergency boot disk with utilities installed for Windows 9x/Me, Windows NT 4.0 Workstation, Windows 2000 Professional, and Windows XP.	Alternative Boot Methods: Using a Startup Disk and Safe/VGA-Only Mode Creating Emergency Disks with OS Utilities Creating Emergency Repair Disk (ERD)

Practice Test Questions

1. To create an emergency startup disk in Windows 95:

   Correct answer: b

2. To go directly to Safe Mode when booting Windows 9x, press:

   Correct answer: d

3. The Mscdex.exe file on the Windows 9x startup disk is used for:

   Correct answer: b

4. What command is used to manage cabinet files?

   Correct answer: d

5. What is the program used by Windows 2000 to create a set of startup disks?

   Correct answer: b

6. What troubleshooting feature is available in Windows 2000 and Windows NT but not in Windows XP?

   Correct answer: c

7. What boot mode disables networking support?

   Correct answer: d

PAGE 206

Objective 2.4	Identify procedures for installing/adding a device, including loading, adding, and configuring device drivers, and required software.	Device Driver Installation: Plug and Play (PNP) and Non-PNP devices, install and configure device drivers, and install different device drivers

Practice Test Questions

1. Which operating system supports Plug and Play?
   Correct answer: c

2. In order for a system to be fully Plug and Play compliant, what must be true?
   Correct answer: a

3. A 16-bit device driver is loaded from:
   Correct answer: a

4. One advantage a 32-bit driver has over a 16-bit driver is that the 32-bit driver:
   Correct answer: c

5. Using Windows 9x, where do you look to find the name of a 32-bit device driver used by a device?
   Correct answer: a

6. You have just installed a new sound card in your Pentium 4 system that runs Windows NT. When your system boots, you find that the sound card was not recognized by the system. What is the likely problem?
   Correct answer: d

7. You cannot locate your CD-ROM drive in My Computer but you can access the driver letter assigned to the CD-ROM. What is the likely reason for this?
   Correct answer: b

PAGE 208

Objective 2.4	Identify procedures for installing/adding a device, including loading, adding, and configuring device drivers, and required software.	Device Driver Installation: Manually install a device driver, search the Internet for updated device drivers, and using unsigned drivers (Driver Signing)

Practice Test Questions

1. Manual installation of a driver can occur using:
   Correct answer: d

2. What does it mean if you manually install a driver and a message pops up and says that the driver does not have a digital signature from Microsoft?
   Correct answer: c

3. If a driver is not Plug and Play compatible and has been manually installed through System.ini, the driver is referred to as a:
   Correct answer: b

4. How can drivers be installed manually in Windows 9x?
   Correct answer: d

5. The way to install a driver using Config.sys is:
   Correct answer: c

6. When you manually update a driver in Windows XP using Device Manager, which of the following are choices? (choose all that apply)
   Correct answer: a, c

7. You have just discovered that a new driver is available for your video card. You are running Windows XP. How should you install the new driver?
   Correct answer: c

PAGE 210

Objective 2.4	Identify procedures for installing/adding a device, including loading, adding, and configuring device drivers, and required software.	Install Additional Windows Components Determine if Permissions are Adequate for Performing the Task

Practice Test Questions

1. A user calls you at lunch the day after you upgrade his computer from Windows 95 to Windows 98 and complains that he cannot find the Solitaire game. How can you resolve his problem?
   Correct answer: c

2. You are running Windows XP and want to install FTP services which are located in the IIS category of Add/Remove Windows Components. You see that the box next to IIS is already checked but you cannot find the FTP service on your computer. What can be the problem?
   Correct answer: b

3. A user running Windows 2000 calls you because his sound card is not working. When you get to his computer, you go to the Device Manager, choose the device properties and go to the Driver tab so you can update the driver, but you don't find an Update Driver button. What is the problem?
   Correct answer: b

4. How can you install the Indexing Service in Windows XP?
   Correct answer: a

5. You try to install the Paint program in Windows XP but cannot run the Add/Remove Windows Components Wizard. What should you do?

Correct answer: c

6. You want to install a new spreadsheet program on your computer, where should you go?

Correct answer: b

7. In Windows XP, how can you easily change the default Java virtual machine?

Correct answer: c

PAGE 212

Objective 2.5	Identify procedures necessary to optimize the operating system and major operating system subsystems.	Virtual Memory Management Disk Defragmentation Files and Buffers Caches Temporary File Management

Practice Test Questions

1. Virtual memory: (select all that apply)

Correct answer: b, d

2. In Windows 9x, the swap file is called:

Correct answer: c

3. The swap file for Windows 2000 is located by default at:

Correct answer: d

4. The options for specifying the paging file in Windows XP include: (select all that apply)

Correct answer: a, b, c

5. The best place to put the Windows XP paging file for performance is:

Correct answer: c

6. You get an error when you run a DOS database program that says "Too Many Open Files," what can you do?

Correct answer: d

7. The optimum size of the paging file in Windows 9x for best performance is:

Correct answer: a

Objective 3.1	Recognize and interpret the meaning of common error codes and startup messages from the boot sequence, and identify steps to correct the problems.	Common Error Messages and and Codes: Boot Failure and Errors (invalid boot disk, inaccessible boot device, missing Ntldr, and bad or missing command interpreter)

Practice Test Questions

1. How can you resolve the error "Invalid sytem disk"?

   Correct answer: c

2. You are trying to boot to Windows 2000 and receive an error that Ntldr is missing. You have another computer that has Windows 2000 installed and you copy Ntldr to a boot floppy. After you have booted to the floppy you type the command: a:\> copy ntldr C:\ntldr and you get the error message "Invalid drive specification." What is wrong?

   Correct answer: b

3. You receive the message "Bad or missing command interpreter" and you verify that C:\command.com is there. You copy a new command.com to c:\ just in case the existing file is corrupted but you get the same error message when you try to reboot. What could be the problem?

   Correct answer: b

4. When is a good time to use Recovery Console? (choose all that apply)

   Correct answer: a, c, d

5. How do you run the Recovery Console?

   Correct answer: b

6. What do you need if you get the error "Inaccessible Disk" when installing Windows XP?

   Correct answer: c

7. Your Windows XP installation gives you an error that the Ntldr file is missing so you insert the installation CD to repair the installation but when you restart the computer, you receive the same error message. What can you do?

   Correct answer: d

Objective 3.1	Recognize and interpret the meaning of common error codes and startup messages from the boot sequence, and identify steps to correct the problems.	Common Error Messages and Codes: Startup Messages (Error in Config.sys Line XX, Himem.sys not loaded, Missing or corrupt Himem.sys, and Device/Service has failed to start) and A device referenced in System.ini, Win.ini, Registry is not found

Practice Test Questions

1. What is the purpose of the Windows 98 command WIN.COM /D:F?

   Correct answer: b

2. When does Windows 98 create the Bootlog.txt file?

   Correct answer: d

3. Which statement about VxDs is true?

   Correct answer: b

4. To temporarily disable a command in Config.sys, you should:

   Correct answer: c

5. Using Windows 9x, from where can device drivers be loaded?

   Correct answer: c

6. How can you load Windows 2000 bypassing entries in System.ini and Win.ini?

   Correct answer: b

7. Which of the following Windows 9x files is built specifically for the current system?

   Correct answer: a

Objective 3.1	Recognize and interpret the meaning of common error codes and startup messages from the boot sequence, and identify steps to correct the problems.	Common Error Messages and Codes: Event Viewer – Event log is full, Failure to start GUI, Windows Protection Error, User-modified settings cause improper operation at startup, and Registry corruption

Practice Test Questions

1. What is the name of the file from which the System.dat was created when Windows 9x was first installed?
   Correct answer: b

2. How often does Registry Checker back up the registry and how many backups does it keep?
   Correct answer: c

3. You get a Windows Protection Error on startup and you cannot boot to Safe Mode, what do you do?
   Correct answer: d

4. What are the five registry files you can restore in Windows 2000/XP if they become corrupt?
   Correct answer: a

5. You have determined that your Boot.ini files are corrupt, so you run Recovery Console. Which of the following commands can you run from Recovery Console to try to fix the problem?
   Correct answer: b

6. Which of the following cannot be used to solve a Windows NT boot problem?
   Correct answer: d

7. Which of the following are possible reasons for a Windows Protection Error?
   Correct answer: a

PAGE 220

Objective 3.1	Recognize and interpret the meaning of common error codes and startup messages from the boot sequence, and identify steps to correct the problems.	Using the Correct Utilities: Dr. Watson, Boot Disk, and Event Viewer

Practice Test Questions

1. Where are the log files created by Dr. Watson stored?
   Correct answer: c

2. How do you start Dr. Watson?
   Correct answer: a

3. What are the log files in Event Viewer? (choose all that apply)
   Correct answer: a, c, d

4. Which is true about Event Viewer?
   Correct answer: c

5. To create a Windows 9x boot disk, you should:
   Correct answer: b

6. An exclamation point sign in an Event Viewer log file indicates:
   Correct answer: c

7. To view a message in Event Viewer, you should:
   Correct answer: a

PAGE 222

Objective 3.2	Recognize when to use common diagnostic utilities and tools. Given a diagnostic scenario involving one of these utilities or tools, select the appropriate steps needed to resolve the problem.	Startup Disks: Required Files for a Boot Disk and Boot Disk with CD-ROM Support

Practice Test Questions

1. Your Windows 2000 system will not boot because of a corrupted Boot.ini file. You do not have a Windows 2000 boot disk for that system, but you do have a Windows 9x boot disk. The C: drive is partitioned with FAT32. What should be on your boot disk to help you out?
   Correct answer: b

2. How do you format a Windows XP floppy so that it is bootable?
   Correct answer: c

3. Which file is needed on a Windows XP boot floppy if the hard disk is a SCSI drive?
   Correct answer: c

4. Which file is needed if you want to access the CD-ROM drive after booting to a floppy?
   Correct answer: d

5. What line is necessary in Config.sys to provide CD-ROM support?
   Correct answer: a

6. You suspect there is a problem with the Msdos.sys file in Windows 98. What file can help you fix the problem?
   Correct answer: d

7. You installed a dual-boot with Windows 98 and Windows 2000 but you have decided to remove the Windows 2000 installation which was on a different partition from Windows 98. You delete the partition but find that the Windows 2000 boot loader still runs when the computer boots. What can you do?
   Correct answer: b

PAGE 224

Objective 3.2	Recognize when to use common diagnostic utilities and tools. Given a diagnostic scenario involving one of these utilities or tools, select the appropriate steps needed to resolve the problem.	Startup Modes: Safe Mode, Safe Mode with Command Prompt, Safe Mode with Networking, Step-By-Step/Single Step Mode, and Automatic Skip Driver (Asd.exe)

Practice Test Questions

1. What is the source of the error message "MS-DOS compatibility mode"?

   Correct answer: a

2. What is the source of the error message "Invalid VxD dynamic link call from IFSMGR" and what do you do to solve the problem?

   Correct answer: a

3. What is one of the first things you should do after booting into Safe Mode?

   Correct answer: a

4. What happens if the Win.com file is missing from the Windows 9x load?

   Correct answer: d

5. What troubleshooting tool can you try if a device causes your computer to hang during startup?

   Correct answer: d

6. Which statement about booting Windows 9x into Safe Mode is not true?

   Correct answer: b

7. What is one way to access Safe Mode under Windows 2000?

   Correct answer: d

PAGE 226

Objective 3.2	Recognize when to use common diagnostic utilities and tools. Given a diagnostic scenario involving one of these utilities or tools, select the appropriate steps needed to resolve the problem.	Diagnostic Tools, Utilities and Resources: User/ Installation Manuals, Internet/Web Resources, training Materials, Task Manager, and Dr. Watson

Practice Test Questions

1. In Windows XP, to view a list of running processes and the amount of CPU they are using, you should:

   Correct answer: b

2. To start Dr. Watson in Windows 98, you should:

   Correct answer: c

3. You are running a program that freezes often and displays an error about Illegal Operation. How can you view detailed information about the errors occurring in the application?

   Correct answer: d

4. Which of the following is not a tab in Windows XP Task Manager?

   Correct answer: a

5. You run Task Manager and notice that a process called System Idle is taking 99% of the CPU time, what should you do?

   Correct answer: c

6. You notice a lot of disk activity when you have several applications loaded even though those applications are not accessing files on the disk. You suspect you may be making heavy use of virtual memory. How can you determine if this is the case?

Correct answer: b

7. Every time you try to run Microsoft Word, you receive a specific error message. You have been unable to resolve the problem yourself. What is the best thing to try next?

Correct answer: c

PAGE 228

Objective 3.2	Recognize when to use common diagnostic utilities and tools. Given a diagnostic scenario involving one of these utilities or tools, select the appropriate steps needed to resolve the problem.	Diagnostic Tools, Utilities and Resources: Boot Disk, Event Viewer, Device Manager, WinMSD, MSD, Recovery CD, and CONFIGSAFE

Practice Test Questions

1. To find out information about device resource usage, you should use: (choose all that apply)

Correct answer: a, b, c

2. The use of a boot disk is usually only necessary when:

Correct answer: c

3. In Windows 2000, to view a summary of DMA channels in use, you should:

Correct answer: a

4. To get a report of resource usage and system information in Windows NT, you should:

Correct answer: c

5. You boot your Windows XP computer and receive a message that a service failed to start. Where do you go to get additional information?

Correct answer: b

6. You have been unable to resolve a problem that started after you installed a new application. You have uninstalled the application but the problem persists. You believe the problem is related to the registry and some configuration files. What tool is most likely to solve this problem?

Correct answer: c

7. You cannot boot the Windows GUI and you think there may be a resource conflict. What tool can help you determine if a resource conflict exists?

Correct answer: a

| Objective 3.2 | Recognize when to use common diagnostic utilities and tools. Given a diagnostic scenario involving one of these utilities or tools, select the appropriate steps needed to resolve the problem. | Eliciting Problem Symptoms from Customers
Having Customer Reproduce Error as Part of the Diagnostic Process
Identifying Recent Changes to the Computer Environment from the User |
|---|---|---|

Practice Test Questions

1. What is something you can do to promote good communication?
Correct answer: d

2. What is something you should do while talking with a customer?
Correct answer: d

3. What is one question to ask a customer?
Correct answer: b

4. What are some things you need to know from the customer?
Correct answer: d

5. What is the first thing you should do when you arrive at a customer's site?
Correct answer: c

6. What do you do if you make a mistake while attempting to repair a PC?
Correct answer: b

7. When interviewing a customer, why is it important to know if the PC has been near a lightning storm recently?
Correct answer: a

Objective 3.3	Recognize common operational and usability problems and determine how to resolve them.	Troubleshooting Windows-Specific Printing Problems: Print spool is stalled, Incorrect/incompatible driver for print, and Incorrect parameter

Practice Test Questions

1. If you can print a test page from the Windows 98 Print window, what is the most likely source of a user's continuing print problem?
Correct answer: d

2. You cannot print from an application or the Windows 98 Print window. What do you do first?
Correct answer: c

3. You are unable to print and several jobs are in the print queue. How do you clear the queue?

   Correct answer: b

4. How do you uninstall a printer's device drivers?

   Correct answer: c

5. What is one source of a problem that would prevent Windows 98 from printing?

   Correct answer: d

6. If you can print from a DOS prompt, but cannot print from Windows, what is the next thing you should do?

   Correct answer: a

7. How can you access the Print Spooler service in Windows XP?

   Correct answer: b

PAGE 234

Objective 3.3	Recognize common operational and usability problems and determine how to resolve them.	Other Common Problems: General Protections Faults, Bluescreen Error (BSOD), Illegal Operation, Invalid Working Directory, System Lock Up, Option (sound card, modem, input device) will not function, Application will not start or load, and Applications don't install

Practice Test Questions

1. When an application fails to load, what should you do first?

   Correct answer: a

2. How can you change the icon of a short-cut object on the desktop?

   Correct answer: a

3. You are running several applications and one of them locks up. What do you do?

   Correct answer: c

4. An application cannot access a device. How can you know if the device is installed properly?

   Correct answer: d

5. In implementing Plug and Play, the bus enumerator inventories the resources required by devices on the bus. Which bus does Windows 95 not support?

   Correct answer: c

6. What is the generic name given to a Windows 2000 STOP error?

   Correct answer: c

7. An application gives an "illegal operations" error. What is one possible cause?

   Correct answer: d

PAGE 236

Objective 3.3	Recognize common operational and usability problems and determine how to resolve them.	Other Common Problems: Cannot Log on to Network (Option – NIC not Functioning) and Network Connection

Practice Test Questions

1. How can you know a PC has a physical connection to an Ethernet hub?
   Correct answer: d

2. How can you verify using Windows 2000 that a PC has good communication over the network?
   Correct answer: a

3. How can you verify that your computer can communicate with another computer on the TCP/IP network?
   Correct answer: a

4. What is a possible cause of a failure to connect to the network?
   Correct answer: d

5. You cannot connect to a network even after a reboot. What is the next thing to do?
   Correct answer: c

6. You can print to a network printer but cannot see another host on the network that should be listed in Network Neighborhood. What might be the cause?
   Correct answer: c

7. How do you share a folder on the network?
   Correct answer: a

PAGE 238

Objective 3.3	Recognize common operational and usability problems and determine how to resolve them.	Viruses and Virus Types: What they are, TSR (Terminate Stay Resident) Programs and Virus, Sources (Floppy, Emails, etc.), and How to determine presence

Practice Test Questions

1. How does a boot sector virus differ from a file virus?
   Correct answer: b

2. How does a virus typically spread over e-mail?
   Correct answer: d

3. What is a macro virus?
   Correct answer: c

4. What can you do to protect against a virus?
   Correct answer: d

5. What is one thing that a virus cannot do?
   Correct answer: d

6. What is the purpose of virus protection in CMOS setup?
   Correct answer: b

7. What is a symptom of a virus being present or having done damage?
   Correct answer: d

PAGE 240

Objective 4.1	Identify the networking capabilities of Windows. Given configuration parameters, configure the operating system to connect to a network.	Configure Protocols: TCP/IP (Gateway, subnet mask, DNS (and domain suffix), WINS, static address assignment, and automatic address assignment (APIPA, DHCP))

Practice Test Questions

1. You are configuring static addressing on a Windows computer. You have to change to the Gateway tab to install the Default Gateway. What operating system are you using?
   Correct answer: a

2. A user complains that he cannot access the Internet with his Windows computer. You check his computer and find that you can access the company web server using the IP address but not the name. Where should you go to fix this?
   Correct answer: b

3. You are a consultant for a small business and they want you to tell them how the IP address is configured. You run IPCONFIG on several machines and find that their IP addresses all start with 169.254. How is the IP address configured?
   Correct answer: d

4. A technician you work with explains to you that he just configured the IP address settings on a customer's computer but it still does not connect to the network. When asked, he tells you he configured the IP address, Default Gateway, and DNS Server. What should he do?
   Correct answer: c

5. A user can access hosts on the the Internet fine but is unable to locate other Windows computers in the corporate network. What might resolve the problem?
   Correct answer: b

6. How do you configure IP address settings in Windows XP?
   Correct answer: d

7. What does DHCP mean?
   Correct answer: b

Objective 4.1	Identify the networking capabilities of Windows. Given configuration parameters, configure the operating system to connect to a network.	Configure Protocols: IPX/SPX (NWLINK), Appletalk, and NetBEUI/NetBIOS

Practice Test Questions

1. What protocol is the default protocol used on a NetWare 4 server?

   Correct answer: c

2. Which protocol is native to Windows computers and is a good choice for small networks not requiring Internet access?

   Correct answer: b

3. How do Windows computers running NetBEUI name computers?

   Correct answer: c

4. With which protocol might you need to configure a frame type?

   Correct answer: b

5. What protocol is used by Macintosh computers?

   Correct answer: c

6. How do you add the NWLink protocol in Windows XP?

   Correct answer: a

7. Which protocol is not supported in Windows 2000 clients?

   Correct answer: c

Objective 4.1	Identify the networking capabilities of Windows. Given configuration parameters, configure the operating system to connect to a network.	Configure Client Options: Microsoft and Novell Verify the Configuration

Practice Test Questions

1. What is the name of the Windows 2000 client supplied by Microsoft that allows access to a NetWare server?

   Correct answer: c

2. You are running a Windows 98 computer and you want the computer to log on to a Windows domain upon start up, what must you do?

   Correct answer: a

3. What must you do for Windows 2000 to log on to a Windows domain?

   Correct answer: b

4. You are trying to make Windows 98 log into a NetWare 3.2 server named NW-SERV1. You have the Client for NetWare Networks installed but it is not working correctly, what can you try to solve the problem?

   Correct answer: c

5. You don't see the Windows server called DB1 in Network Neighborhood, how can you try to connect to that server?

   Correct answer: b

6. You want to verify that your network connection and IP configuration are okay, what can you do?

   Correct answer: c

7. To view all of your network connection IP settings plus the configured DNS server and DHCP server, what can you do? You are running Windows XP.

   Correct answer: b

PAGE 246

Objective 4.1	Identify the networking capabilities of Windows. Given configuration parameters, configure the operating system to connect to a network.	Understand the Use of the Following Tools: Ipconfig.exe, Winipcfg.exe, PING, Tracert.exe, and Nslookup.exe

Practice Test Questions

1. Which utility can you use to verify DNS information?

   Correct answer: b

2. What utility can you use to see the path a packet takes between your computer and *www.course.com*?

   Correct answer: c

3. Your computer was unable to reach a DHCP server when it first booted but you have solved the problem. How can you make your computer try to get an IP address from the DHCP server?

   Correct answer: c

4. Which TCP/IP utility is used to verify that two computers are connected over a network?

   Correct answer: b

5. Which TCP/IP utility is a part of Windows 9x TCP/IP but is not included with Windows 2000 TCP/IP?

   Correct answer: a

6. What is Telnet?

   Correct answer: a

7. You want to view the MAC address of a computer on the network that you just pinged. How can you do this?

   Correct answer: c

PAGE 248

Objective 4.1	Identify the networking capabilities of Windows. Given configuration parameters, configure the operating system to connect to a network.	Share Resources (Understand the Capabilities/Limitations with each OS Version) Setting Permissions to Shared Resources

Practice Test Questions

1. What are the sharing permissions in Windows 2000?
   Correct answer: c

2. Which is installed by default on Windows 2000 but not on Windows 9x?
   Correct answer: b

3. How do you install file and printer sharing for Microsoft Networks?
   Correct answer: a

4. How do you share a file or folder with others on the network?
   Correct answer: b

5. Using Windows 9x, how do you map a drive letter to a network resource?
   Correct answer: d

6. When you share a printer with others on the network, what is required?
   Correct answer: a

7. When using Windows Explorer, how can you tell that an object is network shared?
   Correct answer: b

PAGE 250

Objective 4.1	Identify the networking capabilities of windows. Given configuration parameters, configure the operating system to connect to a network.	Network Type and Network Card

Practice Test Questions

1. What type of networks does Windows 95 support?
   Correct answer: b

2. You have a network card that has a port that looks like a large phone jack. What type of NIC is it?
   Correct answer: b

3. Which is the most popular network architecture for a LAN?
   Correct answer: d

4. What is the most common topology used by Ethernet?
   Correct answer: c

5. Which type of network is not supported by Windows 98?

Correct answer: a

6. Before data can be sent over a network, what happens to it?

Correct answer: a

7. Windows 98 has built-in support for what type of networking?

Correct answer: b

PAGE 252

Objective 4.2	Identify the basic Internet protocols and terminologies. Identify procedures for establishing Internet connectivity. In a given scenario, configure the operating system to connect to and use Internet resources.	Protocols and Terminologies: ISP, TCP/IP, HTTPS, SSL, Telnet, and DNS

Practice Test Questions

1. If a home computer user wants to access the Internet, who should be contacted?

Correct answer: d

2. To be sure your Web transaction is secure, the protocol field of the URL should be:

Correct answer: c

3. SSL keeps transactions safe by which method?

Correct answer: b

4. Jane complains that she can access all of the computers in the company network but cannot access her favorite Web site, *www.bargains4u.com*. What can you check to troubleshoot the problem?

Correct answer: d

5. Which protocol suite is the protocol of the Internet?

Correct answer: b

6. Which of the following is not a communication method for connecting to the Internet through an ISP?

Correct answer: a

7. You want to connect to the Internet through an ISP using dial-up networking, what must you have available to do so?

Correct answer: c

Objective 4.2	Identify the basic Internet protocols and terminologies. Identify procedures for establishing Internet connectivity. In a given scenario, configure the operating system to connect to and use Internet resources.	Protocols and Terminologies: E-mail (POP, SMTP, IMAP), HTML, HTTP, and FTP

Practice Test Questions

1. When a user wishes to send mail, the message is transferred to a server before going on to its destination. What protocol is used to transfer the message from the E-mail client to the server?
   Correct answer: b

2. What protocol is used to transfer a file from a Web server to a Web browser?
   Correct answer: c

3. What is FTP?
   Correct answer: b

4. What organization tracks domain names and IP addresses?
   Correct answer: a

5. What is a URL?
   Correct answer: a

6. What protocol is used to transfer mail from the mail server to the mail client?
   Correct answer: b

7. What protocol will you use to transfer a 2 MB binary file from a server to your workstation?
   Correct answer: d

Objective 4.2	Identify the basic Internet protocols and terminologies. Identify procedures for establishing Internet connectivity. In a given scenario, configure the operating system to connect to and use Internet resources.	Connectivity Technologies: Dial-Up Networking, DSL Networking, ISDN Networking, Cable, Satellite, Wireless, and LAN

Practice Test Questions

1. When configuring a PC to use a modem to an ISP to connect to the Internet, what line protocol is most likely to be used today?
   Correct answer: a

2. Which technology can use standard phone lines? (choose all that apply)
   Correct answer: b, d

3. What LAN technology might you choose in a home network that allows you to carry a laptop from room to room and remain connected?

Correct answer: b

4. When an IP address is assigned to a PC each time it logs onto a network, this is called:

Correct answer: c

5. Which high-speed technology for Internet access is appropriate where there is no cable television and the location is a very long distance from the phone company?

Correct answer: b

6. What technology permits two 64K B channels which can be combined for a 128K connection?

Correct answer: d

7. When using DUN, what is the highest speed connection possible?

Correct answer: c

PAGE 258

Objective 4.2	Identify the basic Internet protocols and terminologies. Identify procedures for establishing Internet connectivity. In a given scenario, configure the operating system to connect to and use Internet resources.	Installing and Configuring Browsers: Enable/disable script support, configure proxy settings, and configure security settings Firewall Protection Under Windows XP

Practice Test Questions

1. Where can you configure scripting support in Internet Explorer?

Correct answer: b

2. Which of the following is not a type of script?

Correct answer: c

3. What type of device acts as an intermediary between a Web client and a Web server?

Correct answer: d

4. What device or program can filter out undesirable packets from reaching a host or network?

Correct answer: a

5. How can you configure Windows XP Internet Firewall Connection to only allow Web server packets into the network?

Correct answer: b

6. Which is true about the Internet Connection Firewall?

Correct answer: c

7. Which of the following can you configure on IE 6? (choose all that apply)

Correct answer: a, b, d

Accelerated graphics port (AGP) — A slot on a system board for a video card that provides transfer of video data from the CPU that is synchronized with the memory bus.

ACPI (Advanced Configuration and Power Interface) — Specification developed by Intel, Microsoft, and Toshiba to control power on notebooks and other devices. Windows 98 supports ACPI.

Active Directory — A Windows 2000 service that allows for a single point of administration for all shared resources on a network, including files, peripheral devices, databases, Web sites, users, and services.

Adapter address — A 6-byte hex hardware address unique to each NIC and assigned by manufacturers. The address is often printed on the adapter. An example is 00 00 0C 08 2F 35. Also called MAC address.

Adapter card — Also called an interface card. A small circuit board inserted in an expansion slot and used to communicate between the system bus and a peripheral device.

Address Resolution Protocol (ARP) — A method used by TCP/IP that dynamically or automatically translates IP addresses into physical network addresses such as Ethernet IDs or Token Ring MAC addresses.

ADSL (asymmetric digital subscriber line) — A method of data transmission over phone lines that is digital, allows for a direct connection, and is about 50 times faster than ISDN.

Advanced Options Menu — A Windows 2000 menu that appears when you press F8 when Windows starts. The menu can be used to troubleshoot problems when loading Windows 2000.

Advanced SCSI programming interface (ASPI) — A popular device driver that enables operating systems to communicate with a SCSI host adapter. (The "A" originally stood for Adaptec.)

Advanced Transfer Cache (ATC) — A type of L2 cache contained within the Pentium processor housing that is embedded on the same core processor die as the CPU itself.

Alternating current (AC) — Current that cycles back and forth rather than traveling in only one direction. Normally between 110 and 115 AC volts are supplied from a standard wall outlet.

Ammeter — A meter that measures electrical current in amps.

Ampere (A) — A unit of measurement for electrical current. One volt across a resistance of one ohm will produce a flow of one amp.

ANSI (American National Standards Institute) — A nonprofit organization dedicated to creating trade and communications standards.

Antivirus (AV) software — Utility programs that prevent infection, or scan a system to detect and remove viruses. McAfee Associates VirusScan and Norton AntiVirus are two popular AV packages.

Asynchronous SRAM — Static RAM that does not work in step with the CPU clock and is, therefore, slower than synchronous SRAM.

AT command set — A set of commands used by a PC to control a modem. AT is the ATtention command, which alerts a modem to prepare to receive additional commands. For example, ATDT means attention and listen for a dial tone.

ATAPI (Advanced Technology Attachment Packet Interface) — An interface standard that is part of the IDE/ATA standards, which allows tape drives and CD-ROM drives to be treated like an IDE hard drive by the OS.

AT system board — A form factor, generally no longer produced, in which the motherboard requires a full-size case.

ATTRIB command — A DOS command that can display file attributes and even lock files so that they are "read-only" and cannot be modified (for example, ATTRIB +R FILENAME).

ATX system board — The most common form factor for PC motherboards, originally introduced by Intel in 1995.

Auto detection — A feature on newer system BIOS and hard drives that automatically identifies and configures a new hard drive in the CMOS setzup.

Autoexec.bat — One startup file on an MS-DOS computer. It tells the computer what commands or programs to execute automatically after bootup.

Back up, Backup — When used as a verb, to make a duplicate copy of important files or data. When used as a noun, refers to the file created when backing up. Backups can be made by saving a file with a different name or by copying files to a different storage media.

Backbone — A network used to link several networks together. For example, several Token Rings and Ethernet LANs may be connected using a single FDDI backbone.

Backside bus — The bus between the CPU and the L2 cache inside the CPU housing.

Backward compatible — Refers to new hardware and software that is able to support older, existing technologies. This is a common choice of hardware and software manufacturers.

Bandwidth — The range of frequencies that a communication cable or channel can carry. In general use, the term refers to the volume of data that can travel on a bus or over a cable.

Bank — An area on the system board that contains slots for memory modules (typically labeled bank 0, 1, 2, and 3).

Base memory — *See* Conventional memory.

Baseband — Relating to a communications system which carries only a single message at a time over wire. Ethernet uses baseband technology. Compare to broadband.

Batch file — A text file containing a series of DOS instructions to the computer, telling it to perform a specific task (for example, Autoexec.bat, which contains a series of startup commands).

Baud rate — A measure of line speed between two devices such as a computer and a printer or a modem. This speed is measured in the number of times a signal changes in one second. *See* bps.

Beam detect mirror — Detects the initial presence of a laser printer's laser beam by reflecting the beam to an optical fiber.

Binary number system — The number system used by computers where there are only two numbers, 0 and 1, called binary digits, or bits.

Binding — Associating an OSI layer to a layer above it or below it. For example, associating a protocol type such as TCP/IP to a NIC driver.

BIOS (basic input/output system) — Firmware that controls much of a computer's input/output functions, such as communication with the floppy drive, RAM chips, and the monitor. Also called ROM BIOS.

Bitmap file — A type of graphics file in which the image is written as a series of 0s and 1s. These files have the extension .bmp and can be loaded into paint programs to be edited and printed.

BNC connector — A connector used on an Ethernet 10Base2 (Thinnet) network. A BNC connector looks like a TV cable connector.

Boot loader menu — A startup menu that gives the user the choice between Windows NT Workstation Version 4.0 and another OS, such as Windows 98.

Boot partition — The hard drive partition where the Windows NT OS is stored. The system partition and the boot partition may be different partitions.

Boot record (of hard drives) — The first sector of each logical drive in a partition that contains information about the logical drive. If the boot record is in the active partition, then it is used to boot the OS. Also called OS boot record or volume boot record.

Boot sector virus — An infectious program that can replace the boot program with a modified, infected version of the boot command utilities, often causing boot and data retrieval problems.

Bootable disk — For DOS, a floppy disk that can upload the OS files necessary for computer startup. It must have the two hidden system files Io.sys and Msdos.sys, and also Command.com.

Booting — The process that a computer goes through when it is first turned on to get the computer ready to receive commands.

Bps (bits per second) — A measure of data transmission speed. (Example: a common modem speed is 56,000 bps or 56 Kbps.)

Break code — A code produced when a key on a computer keyboard is released.

Bridge — A hardware device or box, coupled with software at the data-link layer, used to connect similar networks and network segments. *See* Router.

Briefcase — A Windows 9x system folder used to synchronize files between two computers. When files are transferred from one computer to another, Briefcase automatically updates files on the original computer to the most recent version.

Broadband — Relating to a communications system such as cable modem or ATM networks that carry multiple messages over wire, each message traveling on its own frequency. Compare to baseband.

Buffer — A temporary memory area where data is kept before being written to a hard drive or sent to a printer, thus reducing the number of writes to the devices.

Burst EDO (BEDO) — A refined version of EDO memory that significantly improved access time over EDO. BEDO is not widely used today because Intel chose not to support it. BEDO memory is stored on 168-pin DIMM modules.

Burst SRAM — Memory that is more expensive and slightly faster than pipelined burst SRAM. Data is sent as a two-step process; the data address is sent, and then the data itself is sent without interruption.

Burst transfer — A means of sending data across the bus, with one packet immediately following the next, without waiting for clock beats and/or addressing of the information being sent.

Bus — Strips of parallel wires or printed circuits used to transmit electronic signals on the system board to other devices. Most Pentium systems use a 32-bit bus.

Bus enumerator — A component of Windows 9x Plug and Play that locates all devices on a particular bus and inventories the resource requirements for these devices.

Bus network architecture — A network design in which nodes are connected in line with one another, with no centralized point of contact.

Bus network topology — A network design in which nodes are connected in line with one another, with no centralized point of contact.

Bus speed — The speed or frequency at which the data on the system board is moving.

Cabinet file — A file that contains one or more compressed files, and is often used to distribute software on disk. The Extract command is used to extract one or more files from the cabinet file.

Cable modem — A method of data transmission over cable TV lines that requires a modem and an Ethernet network interface card to receive the transmission.

Cache memory — A kind of fast RAM that is used to speed up memory access because it does not need to be continuously refreshed.

Capacitor — An electronic device that can maintain an electrical charge for a period of time and is used to smooth out the flow of electrical current.

Cards — Adapter boards or interface cards placed into expansion slots to expand the functions of a computer, allowing it to communicate with external devices such as monitors or speakers.

Carrier — A signal used to activate a phone line to confirm a continuous frequency; used to indicate that two computers are ready to receive or transmit data via modems.

CD or CHDIR command — A DOS command to change directories (for example, CD\WINDOWS changes the directory to the Windows directory, and CD\ returns to the Root directory).

CD-R (recordable CD) — A CD drive that can record or write data to a CD. The drive may or may not be multisession, but the data cannot be erased once it is written.

CDRW (rewritable CD) — A CD drive that can record or write data to a CD. The data can be erased and overwritten. The drive may or may not be multisession.

Chain — A group of clusters used to hold a single file.

Checksum — A method of error checking transmitted data, whereby the digits are added up and their sum compared to an expected sum.

Child directory — *See* Subdirectory.

Child, parent, grandparent backup method — A plan for backing up and reusing tapes or removable disks by rotating them each week (child), month (parent), and year (grandparent).

Chip set — A group of chips on the system board that relieves the CPU of some of the system's processing tasks, providing careful timing of activities and increasing the overall speed and performance of the system.

CHS (cylinders, heads, sectors) mode — The traditional method by which BIOS reads from and writes to hard drives by addressing the correct cylinder, head, and sector. Also called normal mode.

Circuit boards — Computer components, such as the main system board or an adapter board, that have electronic circuits and chips.

Classless addresses — Class C network addresses that a service provider owns and then subleases to small companies.

Clean installation — An operating system installation that is not an upgrade; installation is in newly formatted partition.

Client — In a network, a computer that is connected to another computer and uses programs and/or data stored on the other computer.

Clock speed — The speed or frequency that determines the speed at which devices on the system bus operate, usually expressed in MHz. Different components on a system board operate at different speeds, which are determined by multiplying or dividing a factor by the clock speed. The clock speed is itself determined by a crystal or oscillator located somewhere on the system board.

Clone — Originally, a computer that was compatible with IBM computer hardware and MS-DOS software. Today, the word clone often refers to no-name Intel and Microsoft compatibles.

Cluster — One or more sectors that constitute the smallest unit of space on a disk for storing data (also referred to as a file allocation unit). Files are written to a disk as groups of whole clusters.

Cluster chain — A series of clusters used to hold a single file.

CMOS (complementary metal-oxide semiconductor) — One of two types of technologies used to manufacture microchips (the other type is TTL or transistor-transistor logic chips). CMOS chips require less electricity, hold data longer after the electricity is turned off, are slower, and produce less heat than do TTL chips. The configuration or setup chip is a CMOS chip.

COAST (cache on a stick) — Memory modules that hold memory used as a memory cache. *See* Cache memory.

Cold Boot — *See* Hard boot.

Combo card — An Ethernet card that has more than one port to accommodate different cabling media.

Comment lines — Documentation lines that are ignored by a program. A REM in front of a line will comment out an AUTOEXEC command. A semicolon will turn an .ini file line into a comment.

Common access method (CAM) — A standard adapter driver used by SCSI.

Compressed drive — A drive whose format has been reorganized in order to store more data. A compressed drive is really not a drive at all; it's actually a type of file, typically with a host drive called H.

Computer Management Console — a Microsoft Management Console snap-in that contains commonly-used tools for managing a Windows 2000 or Windows XP computer.

Configuration data — Also called setup information. Information about the computer's hardware, such as what type of hard drive or floppy drive is present, along with other detailed settings.

Configuration manager — A component of Windows 9x Plug and Play that controls the configuration process of all devices and communicates these configurations to the devices.

Configuration parameter — In Windows NT, another name for the value names and values of the registry; information in the Windows NT registry.

Connection protocol — In networking, confirming that a good connection is made before transmitting data to the other end. To accomplish this, most network applications use TCP rather than UDP.

Connectionless protocol — When UDP is used and a connection is not required before sending a packet. Consequently, there is no guarantee that the packet will arrive at its destination. An example of a UDP transmission is a broadcast to all nodes on a network.

Console — An administrative tool contains two or more individual administrative tools. For example, Recovery Console contains a set of commands designed to manage a failed Windows 2000 boot, and Computer Management is a console that contains several tools to monitor and manage hardware and software.

Continuity — A continuous, unbroken path for the flow of electricity. A "continuity test" can determine whether or not internal wiring is still intact.

Control blade — A laser printer component that prevents too much toner from sticking to the cylinder surface.

Conventional memory — Memory addresses between 0 and 640K. Also called base memory.

Cooperative multitasking — A type of multitasking whereby the CPU switches back and forth between programs loaded at the same time. One program sits in the background waiting for the other to relinquish control. Also called task switching.

Coprocessor — A chip or portion of the CPU that helps the microprocessor perform calculations and speeds up computations and data manipulations dramatically.

COPY command — A command that copies files from one location to another (for example, COPY File.ext A: is used to copy the file named File.ext to the floppy disk in drive A).

Corrupted files — Data and program files that are damaged for any of a variety of reasons, ranging from power spikes to user error.

CPU (central processing unit) — Also called a microprocessor. The heart and brain of the computer, which receives data input, processes information, and executes instructions.

Cross-linked clusters — Errors caused when files appear to share the same disk space, according to the file allocation table.

Crosstalk — The interference that one wire, in a twisted pair, may produce in the other.

CVF (compressed volume file) — The file on the host drive of a compressed drive that holds all compressed data.

Data cartridge — A type of tape medium typically used for backups. Full-sized data cartridges are 4 × 6 × ⅝ inches in size. A minicartridge is only 3½ × 2½ × ⅝ inches.

Data communications equipment (DCE) — The hardware, usually a dial-up modem, that provides the connection between a data terminal and a communications line.

Data compression — Reducing the size of files by various techniques such as using a shortcut code to represent repeated data.

Data line protectors — Surge protectors designed to work with the telephone line to a modem.

Data path — The number of bits of data transmitted simultaneously on a bus. The size of a bus, such as a 32-bit-wide data path in a PCI bus.

Data terminal equipment (DTE) — This term refers to both the computer and a remote terminal or other computer to which it is attached.

Datagrams — Packets of data that travel between networks from a sender to a receiver. A datagram typically includes an IP header, address information, a checksum, and data.

DEBUG utility — A DOS utility that shows exactly what is written to a file or memory, using the hexadecimal numbering system to display memory addresses and data.

De facto standard — A standard that does not have an official backing, but is considered a standard because of widespread use and acceptance by the industry.

Default directory — The directory that DOS automatically uses to save and retrieve files.

Default drive — The drive that DOS automatically uses to save and retrieve files.

Default gateway — The main gateway or unit that will send or receive packets addressed to other networks.

Default printer — The printer that Windows software will use unless the user specifies another printer.

Defragment — To "optimize" or rewrite a file to a disk in one contiguous chain of clusters, thus speeding up data retrieval.

DEL command — A command that deletes files (for example, DEL A:FILE.EXT deletes the file named File.ext from drive A).

DELTREE command — A command used to delete a directory, all its subdirectories, and all files within it (for example, DELTREE DIRNAME deletes the directory named DIRNAME and everything in it).

Desktop — The initial screen that is displayed when an OS that has a GUI interface is loaded.

Device driver — A small program stored on the hard drive that tells the computer how to communicate with an input/output device such as a printer or modem.

Device ID — Each device has a device ID (i.e. unique string) associated with it that is used to identify the component and install supporting drivers.

Diagnostic cards — Adapter cards designed to discover and report computer errors and conflicts at POST time (before the computer boots up), often by displaying a number on the card.

Diagnostic software — Utility programs that help troubleshoot computer systems. Some DOS diagnostic utilities are CHKDSK and SCANDISK. PC-Technician is an example of a third-party diagnostic program.

Dial-Up Networking (DUN) — A Windows application that allows a PC to remotely connect to a network through a phone line. A Dial-Up Network icon can be found under My Computer.

Differential backup — Backs up only files that have changed or have been created since the last full backup. When recovering data, only two backups are needed: the full backup and the last differential backup.

Digital diagnostic disk — A floppy disk that has data written on it that is precisely aligned, which is used to test the alignment of a floppy disk drive.

Digital signal — A signal that has only a finite number of values in the range of possible values. An example is the transmission of data over a serial cable as bits, where there are only two values: 0 and 1.

Digital subscriber line (DSL) — A type of technology that is used by digital telephone lines that direct connect rather than dial-up.

Digital video disc (DVD) — A faster, larger CD-ROM format that can read older CDs, store over 8 gigabytes of data, and hold full-length motion picture videos.

DIMM (dual inline memory module) — A miniature circuit board used in newer computers to hold memory. DIMMs can hold 16, 32, 64, or 128 MB of RAM on a single module.

Diode — An electronic device that allows electricity to flow in only one direction. Used in a rectifier circuit.

DIP (dual in-line package) switch — A switch on a circuit board or other device that can be set on or off to hold configuration or setup information.

Direct current (DC) — Current that travels in only one direction (the type of electricity provided by batteries). Computer power supplies transform AC current to low DC current.

Direct Rambus DRAM — A memory technology by Rambus and Intel that uses a narrow, very fast network-type memory bus. Memory is stored on a RIMM module. Also called RDRAM or Direct RDRAM.

Directory — An OS table that contains file information such as name, size, time and date of last modification, and the cluster number of the file's beginning location.

Discrete L2 cache — A type of L2 cache contained within the Pentium processor housing, but on a different die, with a cache bus between the processor and the cache.

Disk cache — A method whereby recently retrieved data and adjacent data are read into memory in advance, anticipating the next CPU request.

Disk cloning — Making an exact image of a hard drive including partition information, boot sectors, operating system installation and applications software to replicate the hard drive on another system or recover from a hard drive crash. Also called disk imaging.

Disk compression — Compressing data on a hard drive to allow more data to be written to the drive.

Disk duplexing — An improvement of disk mirroring, whereby redundant data is written to two or more drives, and each hard drive has its own adapter card. This provides greater protection than disk mirroring.

Disk imaging — See disk cloning.

Disk mirroring — A strategy whereby the same data is written to two hard drives in a computer, to safeguard against hard drive failure. Disk mirroring uses only a single adapter for two drives.

Disk striping — Treating multiple hard drives as a single volume. Data is written across the multiple drives in small segments, in order to increase performance and logical disk volume, and, when parity is also used, to provide fault tolerance. RAID 5 is disk striping with an additional drive for parity.

Disk thrashing — A condition that results when the hard drive is excessively used for virtual memory because RAM is full. It dramatically slows down processing and can cause premature hard drive failure.

DISKCOPY command — A command that copies the entire contents of one disk to another disk of the same type, while formatting the destination disk so that the two will be identical (for example, DISKCOPY A: A: uses drive A to duplicate a disk).

Display adapter — See Video controller card.

Display power management signaling (DPMS) — Energy Star standard specifications that allow for the video card and monitor to go into sleep mode simultaneously. See Energy Star systems.

DLL (dynamic-link library) — A file with a .dll file extension that contains a library of programming routines used by programs to perform common tasks.

DMA (direct memory access) controller chip — A chip that resides on the system board and provides channels that a device may use to send data directly to memory, bypassing the CPU.

Docking station — A device designed to connect to a portable, or notebook, computer in order to make it easy to connect the notebook to peripheral devices.

Documentation — Manuals, tutorials, and Help files that provide information that a user needs in order to use a computer system or software application.

Domain — In Windows NT/2000/XP, a logical group of networked computers, such as those on a college campus, that share a centralized directory database of user account information and security for the entire domain.

Domain name — A unique, text-based name that identifies an IP (Internet address). Typically, domain names in the United States end in .edu, .gov, .com, .org, or .net. Domain names also include a country code, such as .uk for the United Kingdom.

Domain Name System or Domain Name Service (DNS) — A database on a top-level domain name server that keeps track of assigned domain names and their corresponding IP addresses.

Dot pitch — The distance between the dots that the electronic beam hits on a monitor screen.

Double conversion — The process by which the inline UPS converts the AC power to battery power in DC form and then back to AC power.

Double-data rate SDRAM (DDR SDRAM or SDRAM II) — A type of memory technology used on DIMMs that runs at twice the speed of the system clock.

Doze time — The time before an Energy Star or "Green" system will reduce 80% of its activity.

DriveSpace — A utility that compresses files so that they take up less space on a disk drive, creating a single large file on the disk to hold all the compressed files.

Dual boot — The ability to boot using either of two different OSs, such as Windows NT and Windows 98. Note that programs cannot be easily shared between Windows NT and the other OS.

Dual ported — When the video chip set (input) and the RAM DAC (output) can access video memory at the same time. A special kind of video RAM is required.

Dual voltage CPU — A CPU that requires two different voltages, one for internal processing and the other for I/O processing.

Dynamic drive — In Windows 2000, a hard drive that uses a 1 MB database written at the end of the drive to hold information about volumes on the drive and RAID setup information.

Dynamic Host Configuration Protocol (DHCP) — The protocol of a server that manages dynamically assigned IP addresses. DHCP is supported by both Windows 9x and Windows NT, and Windows 2000/XP.

Dynamic IP address — An assigned IP address that is used for the current session only. When the session is terminated, the IP address is returned to the list of available addresses.

Dynamic RAM (DRAM) — The most commonly used type of system memory, with access speeds ranging from 70 to 50 nanoseconds. It requires refreshing every few milliseconds.

Dynamic routing — Routing tables that are automatically updated as new information about routes becomes known and is shared by one router with another. Compare to Static routing.

Dynamic VxD — A VxD that is loaded and unloaded from memory as needed.

ECC (error checking and correction) — A chip set feature on a system board that checks the integrity of data stored on DIMMs and can correct single-bit errors in a byte. More advanced ECC schemas can detect, but not correct, double-bit errors in a byte.

ECHS (extended CHS) mode — A mode of addressing information on a hard drive by translating cylinder, head, and sector information in order to break the 528 MB hard drive barrier. Another name for large mode.

ECP (extended capabilities port) — A bidirectional parallel port mode that uses a DMA channel to speed up data flow.

EDO (extended data output) memory — A type of RAM that may be 10–20% faster than conventional RAM because it eliminates the delay before it issues the next memory address.

EEPROM (electrically erasable programmable ROM) chip — A type of chip in which higher voltage may be applied to one of the pins to erase its previous memory before a new instruction set is electronically written.

EISA (extended standard industry architecture) bus — A 32-bit bus that can transfer 4 bytes at a time at a speed of about 20 MHz.

Electrostatic discharge (ESD) — Another name for static electricity, which can damage chips and destroy system boards, even though it might not be felt or seen with the naked eye.

Embedded SCSI devices — Devices that contain their own host adapter, with the SCSI interface built into the device.

Emergency Repair Process — A Windows 2000 process that restores the OS to its state at the completion of a successful installation.

Emergency startup disk (ESD) — One or more floppy disks that contain the files necessary to boot the computer and perform troubleshooting and diagnostic tasks on an operating system that will not boot. *Also see* Rescue disk.

EMI (electromagnetic interference) — A magnetic field produced as a side effect from the flow of electricity. EMI can cause corrupted data in data lines that are not properly shielded.

Emm386.exe — A DOS utility that provides both emulated expanded memory (EMS) and upper memory blocks (UMBs).

Encrypting virus — A type of virus that transforms itself into a nonreplicating program in order to avoid detection. It transforms itself back into a replicating program in order to spread.

Energy Star systems — "Green" systems that satisfy the EPA requirements to decrease the overall consumption of electricity. *See* Green standards.

Enhanced BIOS — A newer BIOS that has been written to accommodate larger-capacity gigabyte drives.

Enhanced IDE technology — A newer drive standard that allows systems to recognize drives larger than 504 MB/528 MB and to handle up to four devices on the same controller.

Enhanced metafile format (EMF) — A format used to print a document that contains embedded print commands. When printing in Windows, EMF information is generated by the GDI portion of the Windows kernel.

Environment — As related to OSs, the overall support that an OS provides to applications software.

Environment subsystems — In Windows NT, a user-mode process in which a subsystem runs an application in its own private memory address space as a virtual machine. (Compare to integral subsystems.)

EPP (enhanced parallel port) — A parallel port that allows data to flow in both directions (bidirectional port) and is faster than original parallel ports on PCs that only allowed communication in one direction.

EPROM (erasable programmable ROM) chip — A type of chip with a special window that allows the current memory contents to be erased with special ultraviolet light so that the chip can be reprogrammed. Many BIOS chips are EPROMs.

ERASE command — Another name for the DEL command.

Error correction — The ability of some modems to identify transmission errors and then automatically request another transmission.

ESCD (extended system configuration data) — A list written to the BIOS chip of what you have done manually to the system configuration that Plug and Play does not do on its own.

ESD (electrostatic discharge) — *See* Electrostatic discharge.

Ethernet — The most popular network topology used today. It uses Carrier Sense Multiple Access with Collision Detection (CSMA/CD) and can be physically configured as a bus or star network.

Event Viewer — In Windows NT/2000/XP, a utility that tracks and logs events as they are performed by the applications, processes, or user actions. Accessed by clicking Start, Programs, Administrative Tools, and then selecting Event Viewer.

Executive services — In Windows NT/2000/XP, a subsystem running in kernel mode that interfaces between the user mode and HAL.

Expanded memory (EMS) — Memory outside of the conventional 640K and the extended 1024K range that is accessed in 16K segments, or pages, by way of a window to upper memory.

Expansion bus — A bus that does not run synchronized with the system clock.

Expansion card — A circuit board inserted into a slot on the system board to enhance the capability of the computer.

Expansion slot — A narrow slot on the system board where an expansion card can be inserted. Expansion slots connect to a bus on the system board.

Extended memory — Memory above the initial 1024 KB, or 1 MB, area.

External cache — Static cache memory, stored on the system board or inside CPU housing, that is not part of the CPU (also called level 2 or L2 cache).

Farad — The unit of measurement for a capacitor.

Fatal system error — An error that prevents Windows NT from loading. An example is a damaged registry.

Fault tolerance — The degree to which a system can tolerate failures. Adding redundant components, such as disk mirroring or disk duplexing, is a way to build in fault tolerance.

FDDI (Fiber Distributed Data Interface) — Pronounced "fiddy." A ring-based network, similar to Token Ring, that does not require a centralized hub. FDDI often uses fiber-optic cabling.

Fiber optic — A medium through which data can be transmitted in the form of light.

Field-replaceable unit — A component in a computer or device that can be replaced with a new component without sending the computer or device back to the manufacturer. Example: a DIMM memory module on a system board.

File — A collection of related records or lines that can be written to disk and assigned a name (for example, a simple letter or a payroll file containing data about employees).

File allocation table (FAT) — A table on a disk that tracks the clusters used to contain a file.

File allocation units — *See* Cluster.

File extension — A three-character portion of the name of a file that is used to identify the file type. The file extension follows the filename under DOS naming conventions.

Filename — The first part of the name assigned to a file. In DOS, the filename can be no more than 8 characters long and is followed by the file extension.

File system — The overall structure that an OS uses to name, store, and organize files on a disk. Examples of files systems are FAT16, FAT32, and NTFS.

File virus — A virus that inserts virus code into an executable program and can spread whenever that program is accessed.

FINGER — A TCP/IP utility that displays the names of users currently logged into a computer.

FireWire — An expansion bus that can also be configured to work as a local bus. It is expected to replace the SCSI bus, providing an easy method to install and configure fast I/O devices. Also called IEEE 1394.

Firmware — Software that is permanently stored in a chip.

Flash memory — A type of RAM that can electronically hold memory even when the power is off.

Flash ROM — ROM that can be reprogrammed or changed without replacing chips.

Flat panel monitor — A desktop monitor that uses an LCD panel.

Flow control — When using modems, a method of controlling the flow of data from a sending PC by having the receiving PC send a message to the sending device to stop or start data flow. Xon/Xoff is an example of a flow control protocol.

FM (frequency modulation) method — A method of synthesizing sound by making a mathematical approximation of the musical sound wave. MIDI may use FM synthesis or wavetable synthesis.

Folder — A Windows directory for a collection of related files (for instance, a person may find it convenient to create a Mydata directory, or folder, in which to store personal files). For example, ATDT means attention and listen for a dial tone.

Formatting (a floppy disk) — To prepare a new floppy disk for use by placing tracks or cylinders on its surface to store information (for example, FORMAT A:). Old disks can be reformatted, but all data on them will be lost.

FPM (fast page mode) memory — An earlier memory mode used before the introduction of EDO memory.

Fragmentation — The distribution of data files, such that they are stored in noncontiguous clusters.

Fragmented file — A file that has been written to different portions of the disk so that it is not in contiguous clusters.

Frame — A small, standardized packet of data that also includes header and trailer information as well as error-checking codes. *See also* Packets.

Front end — In a client/server environment, the application on the client that makes use of data stored on the server.

Frontside bus — The bus between the CPU and the memory outside the CPU housing.

FTP (File Transfer Protocol) — An Internet standard that provides for the transfer of files from one computer to another. FTP can be used at a command prompt, or with a GUI interface, which is available with FTP software or with a Web browser. When using a Web browser, enter the command "ftp" in the browser URL line instead of the usual "http://" used to locate a Web site.

FTP server or FTP site — A computer that stores files that can be downloaded by FTP.

Full backup — A complete backup, whereby all of the files on the hard drive are backed up each time the backup procedure is performed. It is the safest backup method, but it takes the most time.

Full-duplex — Communication that happens in two directions at the same time.

Gateway — A device or process that connects networks with different protocols. *See* Bridge and Router.

General Protection Fault (GPF) error — A Windows error that occurs when a program attempts to access a memory address that is not available or is no longer assigned to it.

Graphics accelerator — A type of video card that has an on-board processor that can substantially increase speed and boost graphical and video performance.

Green standards — Standards that mean that a computer or device can go into sleep or doze mode when not in use, thus saving energy and helping the environment.

Ground — A process by which static electricity can be safely dissipated.

Ground bracelet — An anti-static wrist strap used to dissipate static electricity. Typically grounded by attaching an alligator clip to the computer chassis or to a nearby ground mat.

Ground mat — An antistatic mat designed for electronic workbenches to dissipate static electricity. It often uses a wire attached to the ground connection in an electrical outlet.

GUI (graphical user interface) — A user interface, such as the Windows interface, that uses graphics or icons on the screen for running programs and entering information.

Half-duplex — Communication between two devices whereby transmission takes place in only one direction at a time.

Half-life — The time it takes for a medium storing data to weaken to half of its strength. Magnetic media, including traditional hard drives and floppy disks, have a half-life of five to seven years.

Handshaking — When two modems begin to communicate, the initial agreement made as to how to send and receive data. It often occurs when you hear the modem making noises as the dial-up is completed.

Hard boot — Restart the computer by turning off the power or by pressing the Reset button. Also called cold boot.

Hard copy — Output from a printer to paper.

Hard drive — The main secondary storage device of a PC, a sealed case that contains magnetic coated platters that rotate at high speed.

Hard drive controller — A set of microchips with programs that control a hard drive. Most hard drive controllers today are located inside the hard drive housing.

Hard drive standby time — The amount of time before a hard drive will shut down to conserve energy.

Hard-disk loading — The illegal practice of installing unauthorized software on computers for sale. Hard-disk loading can typically be identified by the absence of original disks in the original system's shipment.

Hardware — The physical components that constitute the computer system, such as the monitor, the keyboard, the system board, and the printer.

Hardware abstraction layer (HAL) — The low-level part of Windows NT/2000/XP, written specifically for each CPU technology, so that only the HAL must change when platform components change.

Hardware cache — A disk cache that is contained in RAM chips built right on the disk controller.

Hardware compatibility list (HCL) — The list of all computers and peripheral devices that have been tested and are officially supported by Windows NT (*See www. microsoft.com/hwtest*).

Hardware interrupt — An event caused by a hardware device signaling the CPU that it requires service.

Hardware profiles — In Windows NT/2000/XP, configuration information about memory, CPU, and OS, for a PC. A PC may have more than one profile. For example, a docking station PC may have two profiles, one with and one without the notebook PC docked.

Hardware tree — A database built each time Windows 9x starts up that contains a list of installed components and the resources they use.

Head — The top or bottom surface of one platter on a hard drive. Each platter has two heads.

Header — Information sent ahead of data being transferred over a network to identify it to receiving protocols. An IP header consists of items such as header and datagram length, flags, checksum, addresses, and so on.

Heap — A memory block set aside for a program's data. If the heap fills up, an "Out of memory" error might occur, even if there is plenty of regular RAM left, especially in 16-bit applications.

Heat sink — A piece of metal, with cooling fins, that can be attached to or mounted on an integrated chip (such as the CPU) to dissipate heat.

Hertz (Hz) — Unit of measurement for frequency, calculated in terms of vibrations, or cycles, per second. For example, a Pentium CPU may have a speed of 233 MHz (megahertz). For 16-bit stereo sound, 44,100 Hz is used.

Hibernation — A power-saving notebook feature. When a computer hibernates, it stores whatever is currently in memory and then shuts down. When it returns from hibernating, it restores everything back to the way it was before the shutdown.

Hidden file — A file that is not displayed in a directory list. To hide or display a file is one of the file's attributes kept by the OS.

High memory area (HMA) — The first 64K of extended memory. The method of storing part of DOS in the high memory area is called loading DOS high.

High-level format — Format performed by the OS that writes a file system to a logical drive. For DOS and Windows 9x, the command used is FORMAT, which writes a FAT and a directory to the drive. Also called OS format.

Himem.sys — A device driver that manages memory above 640K. It is often executed by the line DEVICE = C:\DOS\HIMEM.SYS in a Config.sys file.

Hive — A physical segment of the Windows NT/2000/XP registry that is stored in a file.

Hop count — The number of routers a packet must pass through in a network in order to reach its destination.

Host adapter — The circuit board that controls a SCSI bus that supports as many as eight or 16 separate devices, one of which is a host adapter that controls communication with the PC.

Host drive — Typically drive H on a compressed drive. *See* Compressed drive.

HOSTNAME — A utility that displays or sets the name of a computer.

Hot-swapping — The ability of a computer to use a device, such as a PC Card on a notebook, that is inserted while the computer is running without the computer needing to be rebooted.

Hot-pluggable — A characteristic of 1394 devices that let you plug in the device without rebooting your PC and remove the device without receiving an error message.

HTML (Hypertext Markup Language) — The language used to create hypertext documents commonly used on web sites. HTML documents have an .html file extension.

HTTP (Hypertext Transfer Protocol) — The common transfer protocol used by Internet browsers on the World Wide Web.

Hub — A network device or box that provides a central location to connect cables.

Hypertext — Text that contains links to remote points in the document or to other files, documents, or graphics. Hypertext is created using HTML and is commonly distributed from Web sites.

I/O addresses — Numbers that are used by devices and the CPU to manage communication between them.

I/O card — A card that often contains serial, parallel, and game ports on the same adapter board, providing input/output interface with the CPU.

IBM-compatible — A computer that uses an Intel (or compatible) processor and can run DOS and Windows.

IEEE 1284 — A standard for parallel ports developed by the Institute for Electrical and Electronics Engineers and supported by many hardware manufacturers.

IEEE 1394 — *See* FireWire.

Impact printer — A type of printer that functions by striking a printer head against an ink ribbon in order to create marks on a piece of paper. Types of impact printers include dot matrix and daisy wheel printers.

In-band signaling — In modem communication, the name of the signaling used by software flow control, which pauses transmission by sending a special control character in the same channel (or band) that data is sent in.

Incremental backup — A time-saving backup method that only backs up files changed or newly created since the last full or incremental backup. Multiple incremental backups might be required when recovering lost data.

Infestation — Any unwanted program that is transmitted to a computer without the user's knowledge and that is designed to do varying degrees of damage to data and software. There are a number of different types of infestations, including viruses, Trojan horses, worms, and time bombs, among others.

Initialization files — Configuration information files for Windows. Win.ini and System.ini are the two most important Windows 3.x initialization files.

Instruction set — The set of instructions, on the CPU chip, that the computer can perform directly (such as ADD and MOVE).

Integrated Device Electronics (IDE) — A hard drive whose disk controller is integrated into the drive, eliminating the need for a controller cable and thus increasing speed, as well as reducing price.

Intelligent hubs — Network hubs that can be remotely controlled at a console, using network software. These hubs can monitor a network and report errors or problems.

Intelligent UPS — A UPS connected to a computer by way of a serial cable so that software on the computer can monitor and control the UPS.

Interlace — A display in which the electronic beam of a monitor draws every other line with each pass, which lessens the overall effect of a lower refresh rate.

Interleave — To write data in nonconsecutive sectors around a track, so that time is not wasted waiting for the disk to make a full revolution before the next sector is read.

Internal cache — Memory cache that is faster than external cache, and is contained inside 80486 and Pentium chips (also referred to as primary, Level 1, or L1 cache).

Internal DOS commands — DOS commands whose coding is contained within Command.com and are, therefore, automatically loaded into memory when Command.com is loaded.

Internet — The worldwide collection of over a million hosts that can communicate with each other using TCP/IP. The lowercase internet simply means multiple networks connected together.

Internet Control Message Protocol (ICMP) — Part of the IP layer that is used to transmit error messages and other control messages to hosts and routers.

Internet Printing Protocol (IPP) — A protocol used to send print jobs across the Internet. A printer is addressed by its URL (uniform resource locator)—for example, *www.ourdomain.com/printer4*.

Internet service provider (ISP) — A commercial group that provides a user with Internet access for a monthly fee. AOL, Prodigy, GTE, and CompuServe are four large ISPs.

Internetwork — Two or more networks connected together, such as a LAN and a WAN joined together.

Interrupt handler — A program (either BIOS or a device driver), that is used by the CPU to process a hardware interrupt.

Interrupt vector table — A table that stores the memory addresses assigned to interrupt handlers. Also called a vector table.

Intranet — A private internet used by a large company.

IP (Internet Protocol) address — A 32-bit "dotted-decimal" address consisting of four numbers separated by periods, used to uniquely identify a device on a network that uses TCP/IP protocols. The first numbers identify the network; the last numbers identify a host. An example of an IP address is 206.96.103.114.

IPCONFIG — A command line utility for displaying a computer's TCP/IP configuration.

IPX/SPX — A protocol developed and used by Novell NetWare for LANs. The IPX portion of the protocol works at the network layer, which is responsible for routing, and the SPX portion of the protocol manages error checking at the transport layer.

IRQ (interrupt request number) — A line on a bus that is assigned to a device and is used to signal the CPU for servicing. These lines are assigned a reference number (for example, the normal IRQ for a printer is IRQ 7).

ISA bus — An 8-bit industry standard architecture bus used on the original 8088 PC. Sixteen-bit ISA buses were designed for the 286 AT, and are still used in Pentiums for devices such as modems.

ISDN (Integrated Services Digital Network) — A communications standard that can carry digital data simultaneously over two channels on a single pair of wires, at about five times the speed of regular phone lines.

Isochronous data transfer — A method used by IEEE 1394 to transfer data continuously without breaks.

JPEG (Joint Photographic Experts Group) — A "lossy" graphical compression scheme that allows the user to control the amount of data that is averaged and sacrificed as file size is reduced. It is a common Internet file format. *See* Lossy compression.

Jumper — Two wires that stick up side by side on the system board that are used to hold configuration information. The jumper is considered closed if a cover is over the wires, and open if the cover is missing.

Kernel — Core portion of an operating system that loads applications and manages files, memory, and other resources.

Kernel mode — A Windows NT "privileged" processing mode that has access to hardware components.

Keyboard — A common input device through which data and instructions may be typed into computer memory.

Keys — In Windows 9x, section names of the Windows 9x registry.

Land — Microscopic flat areas on the surface of a CD or DVD that separate pits. Lands and pits are used to represent data on the disc.

Laptop computer — *See* Notebook.

Large mode — A format that supports hard drives that range from 504 MB to 1 GB, mapping the data to conform to the 504-MB barrier before the address information is passed to the operating system.

Legacy — An older device or adapter card that does not support Plug and Play, and might have to be manually configured through jumpers or DIP switches.

Let-through — The maximum voltage allowed through a surge suppressor to the device being protected.

Level 1 cache — *See* Internal cache.

Level 2 cache — *See* External cache.

Line conditioners — Devices that regulate, or condition the power, providing continuous voltage during brownouts and spikes.

Line protocol — A protocol used over phone lines to allow a connection to a network. Also called a bridging protocol. The most popular line protocol is PPP (Point-to-Point Protocol).

Line speed — *See* Modem speed.

Line-interactive UPS — A variation of a standby UPS that shortens switching time by always keeping the inverter that converts AC to DC working, so that there is no charge-up time for the inverter.

Liquid cooling — A method by which an over-clocked CPU can be cooled by running distilled water across it.

Load size — The largest amount of memory that a driver needs to initialize itself and to hold its data. It is almost always a little larger than the size of the program file.

Loading high — The process of loading a driver or TSR into upper memory.

Local bus — A bus that operates at a speed synchronized with the CPU speed.

Local I/O bus — A local bus that provides I/O devices with fast access to the CPU.

Logical block addressing (LBA) — A method in which the operating system views the drive as one long linear list of LBAs, permitting larger drive sizes (LBA 0 is cylinder 0, head 0, and sector 1).

Logical drive — A portion or all of a hard drive partition that is treated by the operating system as though it were a physical drive containing a boot record, FAT, and root directory.

Logical geometry — The number of heads, tracks, and sectors that the BIOS on the hard drive controller presents to the system BIOS and the OS. The logical geometry does not consist of the same values as the physical geometry, although calculations of drive capacity yield the same results.

Logical unit number (LUN) — A number from 0 to 15 (also called the SCSI ID) assigned to each SCSI device attached to a daisy chain.

Lossless compression — A method that substitutes special characters for repeating patterns without image degradation. A substitution table is used to restore the compressed image to its original form.

Lossy compression — A method that drops unnecessary data, but with some image and sound loss. JPEG allows the user to control the amount of loss, which is inversely related to the image size.

Lost allocation units — *See* Lost clusters.

Lost clusters — Lost file fragments that, according to the file allocation table, contain data that does not belong to any file. In DOS, the command CHKDSK/F can free these fragments.

Low insertion force (LIF) — A socket feature that requires the installer to manually apply an even force over the microchip when inserting the chip into the socket.

Low-level format — A process (usually performed at the factory) that electronically creates the hard drive cylinders and tests for bad spots on the disk surface.

LPQ — A command line utility for displaying a computer's TCP/IP configuration.

LPR — A command line utility that sends a print job to a network printer.

MAC (media access control) — An element of data-link layer protocol that provides compatibility with the NIC used by the physical layer. A network card address is often called a MAC address. *See* Adapter address.

Macro — A small sequence of commands, contained within a document, that can be automatically executed when the document is loaded, or executed later by using a predetermined keystroke.

Macro virus — A virus that can hide in the macros of a document file. Typically, viruses do not reside in data or document files.

Main board — *See* System board.

Make code — A code produced by pressing a key on a keyboard.

Master boot record (MBR) (of a floppy disk) — The record written near the beginning of a floppy disk, containing information about the disk as well as the startup operating system programs.

Master boot record (MBR) (on a hard drive) — The first sector on a hard drive, which contains the partition table and other information needed by BIOS to access the drive.

Material safety data sheet (MSDS) — A document that provides information about how to properly handle substances such as chemical solvents including physical data, toxicity, health effects, first aid, storage, disposal, and spill procedures.

MCA (micro channel architecture) bus — A proprietary IBM PS/2 bus, seldom seen today, with a width of 16 or 32 bits and multiple master control, which allowed for multitasking.

MD or MKDIR command — A command used to create a directory on a drive (for example, MD C:\MYDATA).

MEM command — A DOS utility used to display how programs and drivers are using conventional, upper, and extended memory (Example: MEM/C/P).

MemMaker — A DOS utility that can increase the amount of conventional memory available to DOS-based software applications, by loading drivers and TRSs into upper memory.

Memory — Physical microchips that can hold data and programming located on the system board or expansion cards.

Memory address — A number that the CPU assigns to physical memory to keep track of the memory that it has access to.

Memory bus — The bus between the CPU and memory on the system board. Also called the system bus or the host bus.

Memory cache — A small amount of faster RAM that stores recently retrieved data, in anticipation of what the CPU will request next, thus speeding up access.

Memory caching — Using a small amount of faster RAM to store recently retrieved data, in anticipation of what the CPU will next request, thus speeding up access.

Memory leak — A problem caused when an application does not release the memory addresses assigned to it when it unloads, causing the memory heaps to have less and less memory for new applications.

Memory management — The process of increasing available conventional memory, required by DOS-based programs, accomplished by loading device drivers and TSRs into upper memory.

Memory mapping — Assigning addresses to both RAM and ROM during the boot process.

Memory paging — In Windows 9x, swapping blocks of RAM memory to an area of the hard drive to serve as virtual memory when RAM memory is low.

Memory-resident virus — A virus that can stay lurking in memory, even after its host program is terminated.

Minicartridge — A tape drive cartridge that is only 3½ × 2½ × ⅝ inches. It is small enough to allow two drives to fit into a standard 5½-inch drive bay of a PC case.

Minifile system — In windows NT, a simplified file system that is started so that Ntldr (NT Loader) can read files from either a FAT16 or an NTFS file system.

MIRROR command — An old DOS command that saves information about deleted files as they are deleted. This information can be used later by the UNDELETE command to recover a deleted file. The command can be used to save the partition table to a floppy disk.

Mixed mode — A Windows 2000 mode for domain controllers used when there is at least one Windows NT domain controller on the network.

MMX (Multimedia Extensions) technology — A variation of the Pentium processor designed to manage and speed up high-volume input/output needed for graphics, motion video, animation, and sound.

Modem — From MOdulate/DEModulate. A device that modulates digital data from a computer to an analog format that can be sent over telephone lines, then demodulates it back into digital form.

Modem eliminator — A technique that allows two data terminal equipment (DTE) devices to communicate by means of a null modem cable in which the transmit and receive wires are cross-connected, and no modems are necessary.

Modem riser card — A small modem card that uses an AMR or CNR slot. Part of the modem logic is contained in a controller on the system board.

Modem speed — The speed a modem can transmit data along a phone line measured in bits per second (bps). Two communicating modems must talk at the same speed for data transmission to be successful. Also called line speed.

Modulation — Converting binary or digital data into an analog signal that can be sent over standard telephone lines.

Monitor — The most commonly used output device for displaying text and graphics on a computer.

Motherboard — *See* System board.

Mouse — A pointing and input device that allows the user to move a cursor around a screen and select programs with the click of a button.

MP3 — A method to compress audio files that uses MPEG level 3. It can reduce sound files as low as a 1:24 ratio without losing sound quality.

MPC (Multimedia Personal Computer) guidelines — The minimum standards created by Microsoft and a consortium of hardware manufacturers for multimedia PCs.

MPEG (Moving Pictures Experts Group) — A processing-intensive standard for data compression for motion pictures that tracks movement from one frame to the next, and only stores the new data that has changed.

Msdos.sys — In DOS, a program file that contains part of the DOS kernel and controls much of the boot process. In Windows 9x, a text file that contains settings used by Io.sys during booting.

Multibank DRAM (MDRAM) — A special kind of RAM used on video cards that is able to use a full 128-bit bus path without requiring the full 4 MB of RAM.

Multiframe dialog — When a limited token is sent that allows a receiving station to communicate only with the sending station, thus providing continuous communication between the two stations.

Multimedia — A type of computer presentation that combines text, graphics, animation, photos, sound, and/or full-motion video.

Multimeter — Either a voltmeter or an ammeter that can also measure resistance in ohms or as continuity, depending on a switch setting.

Multipartite virus — A combination of a boot sector virus and a file virus. It can hide in either type of program.

Multiplier — On a system board, the factor by which the bus speed or frequency is multiplied to get the CPU clock speed.

Multiscan monitor — A monitor that can work within a range of frequencies, and thus can work with different standards and video cards. It offers a variety of refresh rates.

Multisession — A feature that allows data to be read (or written) on a CD during more than one session. This is important if the disc was only partially filled during the first write.

Multistation access unit (MSAU or MAU) — A centralized device used to connect IBM Token Ring network stations.

Multitasking — When a CPU or an OS supporting multiple CPUs can do more than one thing at a time. The Pentium is a multitasking CPU.

Multithreading — The ability to pass more than one function (thread) to the OS kernel at the same time, such as when one thread is performing a print job while another reads a file.

NBTSTAT — A command line utility used to display connection information for computers running NetBIOS over the TCP/IP protocol.

NetBEUI (NetBIOS Extended User Interface) — A proprietary Microsoft networking protocol used only by Windows-based systems, and limited to LANs because it does not support routing.

NetBT (NetBIOS over TCP/IP) — An alternate Microsoft NetBEUI component designed to interface with TCP/IP networks.

NETSTAT — A command line utility that displays TCP/IP connection information.

Network interface card (NIC) — A network adapter board that plugs into a computer's system board and provides a port on the back of the card to connect a PC to a network.

Network mask — The portion of an IP address that identifies the network.

Node — Each computer, workstation, or device on a network.

Noise — An extraneous, unwanted signal, often over an analog phone line, that can cause communication interference or transmission errors. Possible sources are fluorescent lighting, radios, TVs, lightning, or bad wiring.

Non-interlace — A type of display in which the electronic beam of a monitor draws every line on the screen with each pass. *See* Interlace.

Non-memory-resident virus — A virus that is terminated when the host program is closed. Compare to memory-resident virus.

Nonparity memory — Slightly less expensive, 8-bit memory without error checking. A SIMM part number with a 32 in it (4 × 8 bits) is nonparity.

Nonvolatile — Refers to a kind of RAM that is stable and can hold data as long as electricity is powering the memory.

Normal mode — *See* CHS.

North bridge — That portion of the chip set hub that connects faster I/O buses (e.g., AGP bus) to the system bus. Compare to South bridge.

Notebook — A personal computer designed for travel, using less voltage and taking up less space than a regular PC. Also called a laptop computer.

NSLOOKUP — A command line utility that performs domain name lookup operations.

NT Hardware Qualifier (NTHQ) — A utility found on the Windows NT installation CD-ROM that examines your system to determine if all hardware present qualifies for NT.

NT virtual DOS machine (NTVDM) — An emulated environment in which a 16-bit DOS application or a Windows 3.x application resides within Windows NT/2000/XP with its own memory space or WOW (Win 16 application on a Win 32 platform). *See* WOW.

Ntldr (NT Loader) — In Windows NT, the OS loader used on Intel systems.

Null modem cable — *See* Modem eliminator.

Object linking — A method where one application can execute a command on an object created by another application.

Octet — A traditional term for each of the four 8-bit numbers that make up an IP address. For example, the IP address 206.96.103.114 has four octets.

Ohms — The standard unit of measurement for electrical resistance. Resistors are rated in ohms.

On-board BIOS — *See* System BIOS.

On-board ports — Ports that are directly on the system board, such as a built-in keyboard port or on-board serial port.

Operating system format — *See* High-level format.

OS format — *See* High-level format.

Out-of-band signaling — The type of signaling used by hardware flow control, which sends a message to pause transmission by using channels (or bands) not used for data.

Overclocking — Running a system board at a speed that is not recommended or guaranteed by CPU or chipset manufacturers.

P-A-S-S — An acronym to help remember how to use a fire extinguisher. (Pull the pin, Aim low at the base of the fire, Squeeze the handle of the extinguisher, and Sweep back and forth across the fire.)

P1 connector — Power connection on an ATX system board.

Packets — Network segments of data that also include header, destination addresses, and trailer information. Also called Frames.

Page — Memory allocated in 4K or 16K segments within a page frame.

Page-in — The process in which the memory manager goes to the hard drive to return the data from a swap file to RAM.

Page-out — The process in which, when RAM is full, the memory manager takes a page and moves it to the swap file.

Page fault — An OS interrupt that occurs when the OS is forced to access the hard drive to satisfy the demands for virtual memory.

Page frame — A 64K upper memory area divided into four equal-sized pages through which the memory manager swaps data.

Parallel port — A female port on the computer that can transmit data in parallel, 8 bits at a time, and is usually used with a printer. The names for parallel ports are LPT1 and LPT2.

Parity — An error-checking scheme in which a ninth, or "parity," bit is added. The value of the parity bit is set to either 0 or 1 to provide an even number of ones for even parity and an odd number of ones for odd parity.

Parity error — An error that occurs when the number of 1s in the byte is not in agreement with the expected number.

Parity memory — Nine-bit memory in which the 9th bit is used for error checking. A SIMM part number with a 36 in it (4 2 9 bits) is parity. Older DOS PCs almost always use parity chips.

Partition — A division of a hard drive that can be used to hold logical drives.

Partition table — A table at the beginning of the hard drive that contains information about each partition on the drive. The partition table is contained in the master boot record.

Path — The drive and list of directories pointing to a file.

PC Card — A credit-card-sized adapter card that can be slid into a slot in the side of many notebook computers and is used for connecting to modems, networks, and CD-ROM drives. Also called PCMCIA Card.

PC Card slot — An expansion slot on a notebook computer, into which a PC Card is inserted. Also called a PCMCIA Card slot.

PCI (peripheral component interconnect) bus — A bus common on Pentium computers that runs at speeds of up to 33 MHz, with a 32-bit-wide data path. It serves as the middle layer between the memory bus and expansion buses.

PCI bus IRQ steering — A feature that makes it possible for PCI devices to share an IRQ. System BIOS and the OS must both support this feature.

PCMCIA (Personal Computer Memory Card International Association) card — *See* PC Card.

PCMCIA Card slot — *See* PC Card slot.

PDA (Personal Digital Assistant) — A handheld computer that has its own operating system and applications. The most popular operating systems for PDAs are Palm for Palm Pilot devices and Windows CE.

Peripheral devices — Devices that communicate with the CPU, but are not located directly on the system board, such as the monitor, floppy drive, printer, and mouse.

Physical geometry — The actual layout of heads, tracks, and sectors on a hard drive. *See* Logical geometry.

Physical layer — The OSI layer responsible for interfacing with the network media (cabling).

PIF (program information file) — A file with a .pif file extension that is used by an OS to store the settings of the environment provided to a DOS application.

PING — A TCP/IP utility that sends a message to a computer to test network connectivity to that computer.

Pin grid array (PGA) — A feature of a CPU socket where the pins are aligned in uniform rows around the socket.

Pipelined burst SRAM — A less expensive SRAM that uses more clock cycles per transfer than nonpipelined burst, but does not significantly slow down the process.

Pit — Recessed areas on the surface of a CD or DVD, separating lands, or flat areas. Lands and pits are used to represent data on the disc.

Pixel — Small spots on a fine horizontal scan line that are illuminated to create an image on the monitor.

Plug and Play — A technology in which the operating system and BIOS are designed to automatically configure new hardware devices to eliminate system resource conflicts (such as IRQ and port conflicts).

Plug and Play BIOS — Basic input/output system for Plug and Play devices, which are designed to be automatically recognized by the computer when they are installed.

Polling — A process by which the CPU checks the status of connected devices to determine if they are ready to send or receive data.

Polymorphic virus — A type of virus that changes its distinguishing characteristics as it replicates itself. Mutating in this way makes it more difficult for AV software to recognize the presence of the virus.

Port — A physical connector, usually at the back of a computer, that allows a cable from a peripheral device, such as a printer, mouse, or modem, to be attached.

Port settings — The configuration parameters of communications devices such as COM1, COM2, or COM3, including IRQ settings.

Port speed — The communication speed between a DTE (computer) and a DCE (modem). As a general rule, the port speed should be at least four times as fast as the modem speed.

POST (power-on self test) — A self-diagnostic program used to perform a simple test of the CPU, RAM, and various I/O devices. The POST is performed when the computer is first turned on and is stored in ROM-BIOS.

Power conditioners — Line conditioners that regulate, or condition, the power, providing continuous voltage during brownouts.

Power supply — A box inside the computer case that supplies power to the system board and other installed devices. Power supplies provide 3.3, 5, and 12 volts DC.

Power-on password — *See* Startup password.

PPP (Point-to-Point Protocol) — A common way PCs with modems can connect to an internet. The Windows Dial-Up Networking utility, found under My Computer, uses PPP.

Preemptive multitasking — A type of multitasking whereby the CPU allows an application a specified period of time and then preempts the processing to give time to another application.

Primary cache — *See* Internal cache.

Printer — A peripheral output device that produces printed output to paper. Different types include dot matrix, ink-jet, and laser printers.

Process — An executing instance of a program together with the program resources. There can be more than one process running for a program at the same time. One process for a program happens each time the program is loaded into memory or executed.

Processor speed — The speed or frequency at which the CPU operates. Usually expressed in MHz.

Program — A set of step-by-step instructions to a computer. Some are burned directly into chips, while others are stored as program files. Programs are written in languages such as BASIC and C++.

Program file — A file that contains instructions designed to be executed by the CPU.

Program jump — An instruction that causes control to be sent to a memory address other than the next sequential address.

Program Information File (PIF) — A file used by Windows to describe the environment for a DOS program to use.

Proprietary — A term for products that a company has exclusive rights to manufacture and/or market. Proprietary computer components are typically more difficult to find and more expensive to buy.

Protected mode — An operating mode that supports multitasking whereby the OS manages memory, programs have more than 1024K of memory addresses, and programs can use a 32-bit data path.

Protocol — A set of preestablished rules for communication. Examples of protocols are modem parity settings and the way in which header and trailer information in a data packet is formatted.

PS/2 compatible mouse — A mouse that uses a round mouse port (called a mini-DIN or PS/2 connector) coming directly off the system board.

Quarter-Inch Committee or quarter-inch cartridge (QIC) — A name of a standardized method used to write data to tape. Backups made with the Windows 9x System Tools Backup utility have a .qic extension.

RAID (redundant array of inexpensive disks or redundant array of independent disks) — Several methods of configuring multiple hard drives to store data to increase logical volume size and improve performance, and to ensure that if one hard drive fails, the data is still available from another hard drive.

RAM (random access memory) — Temporary memory stored on chips, such as SIMMs, inside the computer. Information in RAM disappears when the computer's power is turned off.

RAM drive — A RAM area configured as a virtual hard drive, such as drive D, so that frequently used programs can be accessed faster. It is the opposite of virtual memory.

RD or RMDIR command — A DOS command to remove an unwanted directory (for example, RD C:\OLDDIR). You must delete all files in the directory to be removed, prior to using this command.

Read/write head — A sealed, magnetic coil device that moves across the surface of a disk either reading or writing data to the disk.

Real mode — A single-tasking operating mode whereby a program has only 1024K of memory addresses, has direct access to RAM, and uses a 16-bit data path.

RECOVER command — A command that recovers files that were lost because of a corrupted file allocation table.

Recovery Console — A Windows 2000/XP command-interface utility that can be used to solve problems when the OS cannot load from the hard drive.

Rectifier — An electrical device that converts AC to DC. A PC power supply contains a rectifier.

Refresh — The process of periodically rewriting the data for instance, on dynamic RAM.

Registry — A database used by Windows to store hardware and software configuration information, user preferences, and setup information. Use Regedit.exe to edit the registry.

Removable drives — High-capacity drives, such as Zip or Jaz drives, that have disks that can be removed like floppy disks.

Repeater — A device that amplifies weakened signals on a network.

Rescue disk — A floppy disk that can be used to start up a computer when the hard drive fails to boot. *Also see* Emergency startup disk.

Resistance — The degree to which a device opposes or resists the flow of electricity. As the electrical resistance increases, the current decreases. *See* Ohms and Resistor.

Resistor — An electronic device that resists or opposes the flow of electricity. A resistor can be used to reduce the amount of electricity being supplied to an electronic component.

Resolution — The number of spots called pixels on a monitor screen that are addressable by software (example: 1024 2 768 pixels).

Resource arbitrator — A PnP component that decides which resources are assigned to which devices.

Resource management — The process of allocating resources to devices at startup.

RET (resolution enhancement technology) — The term used by Hewlett-Packard to describe the way a laser printer varies the size of the dots used to create an image. This technology partly accounts for the sharp, clear image created by a laser printer.

Retension — A tape maintenance procedure that fast-forwards and then rewinds the tape to eliminate loose spots on the tape.

Reverse Address Resolution Protocol (RARP) — Translates the unique hardware NIC addresses into IP addresses (the reverse of ARP).

REXEC (Remote Executive) — a TCP/IP utility used to execute a program on a remote computer.

RISC (reduced instruction set computer) chips — Chips that incorporate only the most frequently used instructions, so that the computer operates faster (for example, the PowerPC uses RISC chips).

RJ-11 — A phone line connection found on a modem, telephone, and house phone outlet.

RJ-45 connector — A connector used on an Ethernet 10BaseT (twisted pair cable) network. An RJ-45 port looks similar to a large phone jack.

Roaming users — Users who can move from PC to PC within a network, with their profiles following them.

ROM (read-only memory) — Chips that contain programming code and cannot be erased.

ROM BIOS — *See* BIOS.

Root directory — The main directory created when a hard drive or disk is first formatted.

ROUTE - A TCP/IP utility used to display and modify the routing table of a computer.

Route discovery — When a router rebuilds its router tables on the basis of new information.

Router — A device or box that connects networks. A router transfers a packet to other networks when the packet is addressed to a station outside its network. The router can make intelligent decisions as to which network is the best route to use to send data to a distant network. *See* Bridge.

Router table — Tables of network addresses that also include the best possible routes (regarding tick count and hop count) to these networks. *See* Tick count and Hop count.

RPC (Remote Procedure Call) — A TCP/IP function for executing a software module on a remote computer.

RSH (Remote Shell) — A TCP/IP utility used to provide command line access to a computer.

Run-time configuration — A PnP ongoing process that monitors changes in system devices, such as the removal of a PC Card on a notebook computer or the docking of a notebook computer to a docking station.

Safe mode — The mode in which Windows 9x is loaded with minimum configuration and drivers in order to allow the correction of system errors. To enter safe mode, press F5 or F8 when "Starting Windows 95/98" is displayed.

SAM (security accounts manager) — A portion of the Windows NT registry that manages the account database that contains accounts, policies, and other pertinent information about the domain.

SCAM (SCSI configuration automatically) — A method that follows the Plug and Play standard, to make installations of SCSI devices much easier, assuming that the device is SCAM-compatible.

Scanning mirror — A component of a laser printer. An octagonal mirror that can be directed in a sweeping motion to cover the entire length of a laser printer drum.

SCSI (small computer system interface) — A faster system-level interface with a host adapter and a bus that can daisy-chain as many as seven or 15 other devices.

SCSI ID — *See* Logical unit number.

SCSI bus — A bus standard used for peripheral devices tied together in a daisy chain.

SCSI bus adapter chip — The chip mounted on the logic board of a hard drive that allows the drive to be a part of a SCSI bus system.

SC330 (Slot Connector 330) — A 330-pin system board connector used to contain the Pentium III Xeon. Also called Slot 2.

SECC (Single Edge Contact Cartridge) — A type of cartridge that houses the Pentium III processor.

Secondary storage — Storage that is remote to the CPU and permanently holds data, even when the PC is turned off.

Sector — On a disk surface, one segment of a track, which almost always contains 512 bytes of data. Sometimes a single wedge of the disk surface is also called a sector.

Security log — A text file that is used to store security events on a Windows computer. This log file is accessed by Event Viewer.

Segmentation — To split a large Ethernet into smaller segments that are connected to each other by bridges or routers. This is done to prevent congestion as the number of nodes increases.

Sequential access — A method of data access used by tape drives whereby data is written or read sequentially from the beginning to the end of the tape or until the desired data is found.

Serial mouse — A mouse that uses a serial port and has a female 9-pin DB-9 connector.

Serial ports — Male ports on the computer used for transmitting data serially, one bit at a time. They are called COM1, COM2, COM3 and COM4.

Server — A microcomputer or minicomputer that stores programs and data to be used remotely by other computers.

Service Pack — A compilation of software patches and other fixes that have been organized together into a single installation program. Microsoft issues service packs for its operating systems and software every few months.

SGRAM (synchronous graphics RAM) — Memory designed especially for video card processing that can synchronize itself with the CPU bus clock. They are commonly used for modems and mice, and in DOS are called COM1 or COM2.

Shadow RAM or shadowing ROM — The process of copying ROM programming code into RAM to speed up the system operation, because of the faster access speed of RAM.

Signal-regenerating repeater — A repeater that "reads" the signal on the network and then creates an exact duplicate of the signal, thus amplifying the signal without also amplifying unwanted noise that is mixed with the signal.

SIMM (single inline memory module) — A miniature circuit board used in a computer to hold RAM. SIMMs hold 8, 16, 32, or 64 MB on a single module.

Single voltage CPU — A CPU that requires one voltage for both internal and I/O operations.

Single-instruction, multiple-data (SIMD) — An MMX process that allows the CPU to execute a single instruction simultaneously on multiple pieces of data rather than by repetitive looping.

Slack — Wasted space on a hard drive caused by not using all available space at the end of clusters.

Sleep mode — A mode used in many "Green" systems that allows them to be configured through CMOS to suspend the monitor or even the drive, if the keyboard and/or CPU have been inactive for a set number of minutes. *See* Green standards.

SLIP (Serial Line Internet Protocol) — An early version of line protocol designed for home users connecting to the Internet. SLIP lacks reliable error checking and has mostly been replaced by PPP.

SMARTDrive — A hard drive cache program that comes with Windows 3.x and DOS that can be executed as a TSR from the Autoexec.bat file (for example, DEVICE= SMARTDRV.SYS 2048).

SMTP (Simple Mail Transfer Protocol) — A common protocol used to send e-mail across a network.

Snap-in — An administrative tool that is contained within a console. For example, Event Viewer is a snap-in in the Computer Management console.

Socket — A virtual connection from one computer to another such as that between a client and a server. Higher-level protocols such as HTTP use a socket to pass data between two computers. A socket is assigned a number for the current session, which is used by the high-level protocol.

Socket service — On a notebook computer, the socket service allows the notebook computer to detect the insertion and removal of a PCMCIA card.

SODIMM (small outline DIMM) — A small memory module designed for notebooks that has 72 pins and supports 32-bit data transfers.

Soft boot — To restart a PC by pressing three keys at the same time (Ctrl, Alt, and Del). Also called warm boot.

Software — Computer programs, or instructions to perform a specific task. Software may be BIOS, OSs, or applications software such as a word-processing or spreadsheet program.

Software cache — Cache controlled by software whereby the cache is stored in RAM.

Software interrupt — An event caused by a program currently being executed by the CPU signaling the CPU that it requires the use of a hardware device.

South bridge — That portion of the chip set hub that connects slower I/O buses (e.g., ISA bus) to the system bus. Compare to North bridge.

Spanned volumes — Windows 2000 method of linking several volumes across multiple hard drives into a single logical drive.

Spooling — Placing print jobs in a print queue so that an application can be released from the printing process before printing is completed. Spooling is an acronym for simultaneous peripheral operations online.

SSE (streaming SIMD extension) — A technology used by the Intel Pentium III designed to improve performance of multimedia software.

Staggered pin grid array (SPGA) — A feature of a CPU socket where the pins are staggered over the socket in order to squeeze more pins into a small space.

Standby time — The time before a "Green" system will reduce 92% of its activity. *See* Green standards.

Standby UPS — A UPS that quickly switches from an AC power source to a battery-powered source during a brownout or power outage.

Standoffs — Small plastic or metal spacers placed on the bottom of the main system board, to raise it off the chassis, so that its components will not short out on the metal case.

Star network architecture — A network design in which nodes are connected at a centralized location.

Star topology — A network design in which nodes are connected at a centralized location.

Start bit — A bit that is used to signal the approach of data. *See* Stop bit.

Startup BIOS — Part of system BIOS that is responsible for controlling the PC when it is first turned on. Startup BIOS gives control over to the OS once it is loaded.

Startup password — A password that a computer requires during the boot process used to gain access to the PC. Also called power-on password.

Static electricity — *See* Electrostatic discharge.

Static IP addresses — IP addresses permanently assigned to a workstation. In Windows 9x, this can be done under Dial-Up Networking, Server Type, TCP/IP settings. Specify an IP address.

Static RAM (SRAM) — RAM chips that retain information without the need for refreshing, as long as the computer's power is on. They are more expensive than traditional DRAM.

Static routing — When routing tables do not automatically change and must be manually edited. Windows NT and Windows 95 support only static routing. Compare to Dynamic routing.

Static VxD — A VxD that is loaded into memory at startup and remains there for the entire OS session.

Stealth virus — A virus that actively conceals itself by temporarily removing itself from an infected file that is about to be examined, and then hiding a copy of itself elsewhere on the drive.

Stop bit — A bit that is used to signal the end of a block of data.

Streaming audio — Downloading audio data from the Internet in a continuous stream of data without first downloading an entire audio file.

Subdirectory — In DOS, a directory that is contained within another directory. Also called a child directory.

Subnet mask — Defines which portion of the host address within an IP address is being borrowed to define separate subnets within a network. A 1 in the mask indicates that the bit is part of the network address, and a 0 indicates that the bit is part of the host address. For example, the subnet mask 255.255.192.0, in binary, is 11111111.11111111.11000000.00000000. Therefore, the network address is the first two octets and the subnet address is the first two bits of the third octet. The rest of the IP address refers to the host.

Subnetworks or subnets — Divisions of a large network, consisting of smaller separate networks (to prevent congestion). Each subnetwork is assigned a logical network IP name.

Subtree — One of five main keys that make up the Windows NT registry. Examples are HKEY_CURRENT_USER and HKEY_LOCAL_MACHINE.

Suite — As applies to software, a collection of applications software sold as a bundle, whose components are designed to be compatible with one another. An example is Microsoft Office.

Surge suppressor or surge protector — A device or power strip designed to protect electronic equipment from power surges and spikes.

Suspend time — The time before a green system will reduce 99% of its activity. After this time, the system needs a warmup time so that the CPU, monitor, and hard drive can reach full activity.

Swap file — A file on the hard drive that is used by the OS for virtual memory.

Swapping — A method of freeing some memory by moving a "page" of data temporarily to a swap file on the hard drive; it can later be copied from disk back into memory.

Switch — A device that is used to break a large network into two smaller networks in order to reduce traffic congestion. A switch uses MAC addresses to determine which network to send a packet.

Synchronous DRAM (SDRAM) — A type of memory stored on DIMMs that run in sync with the system clock, running at the same speed as the system board. Currently, the fastest memory used on PCs.

Synchronous SRAM — SRAM that is faster and more expensive than asynchronous SRAM. It requires a clock signal to validate its control signals, enabling the cache to run in step with the CPU.

System BIOS — Basic input/output system chip(s) residing on the system board that control(s) normal I/O to such areas as system memory and floppy drives. Also called on-board BIOS.

System board — The main board in the computer, also called the motherboard. The CPU, ROM chips, SIMMs, DIMMs, and interface cards are plugged into the system board.

System-board mouse — A mouse that plugs into a round mouse port on the system board. Sometimes called a PS/2 mouse.

System bus — Today the system bus usually means the memory bus. However, sometimes it is used to refer to other buses on the system board. *See* memory bus.

System clock — A line on a bus that is dedicated to timing the activities of components connected to it. The system clock provides a continuous pulse that other devices use to time themselves.

System disk — A floppy disk containing enough of an operating system to boot.

System File Checker — System File Checker is part of the new Windows 2000 utility to protect system files, called Windows File Protection (WFP).

System partition — The active partition of the hard drive containing the boot record and the specific files required to load Windows NT.

System State data — All files that Windows 2000 requires to load and perform successfully. The System State data is backed up using the Backup utility.

System variable — A variable that has been given a name and a value; it is available to the operating system and applications software programs.

Task switching — *See* Cooperative multitasking.

TCP/IP (Transmission Control Protocol/Internet Protocol) — The suite of protocols developed to support the Internet. TCP is responsible for error checking, and IP is responsible for routing.

Technical documentation — The technical reference manuals, included with software packages and peripherals, that provide directions for installation, usage, and troubleshooting.

Telephony — A term describing the technology of converting sound to signals that can travel over telephone lines.

Telephony Application Programming Interface (TAPI) — A standard developed by Intel and Microsoft that can be used by 32-bit Windows 9x communications programs for communicating over phone lines.

Telnet — A TCP/IP utility used to provide terminal window access to a remote computer.

Temp directory — A location to which inactive applications and data can be moved as a swap file, while Windows continues to process current active applications. (Avoid deleting Temp swap while Windows is running.)

Temporary file — A file that is created by Windows applications, to save temporary data, and may or may not be deleted when the application is unloaded.

Terminating resistor — The resistor added at the end of a SCSI chain to dampen the voltage at the end of the chain. *See* Termination.

Termination — A process necessary to prevent an echo effect of power at the end of a SCSI chain resulting in interference with the data transmission. *See* Terminating resistor.

TFTP (Trivial File Transfer Protocol) — A TCP/IP protocol used for basic file transer functions.

Thread — The smallest part of an application that can be individually scheduled for execution.

Tick count — The time required for a packet to reach its destination. One tick equals 1/18 of a second.

Token — A small frame on a Token Ring network that constantly travels around the ring in only one direction. When a station seizes the token, it controls the channel until its message is sent.

Token ring — A network that is logically a ring, but stations are connected to a centralized multistation access unit (MAU) in a star formation. Network communication is controlled by a token.

Toner cavity — A container filled with toner in a laser printer. The black resin toner is used to form the printed image on paper.

Trace — A wire on a circuit board that connects two components or devices together.

TRACERT — A TCP/IP utility used to display the list of routers a packet encounters from source to destination.

Track — The disk surface is divided into many concentric circles, each called a track.

Trailer — The part of a packet that follows the data and contains information used by some protocols for error checking.

Training — *See* Handshaking.

Transceiver — The bidirectional (transmitter and receiver) component on a NIC that is responsible for signal conversion and monitors for data collision.

Transformer — A device that changes the ratio of current to voltage. A computer power supply is basically a transformer and a rectifier.

Transistor — An electronic device that can regulate electricity and act as a logical gate or switch for an electrical signal.

Translation — A technique used by system BIOS and hard drive controller BIOS to break the 504 MB hard drive barrier, whereby a different set of drive parameters are communicated to the OS and other software than that used by the hard drive controller BIOS.

TREE command — A DOS command that shows the disk directories in a graphical layout similar to a family tree (for example, TREE/F shows every filename in all branches of the tree).

Trojan horse — A type of infestation that hides or disguises itself as a useful program, yet is designed to cause damage at a later time.

TSR (terminate-and-stay-resident) — A program that is loaded into memory but is not immediately executed, such as a screen saver or a memory-resident antivirus program.

UART (universal asynchronous receiver/transmitter) chip — A chip that controls serial ports. It sets protocol and converts parallel data bits received from the system bus into serial bits.

Unattended installation — A Windows 2000 installation that is done by storing the answers to installation questions in a text file or script that Windows 2000 calls an answer file so that the answers do not have to be typed in during the installation.

UNDELETE command — A command that resets a deleted file's directory entry to normal, provided the clusters occupied by the file have not been overwritten and the file entry is still in the directory list.

UNFORMAT command — A DOS command that performs recovery from an accidental FORMAT, and may also repair a damaged partition table if the partition table was previously saved with MIRROR/PARTN.

Universal serial bus (USB) — A bus that is expected to eventually replace serial and parallel ports, designed to make installation and configuration of I/O devices easy, providing room for as many as 127 devices daisy-chained together. The USB uses only a single set of resources for all devices on the bus.

Upgrade installation — A Windows 2000 installation that carries forward all previous operating system settings and applications installed under the previous operating system.

Upper memory — The memory addresses from 640K up to 1024K, originally reserved for BIOS, device drivers, and TSRs.

Upper memory block (UMB) — A group of consecutive memory addresses in RAM from 640K to 1 MB that can be used by device drivers and TSRs.

UPS (uninterruptible power supply) — A device designed to provide a backup power supply during a power failure. Basically, a UPS is a battery backup system with an ultrafast sensing device.

URL (Uniform Resource Locator) — A unique address that identifies the domain name, path, or filename of a World Wide Web site. Microsoft's URL address is *http://www.microsoft.com/*.

User account — The information that defines a computer user. Contains a login name and password and often contains a user's full name. Defines what tasks a user may perform on the system.

User Datagram Protocol (UDP) — A connectionless protocol that does not require a connection to send a packet and does not guarantee that the packet arrives at its destination. (A data packet was once called a datagram.)

User documentation — Manuals, online documentation, instructions, and tutorials designed specifically for the user.

User mode — Provides an interface between an application and an OS, and only has access to hardware resources through the code running in kernel mode.

User profile — A personal profile about the user, kept in the Windows NT registry, which enables the user's desktop settings and other operating parameters to be retained from one session to another.

User State Migration Tool — A utility in Windows XP that helps to migrate user configuration information from one computer to another.

Utility software — Software packages, such as Nuts & Bolts or Norton Utilities, that provide the means for data recovery and repair, virus detection, and the creation of backups.

V.34 standard — A communications standard that transmits at 28,800 bps and/or 33,600 bps.

V.90 — A standard for data transmission over phone lines that can attain a speed of 56 Kbps. It replaces K56flex and x2 standards.

Value data — In Windows 9x, the name and value of a setting in the registry.

VCACHE — A built-in Windows 9x 32-bit software cache that doesn't take up conventional memory space or upper memory space, as SmartDrive does.

Vector table — *See* Interrupt vector table.

VESA (Video Electronics Standards Association) VL bus — A local bus used on 80486 computers for connecting 32-bit adapters directly to the local processor bus.

Video card — An interface card installed in the computer to control visual output on a monitor.

Video controller card — An interface card that controls the monitor. Also called video card or display adapter.

Video driver — A program that tells the computer how to effectively communicate with the video adapter card and monitor. It is often found on a floppy disk or CD that is shipped with the card.

Video RAM or VRAM — RAM on video cards that holds the data that is being passed from the computer to the monitor and can be accessed by two devices simultaneously. Higher resolutions often require more video memory.

Virtual device driver (VDD) or VxD driver — A 32-bit device driver running in protected mode.

Virtual file allocation table (VFAT) — A variation of the original DOS 16-bit FAT that allows for long filenames and 32-bit disk access.

Virtual machines (VM) — Multiple logical machines created within one physical machine by Windows, allowing applications to make serious errors within one logical machine without disturbing other programs and parts of the system.

Virtual memory manager — A Windows 9x program that controls the page table, swapping 4K pages in and out of physical RAM to and from the hard drive.

Virtual memory — A method whereby the OS uses the hard drive as though it were RAM.

Virtual real mode — An operating mode in which an OS provides an environment to a 16-bit program that acts like real mode.

Virus — A program that often has an incubation period, is infectious, and is intended to cause damage. A virus program might destroy data and programs or damage a disk drive's boot sector.

Virus signature — The distinguishing characteristics or patterns of a particular virus. Typically, AV signature updates for new viruses can be downloaded monthly from the Internet.

Voice — A group of samples for a musical instrument stored in a wavetable.

Volatile — Refers to a kind of RAM that is temporary, cannot hold data very long, and must be frequently refreshed.

Volt — A measure of electrical pressure differential. A computer ATX power supply usually provides five separate voltages: +12V, -12V, +5V, -5V, and +3V.

Voltage — Electrical differential that causes current to flow, measured in volts. *See* Volts.

Voltmeter — A device for measuring electrical voltage.

Volumes — In Windows 2000, a partition on a hard drive that is formatted as a dynamic drive.

Wait state — A clock tick in which nothing happens, used to ensure that the microprocessor isn't getting ahead of slower components. A 0-wait state is preferable to a 1-wait state. Too many wait states can slow a system down.

Warm boot — *See* Soft boot.

Wattage — Electrical power measured in watts.

Watts — The unit used to measure power. A typical computer may use a power supply that provides 200 watts.

Window RAM (WRAM) — Dual-ported video RAM that is faster and less expensive than VRAM. It has its own internal bus on the chip, with a data path that is 256 bits wide.

Windows Custom Setup — A setup feature that allows user customization of such things as directory locations, wallpaper settings, font selections, and many other features.

Windows Express Setup — A setup feature that automatically installs Windows in the most commonly used fashion.

Windows File Protection (WFP) — A Windows 2000 feature that protects system files from being corrupted or erased by applications or users.

Windows Internet Naming Service (WINS) — A Microsoft resolution service with a distributed database that tracks relationships between domain names and IP addresses. Compare to DNS.

Windows NT file system (NTFS) — A file system first introduced with Windows NT that provides improved security, disk storage, file compression, and long filenames.

Windows NT registry — A database containing all configuration information, including the user profile and hardware settings. The NT registry is not compatible with the Windows 9x registry.

Windows Protection Error — An error that occurs when an application violates Windows memory access rules or if a real mode driver conflicts with a protected mode driver.

Wireless Access Point — A device used to provide users with a method to access network resources without having to use a wired connection (i.e. Local Area Network). Users access an access point (AP) by way of a wireless network card that has been installed in their computer.

Workgroup — In Windows NT, a logical group of computers and users in which administration, resources, and security are distributed throughout the network, without centralized management or security.

Worm — An infestation designed to copy itself repeatedly to memory, on drive space, or on a network until little memory or disk space remains.

WOW (Win 16 on Win 32) — A group of programs provided by Windows NT/2000/XP to create a virtual DOS environment that emulates a 16-bit Windows environment, protecting the rest of the NT OS from 16-bit applications.

Write precompensation — A method whereby data is written faster to the tracks that are near the center of a disk.

XCOPY command — A faster external DOS COPY program that can copy subdirectories (/S) (for example, XCOPY *.* A:/S).

Zero insertion force (ZIF) — A socket feature that uses a small lever to apply even force when installing the microchip into the socket.

ZIF handle — The small lever on a zero insertion force socket used to apply even force when installing or removing a microchip into the socket.

Zone bit recording — A method of storing data on a hard drive whereby the drive can have more sectors per track near the outside of the platter.

Computer Management Console. *See also* Computer Management tool
  discussed, 158
    Services and Applications, 158
    Storage, 158
    System tools, 158
Computer Management tool, discussed, 184
confidentiality, 88, 230
ConfigSafe, 228
Config.sys, 162, 164, 186, 202, 222, 228. *See also* Msconfig.exe
  commands, 216
  files and buffers, 212
connections. *See also* connectors
  corrosion affecting, 72, 80, 90
connectors. *See also* cable
  BNC connector, 136
  FireWire, 42
  IDU connector, 138
  RJ-11 connector, 44
  RJ-12 connector, 44
  RJ-45 connector, 44, 138, 140
  UDC connector, 138
  USB cable, 42
Control Panel
  accessing, 188
  discussed, 156
cooling systems. *See also* fan
  discussed, 22, 58, 80
  heat sinks, 22, 80
  liquid cooling, 22, 58, 80
  temperature sensors, 80
  thermal compounds, 58, 80
COPY command, 170
corrosion, affecting connections, 72, 80, 90
CPU. *See* central processing unit
customer. *See also* user
  eliciting information from, 230
  interacting with, 230
Cyrix, 100

D

data file. *See also* file
  transferring and configuring, 196
date/time, 122
DB-25 connector, 44
DC. *See* direct current

dead computer. *See also* troubleshooting
  restoring, 72
debug information, memory.dmp, 234
DEFAULT, 168
Defrag.exe command, 170. *See also* defragmentation
  discussed, 182
defragmentation. *See also* hard disk drive
  hard disk drive, 64, 92, 158, 234
DEL command, 172
DELTREE command, 172
Detcrash.log, 198
device. *See also* drivers
  installation, verifying, 196
Device Manager, 82
  discussed, 160, 184, 194, 228
DHCP. *See* Dynamic Host Configuration Protocol
diagnostic tools, discussed, 226, 228
dial-up connection, 148, 256
  networking, 156
Dial-Up Networking (DUN), 256
digital camera
  configure camera, 156
  discussed, 54
digital diagnostic disks, 78
Digital Subscriber Line (DSL), 52
  discussed, 146
DIN port, 44
diode, 6
DIP switch, 2, 72
DIR command, 170
direct current (DC), 6
Direct Methanol Fuel Cell (DMFC), 68
directory
  child directory, 176
  single dot/two dots, 176
  subdirectory, 176
directory structure
  discussed, 176
  root directory, 176
    slash ('') character, 176
Disk Cleanup, 158
  discussed, 182
Disk Defragmenter, 158
Disk Management utility, 174
display
  cleaning, 90
  discussed, 10, 20
  disposal of, 96, 98

dot pitch, 10
  electrical safety, 96, 98
  interlaced display, 10
  LCD panel, 32
  opening, 96
  pixel, 10
  refresh rate, 10
  resolution, 10
  touch screen, 20, 74
  troubleshooting, 82
display options, 156
disposal
  display, 96
  special procedures, 98
.dll files, 152
  Windows 9x/ME, 234
DMA channels, 36
  CMOS settings, 122
  ECP and, 56
  Ultra DMA IDE/ATA interface cable, 46
DMFC. *See* Direct Methanol Fuel Cell
DNS. *See* Domain Name Service
DNS server, 240
.doc files, 178
docking station
  notebook computer, 34
  troubleshooting, 84
documentation, 226
domain name, 254
  Domain Suffix, 240
    .com, 254
    .edu, 254
    .gov, 254
    .net, 254
    .org, 254
Domain Name Service (DNS), 252
DOS. *See also* MSDOS
  boot disc, 192, 222
  command prompt, 156
  directories, 176
  memory management, 14
  mouse driver, 20
  MSD, 82
  partitions, 174
  Windows systems, 152
dot matrix printer, 124, 134. *See also* printer
dot pitch, 10. *See also* display
Dr. Solomon's Software, 238

A+ PC Repair
Total Solution

COURSE TECHNOLOGY PROVIDES THE TOTAL SOLUTION
FOR CERTIFICATION AND SUCCESS!

OURSE TECHNOLOGY offers *everything* you need to prepare or CompTIA's 2003 A+ Certification Exams and embark on a uccessful career as a computer technician.

ll books are written by best-selling author and instructor Jean Andrews.

OMPREHENSIVE TEXTS

Guide to Managing and Maintaining
ur PC, Comprehensive,
urth Edition
BN: 0-619-18617-8

A+ Guide to Hardware: Managing,
Maintaining, and Troubleshooting,
Second Edition
ISBN: 0-619-18624-0

A+ Guide to Software: Managing,
Maintaining, and Troubleshooting,
Second Edition
ISBN: 0-619-18627-5

ANDS-ON PRACTICE

b Manual for A+ Guide to Managing
d Maintaining Your PC,
urth Edition
BN: 0-619-18619-4

Lab Manual for A+ Guide to Hardware:
Managing, Maintaining, and
Troubleshooting, Second Edition
ISBN: 0-619-18626-7

Lab Manual for A+ Guide to Software:
Managing, Maintaining, and
Troubleshooting, Second Edition
ISBN: 0-619-18629-1

DDITIONAL PRACTICAL EXPERIENCE

Computer-Based Training (CBT),
rd Edition
InfoSource
N: 0-619-18621-6

PC Troubleshooting Pocket Guide,
Third Edition
ISBN: 0-619-18620-8

AM PREPARATION

CoursePrep StudyGuide,
ond Edition
N: 0-619-18622-4

A+ CoursePrep ExamGuide,
Second Edition
ISBN: 0-619-18623-2

A+ Hardware CourseCard
ISBN: 0-619-20362-5

A+ Software CourseCard
ISBN: 0-619-20363-3

THE JOB

iece Toolset with ESD Strap
N: 0-619-01655-8

Digital Multimeter
ISBN: 0-619-13101-2